THE ZOHAR

THE

Volume V

THE SONCINO PRESS
London ~ New York

ZOHAR

Translated by

**HARRY SPERLING
MAURICE SIMON**

SECOND EDITION

CONTENTS

PUBLISHERS' NOTE

In presenting to the public the fifth and last volume of the translation of the Zohar, the Publishers feel that a difficult and noteworthy task has been accomplished. They accordingly take this opportunity of calling attention to the predominant share which has to be attributed to one of the collaborators, Mr. Maurice Simon. Besides himself translating a considerable portion—including nearly the whole of the fifth volume—Mr. Simon has carefully revised the rest and has given to it the form in which it has finally appeared. He has also contributed the Appendices, which add so materially to the value of the work.

J. DAVIDSON

THE SONCINO PRESS

THE ZOHAR

KI TAZRIA'

Leviticus XII, I–XIII, 59

AND THE LORD SPOKE UNTO MOSES SAYING, WHEN
A WOMAN, ETC. [42a] R. Abba cited here the verse: "By night
upon my bed I sought him", etc. (S.S. III, I). 'This verse',
he said, 'is spoken by the Community of Israel who in the
exile lies in the dust, in an alien unclean land, and therefore
complains of her bed and beseeches "him whom her soul
loveth" to deliver her from thence. She "seeks him but finds
him not", for it is not his way to unite [42b] with her save
in his temple. She "calls him and he answers not", for She
dwells among other peoples, and only his sons hear his voice.'
R. Isaac interpreted thus: ' "I make plaint to him of my
bed, that he may unite with me to gladden and bless me",
for, as we have learnt, from the union of the King with
the Community of Israel many righteous ones obtain a holy
inheritance and many blessings accrue to the world.' R. Abba
was once going from Kfar Kania to the cave of Lydda, along
with R. Jose and R. Ḥiya. Said R. Jose: 'It is written: "A
virtuous woman is a crown to her husband" (Prov. XII, 4).
The virtuous woman', he said 'is the Community of Israel,
and "she that maketh ashamed" refers to the idolatrous
nations whom God cannot abide, as it says "I abhorred
them" (Lev. XX, 23).' Said R. Abba: 'Assuredly it is so; the
Community of Israel is called a "woman of valour" (ḥayil)
because she is the mistress of so many legions of valiant ones
(ḥayalin).' R. Abba then said: 'Let each of us give some
exposition of the Torah', and he himself commenced with
the verse: "A virtuous woman who can find ?" (Prov. XXXI,
10). 'The "virtuous woman", he said, 'is the Community
of Israel, as we have just explained. "Who shall find": who
shall succeed in being wholly in her and always with her ?
"Far above rubies is her price" (michrah, lit. selling): those
who do not truly and wholeheartedly cleave to her she sells
into the hands of other peoples, and they are removed far
from those precious holy pearls and have no share in them.'

R. Ḥiya then expounded the next verse: "The heart of her
husband trusteth in her, and she shall have no lack of spoil".
'The "husband",' he said, 'is the Holy One, blessed be He,
who hath appointed her to govern the whole world and
placed in her hands all his armoury and warriors; wherefore
she "lacketh not spoil".' R. Jose took the next verse: "She
doeth him good and not evil all the days of her life". 'She
provides good for the world, for the temple of the King
and those who frequent it. When is this ? When those "days
of the heaven" shine upon her and unite with her fitly, these
being then the "days of her life", because the Tree of Life
has sent to her life and shines upon her.' Said R. Abba: 'All
this is well said, and all these verses can be applied to the
Community of Israel.'

IF A WOMAN CONCEIVE SEED. We have learnt that if a
woman conceives the seed first, the child is a male. Said
R. Aha: 'But have we not learnt that God decrees whether
the semen is to be male or female ?' R. Jose replied: 'Indeed,
God distinguishes whether the germ itself comes from a
male or female source,[1] and therefore He decrees whether the
child is to be male or female.' R. Aha also asked why the
word "conceive-seed" is used instead of merely "conceive".
R. Jose answered: 'A woman from the time she becomes
pregnant till she is delivered can talk of nothing but the
child she is to bear, whether it is to be a boy or a girl.'

R. Hizkiah adduced here the verse: "O Lord, how manifold are thy works" (Ps. CIV, 24). 'How manifold', he said,
'are the works of the Holy King in the world ! He is like a
man who takes in his hand a number of [43a] bundles of
seed and sows them all at once, and in time each kind comes
up separately. So the Holy One, blessed be He, accomplished
His work with wisdom; with wisdom He took all together
and sowed them and afterwards they all issued each in its
time, as it says: "In wisdom hast thou made them all".'
R. Abba said: 'They were all secreted in Wisdom, and
they did not issue into being save by certain paths alongside

[1] According to the Zohar, the seed itself contains both a male and a
female element. v. Zohar, Exodus, 161b.

of Understanding (*Binah*), whence they become firmly established. Observe that when a man goes to unite with his wife in sanctity, his holy thought awakens a spirit compounded of male and female, and God signals to a messenger who is in charge of the conception of human beings and entrusts to him that spirit and informs him where to deposit it, and also lays various injunctions on the spirit itself. Then the spirit goes down to earth along with a certain form which bore its image above, and in that form it is created and goes about in this world; and so long as that form is with a man, he retains his form in this world.

'In the book of the sorceries of Asmodai we find that one who knows how to practise magic from the side of the left should rise by the light of the lamp and utter certain incantations and call the unclean sides by their names and prepare his forms for those whom he invites and say he is ready for their commands. Then that man passes out of the dominion of his Master and places himself in charge of the unclean side. And through his incantations two spirits appear in the shape of men which show him how to confer certain benefits or do certain kinds of harm at certain specified times. It is forbidden to a man to abandon any vessel of his house into the possession of the "other side", for many emissaries are in wait to punish such an act, and from that time blessings do not rest upon him—all the more if he assigns to the "other side" the most precious part of himself. For from that time he belongs to it, and when the time comes for the celestial form which has been given to him to depart from this world, the evil spirit to which he clung comes and takes it, and it is never again restored to him.

'When the soul is about to descend to this world, it first goes down to the terrestrial Garden of Eden and sees there the glory of the souls of the righteous, and then it goes down to Gehinnom and sees the wicked who cry "Woe, woe", and find no compassion. That holy form stands by him until he emerges into the world, [43b] after which it keeps him company and grows up with him. Observe that all spirits are compounded of male and female, and when they go forth into the world they go forth as both male and female, and afterwards the two elements are separated. If a man is worthy they are afterwards united, and it is then that he truly meets his mate and there is a perfect union both in spirit and flesh. Hence it is written here: "When a woman conceives seed and bears a male", and not "male and female together", since on account of the ways of the world they are not united (at birth) as they were when they issued from on high, because the first man and his mate sinned before God. Therefore they are separated until, if a man is worthy, it pleases God to restore to him his mate. But if he is not worthy, she is given to another, and they bear children whom they should not.' R. Eleazar said: 'This is not so. All at first comprise both male and female, and they are separated afterwards. But if the woman bears a male, they are then united from the side of the right, and if she bears a female, from the side of the left, this side being then predominant. Hence, if the male child issues from the side of the left, he is effeminate, but if from the side of the right, he has mastery over the female.

'Many myriads are brought forth at every hour, but they are not called souls until they are settled in a body, and this is only after thirty-three days.

'SHE SHALL BE UNCLEAN SEVEN DAYS. Because for seven days spirits do not go in to abide with her; for seven days the spirit seeks for its place in the body, and only on the eighth day does it settle there so that body and soul may appear before the Matrona and unite with Her.

'AND SHE SHALL CONTINUE IN THE BLOOD OF HER PURIFYING THREE AND THIRTY DAYS. These are to allow the spirit to settle in the body. The three extra days are the first three after the circumcision, during which the child is in pain and the spirit cannot settle down in the body.

'SHE SHALL TOUCH NO HALLOWED THING. Every day the Community of Israel takes from the household of the King food for the spirits of men and feeds [44*a*] them in holiness, save for these, the spirits of which have not yet settled in the bodies. But after thirty-three days She tends them like all other human beings, because their spirits are united with their bodies as in all other men. In the case of a female double the number of days is required, because, as stated above, the side of the left is predominant, and therefore it takes twice as long in the case of a female for the spirit to be united with the body.'

R. Judah adduced here the verse: "There is none holy as the Lord, for there is none beside thee, neither is there any rock like our God" (1 Sam. 11, 2). 'Are there then other holy ones or other rocks besides the Lord ? Yes, there are holy ones above, as it is written: "The demand is by the word of the holy ones" (Dan. IV, 14), and Israel are holy below, but none are holy like the Lord, because "there is none beside thee", that is, God's holiness is not like their holiness, for He does not require their holiness, but they could not be holy without Him. Also, "there is no rock (*zur*) like our God", or, as we may translate, "no fashioner like our God", as explained elsewhere; for the Holy One, blessed be He, shapes a form within a form, and finishes it and breathes into it the breath of life and brings it out into the open.'

R. Ḥiya and R. Aha were sitting one night with R. Abba. They rose at midnight to study the Torah, and when they went outside they saw a star strike another star three times and put out its light. They then heard two voices from different directions, one from the north above and one [44b] below, which proclaimed: "Go now in to your places, now the hollow of the abyss is closed and the Holy One, blessed be He, goes into the Garden to have joyous communion with the righteous there". The voice then died away, and R. Aha and R. Abba turned their heads and said: 'Verily this is the hour when the Community of Israel arises to join the Holy King. Verily the Community of Israel meets the Holy One, blessed be He, only with song and praise until morning, and the King twines round her a thread of grace, and not round her alone but round all who accompany her. Let us go and join her.' So they all sat down.

R. Aha then discoursed on the verse: "And the Lord God

said, It is not good that the man should be alone", etc. (Gen. II, 18). He said: 'Was man then alone ? Is it not written, "male and female he created them", and we have learnt that man was created "with two faces" ? What it means, however, is that the male did not concern himself with the female and had no support from her; she was at his side and they were like one from the back. Therefore God sawed him in two and separated the female from him and brought her to the man, so that they should be face to face. And when she was gathered in to man, then God blessed them, like the reader of the service who blesses the bride with seven blessings. Therefore he who unites with the wife of another impairs the [divine] union, for the union of the Community of Israel is with the Holy One, blessed be He, alone, whether it is a time with him of mercy or of judgement. He who joins with the wife of another is like one who denies the Holy One, blessed be He, and the Community of Israel, and therefore he does not obtain forgiveness by repentance until he departs from the world, until he enters repentant into the other world to receive his punishment.' R. Eleazar said: 'He who denies the Community of Israel is not received as a penitent until he has been punished in Gehinnom; all the more so if he denies both the Community of Israel and the Holy One, blessed be He, and all the more so if he caused God the trouble of forming a bastard in the wife of another.' R. Ḥiya said: 'It is written, "Whoso robbeth his father and his mother", etc. (Prov. xxviii, 24). The "father" here', he said, 'is the Holy One, blessed be He, and the "mother" is the Community of Israel; and we have learnt, Whoever enjoys anything of this world without a blessing is like one who robs the Holy One and the Community of Israel. So he who has enjoyment of his wife without a blessing is like one who robs the Holy One and the Community of Israel, because their union is consummated by seven blessings. Further, he is "the companion of the destroyer" (*Ibid.*), because he impairs the celestial form and arrangement: all the more so, then, one who covets the wife of another to cleave to her.' [45a]

R. Abba then discoursed on the verse: "And he said,

Let me go, for the day breaketh" (Gen. XXXII, 26). . . .[1] 'Why was not the angel able to prevail over Jacob ? Because the sun had risen and his strength was crippled. . . . For when the light appears, all the emissaries of punishment are restrained, and then the Community of Israel communes with the Holy One, blessed be He, and that hour is a time of grace for all, and the King holds out to her and all who are with her his sceptre of the thread of grace so that they may be wholly united to the holy King. Observe this. When the Holy One, blessed be He, is in the company of the Community of Israel, if she first makes approaches to him and draws him towards her in the strength of her love and desire, then she is replenished from the side of the right and multitudes from the side of the right are found in all worlds. But if the Holy One, blessed be He, is the first to make advances and she [45*b*] only rouses herself afterwards, then all is on the side of the female and many multitudes arise on the side of the left in all worlds. Hence it is written: "When a woman conceives seed and bears a male", etc., the lower world being on the model of the upper, and in all things a man should concentrate his thoughts above on the Holy One, blessed be He, that grace may abound in the world. Happy are the righteous who know how to concentrate their thoughts on the holy King; of them it is written: "Ye who cleave unto the Lord your God are all alive this day" (Deut. IV, 4).

WHEN A MAN SHALL HAVE IN THE SKIN OF HIS FLESH A RISING OR A SCAB OR A BRIGHT SPOT, ETC. R. Judah here cited the verse: "Look not upon me because I am swarthy, because the sun hath scorched me", etc. (S.S. I, 6). 'When the Moon was hidden in the exile and she saw the yearning of Israel for her, she said, "Look not on me", meaning, "You cannot see me, because I am in darkness—for one thing because the sun has withdrawn his light from me, and for another because "the sons of my mother were incensed against me" (*Ibid.*), these being the emissaries of the side of severity. "They

---

[1] Here follow in the text certain reflections on the conflict of Jacob and the angel which have appeared in substance elsewhere.

made me keeper of the vineyards", that is, of other nations, whereas "my own vineyard"—Israel—I cannot keep. Formerly I kept my own vineyard and through it the others were also kept; now I have to keep the others that my own may be kept among them.' As R. Ḥiya and R. Jose were once going along, they came to a field where there was a balsam tree on the right. Said R. Jose: 'A pall of smoke must come before our eyes; it is forbidden us to look upon any glad sight since the day when the Temple was destroyed.' He then expounded the verse: "The earth is the Lord's and the fulness thereof, the world and they that dwell therein" (Ps. XXIV, I). 'This "earth" ', he said, 'is the holy earth which is called "the land of the living", while "the world" refers to other lands.' R. Ḥiya said: 'The "earth" is as you said; the "fulness thereof" is the souls of the righteous; the "world" is this earth, and "they that dwell therein" are mankind.' Said R. Jose: 'If so, what do you make of the next verse: "For he hath founded it upon the seas and established it upon the waters" ?' He replied: 'Assuredly that "land of the living" is established upon the seas and rivers which issue from that supernal River that proceeds from Eden.'

As they were going along they came across a man standing under a tree whose face was full of the marks of blows. They noticed [46*a*] that his face was all red from the blows. Said R. Ḥiya to him: 'Who are you ?' He replied: 'I am a Jew.' Said R. Jose: 'He must be a sinner, as otherwise his face would not have all those marks, and these are not what are called "chastisements of love".' Said R. Ḥiya: 'Assuredly that is so, for the "chastisements of love" are hidden from view. So with the plague of leprosy, of those marks which are visible to all, it is written, "And the priest shall see and declare him unclean", for assuredly those come from the side of uncleanness and are not chastisements of love. In the same way, he who reproves his neighbour in love should not let other men hear in order that he may not be ashamed; and if he reproves him publicly he does not show true friendship. So God, in reproving a man, acts with him lovingly. At first He smites him inwardly. If he repents, well and good, but if not, he smites him under his garments, and this is called "chastisement of love". If he still does not repent, God smites him on his face where all can see, so that they may know that he is a sinner and not beloved of his Master.' The man thereupon said to them: 'You are in a conspiracy against me: of a surety you are of those who frequent the house of R. Simeon ben Yoḥai, who have no fear of anyone. If my sons were to come up, they would punish you for speaking thus loudly.' They said: 'The Law teaches us to do so, as it says, "Wisdom crieth in the chief places of concourse", etc. (Prov. I, 21). If we were to be afraid to speak words of the Torah before thee, we should be ashamed before God.' The man thereupon lifted up his hands and wept. Meanwhile his sons came up. The youngest one said: 'The support of heaven is here. King Solomon said: "All have I seen in the days of my vanity" (Eccl. VII, 15). In the days of King Solomon the moon was full, and Solomon was the wisest of men and he saw all: he saw "All" attached to the Moon and illuminating her like the sun. Now, when the righteous are numerous in the world, this "All" does not depart from the Sun, and receives all anointing and joy from above to unite with the Moon, for whose sake it is thus enriched. But when sinners are numerous in the world, and the Moon is darkened, the "Righteous One perisheth in his righteousness", that is, he loses all this as he cannot unite with the Moon. Then, too, all the side of the left is aroused, and the prosperity of sinners is prolonged; [46b] hence it is written, "and there is a wicked man who prolongeth his life in his evildoing". Also we may interpret the words, "there is a righteous man that perisheth in his righteousness", to mean that when sinners multiply and judgement impends, the righteous man is seized for their sins, like my father, who has been punished for the sins of the townsfolk who are all law-breakers, because he did not chide them or try to stop them, taking as his guide the verse, "Quarrel not with evildoers, be not zealous against them that work unrighteousness".' His father said: 'In truth God has punished me for this, because I had the power to prevent them and I did not do so, and I did not reprove them either openly or secretly.' His other son then cited the verse: "And the Lord God formed man of the dust of the ground", etc. (Gen. II, 7). 'Man was formed with two inclinations, the good and the evil, one corresponding to Water and the other to Fire. The word "man" (*adam*) indicates a combination of male and female. The dust from which he was formed was that of the Holy Land, of the Sanctuary. "He breathed in his nostrils the breath of life": this is the holy soul which derives from the life above. "And the man became a living soul": he was provided with a holy soul from the supernal "living being" which the earth brought forth. Now, as long as that holy soul is attached to a man, he is beloved of his Master, he is guarded on all sides, he is marked out for good above and below, and the holy divine presence rests upon him. But if he perverts his ways the divine presence leaves him, the super-soul does not cling to him, and from the side of the evil serpent a spirit arises which can abide only in a place whence the heavenly holiness has departed, and so a man becomes defiled and his flesh, his facial appearance and his whole being, is distorted. Observe that because this "living soul" is holy, therefore when the holy land absorbs it, it is called "super-soul" (*neshamah*); it is this which ascends and speaks before the holy King and enters without let or hindrance in all gates, and therefore it is called "speaking spirit".[1] Hence the Torah proclaims, "Keep thy tongue from evil", etc. (Ps. XXXIV, 14), because if a man's lips and tongue speak evil words, those words mount aloft and all proclaim "keep away from the evil word of so-and-so, leave the path clear for the mighty serpent". Then the holy soul leaves him and is not able to speak: it is in shame and distress, and is not given a place as before. Hence it is written, "Whoso keepeth his mouth and his tongue keepeth his soul from troubles" (Prov. XXI, 23). For that soul which was vocal is reduced to silence on account of the evil word. Then the serpent gets ready, and when that evil word finds its way to him, then many spirits bestir themselves, and one spirit comes down from that side and finds the man who uttered the evil word,

---

[1] v. Targum Onkelos, *in loco*.

and lights upon him and defiles him, and he becomes leprous. And just as a man is punished for uttering an evil word, so he is punished for not uttering a good word when he had the opportunity, because he harms that speaking spirit which was prepared to speak both above and below in holiness. All the more so if the people walk in crooked ways and he is able to speak to them and reprove them and does not do so. So David said: "I held my peace from good and my trouble was stirred" (Ps. XXXIX, 3), alluding to his leprosy.' [47a] R. Ḥiya and R. Jose then came and kissed him, and they kept together the whole of that journey.

WHEN A PLAGUE OF LEPROSY IS ON A MAN HE SHALL BE BROUGHT UNTO THE PRIEST. R. Jose said: 'The Companions have studied all the varieties of this plague, and the priest used to know which were chastisements of love and which were a sign that a man was rejected and spurned by his Master; for the plague lights upon mankind according to their works. It is written: "Incline not my heart to any evil thing, to be occupied in deeds of wickedness" (Ps. CXLI, 4).' Said R. Isaac: 'Does God then lead men astray into the ways of sin and evildoing ? If so, how can the Torah say, "*If* thou hearkenest, *if* thou dost not hearken" ? We should, however, translate: "Do not incline, O my heart, to an evil thing (word), for an evil word brings the plague of leprosy upon the world". The Companions have pointed out that the Aramaic translation of leprosy (*segiru*) means "shutting up", and indicates shutting up both above and below. In a similar sense it is written: "He hath defiled the sanctuary of the Lord" (Num. XIX, 20).' Said R. Eleazar: 'He defiles it because the Divine Presence departs from thence and the mighty serpent takes up his abode there and casts filth there and causes defilement, and all because of men's sins.'

AND IF A MAN'S HAIR BE FALLEN OFF HIS HEAD. R. Ḥiya cited here the verse: "Then I saw that wisdom excelleth folly as light excelleth darkness" (Eccl. II, 13). [47b] 'Where', he said, 'is the great wisdom in this remark of king Solomon ? Does not anyone, even one who has no wisdom himself, know that wisdom is superior to folly as light to darkness, and why, therefore, does Solomon say, "Then I saw" ? The truth, however, is that what is meant is that there is an excellence or profit to wisdom from folly itself, for if there were no folly, wisdom and its words would not be recognized. We have learnt that it is incumbent on a man when he learns wisdom to learn a little folly also, since there is a certain benefit to wisdom from it as there is to light from darkness. We have also learnt that this applies to the supernal Wisdom, for R. Simeon said to R. Abba: The supernal Wisdom does not illumine or become illumined save on account of the folly that arises from another place, and but for this it would have no superiority or excellence, and the profit of wisdom would not be discernible. So on earth, if there were no folly there would be no wisdom. Therefore did Rab Hamnuna the Elder, when he instructed the Companions in the secrets of wisdom, also give them a discourse full of folly, that wisdom might benefit therefrom. Therefore it is written: "More precious than wisdom and than honour is a little folly" (Eccl. x, 1).' R. Jose said: 'This means that a little folly reveals and displays the honour of wisdom and the glory of heaven more than anything else. So the benefit of light is only felt from its contrast with darkness, and similarly white is only known and valued from its contrast with black.' R. Isaac said: 'It is the same with sweet and bitter: a man does not know what sweet is until he tastes bitter. [48a]

'We have learnt: Man in the Scripture has four names— *adam*, *geber*, *enosh*, *ish*—and the highest of them is *adam*.' Said R. Judah: 'But is it not written, "When a man (*adam*) shall bring from you an offering" (Lev. I. 2), and who is it that requires to bring an offering ? Is it not a sinner ?' R. Isaac replied: 'The offering is the mainstay of the world, of upper and lower beings, the solace of the Almighty, and who is fitting to offer it ? Surely this man who is called *Adam*.' Said R. Judah: 'If so, what of the verse, "When a man (*adam*) has on the skin of his flesh . . . and it become in the skin of his flesh the plague of leprosy" ?' He replied: 'This one God desires to heal more than all others, and therefore it is written concerning him, "he shall be brought unto the

priest"; it is the duty of anyone who sees him to bring him
to the priest, in order that the holy image may not remain
thus.' Said R. Judah: 'But it is written, "Now Moses the
man (*ish*)"; why is he not called "*adam*" ?' He replied:
'Because he was the "servant of the king", and therefore he
is called *ish* in relation to the supernal Adam. But,' he said,
'why then is it written, "The Lord is a man (*ish*) of war" ?'
He replied: 'The secret of the Lord is to them that fear
him.' Said R. Judah: 'I too am one of them, yet I have not
been privileged to hear this.' Said the other: 'Go to R. Abba,
for I learnt it from him only on condition that I should not
tell.' So he went to R. Abba, and found him discoursing
and saying: 'When is there said to be completeness above ?
When the Holy One, blessed be He, sits on his throne. For
so it is written: "And upon the likeness of the throne was
the likeness as the appearance of a man (*adam*) upon it
above" (Ezek. I, 26); the term "*adam*" indicates wholeness
and completeness.' Said R. Judah: 'God be blessed that
I have found you discoursing thus. Tell me: is it not written,
"The Lord is a man (*ish*) of war" ?' Said R. Abba: 'Your
question is a good one, and the answer is this. At the Red
Sea there was not yet full consummation, and therefore God
was called *ish;* but in the vision of Ezekiel there was full
consummation, and therefore God was called *adam*.' ' "The
law of thy mouth is better to me than thousands of gold and
silver" (Ps. cxix, 72),' exclaimed R. Judah. 'But', he continued, 'it is also written, "O Lord, thou preservest man
(*adam*) and beast" (Ps. xxxvi, 7). Should not the term *ish*
be used here ?' He said: 'This is analogous to the expression:
"From the cedar which is in Lebanon to the hyssop that
springeth out of the wall" (1 Kings v, 13); it is the way of
the Scripture in such cases to mention the two extremes.'
'But,' he went on, 'is it not written: "And there was no man
(*adam*) to till the ground" (Gen. II, 5) ?' He answered:
'Everything in the world was only made for the sake of
man, and all things were kept back until he that was called
Adam should appear, since his form was after the divine
prototype, and when he was created all was complete.'

R. Jose said: 'The *Hayoth* which Ezekiel saw all had the

form of man.' 'But', said R. Judah, 'it is written: "And the face of an eagle . . . and the face of a lion", etc. ?' [48b] He replied: 'All had the face of man, but in this face itself was seen the resemblance of an eagle, etc.'

R. Isaac said: 'Observe, that whoever is under the control of "*adam*" is called "*ish*", because the complete form of Adam was only reached from another previous form. For it has been taught in the profound mysteries of the Book of Concealed Wisdom that when man was created in the holy supernal form there came down with him two spirits from two sides, one from the right and one from the left, which between them formed the complete man. The one from the right was called the holy *neshamah*, as it says: "And he breathed in his nostrils the *neshamah* of life" (Gen. II, 7), while the other was called "living soul" (*nefesh ḥayah*). When man sinned there were formed from this spirit of the left creatures whose body was not complete, and these are called "the plagues of the sons of men", and they hear certain things on high which they communicate to those below. Now it has been taught: From the Lamp of Darkness[1] issued three hundred and twenty-five sparks traced out and linked together from the side of *Geburah*, and when these entered the Body it was called *Ish*.' Said R. Judah: 'Why so ?' R. Isaac could not answer. So they went and asked R. Simeon, who replied: 'Because the lower judgements are attached to the hair of this one,[2] he is called "Stern Judgement", but when the hair is removed he becomes mitigated and the lower judgements are not held in readiness. Therefore he is called clean, as having emerged from the side of uncleanness, and here too it is written: "And if the hair of *ish* be fallen off his head, he is bald, he is clean." Similarly among men, if one is from the side of judgement and is liable to punishment, he is not purified until his hair is removed. So the Levites who came from this side were not purified until their hair was removed; and they required the Priests who came from the side of Lovingkindness to assist them, just as above when that *Ish* desires to be more exhilarated [49a] the supernal

[1] v. Zohar, Gen., 15a.   [2] According to the anthropomorphic symbolism of the *Sifra di-Ẓeniutha*.

Lovingkindness is displayed in him, and he becomes mitigated, and this *Ish* becomes merged in *Adam*.

'AND IF HIS HAIR BE FALLEN OFF FROM THE FRONT PART OF HIS HEAD. This front part is what is called "the face of wrath", and all [angels] who depend from that "face" are bold, stern and cruel. But when the "hair" is removed from the side of that "face", all these are removed and rendered powerless. For, as we have learnt, all those who depend from the "hair of the head" are superior to the others and not bold-faced like them. Hence the faces of the latter are red like fire from the flashing of the Lamp of Darkness.' Rabbi Isaac said: 'This plague is called "reddish-white" (Lev. XIII, 42); it is still a plague if the white is visible and the red has not disappeared. When, however, the whole has become white, mercy is present and judgement departs.'

Rabbi Abba said: 'Sometimes the Female is sullied by the sins of men and sometimes the Male, and the priest knew from which side the punishment came, and he also knew the sacrifices which ought to be brought, as it is written: "The sacrifices of *Elohim* (i.e. sacrifices to avert punishment) are a contrite spirit" (Ps. LI, 18).' [49b] R. Jose quoted the verse: "O thou that hearest prayer, unto thee shall all flesh come" (Ps. LXV, 2). 'This means, at the time when the body is in pain from sickness and blows, and therefore it says "all flesh" and not "all spirit". Similarly it is written: "If there be a plague of leprosy in a man, he shall be brought unto the priest", the "priest" referring to the Holy One, blessed be He, since on Him depends all purification and holiness.' R. Isaac said: 'We have learnt as follows. "Plague" means stern judgement impending over the world. "Leprosy" means the shutting out from the world of the supernal light and goodness. "When it shall be in a man": this is he that is called "man". "He shall be brought unto the priest": this is the earthly priest, who is qualified to open what has been shut up and to kindle the lights, that blessings may through him be spread above and below, and the plague be removed and the light of mercy rest upon all.'

C

R. Abba said: 'I am struck by the way in which men neglect the honour of their Master. It is written concerning Israel: "I have separated you from the peoples to be mine" (Lev. xx, 26), and again, "Ye shall sanctify yourselves and be holy, for I the Lord am holy" (*Ibid.* 7). If they depart from God, where is their holiness, seeing that their thoughts are turned from Him ? And Scripture cries to them saying: "Be not as the horse or as the mule which have no understanding" (Ps. xxxii, 9). In what are human beings distinguished from the horse and the mule ? By sanctification and self-perfection. Hence the marital intercourse of human beings should be at fixed times, that they may concentrate their thoughts on cleaving to the Holy One, blessed be He. As has been pointed out, at midnight God enters the Garden of Eden to have communion with the righteous, and the Community of Israel praises the Holy One, blessed be He, and that is a propitious time to cleave to Him. But as for the Companions who study the Torah, the time of their intercourse is at the time of another intercourse, from Sabbath to Sabbath,[1] for that is the time when all above and below are blessed. But if men abandon Him and act like beasts, where are those holy souls which they derive from above ? King Solomon also cries aloud: "Also without knowledge the soul is not good" (Prov. xix, 2), for they draw upon themselves a soul that is not good from the "other side". He who is inflamed with the evil inclination and turns not his thoughts to God draws upon himself a soul which is not good. Therefore evil diseases light upon men and their appearance testifies that God has rejected them and will not heed them until they [50*a*] amend their ways. Similarly it is written: "When ye be come into the land of Canaan . . . and I put a plague of leprosy in a house of the land of your possession", etc. (Lev. xiv, 34). God loved Israel and brought them into the Holy Land to place His divine presence among them and to make His abode with them, so that Israel should be holy above all other peoples. Now, when the women brought articles for the Tabernacle they used to specify what part each was for: "this is for the holy place, this for the curtain",

[1] *v.* T.B. Ketuboth, 62*b*.

and so forth, and each thing went to its place in holiness. Similarly, whenever anyone makes a thing for idolatrous worship, or the "other side", as soon as he mentions its name in connection with that thing, an unclean spirit rests upon it. Now the Canaanites were idolaters, and whenever they erected a building they used to utter certain idolatrous formulæ, and a spirit of uncleanness rested on the building. But when the Israelites entered the land, God desired to purify them and sanctify the land and prepare a place for His divine presence, and so through that plague of leprosy they used to pull down buildings which had been erected in uncleanness. Now if they had done so merely that they might find hidden treasures, they would have replaced the stones afterwards; but the text says, "and they shall take out the stones . . . and he shall take other mortar", in order that the unclean spirit may pass away and the holiness return and the Shekinah abide in Israel. Therefore, when a man begins to set up a building he should declare that he is building for the service of God. Then the support of heaven is with him, and God assigns holiness to him and bids peace be with him. Otherwise he invites into his house the "other side"—all the more so if his inclination is to the "other side", for then, indeed, an unclean spirit will rest on the house, and that man will not leave this world until he has been punished in that house, and whoever dwells in it may come to hurt. If it is asked, How is one to know such a house ? it is one in which the man who built it has come to harm, he or his family, whether through sickness or loss of money, he and two others after him. Better a man should fly to the mountains or live in a mud hut than dwell there. Therefore God had pity on Israel, who knew nothing of all those houses. He said: "You do not know, but I know them, and I will indicate them with the plague. There is a plague in the house; here is a greater plague which will drive it out." Hence "he shall break down the house, the stones thereof and the timber thereof". We may ask, since the uncleanness has gone, why should he break down the house ? The reason is that as long as the house stands [50b] it belongs to the "other side", and it may return. If that is the case in the Holy Land, how much more so in other lands !' Said R. Eleazar: 'Especially since that evil spirit calls his companions there, and even a hawk's talons could not scratch out the uncleanness from there. Therefore the Scripture says, "Woe unto him that buildeth his house by unrighteousness".'

R. Jose was once going into a house, and as he was crossing the threshold he heard a voice say: 'All now gather, here is one of our adversaries. Let us do him some hurt before he goes out again.' Another voice said: 'We cannot do him anything unless he takes up his abode here.' R. Jose drew back in great fear, saying: 'Assuredly, he who transgresses the words of the Companions endangers his life.' Said R. Ḥiya to him: 'But idolaters and other people live in such houses and come to no hurt ?' He replied: 'They come from the same side as those spirits, but he that fears sin can be hurt by them. And even those others if they live there long will not come out in peace.' Said R. Ḥiya: 'But is it not written, "Their houses are safe from fear" (Job XXI, 9) ?' He replied: 'It may be that they have taken them over from others, and that they were built originally in righteousness.'

THEN HE THAT OWNETH THE HOUSE SHALL COME AND TELL THE PRIEST, THERE SEEMETH TO ME TO BE AS IT WERE A PLAGUE IN THE HOUSE. The meaning of this verse is as follows. When this plague (of leprosy) enters, another (of uncleanness) is revealed, and they attack one another. Hence it says, "*there seemeth*" (lit. is seen) to me. Then the one that was concealed becomes visible and the one that was visible becomes hidden, and then reappears in the form of the leprosy, and this is what the owner "tells" the priest, who takes the hint. Then the priest comes, and the stones and wood are removed, and then the rest are blessed. Therefore it says, "Thou shalt build goodly houses and dwell therein" (Deut. VIII, 12); these are good, but the others were not good. 'But', said R. Judah, 'if that is so, what are we to make of the verse, "Houses full of all good things which thou filledst not" (Deut. VI, 11) ? How could they be full of good if an unclean spirit rested on them ?'

R. Eleazar replied: 'It means, with money, with silver, with gold, and so forth: just as it is said elsewhere, "for the good of all the land of Egypt is yours", although all the houses of Egypt were full of magic and idolatry.' R. Simeon said: 'All this was indeed for the purpose of sanctifying the land and removing from it the unclean spirit, and when the house was destroyed he used to find in it money for building another,[1] and so they were not distressed by the loss of the house, and besides, they dwelt there thenceforth in holiness.'

AND WHEN A MAN OR A WOMAN HATH IN THE SKIN OF THEIR FLESH BRIGHT SPOTS. R. Jose said: 'The "bright spot" is surrounded with many regulations as complicated as the wickerwork of a basket, all depending on the shade of colour.' R. Isaac said: 'Some authorities have formulated three hundred rules regarding the bright spot, and I learnt them all from my father. One black hair renders unclean, being like one witness; two render clean, being like two witnesses.' R. Hizkiah was once studying with R. Simeon. He said: 'It is written, "a reddish-white plague". This is a plague, because the white does not retain its purity.' R. Simeon said: 'Happy are Israel in that God desired to purify them, so that they should not come up for sentence before Him. For like always goes to like, red to red and white to white; right to right and left to left. Of Esau it is written, "and he came forth ruddy", and therefore his own kind rests upon him. [51a] It is true, David is also called "ruddy" (1 Sam. XVI, 12), but whereas Esau's redness came from the "dross of gold", David's came from the brightness of gold. Observe that if there is first redness and then it turns whitish, this is a sign of the commencement of purifying. If white appears first, and then it reddens, this is a sign that uncleanness is commencing. The priest knew all these colours, and if the colour of cleanness appeared, he used to shut up the man to see if another colour would appear, and if not, he would declare him clean.'

As R. Isaac and R. Judah were once walking together, the latter remarked: 'It is written: "Elisha said to Gehazi, The

---

[1] v. Midrash Rabbah, in loco.

leprosy of Naaman shall cleave unto thee and unto thy seed for ever" (2 Kings v, 27). Now, if he sinned, why should his descendants be stricken ?' R. Isaac replied: 'Elisha saw more than most prophets. He saw that Gehazi would never have virtuous offspring, and therefore he cursed all of them. Moreover, he said to him, I served Elijah faithfully, and therefore obtained two portions, but you, villain, have compromised me by swearing falsely and being covetous. You have transgressed the whole of the Law, and therefore deserve to die in this world and the next, but because you have served me, your death shall only be in this world and not in the next.'

R. Jose asked: 'Why should there be leprosy on wool and flax ?' R. Isaac replied: 'It rests on all things and has sway over all. It is written, "She seeketh wool and flax", and therefore the sway of this plague which comes from this same supernal place extends over all, over these two articles, wool and flax.'

R. Isaac was once going to his father's home when he saw a man turning aside from the road with a load on his shoulders. He said to him: 'What is that bundle you have on your shoulders ?' but the man gave him no answer. So he followed him till he saw him enter a cave. He went in after him and saw a cloud of smoke ascend from beneath the ground, while the man went into a hole and he lost sight of him. R. Isaac then left the cave in great fear. As he was sitting there, R. Judah and R. Hizkiah passed by. He went up to them and told them what had happened. Said R. Judah: 'Thank God for delivering you. That cave is where the lepers of Sarunia are, and all the inhabitants of that town are magicians and go into the desert to get black snakes ten years old or more, and through not being careful of them they become leprous, and all their magic arts are in that cave.' They then left the spot. On their way they came across a man who had with him a sick child tied to an ass. They asked him why the boy was tied. He replied: 'I live in a town of the Arameans, and my son here used to learn the Torah every day, and when he came home used to go over what he had learnt. Three years I lived in the same house and observed nothing wrong, but now one day when my son went into the house to repeat his lesson an evil spirit passed before him and distorted his eyes and his mouth and his hands, so that he is not able to speak. So I am going to the cave of the lepers of Sarunia to see if they can show me how to cure him.' R. Judah said to him: [51b] 'Do you know of any other person having come to harm in that house before?' He replied: 'I know that a long time ago a man did come to harm there, but people said that it was just an illness, while others said that it was the evil spirit of the house. Since then many people have been in the house without suffering any harm.' They said: 'This proves the truth of what the Companions said. Woe to those who disregard their words.' Said R. Judah: 'It is written, "Woe to him that buildeth his house without righteousness" (Jer. XXII, 13), because wherever there is righteousness all evil spirits fly from before it. Yet withal, whichever comes first to the place takes possession of it.' Said R. Hizkiah: 'If so, the holy Name is merely on a level with the unclean spirit?' He replied: 'Not so. If the holy spirit is there first, no evil spirits can appear there, much less approach. But if the evil spirit is there first, the holy Name does not rest upon it. Now when the plague of leprosy came, one had to purify the place and drive out the unclean spirit, and afterwards the house was taken down and built up again in holiness with the mention of the holy Name; and still other mortar had to be used and the foundation was removed two handbreadths. Nowadays, however, that the plague does not appear, there being thus no one able to drive out the evil spirit, what is the remedy? The best thing is to remove from the house, but if this cannot be done, it should be rebuilt with fresh wood and stones, and a little away from the previous spot, with the mention of the holy Name.' R. Isaac said to him: 'Why should one take all this trouble in these days, since it is written: "That which is crooked cannot be made straight" (Eccl. I, 15)? Since the destruction of the Temple there is no remedy; hence a man should be very careful.'

They said: 'Let us go along with this man and see.' Said R. Isaac: 'We may not. If we were going to a great and

God-fearing man, like Naaman to Elisha, we could accompany
him. But as he is going to such abandoned and godless people
we must not.' 'But', said R. Judah, 'we have learnt that for
healing sickness anything may be used save the wood of an
Asherah ?'[1] He replied: 'This too is idolatry.' So they went
on their way. The man then entered the cave with his son,
and left him there while he went out to tether his ass. Meanwhile a cloud of smoke came out and struck the boy on the
head and killed him. When the father went in, he found him
dead, so he took him and his ass, and on the next day came
up with R. Isaac and R. Judah and R. Hizkiah. With many
tears he related to them what had happened. Said R. Isaac:
'Did I not tell you many times that it was forbidden to
enter there ? Blessed are the righteous who walk in the way
of truth in this world and in the next.' R. Eleazar said: 'In
all his actions a man should have in mind the holy Name
and declare that all is for the service of God, so that the
"other side" should not rest on him, for this is ever lying
in wait for man. Therefore it was that the warp and the
woof used to become unclean [52*a*] and the "other side"
rested on them.'

R. Eleazar was once going to see his father-in-law, accompanied by R. Abba. He said: 'Let us discourse on the Torah
as we go.' R. Eleazar then took as his text the verse: "Say,
I pray thee, thou art my sister" (Gen. XII, 13). 'This', he
said, 'is very strange. Can we believe that a God-fearing
man like Abram should speak thus to his wife in order that
he might be well treated ? The truth is, however, that Abram
relied on the merit of his wife, and not on his own merit,
to procure for him the money of the heathen, for a man
obtains money through the merit of his wife, as it is written:
"House and riches are an inheritance from fathers, but a
prudent wife is from the Lord" (Prov. XIX, 14). Further,
he saw an angel going before her, who said to him: "Fear not,
Abram, God sent me to procure for her the money of the
heathen and to protect her from all harm". Hence Abram
did not fear for his wife but for himself, since he saw the angel
with her but not with himself. Therefore he said to her: "Say,

[1] *v.* Deut. XVI, 21.

I pray thee, that thou art my sister, that he (the angel) may do good to me in this world, and that my soul may live in the next world for thy sake, if thou departest not from the right way, for otherwise death awaits me in this world." '

R. Abba discoursed on the verse: "As in the day of thy coming forth from the land of Egypt will I show unto him marvellous things" (Mic. VII, 15). He said: 'God will one day bring deliverance to his sons as in the days when He sent to deliver Israel and inflicted plagues on Egypt for their sake. What is the difference between this deliverance and that of Egypt? The deliverance in Egypt was from one king and one country: here it will be from all the kings of the earth. Then God will be glorified in all the world, and all shall know His dominion, as it is written: "The Lord shall be king over the whole earth" (Zech. XIV, 9). And they shall bring Israel as an offering to the Holy One, blessed be He, as it is written, "And they shall bring all your brethren", etc. (Isa. LXVI, 20). Then the patriarchs shall rejoice to see the deliverance of their sons, and so it is written: "As in the days of thy going forth from Egypt I shall show him wonders." '

MEZORAʿ

Leviticus xiv, 1–xv, 33

AND THE LORD SPOKE UNTO MOSES SAYING, THIS
SHALL BE THE LAW OF THE LEPER. R. Abba cited here
the verse: "Be ye afraid of the sword, for wrath bringeth
the punishments of the sword, that ye may know there is a
judgement" (Job xix, 29). 'Observe,' he said, 'that through
the evil tongue of the serpent death came upon the world.
The evil tongue is called a "sharp sword" (Ps. lvii, 5), and
therefore it says, "Be ye afraid of the sword", to wit, of the
evil tongue. Why ? "For wrathful are the punishments of
the sword", to wit, the sword of the Lord, "that ye may
know there is a judgement", for he that hath a sword in his
tongue is punished with the sword; hence it says, "this is
the law of the leper".' [53*a*]

R. Eleazar said: 'When a man is on the point of leaving
this world, his soul suffers many chastisements along with
his body before they separate. Nor does the soul actually
leave him until the Shekinah shows herself to him, and then
the soul goes out in joy and love to meet the Shekinah. If
he is righteous, he cleaves and attaches himself to her. But
if not, then the Shekinah departs, and the soul is left behind,
mourning for its separation from the body, like a cat which
is driven away from the fire. Afterwards both are punished
by the hand of Dumah. The body is punished in the grave
and the soul in the fire of Gehinnom for the appointed
period. When this is completed she rises from Gehinnom
purified of her guilt like iron purified in the fire, and she is
carried up to the lower Garden of Eden, where she is cleansed
in the waters of Paradise and perfumed with its spices, and
there she remains till the time comes for her to depart from
the abode of the righteous. Then she is carried up stage
after stage until she is brought near like a sacrifice to the
altar. Hence it is written, "This shall be the law of the leper
on the day of his cleansing: he shall be brought to the priest",
to wit, to the angelic Priest above. This is the fate of a soul

which has not been defiled overmuch in this world, and which can yet be healed in this way; but otherwise, "that which is crooked cannot be made straight".'

R. Isaac cited the verse: "The sun also ariseth and the sun goeth down" (Eccl. I, 5). 'When a man's soul (*neshamah*)', he said, 'is with him in this world, then it may be said of him that "the sun riseth and the sun goeth down". And when man departs from this world in a frame of repentance then "he hasteth to his place where he ariseth". To those who repent, God grants pardon for all sins save for the evil tongue, as it is written: "This shall be the law of the leper", the word *meẓorah* (leper) being interpreted as *moẓi shem ra'* (slanderer).'[1] R. Ḥiya said: 'Whoever spreads false reports, all his limbs become defiled and he is meet for shutting up, because his evil speech rises aloft and calls down an unclean spirit on him. So it says: "How is the faithful city become an harlot" (Isa. I, 21). Because Jerusalem uttered evil speech, God departed from her and a spirit of murderers abode in her. If that was the fate of Jerusalem the holy city, how much more so must it be that of ordinary men ! Hence it says, "This shall be the law of the leper".' R. Judah said: '*Zoth* (this)[2] indeed shall confront him to punish him for his evil speech.

'ON THE DAY OF HIS CLEANSING HE SHALL BE BROUGHT TO THE PRIEST. This shows that the prayer of an evil speaker does not ascend to the Almighty, but if he repents, then "on the day of his cleansing he shall be brought to the Priest".'

THEN THE PRIEST SHALL COMMAND TO TAKE FOR HIM THAT IS TO BE CLEANSED TWO LIVING CLEAN BIRDS, ETC. When R. Isaac and R. Jose were once studying with R. Simeon, they said to him: 'We know the symbolism of the cedar tree the shoots of which are transplanted in Lebanon, as has been expounded. But what is the point of the hyssop ?' He replied: 'It is written here, "two living clean birds and cedar wood and scarlet [53b] and hyssop".

---

[1] Cf. T.B. Erekhin, 16a; Shab, 97a.   [2] The Shekinah.

"Living" is a reference to two of the "living creatures" (*Ḥayoth*) that Ezekiel saw, denoting the place from which the true prophets draw inspiration. "Cedar wood" we have explained. "Scarlet" indicates the place of Severity, which is associated with him at first. "Hyssop" is the lesser *Vau* which gives sustenance to the Community of Israel. All these again rest upon him because he has been purified.'

R. Judah and R. Isaac were once travelling together. They stopped at a certain field to pray, and then went on. R. Judah then commenced a discourse on the Torah, taking for his text: "She is a tree of life to them that lay hold of her and-happy is every one that retaineth her" (Prov. III, 18). 'The "tree of life" is the Torah, which is a great and mighty tree. It is called Torah (lit. showing) because it shows and reveals that which was hidden and unknown; and all life from above is comprised in it and issues from it. He that "takes hold" of the Torah takes hold of all, above and below. "They that retain her" are those who put the profit of merchandise into the purses of students of the Torah; such become worthy of having a progeny of faithful prophets. Such, too, "retain" her from the beginning, which is Wisdom, to the "end of the body", and become pillars of the faith.'

R. Isaac discoursed on the verse: "And he called unto Moses, and the Lord spake unto him out of the tent of meeting, saying" (Lev. I, 1). 'Who was it that called ? The One who abides in the sanctuary. Moses was greater than Aaron, for Moses was the guest of the King, and Aaron was the guest of the Matrona. Just as a king might appoint for his queen a companion to attend to her and her house, and therefore the companion would never appear before the king without the queen, so of Aaron it is written, "With *zoth* (this, i.e. the Shekinah) shall Aaron come", etc. (Lev. XVI, 3). Moses, however, was invited as a guest by the King himself, and afterwards "the Lord spoke to him". All Aaron's discourse was for the purpose of bringing harmony between the King and the Queen, and therefore he made his dwelling with her to attend to her house, and for this he was perfected after the supernal model and was called "high priest". So he obtained all his requests of the King, and therefore it fell to him to purify all those who came before the Queen, so that there should be none [54*a*] unclean among those who entered the sanctuary. Hence it is written: "And he shall take for him that is to be cleansed two birds", etc.'

R. Judah cited the verse: "He that sitteth in the heavens shall laugh, the Lord shall have them in derision" (Ps. II, 4). The word "laugh", he said, has reference to Isaac, who came from the side of wine, which first smiles and then rages and kills. So God is patient with the wicked: if they turn to Him, it is well, but if not, He destroys them from the future world and they have no share in it.'

R. Ḥiya discoursed on the verse: "Behold a day of the Lord cometh when thy spoil shall be divided in the midst of thee" (Zech. XIV, 1). 'This day', he said, 'has been fixed from the creation of the world for punishing the wicked and for God to take vengeance on those that afflict Israel. That day ever comes and stands before God, and calls upon Him to execute judgement on the heathen.' R. Isaac said: 'God has two Days: one that stays with Him and one that comes before Him, and with these He makes war on all. And when that Day comes to make war, it unites with another Day, and they join arms and make war on high and low, as it is written: "For there is a day to the Lord of Hosts upon all that is proud and haughty and upon all that is lifted up, and it shall be brought low" (Isa. II, 12).' R. Simeon drew a similar lesson from the verse: "And if a woman have an issue of her blood many days", etc. (Lev. XV, 25).' 'The "blood" is that referred to in the verse, "The sword of the Lord is filled with blood" (Isa. XXXIV, 6). "Not in the time of her impurity", as we have learnt, that the wicked bring punishment on the world before its time. "Or if she hath an issue beyond the time of her impurity": this implies an excess of punishment, as it is written, "I will chastise you still more seven times for your sins" (Lev. XXVI, 18). "All the days of the issue of her uncleanness": this means that the wicked with their sins pollute both themselves and the sanctuary, and bring an unclean spirit upon themselves; but in time to come God will purify Israel and remove from them the unclean spirit.'

Once, when R. Hizkiah was studying with R. Eleazar, they rose at midnight, and R. Eleazar discoursed on the verse: "On the day of good be of good cheer, and on the day of evil observe, for God hath made one to match the other" (Eccl. VII, 14). 'When God', he said, 'lavishes kindness on the world, a man should go abroad and show himself, for God's kindness then extends to all. Therefore a man should do kindness that kindness may be shown to him. But at the time when judgement impends over the world a man should not show himself abroad [54b] nor walk alone, for when judgement impends over the world it impends over all, and will strike anyone it lights upon. Therefore on that day look carefully on all sides and go not abroad, for God hath made one to match the other; just as when kindness is abroad it extends to all, so when judgement is over the world it is over all. How many swords, then, suspended from the most high sword, issue forth and, seeing that highest sword red and bloody on all sides, decree punishments and set to work !'

R. Eleazar further discoursed on the verse: "Set me as a seal upon thy heart", etc. (S.S. VIII, 6). 'The Community of Israel says this to the Holy One, blessed be He. The seal is the seal of the phylacteries which a man places on his heart; for by so doing a man makes himself perfect after the supernal model. "For love is strong as death": there is nothing so hard in the world as the separation of the soul from the body when they have to part; and similar is the love of the Community of Israel for the Holy One, blessed be He. "Jealousy is as cruel as Sheol": of all the grades of Gehinnom there is none so hard as Sheol, and he who is jealous of a beloved one finds it harder to part than the Sheol, which is the hardest grade of Gehinnom. "The flashes thereof are flashes of fire": this is the fire that issues from the Shofar, compounded of air and water. And with that flame the Community of Israel sets on fire the world when she is passionate for the Holy One, blessed be He, and woe to him who crosses the path of that flame !' R. Eleazar further discoursed on the verse: "Many waters cannot quench love", etc. (Ibid. 7). 'This', he said, 'is the Right Arm which desires to bind the phylactery on the Left Arm, in accordance with the verse, "that his right hand might embrace me" (S.S. ii, 6). Or again, the "waters" may be the primordial stream from which issue other streams in every direction. "If a man were to give all the substance of his house for love, it would be utterly contemned": this means that if the Holy One, blessed be He, were to offer to the angels all the substance of His house in lieu of His uniting with the Community of Israel, they would contemn it, [55*a*] since they have no joy save in the hour when the Community of Israel unites with the Holy One, blessed be He. When a man puts on the phylactery of the hand, he should stretch out his left arm as though to draw to him the Community of Israel and to embrace her with the right arm, so as to copy the supernal model, as it is written, "O that his left hand were under my head and his right hand embraced me" (S.S. ii, 6), for then is that man wholly sanctified.'

R. Hizkiah spoke on the verse: "Hear righteousness, O Lord, attend unto my cry" (Ps. xvii, 1). He said: 'Beloved is the Community of Israel before the Holy One, blessed be He, and whenever she comes before Him, He is ready to receive her. Hence David said: "I am linked with the Community of Israel, being before Thee as She is, and therefore, hearken, O Lord, unto Righteousness first, and then give ear unto my prayer".' He continues: ' "Without feigned lips." What is this ? We have learnt that every word of prayer that issues from a man's mouth ascends aloft through all firmaments to a place where it is tested. If it is genuine, it is taken up before the Holy King to be fulfilled, but if not, it is rejected, and an alien spirit is evoked by it. So it is written of Joseph, "His feet they hurt with fetters . . . until the time that his word came", that is, until the word of Joseph's prayer came to heaven and was tested; and then, "the king sent and loosed him".'

Meanwhile day had arrived. Said R. Eleazar: 'It is now time for the Community of Israel to be united with her Spouse. Happy are the righteous who study the Torah by night and then come to unite themselves with the Holy One, blessed be He, and the Community of Israel.' R.

Eleazar continued: 'It is written: "Thus shall ye separate the children of Israel from their uncleanness" (Lev. xv, 31). When an unclean spirit is roused below, it rouses another unclean spirit above which obtains permission to go down to the world, when the spirit of holiness which used to come down and smite it is no longer there. Then judgement confronts sinners, and there are two harmful spirits in the world, one of judgement and one of uncleanness.' Said R. Eleazar: 'Here I must say something that I have learnt from my father. Just as when an unclean spirit rests upon a house, God sends a plague of leprosy to attack it and so cause the house to be purified, so if a spirit of uncleanness rests on a man and God desires to purify him, He rouses a spirit of stern judgement which contends with that unclean spirit until [55b] it is expelled. Nor does that spirit of judgement depart until it has loosened the bodily frame. Then at last is the man purified and freed from the unclean spirits. Therefore we have learnt that if a man wants to defile himself, heaven helps to defile him,[1] and woe to a man when an unclean spirit is found in him all his life, for this indeed shows that God desires to clear him out of the world (to come). Happy are the righteous on whom rests a spirit of holiness in this world and in the world to come'.

When it was full day they went on their way, and R. Eleazar discoursed on the verse: "And Jacob went on his way, and the angels of God met him" (Gen. XXXII, 1). 'Observe', he said, 'that all the time that Jacob was with Laban God did not speak with him (save at the very end, when he was about to depart), but as soon as he had left him the angels came to meet and to escort him. It says that the angels met him (bo, lit. in him), not that he met them. This is to indicate that they were some from the side of mercy and some from the side of judgement, and they met and were united "in him". Hence he called the place maḥa-naim (lit. two camps). It is written of Esau, "And the first came forth red" (Gen. xxv. 25). Though Esau came forth first, he was not really the elder, since at the time of pro-creation Isaac's thoughts were [56a] first centred on mercy,

---

[1] T.B. Yoma, 38b.

represented by Jacob, and afterwards on judgement, represented by Esau. Hence Jacob was really created first.
R. Judah used to teach as follows. Esau is called "first", and
God is also called "first", as it is written, "I am the first
and I am the last" (Isa. XLIV, 6). The "first" will one day
punish the "first" and rebuild the other "first", to wit, "A
glorious throne set on high from the first, the place of our
Sanctuary" (Jer. XVII, 12). We have learnt: One day the walls
of Jerusalem will reach on high to the throne of the King,
as it is written, "At that time they shall call Jerusalem the
throne of the Lord" (Jer. III, 17).'

AḤARE MOTH

Leviticus XVI, 1–XVIII, 30

AND THE LORD SPOKE UNTO MOSES AFTER THE DEATH OF THE TWO SONS OF AARON. R. Judah said: 'Since it says here, "the Lord spoke unto Moses", why does it repeat in the next verse, "And the Lord said unto Moses, Speak to Aaron thy brother", etc. ? The same question arises in other places (e.g. Lev. I, 1; Exodus XXIV, 1), and in all cases the answer is the same, that the reference is first to one grade (of the Deity) and then to another; but all are equivalent and come from one root.'

R. Isaac remarked: 'One verse says, "Serve the Lord with fear, and rejoice with trembling" (Ps. II, 11), and another verse says, "Serve the Lord with gladness, come before him with rejoicing" (Ps. C, 2). The apparent contradiction is explained as follows. When a man comes to serve his Master he should do so first in fear, and through that fear he will afterwards perform the precepts of the Law in joy. It says, "rejoice in trembling", because it is forbidden to a man to rejoice overmuch in this world, but in the words and the precepts of the Torah it is quite right that he should rejoice.' R. Abba said: 'The word "fear" [56b] here esoterically alludes to the Holy One, blessed be He, as in the verse, "The fear of the Lord is the beginning of knowledge" (Prov. I, 7).' R. Eleazar said: 'If a man desires to serve his Master, from what place should he commence and in what place should he first aim at unifying the name of his Master ? In "fear", with which the ascent heavenwards commences.'

Another interpretation is as follows. R. Jose said: 'Why does the text say, "after the death of the two sons of Aaron", and not "after the death of Nadab and Abihu", since we know they were his sons ? The reason is to show that they had not yet emerged from the guardianship of their father, but they thrust themselves forward in his lifetime.'

R. Ḥiya said: 'One day I was on my way to visit R. Simeon

to learn from him the portion of the Passover. In a certain mountain which I passed I saw some clefts in a rock and two men sitting in one. As I went along I caught the sound of their voices saying: "A song, a psalm of the sons of Korah." Why both song and psalm ? We have learnt in the name of R. Simeon that this is a double song, and therefore superior to other songs. So, too, with the expressions, "A psalm, a song for the Sabbath day" (Ps. xcii, 1), or "Song of songs" (S.S. 1, 1): the doubling is a sign of pre-eminence. This is the song of the Holy One, blessed be He, which was sung by the sons of Korah, those who sat at the doorway of Gehinnom.[1] Therefore this Psalm is recited (in the morning prayers) on the second day of the week. I went up to them and asked them what they were doing in that place. They said: "We are pedlars, and two days in the week we go into a solitary place and study the Torah, because on other days people will not let us." I said to them: "Happy is your portion." They continued: "Whenever the righteous are removed from the world, punishment is removed from the world and the death of the righteous atones for the sins of the generation. Therefore we read the section dealing with the death of the sons of Aaron on the Day of Atonement that it may atone for the sins of Israel. God says: Recount the death of these righteous ones, and it will be accounted to you as if you brought an offering on that day to make atonement for you. For we have learnt that so long as Israel are in captivity, and cannot bring offerings on that day, the mention of the two sons of Aaron shall be their atonement. For so we have learnt, that Abihu was equal to his two brothers Eleazar and Ithamar, and Nadab to all together, and Nadab and Abihu were reckoned as equal to the seventy elders who were associated with Moses; and therefore their death was an atonement for Israel." '

R. [57a] Hizkiah quoted in this connection the verse: "Therefore thus saith the Lord to the house of Jacob who redeemed Abraham" (Isa. xxix, 22). 'We might think', he said, 'that the words "to the house of Jacob" are misplaced,

---

[1] According to another reading, "regarding those who sat", etc. Cf. T.B. Baba Bathra, 74a.

but really the verse is to be taken as it stands. For when Abram was cast into the furnace of the Chaldeans the angels said before God: How shall this one be delivered, seeing that he has no merit of his ancestors to rely upon ? God replied: He shall be delivered for the sake of his sons. But, they said, Ishmael will issue from him ? There is Isaac who will stretch forth his neck on the altar. But Esau will issue from him ? There is Jacob who is the complete throne and all his sons who are perfect before me. They said: Assuredly through this merit Abraham shall be delivered. Hence it is written: "Jacob who redeemed Abraham". The verse continues: "Jacob shall not now be ashamed . . . but when he seeth his children the work of my hands", etc. The reference here in "his children" is to Hananiah, Mishael and Azariah, who cast themselves into the fiery furnace. We have learnt that when they were bound in order to be cast into the fire, each of them lifted up his voice and quoted a verse of Scripture in the presence of all the princes and rulers. Hananiah said: "The Lord is on my side, I will not fear what man can do to me", etc. (Ps. cxviii, 6). Mishael said: "Therefore fear thou not, O Jacob my servant, saith the Lord", etc. (Jer. xxx, 10). When those present heard the name of Jacob they all laughed in scorn. Azariah said: "Hear, O Israel, the Lord our God the Lord is one" (Deut. vi, 4). At that moment God assembled His court and said to them: For the sake of which of those verses shall I deliver them ? They replied: "They shall know that thou alone whose name is the Lord art most high over all the earth" (Ps. lxxxvii). God then turned to His Throne and said: With which of these verses shall I deliver them ? The Throne replied: With the one at which they all laughed: as Jacob stood by Abraham in the furnace, so let him stand by these. Hence it is written in connection with them, "Not now shall Jacob be ashamed". Now why were these delivered ? Because they prayed to God and unified His name in the fitting manner. The two sons of Aaron brought strange fire on the altar and did not unify God's name in the fitting manner, and therefore they were burnt.'

R. Isaac said: 'It is written here, "After the death of the

two sons . . . and they died". Why this double mention of
their death ? One referring to their actual death, the other
to their having no children, for he who has no children is
counted as dead.'[1] R. Abba derived the same lesson from
this verse, "And Nadab and Abihu died . . . and they had
no children and Eleazar and Ithamar ministered," etc.
(Num. III, 4). He said further that they did not die like others
who have no children: they died only their own death but
not that of their souls, [57b] because their souls entered into
Phineas; wherefore it refers to Phineas as "these" (Ex. VI,
25). R. Eleazar said: 'For this reason whenever Phineas is
mentioned he is always called "the son of Eleazar the son
of Aaron the Priest" (v. Num. XXV, 7; Judges XX, 28). . . .[2]

'It has been taught in the name of R. Jose that on this
day of Atonement it has been instituted that this portion
should be read to atone for Israel in captivity. Hence we
learn that if the chastisements of the Lord come upon a
man, they are an atonement for his sins, and whoever sorrows
for the sufferings of the righteous obtains pardon for his
sins. Therefore on this day we read the portion commencing
"after the death of the two sons of Aaron", that the people
may hear and lament the loss of the righteous and obtain
forgiveness for their sins. For whenever a man so laments
and sheds tears for them, God proclaims of him, "thine
iniquity is taken away and thy sin purged" (Isa. VI, 7).
Also he may be assured that his sons will not die in his lifetime, and of him it is written, "he shall see seed, he shall
prolong days" (Isa. LIII, 19).'

R. Simeon said: 'I am amazed to see how little men pay
heed to the will of their Master, and how they allow themselves to be wrapt in sleep until the day comes which will
cover them with darkness, and when their Master will
demand [58a] reckoning from them. The Torah calls aloud
to them, but none inclines his ear. Mark now that in future
generations the Torah will be forgotten, and there will be

---

[1] T.B. Nedarim, 64b.   [2] The text here expounds the significance of the
Yod with which the name Pinchas is written in Numbers XXV, 7, finding
in it an indication that by his zeal in the matter of Zimri he rectified the
misdeed of Nadab and Abihu, and reunited the letters of the Divine Name.

none to close and open. Alas for that generation ! There will be no generation like the present until the Messiah comes and knowledge shall be diffused throughout the world. It is written: "A river went forth from Eden" (Gen. II, 10). It has been laid down that the name of that river is Jubilee, but in the book of Rab Hamnuna the Elder it is called Life, because life issues thence to the world. We have also laid down that the great and mighty Tree in which is food for all is called the Tree of Life, because its roots are in that Life. We have learnt that that river sends forth deep streams with the oil of plenitude to water the Garden and feed the trees and the shoots. These streams flow on and unite in two pillars which are called Jachin and Boaz. Thence the streams flow on and come to rest in a grade called Zaddik, and from hence they flow further till they all are gathered into the place called Sea, which is the sea of Wisdom. But the current of that river never ceases, and therefore the streams flow back to the two pillars, Neẓaḥ and Hod, whence they traverse that Zaddik to find there blessings and joy. The Matrona is called the "time" of the Zaddik, and therefore all who are fed below are fed from this place, as it is written: "The eyes of all wait on thee and thou givest them their meat in due season" (Ps. CXLV, 15). When these two are joined, all worlds have gladness and blessing, and there is peace among upper and lower beings. But when through the sins of this world there are no blessings from these streams, and the "time" sucks from the "other side", then judgement impends over the world and there is no peace. Now when mankind desire to be blessed, they can only be so through the priest, when he arouses his own Crown and blesses the Matrona, so that there are blessings in all worlds. We have learnt that at that time Moses inquired of God concerning this, saying: If the sons of men shall return to Thee, through whom shall they be blessed ? and God replied: Do not ask Me. Speak to Aaron thy brother, for in his hands are delivered blessings above and below.'

R. Abba said: 'There are times when God is propitious and ready to dispense blessing to those that pray to Him, and times when He is not propitious and judgement is let loose on the world, and times when judgement is held in suspense. There are seasons in the year when grace is in the ascendant, and seasons when judgement is in the ascendant, and seasons when judgement is in the ascendant but held in suspense. Similarly with the months [58b] and similarly with the days of the week, and even with the parts of each day and each hour. Therefore it is written: "There is a time for every purpose" (Eccl. III, 1), and again, "My prayer is unto thee, O Lord, in an acceptable time" (Ps. LXIX, 14). Hence it says here: "Let him not come at every time to the Sanctuary".' R. Simeon said: 'This interpretation of the word "time" is quite correct and here God warned Aaron not to make the same mistake as his sons and try to associate a wrong "time" with the King, even if he should see that the control of the world has been committed for the time to the hands of another, and though he has the power to unify with it and bring it near to Holiness.[1] And if he wants to know with what he should enter, the answer is, with *zoth* (this‑ =Shekinah), for that is the "time" which is attached to my name by the letter *yod* which is inscribed in my name. R. Jose taught: Verily it is as the Holy Lamp (R. Simeon) explained the verse, "He hath made everything (*kol*) beautiful in its time (*be'itto*)"; that is to say, "He hath made *kol* (*Yesod*) beautiful in *'eth* (Malkuth), and none should interpose between them"; and therefore Aaron was warned that he should not come at every "time" into the Sanctuary, but only with *zoth*.'

Once when R. Eleazar was studying with his father he said to him: 'It is written of the sons of Aaron that a fire went forth from the Lord and consumed them, and also of the assembly of Korah that a fire went forth from the Lord and consumed them (Num. XVI, 35). Were they then in the same category ?' R. Simeon replied: 'There is a difference, because of the assembly of Korah it says that "they perished from the congregation", but this word is not used of the sons of Aaron.' He further asked him: 'Since it says, "let

[1] Al. "Yet it is not so far committed that this power should be united and brought near to Holiness (i.e. that its name should be linked with God as the name *Adonay* is)."

him not come at all times into the sanctuary", why does it
not specify at which time he should come ?' He replied: 'As
we have explained, there was a certain time which was known
to the priests, and here these words are inserted only as a
warning to Aaron, as we have explained.' He replied: 'That
is what I thought, only I wanted to make certain.' R. Simeon
continued: 'Eleazar, my son, note that all the offerings were
acceptable to God, but none so much as the incense, wherefore it was taken into the inmost shrine with the greatest
privacy, and the severest punishment was inflicted for its
misuse.' R. Simeon then expounded the verse: "In fragrance
thine ointments are good" (S.S. 1, 3). 'This fragrance is the
odour of the incense, which is more subtle and intimate
than any other, and when it ascends to unite with the anointing oil of the streams of the Source they stimulate one another,
and then those oils are good for giving light, and the oil
flows from grade to grade through those grades which are
called the Holy Name; hence it is written, "therefore do
maidens love thee" (*Ibid.*), where *'alamoth* (maidens) may
be read *'olamoth* (worlds); and from thence blessings spread
over all below. [59a] And because this incense is bound
up with the supernal ointment more closely it is more
esteemed by the Almighty Holy One, blessed be He, than
all offerings and sacrifices. The verse continues: "Draw me,
we will run after thee". Therefore the Community of
Israel says: "I am like incense and thou art like oil, draw me
after thee, and we shall run, I and all my hosts. Let the King
bring me to his chambers that we may all be glad and rejoice
in thee".'

FOR I WILL APPEAR IN THE CLOUD UPON THE MERCY
SEAT. R. Judah said: 'Happy are the righteous that God
seeks to honour them. If a man rides on the horse of an
earthly king he is put to death, but God let Elijah ride upon
His, as it is written: "And Elijah went up in a whirlwind
into heaven" (2 Kings II, 11); and He also took Moses into
the cloud, though it is written here, "in the cloud I shall
appear on the mercy seat". We have learnt that this was the
place where the Cherubim abode. We have learnt that three

times a day a miracle was accomplished with their wings. When the holiness of the King descended upon them they of themselves raised their wings and spread them out so as to cover the mercy seat. Then they folded their wings and stood rejoicing in the divine presence.' R. Abba said: 'The high priest did not see the divine presence when he entered the sanctuary, and but a cloud came down, and when it lighted on the mercy seat the Cherubim beat their wings together and broke out into song. What did they chant? "For great is the Lord and highly to be praised, he is to be feared above all gods" (Ps. xcvi, 4). When they spread out their wings they said: "For all the gods of the peoples are idols, but the Lord made the heavens" (*Ibid.* 5). And when they covered the mercy seat they said: "Before the Lord for he cometh to judge the earth, he shall judge the world with righteousness and the peoples with equity" (Ps. xcviii, 9). Then the priest used to hear their voice in the sanctuary, and he put the incense in its place with all devotion in order that all might be blessed.' R. Jose said: 'The word "equity" (*mesharim*, lit. equities) in the above quoted verse indicates that the Cherubim were male and female.' R. Isaac said: 'From this we learn that where there is no union of male and female men are not worthy to behold the divine presence.' [59b]

It has been taught in the name of R. Jose: Once the people were short of rain and they sent a deputation to R. Simeon, R. Jesse, R. Hizkiah and the rest of the Companions. R. Simeon was on the point of going to visit R. Pinchas ben Jair, along with his son R. Eleazar. When he saw them he exclaimed: ' "A song of ascents; Behold how good and how pleasant it is for brethren to dwell together in unity" (Ps. cxxxiii, 1). The expression "in unity",' he said, 'refers to the Cherubim. When their faces were turned to one another, it was well with the world—"how good and how pleasant", but when the male turned his face from the female, it was ill with the world. Now, too, I see that you are come because the male is not abiding with the female. If you have come only for this, return, because I see that on this day face will once more be turned to face. But if you have come to learn the Torah, stay with me.' They said: 'We have come for both purposes. Let, therefore, one of us go and take the good news to our fellows, and we will stay here with our Teacher.' As they went along he took as his text, "I am black but comely, O ye daughters of Jerusalem" (S.S. 1, 5). 'The Community of Israel says to the Holy One, blessed be He: I am black in captivity but I am comely in religious practices, for although Israel are in exile they do not abandon these. "I am black like the tents of Kedar", to wit, the sons of Keturah, whose faces are always swarthy, and yet I am like the curtains of Solomon, like the brightness of the skies. "Look not upon me because I am swarthy." Why am I swarthy? Because the sun hath gazed hard on me, but not looked upon me to illumine me as he should have done. "My mother's sons were angry with me." These words are said by Israel, and refer to the Chieftains appointed over the other nations. Or they may still be spoken by the Community of Israel, and allude to the verse, "For he hath cast from earth to heaven the beauty of Israel" (Lam. II, 1). Or again, the words, "how good, how pleasant it is for brethren to dwell together in unity" may refer to the Companions when they sit together and there is no discord between them. At first they are like combatants who seek to kill one another, but afterwards they become friends and brothers.[1] Then God says: "Behold how good", etc., and He himself listens to them and delights in their converse. You, therefore, Companions that are gathered here, as you have been close friends hitherto, so may you never part until God shall give you glad greeting, and for your sake may there be peace in the world.'

They then went on their way till they reached R. Pinchas ben Jair. R. Pinchas came out and kissed him, saying: 'I am privileged to kiss the Shekinah.' He prepared for them couches with awnings. Said R. Simeon: 'The Torah does not require this.' So he removed them and they sat down. Said R. Pinchas: 'Before we eat let us hear something from the great Master, for R. Simeon always speaks his mind; he is a man who says what he has to say without fear of heaven

[1] v. T.B. Kiddushin, 30b.

or earth. He has no fear of heaven since God concurs [60a] with him, and he is no more afraid of men than a lion of sheep.'

R. Simeon then turned to R. Eleazar his son, saying: 'Stand up and say something new in the presence of R. Pinchas and the rest of the Companions.' R. Eleazar thereupon arose and began with the text: "And the Lord spoke unto Moses after the death of the two sons of Aaron" (Lev. XVI, I). 'This verse', he said, 'seems superfluous, seeing that the text proceeds, "And the Lord said to Moses, speak unto Aaron thy brother", which should properly be the beginning of the section. The explanation is this. When God gave the incense to Aaron, he desired that no other man should use it in his lifetime. He said to him: "Thou desirest to increase peace in the world. By thy hand shall peace be increased above. Therefore the incense of spices shall be delivered to thy hand from now onwards, and in thy lifetime no other shall use it." Nadab and Abihu, however, thrust themselves forward to offer it. We have learnt that Moses worried himself to find out what was the cause of their misfortune. Hence God spoke to him after their death and said to him: "The cause is that they 'drew near to the Lord', and thrust themselves forward in the lifetime of their father." Now if the sons of Aaron brought this upon themselves through thrusting themselves forward in the lifetime of their father, what should I deserve if I thrust myself forward before my father and R. Pinchas and the rest of the Companions ?' Hearing this, R. Pinchas came up to him and kissed him and blessed him.

R. Simeon then discoursed on the verse: "Behold it is the litter of Solomon, threescore mighty men are round about it", etc. (S.S. III, 7). He said: 'The "litter" here is the throne of glory of the King, Solomon, the "king to whom all peace belongs". Threescore mighty men are round about it, clinging to its sides as emissaries from stern judgement; they are called the sixty rods of fire wherewith that Youth[1] is girt. On its right hand is a flashing sword, on its left hand coals of fire with seventy thousand consuming

[1] Metatron.

flames. Those threescore are armed with deadly weapons
from the armoury of the supernal Might of the Holy One,
blessed be He. They all "handle the sword and are expert
in war": they are ever ready to execute judgement and are
called the "lords of wailing and howling". And from whence
do they receive all this ? "From fear": that is, from the place
called "the fear of Isaac". And when ? "In the night": at
the time when they are commissioned to execute judgement.
We have learnt that a thousand and five hundred bearers
of arms with authority to smite are attached to the side of
those mighty ones. In the hands of him who is called "Youth"
there are four mighty keys. Sea monsters go forth beneath
the ship [60b] of this mighty sea in four directions, and each
has four aspects. A thousand rocks rise and sink every day
from the tide of that sea. Afterwards they are uprooted from
it and go to another sea. There is no number to those that
cling to her hair. Two sons suck from her every day who are
called "spies of the land", and two daughters are at her
feet, and these cling to the sides of that litter. In her left
hand are seventy branches that grow among the fishes of the
sea, all red as a rose, and above them all is one of a still
deeper red. This one goes up and down and all hide in her
hair. When the master of the evil tongue comes down he
becomes a serpent leaping over the hills and mountains until
he finds prey to consume. Then he becomes mollified and
his tongue turns to good. Israel furnish him with prey and
then he returns to his place and enters into the hollow of
the great abyss. When he ascends, there also ascend demons
girt with spear and sword without number, who surround
the sixty who are round the litter, so that myriads of myriads
stand round this litter above, all being nurtured by it and
doing obeisance to it, and below there go forth from it
myriads who wander about the world until the trumpet blows
and they assemble. These cling to the uncleanness of the
nails. This litter embraces them all. Its feet take hold of the
four corners of the world; it is found in heaven above and
in the earth below. It is called *Adonay*, the lord of all, this
name being inscribed among its hosts. Therefore the priest
must concentrate his thought on heavenly things to unify

the holy name from the fitting place. Hence we have learnt
that Aaron was to come to the sanctuary with *zoth*. With
this he was to bring the holiness to its place, and from this
place man must fear God. Hence it is written, "O that they
were wise, that they considered *zoth*" (Deut. XXXII, 29);
that is to say, if men consider how *zoth* is surrounded by
her hosts who stand ready before her to punish sinners, then
at once they would "consider their latter end", be careful
of their acts and not sin before the Holy One, blessed be He.'
R. Simeon further said: 'If a man studies the Torah and
guards this *zoth*, then *zoth* protects him and makes a covenant
with him regarding his own covenant that it shall not depart
from him or from his sons or his sons' sons for ever, as it is
written: "And as for me, this (*zoth*) is my covenant with
them", etc.'

They then sat down to eat, and in the course of the meal
R. Simeon said to the Companions: 'Let each one enunciate a
new idea concerning the Torah at the table before R. Pinchas.'

R. Hizkiah then began with the text: "The Lord God
hath given me the tongue of them that are taught, that I
should know how to sustain with words him that is weary"
(Isa. L, 4). 'Happy are Israel in that God has chosen them
above all other peoples and called them "holy" [61a] and
given them as their portion union with the holy name. How
do they effect this union ? By their attainments in the Torah,
for knowledge of the Torah means union with the Holy One,
blessed be He. We have learnt in the presence of our Master:
What is holiness ? The consummation of the whole which
is called Supernal Wisdom. From thence issue streams and
fountains in all directions till they reach this *zoth*. And when
this *zoth* is blessed from the supernal place called Holiness
and Wisdom, it is called "the spirit of holiness"; and when
mysteries of the Torah proceed from it, it is called "the
language of holiness". When the holy oil flows to those two
pillars[1] that are called "the disciples of the Lord", it is
gathered in there, and when it issues thence through the
grade called Yesod to this lesser Wisdom, it is called "the
tongue of the disciples", and it goes forth to arouse the

---

[1] *Nezah* and *Hod*.

superior holy saints. Hence it is written, "The Lord has
given me the tongue of disciples", and why ? "To know how
to sustain with words him that is weary". God gives this
tongue to the Sacred Lamp, R. Simeon, nay more, He raises
him higher and higher: therefore he speaks his mind openly
without concealment.'

R. Jesse then took the text: "And the Lord gave Solomon
wisdom as he had promised him, and there was peace between
Hiram and Solomon" (1 Kings v, 26). 'What is the connection between these two statements ? The answer is this:
"God gave Solomon wisdom"; and how did Solomon display this wisdom that God gave him ? First in this way, that
he made Hiram assume a more modest frame of mind. For
we have been taught that Hiram at first set himself up as a
god, as it is written: "Thou hast said, I am a god, I sit in the
seat of God" (Ezek. xxviii, 2). Solomon, however, with his
wisdom induced him to give up these claims, and he deferred
to him, and therefore it is written, "and there was peace
between Hiram and Solomon". We have also learnt that
R. Isaac said in the name of R. Judah that Solomon sent
him a carriage which took him down to the seven circuits
of Gehinnom and brought him up again. We have also
learnt that Solomon inherited the Moon complete on all
sides. So R. Simeon ben Yoḥai surpasses all others in wisdom,
and none can rise save they make peace with him.'

R. Jose took as his text the verse: "O my dove that art in
the clefts of the rock, in the covert of the steep place" (S.S.
II, 14). 'The "dove" here is the Community of Israel, which
like a dove never forsakes her mate, the Holy One, blessed
be He. "In the clefts of the rock": these are the students
of the Torah, who have no ease in this world. "In the covert
of the steep place": these are the specially pious among
them, the saintly and God-fearing, from whom the Divine
Presence never departs. The Holy One, blessed be He,
inquires concerning them of the Community of Israel,
saying, "Let me see thy countenance, let me hear thy voice,
for sweet is thy voice"; for above only the voice of those
who study the Torah is heard. We have learnt that the
likeness of all such is graven above before the Holy One,

blessed be He, who delights Himself with them every day
and watches them, and that voice rises and pierces its way
through all firmaments until it stands before the Holy One,
blessed be He. And now the Holy One, blessed be He, has
graven the likeness of R. Simeon above, and his voice rises
higher and higher and is crowned with a holy diadem, and
God crowns him in all worlds and glories in him.'

R. Ḥiya took as his text: "That which is hath been already
and that which is to be", etc. (Eccl. III, 15). 'This is explained
by what we have learnt, that before God created this world
He created others and destroyed them, until [61b] He consulted the Torah, and through it made the proper adjust-
ments and became crowned. Thus all that was to be in this
world was before Him fully prepared. We have learnt, too,
that all men of all generations stood before Him in their
likenesses before they came into the world, and even all the
souls of men were traced out before Him in the firmament
in the similitude of their shape in this world. All, too, that
they afterwards learnt in this world they already knew before
they came into it. All this, however, applies only to the truly
virtuous. Those who did not turn out virtuous in this world
even there were far from the Holy One, blessed be He, being
in the hollow of the abyss, whence they came down into the
world before their time. And as they proved to be stiff-necked
in this world, so, we have learnt, they were before they came
into the world. They threw away the holy portion which
was given them and went and defiled themselves with the
hollow of the abyss and took their portion from thence and
came down into the world before their time. If such a one
deserves well afterwards and repents before his Master, he
takes his own proper portion, namely, "that which hath
been already". Now we may ask concerning the sons of
Aaron, the like of whom were not in Israel, how they could
perish from the world as they did. Where was their own
merit, the merit of their father, the merit of Moses? We
have, however, learnt from the Sacred Lamp that God was
indeed solicitous for their honour, and so their bodies were
burnt within but their souls did not perish.[1] Phineas, too,

---

[1] v. T.B. Sabbath, 113b, where the reverse is stated.

was already in existence who was to repair the damage; whence it is written, "that which is to be already was". We have learnt that all the truly virtuous before they come into the world are prepared above and called by their names. And R. Simeon ben Yohai from the first day of Creation was stationed before the Holy One, blessed be He, and God called him by his name, happy is his portion above and below !'

R. Abba took as his text the verse: "While the king sat at his table, my spikenard sent forth its fragrance" (S.S. I, 12). 'This has been applied by the Companions to the children of Israel when at the giving of the Law they sent forth a sweet fragrance which will bestead them in all generations by saying "we will do and we will hear". Or we may translate "my spikenard forsook its fragrance", applying the words to the making of the calf. There is, however, also an esoteric allusion in this verse. It says "A river went forth from Eden to water the garden" (Gen. II, 10). This stream first issues in a path which none knoweth. Then Eden joins with it in perfect union, and then fountains and streams issue and crown the holy Son, who thereupon assumes the inheritance of his Father and Mother, and the supernal King regales himself with royal delights. Then "my spikenard gives forth its fragrance": this is *Yesod*, who sends forth blessings at the union of the Holy King [62a] and the Matrona, and so blessings are dispensed to all worlds and upper and lower are blessed. And now the Sacred Lamp is crowned with the crowns of that grade, and he and the Companions send up praises from earth to heaven wherewith She is crowned. Now blessings must be brought down from heaven on to the Companions through that grade. Let, therefore, R. Eleazar his son expound to us some of the profound ideas which he has learnt from his father.'

R. Eleazar then cited the verse: "And he looked and behold a well in a field," etc. (Gen. XXIX, 2). 'These verses', he said, 'have an esoteric meaning which I have learnt from my father. The "well" is the same as that of which it is written, "the well which princes digged" (the Shekinah). The three flocks lying by it are *Nezah*, *Hod*, and *Yesod*, and from them the well is ever full of blessings. "Out of that

well they watered the flocks": this means that from it the
lower worlds are sustained. "The stone upon the well's
mouth was great": this is rigorous Judgement, which stands
by it from the "other side" to suck from it. But "thither
all the flocks gather": these are the six Crowns of the King,
which gather together and draw blessings from the Head of
the King and pour them upon her, and thereby they "roll
away" the stern judgement and remove it from her. Then
they "water the flock", that is, pour out blessings in that
spot for higher and lower, and then "put the stone again
upon the well's mouth in its place": that is to say, judgement
returns to its place, because it is necessary for the upholding
of the world. And now God has poured upon you blessings
from the source of the stream, and from you all of this
generation are blessed. Happy are ye in this world and in
the world to come !'

R. Simeon then spoke on the verse: "Let the saints exult
in glory, let them sing for joy upon their beds" (Ps. CXLIX, 5).
'We have learnt', he said, 'that the knot of faith is tied with
thirteen attributes, and in addition the Torah is crowned
with thirteen "measures", [rules of interpretation] and
the holy name is crowned therewith. Similarly, when
Jacob desired to bless his sons, he said that his sons should
be blessed with the bond of faith; it is written, "all these are
the tribes of Israel, twelve, and this (zoth)", etc. (Gen. XLIX,
28); thus there were thirteen, the Shekinah being joined
with them. We have learnt that all those "measures" ascend
and rest upon a certain head, and the pious inherit all that
glory from above, as it is written, "Let the saints exult in
glory", in this world, "and let them sing for joy upon their
beds"—in the next world. "The high praises of God are in
their mouths", to tie the bond of faith in fitting manner; and
so "a two-edged sword is in their hand", to wit, the sword
of the Holy One, blessed be He, which flashes with two
judgements. Now R. Pinchas ben Jair is the crown of Lovingkindness, the high attribute, and therefore he inherits the
glory from on high and ties the celestial and holy bond, the
bond of faith. Happy is his portion in this world and in
the world to come. Of this table it is said: "This is the table

that is before the Lord" (Ezek. XLI, 22).' R. Pinchas then
rose and kissed and blessed him, and R. Eleazar and all the
Companions, and took the cup and said the benediction
and the psalm, "Thou preparest a table before me in the
presence of mine enemies" (Ps. XXIII, 5). All that day they
gladdened themselves [62b] with words of the Torah, and
the joy of R. Simeon was great. R. Pinchas took R. Eleazar
and did not leave him all that day and night, saying: 'All
this great joy and gladness is of my portion, and they will
make proclamation concerning me to that effect in the other
world.'

When they rose to depart R. Pinchas would not at first
let R. Eleazar go, but he accompanied R. Simeon and all
the Companions on their way. As they went along R. Simeon
said: 'It is time to work for the Lord.' R. Abba came and
asked him: 'It is written, AND AARON SHALL CAST LOTS
UPON THE TWO GOATS. What', he asked, 'is the meaning
of these lots, and why had Aaron to cast them?' R. Simeon
began his reply by citing the verse: "And he took from them
Simeon and bound him before their eyes" (Gen. XLII, 24).
'Why did Joseph take Simeon rather than any other one
of the brothers ? The reason was that Joseph said to himself:
Simeon and Levi everywhere open the door to judgement.
So it was with me and so it was with Shechem. It is therefore
meet that I should take this one so that he should not rouse
contention among all the tribes. The question has also been
asked why Simeon associated himself with Levi rather than,
say, with Reuben, who was also his full brother. The reason
was that he saw that Levi came from the side of judgement
and he himself was attached to the side of stern judgement.
He therefore thought that if Levi joined him they would
be able to conquer the world. What then did God do ? He
took Levi for his portion, and made Simeon isolated.

'We have learnt that on the side of the Mother there are
two emissaries attached to her left hand who roam about
the world to spy it out. Now Israel are God's portion, and
from His great love for them He gave them one day in the
year to cleanse and purify them from all their sins, and therefore on this day they are crowned and are safe from all

executioners and all hostile emissaries. It is written that
Aaron shall cast lots upon the two he-goats. Why is one of
these for the Lord ? Because God said, Let one abide by
me and the other roam about the world; for if the two were
combined the world would not be able to stand against
them. The second one therefore goes forth, and when he
finds Israel absorbed in religious service and pious deeds and
all at peace with one another he can see no opportunity
to bring a charge against them. We have learnt that there
are many demons under his control, whose office it is to
spy out the earth for those [63*a*] who transgress the commands of the Law; but on that day there is no opening for
any accusation against Israel. When that he-goat reaches
the rock (of Azazel) there is great rejoicing and the emissary
who went forth to accuse returns and declares the praises
of Israel, the accuser becoming the defender. And not only
on this day, but whenever Israel desire to be cleansed of
their sins, God shows them how to restrain the accusers by
means of the offerings which are brought before the Holy
One, blessed be He, and then they cannot harm. But this
day is more efficacious than all; and just as Israel appease
all below, so all those who have accusations to bring (above)
are appeased, though all the service is to the Holy One.
We have learnt that at the hour of which it is written that
Aaron should take the two he-goats, all those (accusers)
above rouse themselves and seek to go forth into the world,
and when Aaron brings near those below those above are
also brought near. The lots are then produced for both sides;
and as the priest casts lots below so the Priest casts lots
above; and just as below one is left for the Holy One and
one is thrust out to the wilderness, so above one remains
with the Holy One, blessed be He, and one goes forth into
the supernal wilderness; so the two are connected. It is
written later:

'AND AARON SHALL LAY HIS TWO HANDS ON THE
HEAD OF THE LIVE GOAT AND CONFESS OVER HIM, ETC.
He must use both hands in order that the Holy One may
concur with him. The he-goat is called "live", to include

the one above. The words "over him" mean that the
sins shall all be left on the goat.' R. Abba asked how this
could be reconciled with the verse which says, "And they
shall no more sacrifice their sacrifices unto the he-goats
after which they go a-whoring" (Lev. XVII, 7). He replied:
'It does not say there that they should not sacrifice he-goats,
but *to* he-goats. So here, the goat bore on itself all their
iniquities, but the offering was brought only to the Holy One,
blessed be He, and through the offering upper and lower are
appeased and judgement has no sway over Israel.

'AND SHALL SEND HIM AWAY BY THE HAND OF A MAN
THAT IS IN READINESS. The words "in readiness" contain a hint that [63b] for every kind of action there are men
specially fitted. There are some men specially fitted for the
transmission of blessings, as, for instance, a man of "good
eye". There are others, again, who are specially fitted for the
transmission of curses, and curses light wherever they cast
their eyes. Such was Balaam, who was the fitting instrument
of evil and not of good, and even when he blessed his blessing
was not confirmed, but all his curses were confirmed, because
he had an evil eye. Hence, as we have learnt, a man should
turn aside a hundred times in order to avoid a man with an
evil eye. So here, "a man that is in readiness" means a man
who is marked out by nature for this service. The priest was
able to tell such a man because he had one eye slightly
larger than the other, shaggy eyebrows, bluish eyes and a
crooked glance. This was the kind of man fitted for such a
task. In Gush Halba[1] there was a man whose hands brought
death to whatever they touched, and none would come near
him. In Syria there was a man whose look always brought
ill hap, even though he meant it for good. One day a man
was walking in the street with a beaming countenance when
this man looked at him and his eye was knocked out. Thus
different men are fitted either for one thing or the other.
Hence it is written, "He that hath a good eye shall be
blessed" (Prov. XXII, 9), or, as we should rather read by a
change in the vowelling (*yebarech* for *yeborach*), "shall bless".

[1] = Gischala, in Galilee.

We have learnt that the man who took the goat to the wilderness used to go up on a mountain and push it down with both his hands, and before it was half way down all its bones were broken,[1] and the man used to say: "So may the iniquities of thy people be wiped out", etc. And when the accuser of Israel was thus made into its advocate, the Holy One, blessed be He, took all the sins of Israel and all the records of them above and threw them into the place called "depths of the sea", as it is written: "Thou wilt cast all their sins into the depths of the sea" (Mic. VII, 19).

'AND OF THE CONGREGATION OF THE PEOPLE OF ISRAEL HE SHALL TAKE TWO HE-GOATS FOR A SIN-OFFERING. This offering was to be taken from all of them, so as to make atonement for all of them, [64*a*] and it was not sufficient that it should be taken from one individual. From whence, then, was it taken ? They used to take the money for it from the boxes in the Temple court,[2] which contained the contributions of all. The other goat, which was left to the Lord, was brought as a sin-offering first of all, being attached to a certain grade, and afterwards the other offerings were brought and Israel were left purified of all the sins which they had committed against God. On that day many doors were opened facing Israel to receive their prayers. On that day the priest was crowned with many crowns, and his service was more precious than at any other time, since he gave portions to all in those offerings of the Holy One, blessed be He. On that day lovingkindness was awakened in the world by the hand of the priest bringing offerings.'

Having gone some way, they sat down in a field and prayed. A fiery cloud came down and surrounded them. Said R. Simeon: 'We see that God's favour is in this place, so let us stay here'. They therefore sat down and discoursed on the Torah. R. Simeon quoted the text: "As cold waters to a thirsty soul, so is good news from a far country" (Prov. XXV, 25). 'King Solomon', he said, 'composed three books corresponding to three supernal attributes—the Song of Songs to Wisdom, Ecclesiastes to Understanding, and

[1] *v.* T.B. Yoma, 67*a*.   [2] *v.* Mishnah, Shekalim, IV, 2.

Proverbs to Knowledge. Why does Proverbs correspond to Knowledge ? Because all its verses are in parallel form, one half balancing the other, and when we examine them we find that they can be placed in either order. Thus here we have two things, "cold waters" and a "good report", either of which may be compared to the other as a source of comfort and refreshment.' As they were sitting a man came up and told them that the wife of R. Simeon had recovered from her illness; and at the same time the Companions heard a voice saying that God had forgiven the transgressions of the generation. Said R. Simeon: 'This is a fulfilment of the verse about "a good report from a distant country"; it is as refreshing to the spirit as cool waters to a thirsty soul.' He then said: 'Let us rise and pursue our way, since God is performing miracles for us.' He then continued his exposition, saying: 'The "cold waters" mentioned here refer to the Torah, since he who studies the Torah and sates his soul with it will hear "a good report from a distant land", to wit, the promise of many good things in this world and the next from God, who was at first far from him, and also from the place where men were previously at enmity with him, from that place [64b] greeting of peace shall be given to him.'

AND HE SHALL GO OUT UNTO THE ALTAR THAT IS BEFORE THE LORD. R. Judah quoted here the verse: "God, even God the Lord hath spoken, and called the earth from the rising of the sun unto the going down thereof" (Ps. L, 1). 'We have learnt', he said, 'that a thousand and five hundred and fifty myriads of choristers chant hymns to God when day breaks, and a thousand and five hundred and forty-eight at midday, and a thousand and five hundred and ninety myriads at the time which is called "between the evenings".' R. Jose said that when day dawns all the "lords of shouting" utter words of praise to greet it, because then all are exhilarated and judgement is mitigated. At that moment joy and blessing is in the world, and the Holy One, blessed be He, awakens Abraham[1] and has joyous communion with him, and gives him sway over the world. At the time called "between the evenings" all those angels called "masters

---

[1] Ḥesed.

of howling" are vocal, and contention is rife in the world. That is the time when the Holy One arouses Isaac[1] and rises to judge the guilty who transgress the precepts of the Law. Seven rivers of fire issue forth and descend on the heads of the wicked, along with burning coals of fire. Then Abraham returns to his place and the day departs and the sinners in Gehinnom groan as they say: "Woe unto us, for the day declineth, for the shadows of evening are stretched out" (Jer. vi, 4). At that time, therefore, a man should be careful not to omit the afternoon prayer. When night comes, those other fifteen hundred and forty-eight myriads are summoned from without the curtain and chant hymns, and then the underworld chastisements are aroused and roam about the world. These chant praises until midnight, a watch and a half. Then all the others assemble and sing psalms, after the north wind has risen and gone forth, until daylight comes and the morning rises, when joy and blessing return to the world.' R. Abba said that there are three leaders for all of the choirs. Over those who sing in the morning is appointed one named Heman, under whom there are many deputies for ordering their song. Over those of the evening there is appointed one named Jeduthun, who also has many deputies under him. At night time, when all from without the curtain arise, they are in disorder until midnight, when all gather together and the lead is taken by one called Asaph, to whom all the deputies are subordinate till morning comes. Then that "lad"[2] who sucks from his mother's breasts rises to purify them and enters to minister. That is a time of favour when the Matrona converses with the King, and the King stretches forth [65a] a thread of blessing and winds it round the Matrona and all who are joined with her. These are they that study the Torah at night time after midnight. R. Simeon said: 'Happy he who comes with the Matrona at the hour when she goes to greet the King and to converse with Him, and He stretches out his right hand to receive her. This hour is called "the uttermost parts of the sea" (Ps. cxxxix, 9), when her chastisements depart and she enters under the wings of the King, with all those that are attached to her.

[1] *Geburah*.   [2] Metatron.

At that time the Patriarchs invite the Matrona and advance to converse with her, and the Holy One, blessed be He, joins them. Hence it is written: "God, even God the Lord hath spoken and called the earth", etc. The first "God" here (*El*) refers to the light of Wisdom which is called Lovingkindness; the second "God" (*Elohim*) to Might: and "the Lord" to Mercy.'

When R. Eleazar was once studying with his father he asked him why the name YHVH is sometimes pointed with the vowels of ELOHIM, and read so. R. Simeon answered: 'The name YHVH everywhere indicates mercy, but when the wicked turn mercy into judgement, then it is written YHVH and read Elohim. There is, however, a deeper explanation, as follows. There are three grades (of Judgement) which though essentially one can yet be distinguished. All plants and lamps are illumined and fired, watered and blessed from that perennial Stream in which all is comprised, and which is called the Mother of the Garden of Eden. In itself this is Mercy, but being called Mother it is also the source of Judgement. This is represented by the name YHVH read as ELOHIM, and this is the first grade. Then we have the grade of *Geburah* itself, which is properly called *Elohim*. Thirdly we have *Ẓedek* (Righteousness), which is the final Crown and the Court of Justice of the King, and this is called *Adonay*, being also written so; and the Community of Israel is also called by this name.'

R. Eleazar then asked his father to explain to him the name EHYEH ASHER EHYEH (I am that I am). He said 'This name is all-comprehensive. [65b] The first *Ehyeh* (I shall be) is the comprehensive framework of all when the paths are still obscure, and not yet marked out, and all is still undisclosed. When a beginning has been made and the Stream has started on its course, then it is called *Asher Ehyeh* (That which I shall be), meaning: Now I am ready to draw forth into being and create all, now I am the sum total of all individual things. "That I am": to wit, the Mother is pregnant and is ready to produce individual things and to reveal the supreme Name. We find it stated in the book of King Solomon that the *Asher* (That) is the link that completes the joyful union. Observe now how the divine utterance[1] went from grade to grade to teach the secret of the holy name to Moses. First came *Ehyeh* (I shall be), the dark womb of all. Then *Asher Ehyeh* (That I Am), indicating the readiness of the Mother to beget all. Then, after the creation had commenced, came the name *Ehyeh* alone (*Ibid.*), as much as to say: Now it will bring forth and prepare all. Finally when all has been created and fixed in its place the name *Ehyeh* is abandoned and we have YHVH (*Ibid.* 15), an individual name signifying confirmation. Then it was that Moses knew the Holy Name, as it is both disclosed and undisclosed, and attained to an insight to which no other man has ever attained, happy is his portion !'

R. Eleazar came and kissed his hand. He said: 'Eleazar my son, from now onward be careful not to write the Holy Name save in the manner prescribed, since whoever does not know how to write the Holy Name in the manner prescribed so as to tie the bond of faith and unify the Holy Name, of him the Scripture says, "he hath despised the word of the Lord and hath broken his commandment", etc. (Num. xv, 31), even though he only left out one stroke from one letter. See, now, the *Yod* signifies the first framework of all, undisclosed from all sides. The *Yod* then produces the perennial stream indicated by *Hé*, and also a son and daughter, *Vau* and *Hé*, as explained elsewhere. Happy the lot of the righteous who know the profound secrets of the Holy King and are meet to give thanks to Him !'

R. Judah said: 'In the verse from the Psalms quoted above, the three names "God", "God", "the Lord" indicate the complete triad of the holy Patriarchs. God "called the earth", that the Community of Israel might perfect the gladness. And from what place does He join her ? "Out of Zion the perfection of beauty" (Ps. L, 2). For, as we have learnt, Jerusalem is the centre of the earth and a (heavenly) place called Zion is above it, and from this place it is blessed, [66a] and the two are indissolubly linked together.

'AND HE SHALL GO OUT UNTO THE ALTAR WHICH IS BEFORE THE LORD, AND MAKE ATONEMENT FOR IT.

[1] In Ex. III, 14.

We have learnt that just as the priest makes atonement below on this day, so also it is above, nor does the Priest above commence his service until the priest below has done so; for from below the sanctification of the Holy King commences to ascend, and then all worlds are one before the Holy One, blessed be He.' Said R. Judah: 'If Israel only knew why God visits their sins upon them more than those of other nations, they would perceive that He does not collect from them a hundredth part of His due. Many are the Chariots, Powers and Rulers that God has to serve Him. Now when He placed Israel in this world He crowned them with holy crowns and placed them in the holy land that they might devote themselves to His service, and He made all the celestials depend upon Israel, so that there is no joy or service before Him until Israel commence below; and when Israel neglect the service, it is suspended above, and there is no service either in earth or in heaven. And if this was so when Israel were in their own land, how much more so subsequently ! If Israel but knew, says God, how many hosts and multitudes are held up through them, they would see that they are not worthy to survive for an instant. Therefore "the priest shall go out to the altar which is before the Lord"—this is the supernal Altar—and then "make atonement for it", and then "he shall come forth and offer his burnt offering and the burnt offering of the people" (v. 24).'

It is written: "And he shall make atonement for the holy place because of the uncleanness of the children of Israel" (v. 16). R. Eleazar said: 'The wicked cause imperfection above and arouse judgement and bring defilement on the Sanctuary, so that the mighty Serpent shows himself. So on this day the priest has to purify all and put on his holy crown so that the King may come to abide with the Matrona and to awaken joy and blessing in the world. Thus completeness both above and below can be realized only through the priest, when he awakens his own proper Crown. So when the joy of union comes to the King and the Matrona, all the ministers and attendants of the palace rejoice, and all the sins that they committed against the King are forgiven.

Hence it is written, "No man shall be in the tent of meeting when he goeth in to make atonement in the holy place until he goeth out", to wit, when he goes in to unite them; and at that moment "he shall make atonement for himself and his house".'

R. Isaac said: 'When Israel are in captivity, God, if one may say so, is with them in captivity, for the Shekinah never leaves them. It was with them in Babylon and returned with them from the captivity; and for the sake of those righteous [66b] who were left in the land it abode in the land, as it never left them.' R. Judah said: 'The Matrona returned to the King and everything was gloriously restored, and therefore they were called "the men of the great Synagogue". We have learnt that if Israel in exile show themselves deserving, God will have mercy on them and hasten to bring them forth from exile, and if not He keeps them there until the appointed time,[1] and if when that comes they are still not worthy He has regard to the honour of His Name and does not forget them in exile, as it is written: "I shall remember my covenant with Jacob", etc. (Lev. xxvi, 42).' R. Isaac said: 'When the Holy King shall remember Israel for the sake of His Name and restore the Matrona to her place, then, as the Scripture says, "no man shall be in the tent of meeting when He comes to make atonement for the holy things", just as it is written of the priest when he went in to unify the Holy Name and to join the King with the Matrona.' R. Judah said: 'It has been taught that the priest entered into one degree and bathed his flesh. Then he left that grade and entered into another and bathed, making peace between the two. Thus at every step he had to perform some fitting ceremony, and wear corresponding garments, until he had properly completed the service, bringing blessing above and below. When all was linked together, [67a] all faces were illumined. Then all fell on their faces and trembled and said, "Blessed be the name of his glorious kingdom for ever and ever". Their voices joined that of the priest and he replied, "Ye shall be clean" (v. 30); only the High Priest said this, not the other priests or the people.

[1] v. T.B. Sanhedrin, 98a.

'FROM ALL YOUR SINS SHALL YE BE CLEAN BEFORE
THE LORD. It has been taught: From the beginning of the
(seventh) month the books are opened and the judges sit in
judgement, until the day which is called "the ninth of the
month" (Lev. XXIII, 32), when all judgements are submitted
to the Supreme Judge, and a Throne of mercy is set for the
Holy King. Then it is meet for Israel below to rejoice before
their Master because on the next day He intends to try them
from the holy throne of Mercy, of forgiveness, and to purify
them from all the sins recorded in the books that are open
before Him. Hence it is written, "from all your sins before
the Lord".

'When the public recited this verse (in the Temple
service) they went up to this point but no further, and none
was permitted to say the word "Ye shall be clean" save
the High Priest alone who was linking the Holy Name together through his utterance. When he had done so a voice
came down and struck him and a word flowed into his
mouth and he said "Ye shall be clean". He then performed
his service and all the celestials that were left there were
blessed. Then he bathed himself and washed his hands in
preparation for another service, in which he was to enter
into a place more holy than all. The other priests, the Levites
and the people stood around him in three rows and lifted
their hands over him in prayer, and a golden chain was
tied to his leg. He took three steps and all the others came
to a stand and followed him no further. He took three more
steps and went round to his place; three more and he closed
his eyes and linked himself with the upper world. He went
into the inner place and heard the sound of the wings of
the Cherubim chanting and beating their wings together.
When he burnt the incense the sound ceased and they folded
their wings quietly, if the priest was worthy and joy was
found above. Here, too, at that moment there went forth a
sweet odour as from hills of celestial pure balsam, and the
scent was brought into his nostrils, gladdening his heart.
Then all was silent and no accuser was found there. Then
the priest offered his prayer with fervour and joy. When he
finished, the Cherubim raised their wings again and resumed

their chant. Then the priest knew that his service had been acceptable, and it was a time of joy for all, and the people knew that his prayer had been accepted. Happy the portion of the priest in that through him joy upon joy was diffused on that day both above and below !'

R. Ḥiya discoursed on the verse: "(With) my soul have I desired thee in the night, yea, with my spirit within me will I seek thee early" (Isa. xxvi, 9). 'It does not say here,' he remarked, "my soul desires thee", but "my soul I desire thee'. The explanation is, as we have learnt, that God is the soul and spirit of all, and Israel here calls Him so and says, "I desire thee in order to cleave to thee and I seek thee early to find thy favour".' R. Jose said: 'When a man is asleep at night his soul goes and testifies to all that he has done during the day. Then the body says to the soul "I desire thee at night" [67b] and to the spirit "I shall seek thee early". Alternatively, the Community of Israel says to the Holy One, blessed be He, "While I am in exile among the nations and withhold myself from all evil communication with them, my soul desires thee to restore me to my place, and although they subject my sons to all kinds of oppression the holy spirit does not depart from me nor do I cease to seek thee and do thy commandments.' R. Isaac said: 'Israel says before God: While my soul is still within me I desire thee at night (the exile), because at such time the soul is constrained to yearn for thee, and when the holy spirit awakens within me I shall seek thee early to do thy will.' R. Hizkiah said that "soul" refers to the Community of Israel and "spirit" to the Holy One, blessed be He.

When R. Abba was studying with R. Simeon, the latter once rose at midnight to study the Torah, and R. Eleazar and R. Abba rose with him. R. Simeon discoursed on the verse: "As a hind panteth after the water-courses so my soul panteth for thee, O Lord" (Ps. XLII, 2). 'Happy are Israel,' he said, 'for that God gave them the Holy Law and caused them to inherit holy souls from a holy place, that they might keep His commandments and delight themselves in His Law. For the Torah is called a delight, and this is what is meant by the saying that God comes to delight

Himself with the righteous in the Garden of Eden, to wit, to regale Himself from the selfsame stream as the righteous. And whoever studies the Torah is privileged to delight himself along with [68a] the righteous from the waters of this stream. So we are told here that the "hind", to wit, the Community of Israel, pants for the water brooks to receive a draught from the sources of the stream at the hands of the Righteous One. What are these sources? One is above, of which it is written, "And a river went forth from Eden to water the Garden", etc., and from there it flows forth and waters the Garden and all the streams issue from it and meet again in two sources called Neẓah and Hod, and these pour forth water into that grade of Ẓaddik which goes forth from thence and waters the Garden. Observe that the soul and the spirit are inseparable. We have learnt that the perfect service offered by man to God consists in loving Him with his soul and his spirit. As these cleave to the body and the body loves them, so a man should cleave to God with the love of his soul and his spirit. Hence it says, "With my soul I have desired thee and with my spirit I seek thee early". It has been taught: Happy is the man who loves the Almighty with such a love; such are the truly virtuous for whose sake the world is established and who can annul all evil decrees both above and below. We have learnt that the virtuous man who with his soul and his spirit cleaves to the Holy King above with fitting love has power over the earth below, and whatever he decrees for the world is fulfilled, just as Elijah decreed concerning the rain. When the holy souls come down from heaven to earth and the virtuous of the world withdraw themselves from the King and the Matrona, few are they who at that time stand before the King and on whom the King deigns to look. For, as we have stated, at the time when God breathed spirit into all the hosts of the heavens, they all came into being and existence, but some were held back until the Holy One, blessed be He, [68b] sent them below, and these have sway both above and below. Hence Elijah said: "As the Lord liveth before whom I have stood" (1 Kings XVII, 1), not "before whom I *am standing*". Afterwards he returned to his place and ascended to his chamber, but the others do not ascend until they die, because they did not stand before God previously. Therefore Elijah and all those who cleave to the King were made messengers of the heavenly King, as we find in the book of Adam that all holy spirits above perform God's messages and all come from one place, whereas the souls of the righteous are of two degrees combined together, and therefore they ascend to a greater height. This applies to Enoch and Elijah. We have learnt that a hundred and twenty-five thousand grades of souls of the righteous were decided upon by the Almighty before the world was created, and these are sent into this world in every generation and they fly about the world and are "bound in the bundle of the living", and through them God will resurrect the world.

'YE SHALL AFFLICT YOUR SOULS, that Israel may be meritorious in the eyes of God and that their whole intent may be to cleave to Him so that their sins may be forgiven. The word "souls" (instead of "soul") indicates that one should eat and drink and feast on the ninth day so as to make the affliction double on the tenth.

'FOR ON THIS DAY SHALL HE ATONE FOR YOU. This indicates, as we have learnt, that on this day the Ancient Holy One reveals himself to make atonement for the sins of all.'
    R. Abba expounded in this connection the verse: "There was a little city and few men within it, and there came a great king against it and besieged it", etc. (Eccl. IX, 14, 15). 'The "little city",' he said, 'has here its well-known esoteric meaning (*Malkuth*); it is so called because it is the last and the lowest of all (the grades). There are "few men within it", for few are those who succeed in ascending to it and abiding in it. "A great king comes to it": this is the Holy One, blessed be He, who comes to unite with it, and He "surrounds it" with walls, "and builds great bulwarks for it", so that it is called "the holy city", and all the treasure of the King is placed there, and therefore it alone is crowned with all the diadems of the King. "He finds therein a poor wise man", or, as we should rather say, "a prudent (*misken*)

wise man", a man crowned with the crowns of the Law and
the precepts of the King, and endowed with wisdom to
interpret aright the service of his Master. He "shall escape
to that city in his wisdom", but "no man remembereth
that man" to follow his example in keeping the precepts
of the Law and studying the Torah. [69a] "Then said I,
Wisdom is better than strength", because in the other
world none are permitted to enter save those truly virtuous
who study the Torah day and night and are crowned with
the precepts of the Law. "But the poor man's wisdom is
despised and his words are not heard", since mankind pay
no heed to him and have no desire to associate with him and
listen to him. For so we have learnt, that to listen to the
words of the Torah is like receiving it from Sinai, no matter
from whom it comes, and he who inclines his ear to listen
gives honour to the Holy King and to the Torah.'

One day, as the Companions were walking with R. Simeon,
he said: 'I see all other peoples elevated and Israel degraded.
What is the reason ? Because the King has dismissed the
Matrona and put the handmaid in her place. Who is the
handmaid ? This is the alien Crown whose firstborn God
slew in Egypt.' R. Simeon wept, and continued: 'A king
without a queen is no king. If a king cleaves to the handmaid
of the queen, where is his honour ? A voice will one day
announce to the Matrona, "Rejoice greatly, O daughter of
Zion, shout, O daughter of Jerusalem, for thy king cometh
unto thee; he is just and having salvation", etc. (Zech. IX, 9);
as if to say: The Righteous One (*Zaddik*) will be saved, he
that was hitherto poor and riding on an ass, viz., as we have
explained, the lower Crowns of the heathen nations whose
firstborn God killed in Egypt. It is the *Zaddik*, as it were,
who will be saved, because till now he was without *Zedek*
(righteousness), but now they will be joined.' R. Isaac here
asked R. Simeon to explain how it is that some say the world
is founded on seven pillars and some on one pillar, to wit,
the *Zaddik*. He replied: 'It is all the same. There are seven,
but among these is one called *Zaddik* on which the rest are
supported. Hence it is written: "The righteous one (*Zaddik*)
is the foundation of the world" (Prov. X, 25). This handmaid',

resumed R. Simeon, 'will one day rule over the holy land below as the Matrona once ruled over it, but the Holy One, blessed be He, will one day restore the Matrona to her place, and then who shall rejoice like the King and the Matrona ?—the King, because he has returned to her and parted from the handmaid, and the Matrona because she will be once more united to the King. Hence it is written: "Rejoice exceedingly, O daughter of Zion", etc. Observe now that it is written, "This shall be to you a statute for ever" (Lev. XVI, 29). This promise is a decree of the King, fixed and sealed. [69b]

'IN THE SEVENTH MONTH ON THE TENTH DAY OF THE MONTH. The allusion of the "tenth" is as we have explained. We have learnt that on this day all joy and all illumination and all forgiveness depend on the Supernal Mother from whom issue all springs. Then all the lights shine with glad brightness until all is firmly established, and all judgements are also bathed in light and punishment is not inflicted.

It is written: "Howbeit (ach) on the tenth day of this seventh month is the day of atonement, and ye shall afflict your souls" (Lev. XXIII, 27). What is the force here of the word ach (only) ? When used in connection with the Passover (Ex. XII, 15) we derive from it the lesson that on half of the day preceding the Passover the eating of leaven is permitted and on half it is forbidden.[1] Shall we say that here also it teaches that half the day eating is permitted and half forbidden ?' R. Simeon replied: 'It goes here with the words "ye shall afflict your souls", and signifies that the real affliction is only in the second half of the day.'

FOR ON THIS DAY HE SHALL ATONE FOR YOU. R. Eleazar said: 'We should expect here, "I shall atone for you". The "he", however, signifies that the Jubilee sends forth streams to water and replenish ail on this day, and this "for you", to purify you from all sins, so that judgement should have no power over you.' R. Judah said: 'Happy are Israel in that God took pleasure in them and sought

[1] v. T.B. Pesaḥim, 28b.

to purify them so that they might belong to his Palace and dwell therein.'

R. Judah cited here the verse: "A song of ascents. Out of the depths have I cried unto thee, O Lord" (Ps. cxxxi). 'We have learnt', he said, 'that when God was about to create man, He consulted the Torah and she warned Him that he would sin before Him and provoke Him. Therefore, before creating the world God created Repentance, saying to her: "I am about to create man, on condition that when they return to thee from their sins thou shalt be prepared to forgive their sins and make atonement for them". Hence at all times Repentance is close at hand to men, and when they repent of their sins it returns to God and makes atonement for all, and judgement is suppressed and all is put right. When is a man purified of his sin ?' R. Isaac said: 'When he returns to the Most High King and prays [70a] from the depths of his heart, as it is written, "From the depths I cried unto thee".' R. Abba said: 'There is a hidden place above, which is "the depth of the well", whence issue streams and sources in all directions. This profound depth is called Repentance, and he who desires to repent and to be purified of his sin should call upon God from this depth. We have learnt that when a man repented before his Master and brought his offering on the altar, and the priest made atonement for him and prayed for him, mercy was aroused and judgement mitigated and Repentance poured blessings on the issuing streams and all the lamps were blessed together, and the man was purified from his sin.'

(AFTER THE DOINGS OF THE LAND OF EGYPT IN WHICH YE DWELT SHALL YE NOT DO.) The Holy One, blessed be He, has produced ten holy crowns above wherewith He crowns and invests Himself, and He is they and they are He, being linked together like the flame and the coal. Corresponding to these are ten crowns beneath, which are not holy, and which cling to the uncleanness of the nails of a certain holy Crown called Wisdom, wherefore they are called "wisdoms". We have learnt that these ten species of wisdom came down to this world, and all were concentrated

in Egypt, save one which spread through the rest of the world.[1]
They are all species of sorcery, and through them the Egyptians
were more skilled in sorcery than all other men. When the
Egyptians desired to consort with the demons, they used to go
out to certain high mountains and offer sacrifices and make
trenches in the ground and pour some of the blood around the
trenches and the rest into them and put flesh over it, and
bring offerings to the demons. Then the demons used to
collect and consort with them on the mountain. Israel, being
subject to the Egyptians, learnt their ways and went astray
after them; hence God said to them: "After the doings of the
land of Egypt in which ye have dwelt shall ye not do", and
also, "And they shall no more sacrifice their sacrifices unto
the satyrs after whom they go a-whoring", since, as we have
learnt, the demons used to appear to them in the form of he-
goats. R. Ḥiya said: 'This is the last of the unholy crowns,
as we have learnt.' R. Isaac said, in the name of R. Judah,
that the souls of the wicked are the demons of this world.
Said R. Jose: 'If so, the wicked are well off; where is their
punishment in Gehinnom ? Where is the evil in store for
them in the other world ?' R. Ḥiya replied: 'We have learnt
and laid down that when the souls of the wicked leave this
world many executioners of judgement await them and
take them to Gehinnom, and subject them there to three
tortures every day. Afterwards they go about the world
in company with them and mislead the wicked, from whom
repentance is withheld, and then return to Gehinnom and
punish them there, and so every day'. [70b]

R. Isaac said: 'Happy are the righteous in this world and
in the next, because they are altogether holy. Their body is
holy, their soul is holy, their spirit is holy, their super-soul
is holy of holies. These are three grades indissolubly united.
If a man does well with his soul (*nefesh*), there descends
upon him a certain crown called spirit (*ruah*), which stirs
him to a deeper contemplation of the laws of the Holy
King. If he does well with this spirit, he is invested with
a noble holy crown called super-soul (*neshamah*), which
can contemplate all.

[1] *v*. T.B. Kiddushin, 49*b*.

'In the book of King Solomon it is written that God has made three abodes for the righteous. One is for the souls of the righteous which have not yet left this world and are still here, and when the world is in need of mercy and the living afflict themselves, these pray for mankind and go and inform those that sleep in Hebron,[1] who being thus awakened go into the terrestrial Paradise where are the souls of the righteous in their crowns of light, and take counsel of them and decide what shall be, and God carries out their desire and has pity on the world. These souls of the righteous are in this world to protect the living and know their troubles, and these are they of whom the Companions say that the dead know the sorrows of the world and the punishment of the wicked. The second rank belongs to the terrestrial Paradise. In it God has made excellent chambers after the pattern of those of this world and of the celestial world, and palaces of two colours without number and sweet-smelling herbs that grow afresh every day. In that place abides that which is called the "spirit" of the righteous, each one being clad in a precious garment after the pattern of this world and of the upper world. The third grade is that holy celestial abode which is called "the bundle of the living", where that holy superior grade called the super-soul (neshamah) regales itself with the supernal delights. Now we have learnt that when the world requires mercy and those righteous ones take note of it, that soul of theirs which is in the world to shield mankind flits about the world to tell the spirit, and the spirit ascends and tells the super-soul, and this tells the Holy One, blessed be He. Then God has pity on the world and the reverse process takes place, the super-soul telling the spirit and the spirit the soul. Thus when the world requires mercy, the living go and inform the spirits of the righteous and weep over their graves, in order that soul may cleave to soul, [71a] and the souls of the righteous then come together and go and inform the sleepers of Hebron of the sorrows of the world, and then all enter the gateway of Paradise and inform the spirit, and those spirits which are crowned in Paradise

[1] The patriarchs.

like celestial angels join them and inform the super-soul, and this informs the Holy One, blessed be He, and God has mercy on the world for their sakes; and regarding this Solomon said: "Wherefore I praised the dead which are already dead more than the living that are still alive" (Eccl. IV, 2).'

Said R. Ḥiya: 'I wonder if anyone knows how to inform the dead besides us.' R. Abba replied: 'The sufferings of men tell them, the Torah tells them. For when there is none who knows how to do this, they take out the Scroll of the Law to the graveyard, and the dead are curious to know why it has been brought there; and then Duma informs them.' R. Jose added: 'They then know that the world is in trouble and the living are not meet nor know how to inform them. Then they all lament for the dishonour done to the Torah in bringing it to such a place. If men repent and weep with all their heart and return to God, then they all gather together and seek mercy and inform the sleepers of Hebron, as we have said. But if they do not repent, then woe to them for that they have assembled for nothing, and have caused the holy Torah to go into banishment without repentance, and they all go to remind God of their sins. Therefore men should not go thus to the graveyard without repentance and fasting.' R. Abba said: 'There should be three fasts.' R. Jose, however, said that one is sufficient, namely on the same day, provided they are very contrite'.

R. Judah taught: One day R. Hizkiah and R. Jesse were going together when they came to Gischala, which they found in ruins. They sat down near to the graveyard, R. Jesse having in his hand the cylinder of a Scroll of the Law which had been torn. While they were sitting, a grave began to stir near them and to cry: Alas, alas, that the world is in sorrow, since the Scroll of the Law comes into exile hither, or else the living have come to mock us and to shame us with their Torah! R. Hizkiah and R. Jesse were greatly alarmed. Said the former: Who art thou? I am dead, was the reply, but I have been awakened by the Scroll of the Law. For once the world was in trouble and the living came here to awaken us with a Scroll of the Law, and I and my

companions approached the sleepers of Hebron, and when
they joined the spirits of the righteous in Paradise it was
found that the Scroll of the Law which they brought before
us was faulty and so belied the name of the King, there
being a superfluous *vau* in one place. So the spirit said that
since they had belied the name of the King they would not
return to them, and they thrust me and my companions
out of the assembly, until a certain elder who was among
them went and brought the Scroll of Rab Hamnuna the
Elder. Then R. Eleazar the son of R. Simeon who was
buried with us awoke and entreated for them in Paradise
and the world was healed. And from the day that they caused
R. Eleazar to leave his grave with us and join his father
there is none of us that has wakened to stand before the
sleepers of Hebron, for we remember with fear the day
when they rejected me and my companions. And now that
you have come to us with a Scroll of the Law in your hands,
I presume that the world is in trouble and therefore I am
in fear and trembling as I think: Who will go and tell those
sainted ones, the sleepers of Hebron. R. Jesse thereupon let
go of the stick of the Scroll and R. Hizkiah said: God forbid,
the world is not in trouble, and we have not come on that
account.

R. Hizkiah and R. Jesse then rose and went on their way.
'Verily,' they said, 'when there are no righteous in the
world, the world is sustained only by the Scroll of the Law.'

R. Jesse asked: 'Why, when rain is wanted, do we go to
the graveyards, seeing that it is [71b] forbidden to "inquire
of the dead" (Deut. XVIII, 11) ?' He replied: 'You have not
yet seen the "wing of the Bird of Eden".[1] The "dead" here
are those of the sinners of the heathens who are forever
dead, but of Israel who are truly virtuous Solomon says
that "they have died aforetime", but now they are living.
Further, when other peoples visit their dead, they do so
with divinations to summon demons to them, but Israel
go with repentance before the Lord, with a contrite heart
and with fasting, in order that the holy souls may beseech
mercy for them. Therefore we have learnt that the righteous

[1] R. Simeon.

man, even when he departs from this world, does not really disappear from any world, since he is to be found in all of them more than in his lifetime. For in his lifetime he is only in this world, but afterwards he is in three worlds. So we find that Abigail said to David: "May the soul (*nefesh*) of my lord be bound in the bundle of life" (1 Sam. xxv, 29); she did not say "super-soul" (*neshamah*), because all three are bound together, and so even the *nefesh* of the righteous is in "the bundle of the living".'

R. Eleazar said: 'The Companions have laid down that it is forbidden to remove a Scroll of the Law even from one synagogue to another, all the more to bring it out into the street. Why then do we do so when praying for rain ?' R. Judah replied: 'As we have explained, that the dead may be awakened and entreat for the world.' R. Abba said: 'The Shekinah also was driven from place to place until she said: "O that I had in the wilderness a lodging place of wayfaring men", etc. (Jer. ix, 1). So here, the Scroll is first taken from synagogue to synagogue, then into the street, then to "the wilderness, the lodging place of wayfaring men".' R. Judah said: 'In Babylon they are afraid to take it even from synagogue to synagogue.' It has been taught that R. Simeon said to the Companions: 'In my days the world will not require this.' R. Jose said to him: 'The righteous shield the world in their lifetime, and after their death even more than in their life. For so God said (to King Hezekiah): "I will defend this city to save it for my own sake and for my servant David's sake" (Isa. xxxvii, 35), but in David's lifetime He did not say so.' R. Judah said: 'Why does God put David here on a par with Himself ? Because David was found worthy to be attached to the Holy Chariot of the Patriarchs, and therefore all is one. [72*b*]

R. Isaac said: 'The Egyptians used to serve the power called "handmaid" and the Canaanites the power called "the captive which is behind the mill", and all used to misuse holy words and practise their arts therewith; therefore the Israelites were commanded: "After the doings of the land of Egypt shall ye not do", etc.' R. Judah said that they caused evil demons to rule over the land, as it says, "and the land was defiled". We have learnt that one day God will purify His land of all the uncleanness wherewith the heathen have defiled it, like one who cleans a garment, and will cast out all those that are buried in the holy land, and purify it from the "other side", since, if one may say so, it went a-whoring after the Chieftains of the peoples and received their uncleanness. R. Simeon purified the streets of Tiberias, removing all dead bodies from there.'[1] R. Judah said: 'Happy he whose lot it is during his lifetime to abide in the holy land; for such a one draws down the dew from the heavens above upon the earth, and whoever is attached to this holy land in his lifetime becomes attached afterwards to a supernal holy land. But of those who do not live there but are brought there to be buried, the Scripture says: "Ye have made my inheritance an abomination" (Jer. II, 7). His spirit leaves him in a strange land and his body comes to rest in the holy land; he turns holy into profane and profane into holy. But if one dies in the holy land his sins are forgiven and he is taken under the wings of the Shekinah. Further, if he is worthy, he continually draws to himself a holy spirit, but he that lives in a strange land draws to himself a strange spirit. We have learnt that when R. Hamnuna the Elder went up to Eretz Israel he was accompanied by twelve members of his academy. He said to them: If I go on this way it is not for myself, but to restore the pledge[2] to its owner. We have learnt that all who do not attain to this in their lifetime restore the pledge of their Master to another'. R. Isaac said: 'Consequently, if anyone takes those evil spirits or foreign powers into the land it becomes defiled, and woe to that man and his soul, because the holy land does not receive him again.'

MY JUDGEMENTS SHALL YE DO AND MY STATUTES SHALL YE KEEP. R. Abba said: 'Happy are Israel in that God has chosen them above all peoples, and for the sake of His love has given them true laws, planted in them the tree of life, and made His divine Presence abide with them. Why ? Because Israel are stamped with the holy impress

---

[1] v. T.B. Sabbath, 33b, 34a.   [2] His soul.

on their flesh, and they are marked as being His and belonging to His temple. Therefore all who are not stamped with the holy sign [73*a*] on their flesh are not His, and they are marked as coming from the side of uncleanness, and it is forbidden to associate with them or to converse with them on matters of the Holy One, blessed be He. It is also forbidden to impart to them knowledge of the Torah, because the Torah consists wholly of the name of the Holy One, blessed be He, and every letter of it is bound up with that Name.' R. Simeon said: 'We are told in regard to the paschal lamb that no stranger who is uncircumcised may eat it. If this is so with the paschal lamb because it is the symbol of some holy thing, how much more must it be so with the Torah, which is holy of holies.'

R. Eleazar once said to his father: 'We have learnt that it is forbidden to teach the Torah to a heathen, and the Companions in Babylon have well connected this rule with the text, "He hath not dealt so with any nation" (Ps. CXLVII, 20). But in the preceding verse, why, after saying, "He sheweth his word unto Jacob" does it add "His statutes and his judgements to Israel" ?' He replied: 'Eleazar, God has given this holy celestial portion to Israel and not to the nations. And Israel themselves are in two grades, corresponding to the two grades of the Torah, the disclosed and the undisclosed. To all who have been circumcised and stamped with the holy impress, we impart those things in the Torah which are on the surface, the letters and the plain contents and the precepts, and no more. This is indicated in the words, "He telleth his words to Jacob". But if the Israelite rises to a higher grade, then "His statutes and his judgements to Israel": these are the allegories of the Torah and the hidden paths of the Torah and the secrets of the Torah, which should only be revealed to those of a higher degree. But to impart even a little letter to one who is not circumcised is like destroying the world and repudiating the Holy Name of the Holy One, blessed be He. Hence it is written, "This is the law which Moses set before the children of Israel" (Deut. IV, 44), and not before other peoples. Peace be upon the fathers of the world, Hillel and

Shammai, who thus dealt with Onkelos[1] and refused to impart to him any knowledge of the Torah until he was circumcised. See now. The very first thing taught to children, the *Aleph Beth*, transcends the comprehension and the mind of man, and even of the higher and highest angels, because the Holy Name is concealed in the letters. A thousand and four hundred and five worlds are suspended from the point of the *aleph*, and seventy-two holy names traced in their full spelling, which uphold heaven and earth, upper and lower beings, and the Throne of the King, are suspended along the stroke of the *aleph*, while the mystery of Wisdom and the hidden paths and the deep rivers and the ten Words all issue from the lower point of the *aleph*. From this point *aleph* begins to extend into *beth*, and there is no end to the wisdom that is here inscribed. Therefore [73*b*] the Torah is the support of all and the link that binds all in faith, and he who is circumcised is attached to that link and he who is not circumcised is not. Of such it is written, "No stranger shall eat of the holy thing" (Lev. XXII, 10), for an unclean spirit comes from his side and mingles itself with the holiness. Blessed be the Merciful One who has separated Israel from them and their uncleanness.' R. Eleazar then came and kissed his hands.

R. Hizkiah said: 'It is written, "God will not forsake his people for the sake of his great name" (1 Sam. XII, 22), since Israel is linked to God, and by what? By the holy impress on their flesh. We have learnt that the Torah is called "covenant", and God is called "covenant", and this impress is called "covenant", and so all is inseparably linked together.' R. Jesse asked whence we derive the statement that God is called covenant. He replied: 'From the text, "And he remembered for them his covenant" (Ps. CVI, 45), as has been explained.

'The "statutes" mentioned above are ordinances of the King, and the "judgements" are the edicts of the Torah.' R. Judah said that all those ordinances which come from the place called "Righteousness" are called "my statutes", and they are the edicts of the King, and those that come from

---

[1] The reputed author of the Aramaic version of the Pentateuch.

the place called "judgement" are called his "judgements",
the judgements of the King who is enthroned in the place
where two sections, judgement and mercy, meet. We have
learnt that even though one is circumcised, if he does not
carry out the precepts of the Torah he is like a heathen in
all respects, and it is forbidden to teach him the precepts
of the Torah. He is called "an altar of stones" because of
the hardness of his heart, and therefore his circumcision
does not avail him aught. [74*a*]

THE NAKEDNESS OF THY FATHER AND THE NAKED-
NESS OF THY MOTHER SHALT THOU NOT UNCOVER.
R. Ḥiya cited the verse: "As the apple tree among the trees
of the wood, so is my beloved among the sons" (S.S. II, 3).
'Why', he said, 'does the Community of Israel praise God
by comparing Him to an apple tree ? Because it combines
all excellences. As it is healing for all, so is God healing for
all; as it combines two colours, so God combines two attributes; as the apple has a more delicate scent than other trees,
so of God it is written, "His scent is like Lebanon" (Hosea,
XIV, 5); as the apple has a sweet taste, so of God it is written,
"His mouth is most sweet" (S.S. V, 16). And the Holy One,
blessed be He, praises the Community of Israel by comparing
her to a lily, for reasons which have been explained elsewhere.'
R. Judah said: 'When the righteous abound in the world,
the Community of Israel emits sweet odours and is blessed
in the Holy King and her face shines. But when the wicked
abound she does not send forth good odours, and she receives
a bitter taste from the other side, and her face is darkened.'
R. Jose said: 'Of the time when the righteous abound it is
said, "His left hand is under my head and his right hand
doth embrace me" (S.S. II, 6). But of the time when sinners
abound it is written, "He hath drawn back his right hand"
(Lam. II, 3).' R. Hizkiah said: 'The King separates from
the Matrona, and in regard to this it is written, "the nakedness of thy father and thy mother shalt thou not uncover".'

When R. Eleazar was once studying with his father he
said: 'If an Advocate comes down to the world, he is
to be found in the Matrona, and if there is an Accuser

who assails the world, it is the Matrona that he assails. Why is this?' He replied with a parable. 'A king once had a son from a queen. As long as the son was obedient to the king the latter consorted with the queen. But when the son was not obedient to the king he separated from the queen. So it is', he said, 'with the Holy One, blessed be He, and the Community of Israel. As long as Israel perform the will of God the Holy One makes His abode with the Community of Israel. But when Israel do not perform the will of God He does not make His abode with the Community of Israel, because Israel is the firstborn of the Holy One, blessed be He, and the Community of Israel is their mother. All the time that Israel is kept away from the temple of the king, the Matrona, if one may say so, is kept away with them. Why is this? Because the Matrona did not in time apply the lash to this son to keep him in the right path. For the King never punishes his son, but leaves it in the hand of the Matrona to punish him and to lead him in the straight way before the King. [74b] It is written, "A wise son maketh a glad father, but a foolish son is the heaviness of his mother" (Prov. x, 1). As long as this son goes in the right way and is wise he rejoices his father, the Holy King, but if he perverts his way he is the heaviness of his mother, to wit, the Community of Israel. Never was there such joy before the Holy One, blessed be He, as on the day when Solomon attained to wisdom and composed the Song of Songs. Then was the face of the Matrona brightened, and the King came to make his abode with her, so that she became more beautiful and exalted than ever. Why was this? Because she had produced this wise son for the world.[1] When she produced Solomon she produced all Israel, and all were in high degrees, virtuous like Solomon, and God rejoiced in them and they in Him. On the day when Solomon completed the temple below the Matrona prepared the house above, and they made their abode together and her face was bright with perfect joy, and then there was gladness for all above and below. But when this son does not conform to the will of the King, then there is uncovering of nakedness on all sides, because

[1] Al. "King".

the King parts from the Matrona and the Matrona is kept away from the palace; for is not their separation a kind of nakedness ? Hence it is written, "the nakedness of thy father and thy mother shalt thou not uncover". [75*a*]

THE NAKEDNESS OF THY FATHER'S WIFE SHALT THOU NOT UNCOVER. Who is meant by "thy father's wife" ? Said R. Simeon: 'We have learnt: As long as the Matrona is with the King and giveth suck to thee, she is called "thy mother". Now, however, that she is banished with thee and is removed from the King, she is called "thy father's wife". She is his wife, because he has not divorced her, although she is in exile. Therefore the text enjoins concerning her twice—once in reference to the time when she is still with the King and is called "thy mother", and once in reference to the time when she is banished from the King's palace and is called the wife of the King. Although she is far from him, thou shalt not cause her to remove from thee, lest thine enemies gain dominion over thee and she do not protect thee in the captivity. Hence "thou shalt not uncover the nakedness of thy father's wife". Why ? Because "it is thy father's nakedness": because although she is removed from the King, yet he is constantly watching over her, and therefore thou must be careful before her and not sin against her.'

R. Simeon here quoted the verse: "For the Lord thy God walketh in the midst of thy camp to deliver thee", etc. (Deut. XXIII, 14). 'This', he said, 'refers to the Shekinah, which is in the midst of Israel, and especially in the captivity, to protect them continually and on all sides from all other peoples, that they should not destroy them. For so it has been taught, that [75*b*] the enemies of Israel have no power over them until Israel weaken the might of the Shekinah in face of the Chieftains who are appointed over the other nations. Then only the latter have power over them and enact cruel decrees against them. But when they return in repentance to her she breaks the power of all those Chieftains and of the enemies of Israel and avenges them on all. Hence "thy camp shall be holy": a man must not defile himself by

sin and transgress the commands of the Law. We have
learnt that there are two hundred and forty-eight members
in the human body, and all are defiled when he is defiled,
that is, when he is minded to be defiled. We have learnt that
for three things Israel are kept in captivity: because they
pay scant respect to the Shekinah in their exile, because they
turn their faces away from the Shekinah, and because they
defile themselves in the presence of the Shekinah.'

THE NAKEDNESS OF THY SISTER . . . THOU SHALT
NOT UNCOVER. R. Abba was once going from Cappadocia
to Lydda in company with R. Jose. As they were going they
saw a man approaching with a mark on his face. Said R.
Abba: 'Let us leave this road, because that man's face testifies
that he has transgressed one of the precepts of the Law
against illicit intercourse.' Said R. Jose: 'Suppose this mark
was on him from his boyhood; how can it show that he has
transgressed by illicit intercourse ?' R. Abba replied: 'I can
see that he has by his face.' R. Abba then called him and
said: 'Tell me, what is that mark on your face ?' He replied:
'I beg of you, do not punish me further, because my sins
have caused this.' 'How is that ?' said R. Abba. He replied:
'I was once travelling with my sister, and we turned in to
an inn, where I drank much wine. All that night I was in
company with my sister. When I got up in the morning
I found the host quarrelling with another man. I interposed
between them and received blows from both, one on one
side and one on the other, and was severely wounded, but
was saved by a doctor who was living among us.' R. Abba
asked who the doctor was, and he replied: 'It was R. Simlai.'
'What medicine did he give you ?' asked R. Abba. He replied:
'Spiritual healing. From that day I repented, and every day
I looked at myself in a mirror and wept before the Almighty
for my sin, and from those tears my face was healed.' Said
R. Abba: 'Were it not that you might cease repenting,
I would cause that scar to be removed from your face.
However, I will say over you the verse, "And thine iniquity
is taken away and thy sin purged" (Isa. vi, 7). Repeat that
three times.' He repeated it three times and the mark

vanished; whereupon R. Abba said: 'In sooth, your Master was fain to remove it from you, which shows that you have truly repented.' He said: 'I vow from this day to study the Torah day and night.' R. Abba asked him what his name was, and he said 'Eleazar'. Said R. Abba: 'Eleazar, God is thy help; as thy name is so art thou.' He then sent him away with a blessing.

Some time after, R. Abba, as he was on his way to R. Simeon, went into the town where this man lived. He found him expounding the verse: "A brutish man knoweth not, neither doth a fool understand this" (Ps. XCII, 6). 'How stupid', he said, 'are mankind that they take no pains to know the ways of the Almighty by which the world is maintained. What prevents them ? Their stupidity, because they do not study the Torah; for if they were to study the Torah they would know the ways of the Holy One, blessed be He. "A fool doth not understand this": to wit, [76a] the ways of "this" (zoth, the Shekinah), in the world, how it judges the world. For they only see the punishments of this zoth alighting on the righteous and not alighting on the wicked who transgress the precepts of the Torah, and who inherit this world in every direction, as it is written, "the wicked spring as the grass". Nor should we know better, did not King David enlighten us in the second part of the verse, saying, "It is that they shall be destroyed for ever"; that is, to be destroyed in the other world, where they shall be dust under the feet of the righteous.' He further discoursed on the verse: "My leanness riseth up against me, it testifieth to my face" (Job XVI, 8). 'Observe', he said, 'that if a man transgresses the precepts of the Law, the Torah itself goes up and down and makes marks on that man's face so that all both above and below look at him and heap curses on his head. We have learnt that all the eyes of the Lord which go to and fro in the world to observe the ways of mankind look well at the face of that man and exclaim: Alas, alas ! Alas for him in this world, alas for him in the world to come. Keep away from So-and-so because his face testifies against him that an unclean spirit rests upon him. If during the days that that testimony is upon his face he begets a son, he instils in him a spirit from the unclean side; and such become the shameless sinners of the generation, to whom their Master allows scope in this world in order to destroy them in the next. But if a man is virtuous and studies the Torah day and night, then God weaves around him a thread of grace and sets a mark on his face which makes all afraid of him both above and below.' Said R. Abba to him: 'All this is very true; from whence have you learnt it ?' He replied: 'So I have been taught, and I have also been taught that this evil heritage is transmitted to all his sons, if they do not repent, for repentance overcomes everything. For this remedy was given me once when I bore a mark on my face, until one day as I was going along I met a certain saintly man through whom this mark was removed from me.' 'What is your name ?' asked R. Abba. He replied: 'My name is Eleazar', and he divided it into *El ezer* (God is help). Said R. Abba to him: 'Blessed be God that I have been privileged to see thee thus. Blessed art thou in this world and the next. I am the man who met you.' He thereupon prostrated himself before him and brought him into his house and prepared for him special bread and flesh from a fatted calf.

After they finished eating the man said: 'Rabbi, I want you to tell me something. I have a red heifer, the mother of the calf the flesh of which we have just eaten. One day before it had calved I was going with it to the pasture when a man met me and said to me: What is the name of that cow ? I replied that I had never given it a name. He said: It will be called Bathsheba the mother of Solomon if you shall succeed in repenting. Before I could turn my head he was gone, and I thought his remark very ridiculous. [76b] Now, however, that I have become a student of the Torah I have been thinking again over that remark, but since R. Simlai departed this world there has been none who can enlighten us on questions of the Torah like him, and I am afraid to put forth any opinion of my own which I have not learnt from a teacher, and I can see that there is a hidden meaning in this remark though I do not understand it.' 'Truly', replied R. Abba, 'it has a hidden meaning with reference both to the upper and the lower world. A certain divine grade is called *Bath sheba* (daughter of seven) in the mystery of Wisdom, and is symbolized by the seven kine, the seven burnings, the seven sprinklings, the seven washings, the seven unclean, the seven clean, the seven priests.[1] This was the hidden meaning in that man's remark.' He said: 'Thank God for granting me to hear this, and for giving me His greeting of peace, and bringing me near to Him when I was far away.' Said R. Abba to him: ' "Peace be unto thee and peace to thy house and peace to all that thou hast" (1 Sam. xxv, 6).'

THOU SHALT NOT UNCOVER THE NAKEDNESS OF THY FATHER'S SISTER. We have learnt elsewhere that Adam separated from his wife a hundred and thirty years[2] after Cain killed Abel. R. Jose said: 'When death was decreed for him and for all mankind, he said: Why should I beget children for confusion ? and he therefore separated from his wife. Then two female spirits used to come to him and they bore from him. Their offspring were demons and were called "plagues of the children of men". We have learnt that when man came down to earth in the supernal likeness all who saw him, both higher and lower beings, came to him and made him king of this world. Eve bore Cain from the filth of the serpent, and therefore from him were descended all the wicked generations, and from his side is the abode of spirits and demons. Therefore all spirits and demons are half of the class of human beings below and half of the class of angels above. So, too, those that were born from Adam afterwards were half of the lower and half of the upper sphere. After these were born from Adam, he begat from those spirits daughters with the beauty of the heavenly beings and also with the beauty of the lower beings, so that the sons of God went astray after them. One male came into the world from the side of the spirit of the side of Cain, and they called him Tubal Cain. A female came with him who was called Naamah, from whom issued other spirits and

---

[1] The reference is, apparently, to the section of the Red Heifer, Num. xix
[2] v. T.B. Erubin, 18b.

demons; these hover in the air and tell things to those others
below. This Tubal Cain produced weapons of war, and this
Naamah clung to her own side, and she still exists, having
her abode among the waves of the great sea. She goes forth
and makes sport with men and conceives from them through
their lustful dreams. From that lust she becomes pregnant
and brings forth further species in the world. The sons
whom she bears from human beings show themselves to the
females of mankind, who become pregnant from them and
bring forth spirits, and they all go to the ancient Lilith, who
brings them up. She goes out into the world and seeks [77a]
her little ones, and when she sees little children she cleaves
to them in order to kill them and to insinuate herself into
their spirits. There are, however, three holy spirits which
fly in front of her and take that spirit from her and set it
before the Holy One, blessed be He, and there they are
taught before Him. Thus they guard that child and she cannot hurt him. But if a man is not holy, and draws upon himself
a spirit from the unclean side, she comes and makes sport
with that child, and if she kills him she enters into his spirit
and never leaves it. You may say: What about those others
whom she has killed, although the three angels confronted
her and took from her their spirits ? Since they were not on
the side of uncleanness, why had she power to kill them ?
This happens when a man does not sanctify himself, but
yet does not purposely try to defile himself nor actually do
so. In such cases she has power over the body but not the
spirit. Sometimes it happens that Naamah goes forth to
have intercourse with men and a man is linked with her in
lust, and then suddenly wakes and clasps his wife though his
mind is still full of the lust of his dream. In that case the
son so born is of the side of Naamah, and when Lilith goes
forth she sees him and knows what has happened, and brings
him up like the other children of Naamah, and he is often
with her, and she does not kill him. This is the man who
receives a blemish on every New Moon. For Lilith never gives
them up, but at every New Moon she goes forth and visits
all those whom she has brought up and makes sport with
them; hence this man receives a blemish at that time. These

things King Solomon revealed in the book of Asmodai, and we find therein a thousand and four hundred and five manners of defilement which can affect mankind. Alas for mankind that they close their eyes and observe not nor take any heed how they are preserved in the world ! Counsel and healing are before them but they heed not, for they cannot deliver themselves save by the counsel of the Torah, as it is written: "Ye shall sanctify yourselves and ye shall be holy, for I am the Lord your God."

'We have learnt that when Cain and Abel were removed, Adam returned to his wife and was clothed with a fresh spirit and begat Seth, with whom commenced the generations of righteous men in the world. God showed lovingkindness to the world, and with each one a female was born to popu-late the world, after the supernal pattern. For so we have affirmed in the secret doctrine of the Mishnah, that "if a man taketh his sister, his father's daughter or his mother's daughter, it is ḥesed" (lit. lovingkindness); truly so, and after ḥesed had appeared, roots and stocks came forth from beneath the highest, and branches spread and that which was near receded afar. This was at the beginning, in the hidden development of the world, but subsequently human beings who behave so "shall be cut off before the eyes of the children of their people". [77b]

'We have learnt that the upper Hé was conceived from the love of its inseparable companion Yod, and brought forth Vau. When this Vau came forth, its mate came forth with it. Lovingkindness came and parted them, and there came forth roots from beneath the Highest, and branches spread and grew and the lower Hé was produced. It spread its branches higher and higher until it joined the upper tree and Vau was linked with Hé. Who caused this ? Ḥesed. But the union of Yod with the upper Hé is not caused by Ḥesed but by mazzal (lit. luck). In this way Yod is linked with Hé, Hé with Vau, Vau with Hé, and Hé with all, and all forms one entity, of which the elements are never to be separated. He who causes separation between them, as it were, lays waste the world and is called "the nakedness of all". In time to come God will restore the Shekinah to its place, and there will be a complete union, as it is written: "On that day the Lord shall be one and his name one" (Zech. XIV, 9). It may be said: Is He not now one ? No; for now through sinners He is not really one; for the Matrona is removed from the King and they are not united, and the supernal Mother is removed from the King and does not give suck to Him, because the King without the Matrona is not invested with His crowns as before. But when He joins the Matrona, who crowns Him with many resplendent crowns, then the supernal Mother will also crown Him in fitting manner. But now that the King is not with the Matrona, the Supernal Mother keeps her crowns and witholds from Him the waters of the Stream and He is not joined with Her. Therefore, as it were, He is not one. But when the Matrona shall return to the place of the temple and the King shall be wedded with her, then all will be joined together without separation, and regarding this it is written, "On that day the Lord shall be one and his name one". Then "saviours shall come up on Mount Zion to judge the mount of Esau" (Obad. I, 21), as it has been taught: R. Simeon said, The Matrona will not enter her temple in joy until the kingdom of Esau has been brought to judgement and she has taken vengeance on it for causing all this. Therefore "they shall judge the mount of Esau" first, and then "the kingdom shall be the Lord's" (*Ibid.*), the kingdom being the Matrona.'

THE NAKEDNESS OF THY FATHER'S BROTHER THOU SHALT NOT UNCOVER. R. Judah taught that this refers to Israel below, and "the mother's sister" to Jerusalem below; for it was for these sins that Israel was destined to go into exile among the peoples and the earthly Jerusalem to be destroyed. Concerning this we have learnt that God showed His love for Israel by calling them brothers, as it is written, "For my brethren and companions' sake I will speak peace concerning thee" (Ps. CXXII, 8), the esoteric meaning of which is as follows, as explained by R. Simeon in the name of R. Judah. The word "companion" refers to one who never parts, and so the supernal Mother is called "companion" because the love of the Father never departs from her, [78*a*] whereas the lower Mother is called "bride" (daughter-in-law) and "sister". In this passage it refers to her as "the daughter of thy father" and "the daughter of thy mother". If she is from the side of the Father she is called Wisdom (*Hokhmah*), and if from the side of the Mother she is called Understanding (*Binah*); and in either case she is from both the Father and the Mother; and this is hinted in the words "born at home", to wit from the side of the Father, "or born abroad", to wit, from the side of the Mother. R. Abba, however, said that "born at home" means coming from the River that issues from Eden, and "born abroad" from the Small of Countenance. R. Judah said that Israel are called "brothers" to the Holy One, blessed be He, because His love never departs from them. The earthly Jerusalem is called "thy mother's sister". It is written, "Jerusalem that art builded as a city that is compact together" (Ps. CXXII, 3). It is so called because the King is joined to it from six sides and all the crowns of the King are comprised in it. "Whither the tribes went up, even the tribes of *Jah*": these are the twelve boundaries which spread from that great and mighty Tree, and which it inherited from the side of the Father and the Mother. "For there are set thrones for judgement, thrones for the house of David": that he may inherit the holy kingdom, he and his sons for all generations. Thus this is a hymn which David composed concerning the holy supernal kingdom. R. Hizkiah said: 'The whole has a supernal reference, to show that he who impairs below impairs above. It is written: "The nakedness of thy daughter-in-law thou shalt not uncover". If the disciples of the wise who know the inner meaning of this commit an offence below, then, as it were, they cause a blemish in the Bride above; but in regard to the mass of men the verse has its literal significance, and for this sin the Shekinah departs from them.' [78*b*]

R. Simeon said to R. Eleazar: 'See now. These twenty-two letters which are inscribed in the Torah are all illustrated in the Ten Creative Utterances. Each of those ten, which are the crowns of the King, is traced in certain letters. Hence the Holy Name is disguised under other letters and each

Utterance lends to the one above it certain letters, so that they are comprised in one another. Therefore we trace the Holy Name in other letters not its own, one set being concealed in the other, though all are linked together. He who desires to know the combinations of the holy names must know the letters which are inscribed in each crown and then combine them. I myself trace them from the profound book of Solomon, and so I am able to do it and reveal them to the Companions. Blessed are the righteous in this world and the next, because God desires to honour them and reveals to them profound secrets of the Holy Name which He does not reveal to the celestial holy ones (angels). And therefore Moses was able to crown himself among those holy ones and they were not able to touch him, though they are like a burning flame and coals of fire. For otherwise how could Moses have stood among them ? When God commenced to speak with Moses, the latter desired to know His holy names, disclosed and undisclosed, each one in fitting manner, and thus he came closer and learnt more than any other man. When Moses entered into the cloud and came among the angels, one named Gazarniel came up to him with flames of fire, with flashing eyes and burning wings, and sought to wound him. Then Moses mentioned a certain holy name which was traced with twelve letters, and the angel was utterly confused; and so with all the others.

'THOU SHALT NOT UNCOVER THE NAKEDNESS OF A WOMAN AND HER DAUGHTER. We have explained these prohibitions to refer to the adornments of the Matrona, but they also have their literal meaning because they are necessary for the right ordering of society, and if a man transgresses one of them, woe for him and woe for his soul, because he uncovers other nakednesses. We have learnt that the last of the Ten Commandments, "Thou shalt not covet thy neighbour's wife", comprises all the others, and he who covets his neighbour's wife is like one transgressing the whole of the Law. Nothing, however, can stand in the way of repentance, especially if a man receives his punishment, like King David.' R. Jose said: 'We have learnt that if a man sins and gives up the fruit of his sin, his repentance brings him to a higher grade than before; but if he does not give up the fruit of his sin, his repentance does not avail him. If that is the case, it may be asked why did not David part from Bathsheba ?' He replied: 'Bathsheba was his by right, and he only took his own, her husband having died. For it has been taught that Bathsheba was destined for David from the Creation, and what kept her from him was his marrying the daughter of King Saul. On that day Uriah obtained her by a special grace, though she was not really his. Afterwards David came and took his own; and it was because David anticipated matters by killing Uriah that God was displeased with him, and He punished him that he might be established in the supernal holy kingdom.'

I AM THE LORD. R. Jose taught: 'This means, "I am the Lord who will one day bestow a good reward on the righteous in the time to come; I am the Lord who will one day punish the wicked in the time to come". It is written, "I kill and make alive" (Deut. XXXII, 39); although [79a] I am in the attribute of mercy, the wicked turn me to the attribute of judgement.' R. Simeon said: 'Sinners cause imperfection above, as we have explained.'

THOU SHALT NOT APPROACH A WOMAN TO UNCOVER HER NAKEDNESS AS LONG AS SHE IS IMPURE BY HER UNCLEANNESS. R. Judah taught: 'The generation of whom R. Simeon is one are all righteous, saintly and fearful of sin, and the Shekinah abides among them as among no other generation. Therefore these things are stated openly and not concealed, whereas in former generations supernal mysteries could not be revealed, and those who knew them were afraid to utter them. For when R. Simeon expounded the mysteries of this verse all the Companions were in tears, and his meaning was clear to them. For one day R. Jesse mockingly repeated R. Simeon's words, "An egg of truth[1] which issues from a bird which abides in fire and bursts forth on four sides; two go forth from there, one is depressed and

---

[1] The primordial *Yod*.

one overflows into a great sea".' R. Abba said to him: 'You
have turned sacred into profane before R. Simeon.' Said
R. Simeon: 'Before the egg breaks open, you shall depart
from this world; and so it came to pass in the Chamber of
R. Simeon.[1] We have learnt that in the days of R. Simeon
one man used to say to another: Open thy mouth that thy
words may spread light. In the holy Chamber it was said:
Here it is fitting to reveal what concerns this subject. When
the mighty Serpent above rouses himself on account of the
sins of the generation, he joins himself to the Female and
injects filth into her. Then the Male parts from her because
she is defiled, and it is not fitting for the Male to approach
her, for pity would be if he were defiled with her. We have
learnt that a hundred and twenty-five species of uncleanness
came down into the world and are connected with the side
of the mighty Serpent, and twenty-seven chiefs of them
attach themselves to females and cling to them. Alas, then,
for a man who touches such a woman at that time, for through
this sin he awakens the supernal Serpent and casts filth into
a holy place, and punishments are let loose on the world
and all is defiled. We have learnt that the Serpent injected
twenty-four kinds of uncleanness into the female when he
was joined to her, so that twenty-four punishments are
roused above and twenty-four below. The hair and the
nails grow, and therefore when a woman comes to purify
herself she must cut off the hair which grew in the days
of her uncleanness and cut her nails with all the filth that
clings to them. For, as we have learnt, the filth of the nails
arouses another filth, and therefore they must be hidden
away.[2] He who hides them away completely, as it were,
awakens lovingkindness in the world, for they even provide
opportunity for sorcerers to exercise their magic on account
of the demons attached to them, [79b] and a person stepping
on them with his foot or his shoe may come to harm. If
this is true of this remnant of a remnant of filth, how much
more of the woman who was joined with the Serpent ! Alas
for the world which inherited that filth from her ! Therefore
it is written, "To a woman in the separation of her

[1] v. Zohar, Numbers, 144a. [2] v. T.B. Moed Katon, 18a; Niddah, 17a.

uncleanness thou shalt not draw near". Happy the generation
in which R. Simeon lived ! To it the words apply, "Happy art
thou O land, when thy king is a free man". This is R. Simeon,
who holds his head erect to expound doctrine and fears not,
like a free man who says what he wants to say without fear.'

R. Simeon said: 'It is written: "And it shall come to pass
that from one new moon to another, and from one Sabbath
to another", etc. (Isa. LXVI, 23). Why is "new moon" put
side by side with "Sabbath" ? Because both are of one grade,
being the time when one is joined to the other. On Sabbath
there is joy and an additional soul, because the Ancient One
reveals Himself and the wedlock is prepared. So, too, at the
renewal of the moon, because the sun illumines her with
the joyful light of the Ancient One above. Therefore the
offering of new moon is an atonement above.

'It is written, "The burnt offering of the Sabbath beside
(*'al*, lit. upon) the continual burnt offering" (Num. XXVIII,
10). The word *'al* here signifies that the thought should
be directed to the very highest more than on other days.
Similarly it is written, "And Hannah prayed to (*'al*, lit. upon)
the Lord" (1 Sam. I, 19), because children depend upon the
holy *mazzal*, as we have pointed out.' R. Jose found R. Abba
similarly interpreting the words, "Cast thy burden upon
the Lord" (Ps. LV, 23), because food also depends on *mazzal*.
R. Judah expounded similarly the verse, "For this (*'al zoth*)
let every one that is godly pray to thee" (*Ibid*. XXXII, 6):
verily, to that which is above *zoth*.

R. Isaac said: 'Happy are the righteous in that many
precious treasures are stored up for them in the other world,
where God will have joyous converse with them, as we have
laid down. Happy their portion in this world and the [80a]
next, as it is written: "But let all those that put their trust
in thee rejoice, let them ever shout for joy because thou
defendest them, let them also that love thy name be joyful
in thee" (Ps. V, 12).'

KEDOSHIM

Leviticus XIX, I–XX, 27

YE SHALL BE HOLY, ETC. R. Eleazar cited here the text: "Be ye not as the horse or as the mule which have no understanding", etc. (Ps. XXXII, 9). 'How often', he said, 'does the Torah warn men, how often does it cry aloud on all sides to rouse them, yet they all sleep in their sins¹ and heed not ! With what face will they rise on the day of judgement when the Most High King will visit upon them their neglect of the Torah in not listening to her call, since they are full of blemishes and know not the faith of the Heavenly King. Alas for them and for their souls ! For the Torah has warned them saying: "Whoso is simple let him turn in hither; as for him that is void of understanding (lit. heart), she saith to him" (Prov. IX, 4). Why is he called "void of heart" ? Because he has no faith; since he who does not study the Torah has no faith and is wholly blemished. It is the supernal Torah which "saith to him", and calls him "void of heart". Similarly we have learnt that if a man does not study the Torah it is forbidden to go near him, to associate with him, to do business with him, all the more so to walk in the road with him. We have learnt that if a man walks abroad and no words of Torah accompany him, his life is forfeit; still more one who goes with a man who has no faith and heeds neither the honour of his Master nor his own, being regardless of his soul. Hence it is written: "Be not as the horse or as the mule", etc. Happy are the righteous who study the Torah and know the ways of the Holy One, blessed be He, and sanctify themselves with the holiness of the King and become holy throughout, thereby drawing down a holy spirit from above, so that all their children are truly virtuous and are called "sons of the king". Woe to the wicked who are shameless and do shameless deeds, for which their children inherit an unclean soul from the unclean side. "Be not like a horse or a mule", which are lustful

¹ Al. "in their dens".

above other creatures, for "they which have no understanding" fall a prey to the "dogs which are greedy and
can never have enough" (Isa. LVI, 11), and which are ready
to "shepherd them that have no understanding" (*Ibid.*)
[80b] into Gehinnom. Why does all this come upon them ?
Because they do not duly sanctify themselves in wedlock.
God said: Of all peoples I desired to attach to myself only
Israel; hence, "Ye shall be holy".'

YE SHALL BE HOLY FOR I THE LORD AM HOLY. R. Isaac
cited here the verse: "Ah land of the rustling of wings", etc.
(Isa. XVIII, 1). 'When God', he said, 'came to create the
world and reveal what was hidden in the depths and disclose
light out of darkness, they were all wrapped in one another,
and therefore light emerged from darkness and from the
impenetrable came forth the profound. So, too, from good
issues evil and from mercy issues judgement, and all are
intertwined, the good impulse and the evil impulse, right
and left, Israel and other peoples, white and black—all
depend on one another.' Said R. Isaac in the name of R.
Judah: 'The whole world is like a garland of variegated
flowers; when it is tried, it is judged with judgement
mingled with mercy; otherwise it could not stand an instant.
We have learnt that when judgement is suspended over the
world and righteousness is crowned with its judgements,
many winged messengers arise to meet the lords of stern
judgement and to obtain sway over the world, and they spread
their wings on both sides to overshadow the earth, which is
then called "the land of the rustling of wings".' R. Judah
said: 'I perceive that all mankind are shameless save the
truly virtuous. So, if one may say so, it is throughout: if
one commences to purify himself he is supported from above
and similarly if he commences to defile himself.'[1]

As R. Jose was once on the road he met R. Ḥiya and said
to him: 'In reference to the verse, "Therefore I have sworn
to the house of Eli that the iniquity of Eli's house shall not
be purged with sacrifice nor offering for ever" (1 Sam. III, 4),
the Companions, you know, have stated that it will not be

[1] *v.* T.B. Yoma, 38b.

purged with sacrifices nor offering, but it can be purged with words of Torah.[1] Why is this ? Because the words of the Torah rise above all offerings.' He replied: 'This is truly so, and if a man studies the Torah it benefits him more than all sacrifices and burnt-offerings, and even though punishment has been decreed against him from above, it is annulled. Therefore it is that words of the Torah are not susceptible to uncleanness,[2] because it can itself purify those who are unclean. We know this from the verse: "The fear of the Lord is clean, enduring for ever" (Ps. XIX, 9).' Said R. Jose: 'But it says here "the fear of the Lord", and not "the Torah" ?' He replied: 'It means the same thing, because the Torah comes from the side of *Geburah* (Might).' Said R. Jose: 'Rather derive it from here: "The fear of the Lord is the beginning of wisdom" (*Ibid.* CXI, 10). It is written: "The fear of the Lord is pure", and the Torah is called "holiness", as it is written, "I the Lord am holy", and the Torah is the supernal holy Name. Therefore [81*a*] he who studies it is first purified and then sanctified. We have learnt that the holiness of the Torah surpasses all other sanctifications, and the holiness of the superior recondite wisdom is highest of all.' He said to him: 'There is no Torah without wisdom and no wisdom without Torah, both being in the same grade, the root of the Torah being in the supernal Wisdom by which it is sustained. As they were going along they came across a man riding on a horse through a garden, and as he raised his hand he broke off the branch of a tree. Said. R. Jose: 'This illustrates the verse: "Ye shall sanctify yourselves and become holy"; if a man sanctifies himself below, he is further sanctified above.'

R. Abba taught: 'This section sums up the whole Torah, and is the seal of truth. In this section are contained profound mysteries of the Torah relative to the Ten Commandments and divine decrees and penalties and precepts, so that when the Companions came to this section they used to rejoice.'

Said R. Abba: 'Why does the section of "holiness" follow immediately upon the section dealing with sexual offences ? Because we have learnt that whoever preserves himself from

[1] *v.* T.B. Rosh Hashanah, 18*a*.   [2] *v.* T.B. Berachoth, 22*a*.

these offences shows that he was begotten in holiness; all
the more so if he sanctifies himself with the holiness of
his Master. The Companions have indicated the proper
time of marital intercourse for all classes. He who desires
to sanctify himself according to the will of his Master should
not have intercourse save from midnight onwards, or at
midnight, for at that time the Holy One, blessed be He, is
in the Garden of Eden, and greater holiness is abroad,
wherefore it is a time for a man to sanctify himself. This is
the rule for the ordinary man. But students who know the
ways of the Torah should rise at midnight to study and to
join themselves with the Community of Israel to praise the
holy name and the holy King; and their time of intercourse
is at that hour on the night of the Sabbath[1] when grace
abounds, that they may obtain favour from the Community
of Israel and the Holy One, blessed be He, and those are
called holy.'

R. Abba quoted here the verse: "Who is like thy people
Israel, one nation in the earth?" (1 Sam. VII, 23). 'God', he
said, 'chose Israel alone of all peoples, and made them one
unique nation in the world and called them "one nation",
after His own name. He gave them many precepts to be
crowned withal, including the phylacteries of the head and
the arm, wherewith a man becomes one and complete.
For he is only called "one" when he is complete, and not
if he is defective, and therefore God is called One when He
is consummated with the Patriarchs and the Community
of Israel. When, therefore, the Israelite puts on his phylacteries and wraps himself in the fringed garment, he is crowned
with holy crowns after the supernal pattern and is called
"one", and it is fitting that One should come and attend
to one. And when is a man called "one"? When he is male
with female and is sanctified with a high holiness and is
bent upon sanctification; [81b] then alone he is called one
without blemish. Therefore a man should rejoice with his
wife at that hour to bind her in affection to him, and they
should both have the same intent. When they are thus
united, they form one soul and one body: one soul through

[1] *v.* T.B. Ketuboth, 62b.

their affection, and one body, as we have learnt, that if a man is not married he is, as it were, divided in halves, and only when male and female are joined do they become one body. Then God rests upon "one" and lodges a holy spirit in it: and such are called "the sons of God", as has been said.'

YE SHALL FEAR EVERY MAN HIS MOTHER AND HIS FATHER, ETC. The fear of mother and father is here put side by side with the keeping of the Sabbath. Said R. Jose: 'It is all one; he who fears one keeps the other. Why is the mother here placed before the father? As we have learnt, because she has not so much power as the father.' R. Isaac connected this with the preceding words, "ye shall be holy": when a man comes to sanctify himself together with his wife, it is the female who deserves the greater credit for that sanctification, and therefore the mother is placed first here.' R. Judah pointed out that in another place the father is placed before the mother, the object being to indicate that both contributed equally to producing the son. The verse continues: AND YE SHALL KEEP MY SABBATHS, to show that one precept is of equal weight with the other. [82a] R. Simeon said: 'When a man sanctifies himself below, as, for instance, the Companions who sanctify themselves from Sabbath to Sabbath at the hour of the supernal wedlock, when grace abounds and blessings are at hand, then all cleave together, the soul of Sabbath and the body that has been prepared for Sabbath. Therefore it is written, "Ye shall fear every one his mother and his father", who form one wedlock in the body at that hour which has been sanctified. "Ye shall keep my sabbaths": the plural refers to the upper and the lower Sabbath which invite the soul to that body from that supernal wedlock. We may also translate "Ye shall *wait for* my sabbaths", this being an admonition to those who wait for their marital intercourse from Sabbath to Sabbath, as it is written, "the eunuchs who keep my sabbaths" (Isa. LVI, 4), for so we may call the Companions who emasculate themselves all the other days of the week in order to labour in the study of the Torah and wait from

Sabbath to Sabbath. We may also take "father and mother" here to refer to the Body, and "my sabbaths" to the Soul, both of which cleave together.' [83b]

TURN YE NOT UNTO IDOLS NOR MAKE TO YOURSELVES MOLTEN GODS. R. Ḥiya adduced in this connection the verse: "Turn not unto the stubbornness of this people" (Deut. IX, 27). 'How', he said, 'could Moses address such a request to the Almighty who observes all things and passes all deeds in judgement ? The answer is as follows. If a man performs a religious action, that action ascends and stands before the Almighty and says: I am from So-and-so who has performed me; and God then sets it before Him that He may look upon it all the day and treat the doer well for its sake. Similarly, if a man transgresses a precept of the Law, that action ascends and stands before the Almighty and says: I am from So-and-so who has performed me; and God sets that action where the sight of it will remind him to destroy that man. But if the man repents, then He removes that sin to where He will not observe it. Hence Moses said to God: "Turn not to the wickedness of this people, nor to their wickedness nor to their sin".'

R. Jose the younger once went in to see R. Simeon and found him expounding the verse: "And the man said: The woman whom thou gavest to be with me, she gave me of the tree and I did eat" (Gen. III, 12). 'The expression "with me",' he said, 'indicates that Adam and Eve were created together with one body.' Said R. Jose to him: 'If so, what of the words of Hannah to Eli: "I am the woman who stood with thee here" (1 Sam. 1, 26) ?' He replied: 'It does not say here "was given".' 'But,' said the other, 'what of the verse, "And the Lord God said, It is not good that the man should be alone, I will make him an help meet for him" (Gen. II, 18), which implies that she was not made until then ?' He replied: 'Adam was indeed alone in so far as he had no support from his female, because she was fixed in his side, as we have explained. Hence God did not say "I will *create* a help", but "I will *make*", that is, fashion; and so God did by taking one of his sides and fashioning it and bringing it to him. Then Adam cohabited with his wife, and she became a support to him.

'We have learnt that the beauty of Adam was like an emanation from the supernal effulgence, and the beauty of Eve such that no creature could look steadily at her. Even Adam could not look steadily at her until they had sinned and their beauty had been diminished. Then only did Adam gaze steadfastly at her and "know" her. We have learnt that it is forbidden to a man to gaze at the beauty of a woman[1] lest evil thoughts should be provoked in him and he should be incited [84a] to something worse.' When R. Simeon went through the town, followed by the Companions, if he saw a beautiful woman he used to lower his eyes and say to the Companions, Do not turn. Whoever gazes at the beauty of a woman by day will have lustful thoughts at night, and if these gain the better of him he will transgress the precept, "Ye shall not make to yourselves molten gods". And if he has intercourse with his wife while under the influence of those imaginings, the children born from such union are called "molten gods". R. Abba said: 'It is forbidden to a man to fix his gaze upon heathen idols and upon Gentile women, or to receive benefit or healing from them.'

R. Abba discoursed on the verse: "Turn unto me and have mercy upon me, give thy strength unto thy servant" (Ps. LXXXVI, 15). 'Had God, then', he said, 'nothing more beautiful than David to turn to ? It is, however, as we have learnt, that God has another David who is in command of many celestial hosts and legions: and when God desires to be gracious to the world He looks upon this David with a smiling countenance, and he in turn sheds light and grace upon the world through his beauty, his head being a skull of gold broidered with seven ornaments of gold. And through God's great love for him, He tells him to turn his eyes towards Him and look at Him, because they are very beautiful; and when he does so, His heart is, as it were, pierced with shafts of supernal love. And for the sake of that celestial David, beautiful, beloved and desired of God, David said: "Turn

[1] v. T.B. Berachoth, 24a et passim.

to me and be gracious unto me". Similarly, when Isaac said to Jacob, "Behold the smell of my son is as the smell of a field which the Lord hath blessed", this, we are told, was because the Garden of Eden entered with Jacob. Here, too, we may ask, how could the Garden of Eden enter with him, seeing that it is of immense extent in length and breadth, with many compartments and residences ? The truth is that God has another holy Garden of which He is specially fond, and which He guards Himself and which He appoints to be continually with the righteous; and this it was that entered with Jacob. Similarly when we are told that the whole land of Israel came and folded itself under Abram,[1] this refers to another holy supernal land which God has and which is also called "the land of Israel". This is below the grade of Jacob and has been transmitted by God to Israel out of His love for them to abide with them and to lead and protect them, and it is called "the land of the living".

'It is forbidden to a man to gaze upon a place which God loathes, and even on one which God loves. For instance, it is forbidden to gaze upon the rainbow,[2] because it is the mirror of the supernal form. It is forbidden to a man to gaze upon the sign of the covenant upon him, because this is emblematic of the Righteous One of the world. It is forbidden to gaze upon the fingers of the priests when they spread out their hands to bless the congregation,[3] because the glory of the most high King rests there. If one must not gaze at a holy place, [84b] how much less may he at an unclean and loathsome one ! Therefore, "turn not to the idols".' R. Isaac said: 'If it is forbidden to look at them, how much more to worship them !

'The injunctions in this section correspond to those in the Ten Commandments. Thus: "Ye shall not turn to the idols" corresponds to "Thou shalt have no other gods before me"; "nor make to yourselves molten gods" to "thou shalt not make unto thee any graven image"; "I am the Lord your God" to "I am the Lord thy God"; "ye shall fear every

---

[1] v. Midrash Rabbah on Genesis XIII, 15. [2] v. T.B. Hagigah, 16a.
[3] v. Ibid.

one his mother and his father" to "honour thy father and thy mother"; "and ye shall keep my sabbaths" to"remember the Sabbath day to keep it holy"; "ye shall not swear by my name falsely" to "thou shalt not take the name of the Lord thy God in vain"; "ye shall not steal" to "thou shalt not steal"; "neither shall ye deal falsely nor lie to one another" to "thou shalt not bear false witness against thy neighbour"; "the adulterer and the adulteress shall surely be put to death" (xx, 10) to "thou shalt not commit adultery"; "neither shalt thou stand against the blood of thy neighbour" to "thou shalt not murder". Thus the Law is summed up in this section.' R. Ḥiya asked: 'Why in the Ten Commandments is the singular (thou) used and here the plural (you)? Because in the whole of their existence Israel were never so united in heart and mind in devotion to God as on that day when they stood before Mount Sinai; hence they were addressed there as a single individual, but later they were not so single-hearted.'

R. Eleazar once went to pay a visit to R. Jose ben R. Simeon ben Lakunia, his father-in-law, accompanied by R. Ḥiya and R. Jose. On reaching a certain field they sat down under a tree, and R. Eleazar said: 'Let each of us give a discourse on the Torah.' He himself commenced with the text: "Yet I am the Lord thy God from the land of Egypt, and thou shalt know no god but me" (Hos. xiii, 4). He said: 'Was God then their king only from the land of Egypt and not previously? Did not Jacob say to his sons, "Remove the strange gods from your midst" (Gen. xxxv, 2)? The truth is that Israel never paid such recognition to the glory of God as in the land of Egypt, where they were so bitterly oppressed and yet did not change their customs; nay more, they saw every day much magic and sorcery which might have seduced them, and yet they turned aside neither to the right nor to the left, although they did not actually know much of the glory of God, but only adhered to the customs of their fathers. Afterwards they saw many wonders and miracles, and therefore God said to them, "I am the Lord thy God from the land of Egypt", where His glory was revealed to them by the sea, and they saw the brightness of His glory face to face, so that they should not say it was another God who spoke with them, but should know that it was the same one who brought them out of the land of Egypt, whom they had seen in the land of Egypt, who had slain their enemies there and wrought the ten plagues there.'

He further discoursed on the verse: THOU SHALT NOT OPPRESS THY NEIGHBOUR, NOR ROB HIM; THE WAGES OF A HIRED SERVANT SHALL NOT ABIDE WITH THEE ALL NIGHT UNTIL MORNING. 'The reason for this last injunction is to be found in the verse, "In his day thou shalt give him his hire, and the sun shall not go down upon him" (Deut. XXIV, 15): that is to say, that thou be not gathered in from the world on his account before thy time cometh. From this we learn another thing, that if one restores the soul of a poor man, even [85a] if his time has arrived to depart from the world, God restores his soul and gives him a further lease of life. To withhold the wage of a poor man is like taking his life and the life of his household. As he diminishes their souls, so God diminishes his days, and cuts off his soul from the other world. For all the breaths which issue from his mouth for the whole of that day ascend and stand before the Almighty, and afterwards his soul and the souls of his household ascend and stand in those breaths. Thus, even if length of days and many blessings had been decreed for that man, they are all withdrawn, nor does his soul mount aloft. Therefore R. Abba said: God save us from them and from their plaint ! And the same is true even if it is a rich man, and his right is withheld from him. Hence R. Hamnuna, when a hired worker had finished his work, used to give him his wage and say to him: Take your soul which you have entrusted to my hand ! Take your deposit ! And even if the other asked him to keep it for him, he was unwilling to do so, saying: It is not fitting that your body shall be deposited with me, still less then your soul, which should be deposited only with God. Why is it written, "On his day thou shalt give him his hire" ? Because every day is under the surveillance of another, a supernal Day, and if he does not give him his soul on that day, it is as if he impairs that supernal Day.'

R. Ḥiya discoursed on the next verse: THOU SHALT
NOT CURSE THE DEAF NOR PUT A STUMBLING BLOCK
BEFORE THE BLIND. 'This verse can be taken literally,
but all this section has also other significations, and each set
is connected with the other. See now. If a man curses his
neighbour in his presence, it is as if he spills his blood.
When, however, he curses him not in his presence, the
voice of his words ascends, and is joined by many emissaries
of judgement until the place of the great abyss is aroused.
Woe, therefore, to him who lets an evil word issue from his
mouth. The words, "thou shalt not put a stumbling block
before the blind" we interpret of one who leads another
into sin,[1] and also of one who strikes his grown-up son;
or again, of one who not being competent gives decisions
on points of Jewish law, because he causes his fellow-man
to come to grief in the future world. For we have learnt
that he who walks straightly in the path of the Torah and
who studies it in the fitting manner has ever a goodly portion
in the world to come, since the word of Torah which issues
from his lips flits about the world and goes aloft, where
many angels join it, and it is crowned with a holy crown and
bathed in the light of the world to come, so that there
proceeds from it a celestial light which crowns him during
the whole of the day. But if a man studies the Torah not
in the true and [85b] proper manner, his words stray from
the path and no angels join them, but they are thrust away
by all and find no resting place. Who is the cause of this?
The one who led him astray from the right path. If a man,
however, desires to study the Torah and cannot find a
proper teacher, and yet out of his love for the Torah he
pores over it and babbles it ignorantly, all his words ascend
and God rejoices in them and plants them around the River,
where they grow into mighty trees and are called "willows
of the brook". Happy are those who know the ways of
the Torah and study it in the proper manner, for they plant
trees of life which are superior to all healing medicines.
Therefore it says, "The law of truth was in his mouth"
(Mal. II, 6). For there is a law which is not of truth, namely,

[1] v. T.B. Moed Katon, 17a.

of him who gives decisions without being qualified, and one who learns from him learns something which is not truth. None the less it behoves a man to learn Torah, even from one who is not qualified, in order that thus his interest may be aroused and he may eventually learn from one who is qualified and walk in the straight path of the Torah.'

R. Jose then discoursed on the next verse: YE SHALL DO NO UNRIGHTEOUSNESS IN JUDGEMENT, ETC. IN RIGHTEOUSNESS SHALT THOU JUDGE THY NEIGHBOUR. 'Two grades are here mentioned, "judgement" and "righteousness". What is the difference between them ? One is mercy and one judgement, and one is established by the other. When "righteousness" is aroused it deals out sentence to all impartially without indulgence; but when "judgement" is aroused, clemency is also in it. I might then think that judgement alone should be used; therefore the verse says, "In righteousness shalt thou judge thy neighbour", not sentencing one and passing over another, but treating all equally. Should, then, righteousness alone be used ? No: the verse tells us "thou shalt judge", implying that both must be together. Why so ? Because God is there, and therefore the trial must be without flaw: as he does below, so does God do above. For God sets up His throne of judgement when the judges sit on earth, and it is from there that God's Throne is established, that Throne consisting of righteousness and judgement. Hence if a judge offends against these, he, as it were, impairs the Throne of the King, and then God leaves the judges and does not remain among them.' [86a]

They then rose, and as they went along R. Eleazar cited the verse: THOU SHALT NOT GO UP AND DOWN AS A TALE-BEARER AMONG THY PEOPLE, ETC. 'All these rules', he said, 'have been commented on by the Companions. Let us, however, also give some exposition of this section. It is written: YE SHALL KEEP MY STATUTES. THOU SHALT NOT LET THY CATTLE GENDER WITH A DIVERSE KIND, ETC. It is written: "Ye are my witnesses said the Lord, and my servant whom I have chosen" (Isa. XLIII, 10). Israel are called witnesses and the heaven and earth are called witnesses, as it says, "I testify against you heaven and earth" (Deut. xxx, 19). Israel witness against one another and heaven and earth against all. Observe now. When God created the world, He assigned all things to their respective sides, and appointed over them celestial powers, so that there is not even a tiny herb without such a super-visor,[1] and whatever they do is done through the power of that heavenly control, and all are rigidly assigned, and none [86b] leaves its appointed sphere. All are guided by another superior regulation which gives to each its portion, which comes from the heavens, and all together are called "the statutes of the heavens". Hence it is written, "Ye shall keep my statutes", because each power is appointed over a certain sphere in the world in virtue of a certain statute. Therefore it is forbidden to confound species and mate them one with another, because this dislodges the heavenly power from its place and is a defiance of the celestial household. The word *kilaim* (divers kinds) may be connected with *kele* (prison), and it also bears the meaning of preventing, indicating that one who does this prevents the celestial powers from carrying out their function, and throws them into confusion. As has been said, he alters the commands of the King, and exchanges the Tree of Life, by which all is perfected and on which faith depends, for another place.

'We have learnt that in all things a man should act after the supernal model and perform the right thing, and that if he alters it he draws upon himself something which he would better have avoided. When a man does things below in the right way, he draws upon himself a celestial holy spirit. But if he does things in a crooked way, he draws upon himself another spirit which leads him astray to an evil side. What brings upon him this evil spirit ? The action which he exhibited in the other side. Such is he who joins wool and flax. (In the case of the fringes, however, this is allowed,[2] because when making these a man is in the category of completeness, and therefore he does no wrong.) But if one joins them when he is not in the category of completeness,

---

[1] *v.* Bereshith Rabbah, 10.   [2] *v.* T.B. Yebamoth, 4*a et passim.*

he brings an unwelcome spirit on himself. We have a proof of this in Cain and Abel, because they came from different sides; therefore the offering of Cain was rejected for that of Abel. Another proof is in the prohibition to plough with an ox and an ass, which are names given to two different sides. These must not be mingled together, lest the junction should harm the world, whereas he who keeps them separate benefits the world. So, too, he who keeps flax and wool separate. [87a] Cain was of the type of *kilaim* because he came partly from another side which was not of the species of Adam and Eve; and his offering also came from that side. In the case of Abel the two sides were joined in the womb of Eve, and because they were joined no benefit came to the world from them and they perished. Hence he who makes this union arouses both sides together and may come to harm, and a wrong spirit rests on him. Israel, however, ought to call down upon themselves a holy spirit, so as to be at peace in this world and the next. Therefore the High Priest on the Day of Atonement wore only linen garments when he came to clear away the ashes from the altar (Lev. VI, 10), because the burnt-offering is an atonement for evil thoughts; but when he went into the Sanctuary, the place where there was completeness and all services of completeness, it mattered not if he wore wool and flax together, because there all the different celestial species were found together in harmony, and similarly all kinds of holy vessels were there in combination, after the supernal model.

R. Ḥiya followed him with a discourse on the text: WHEN YE SHALL HAVE COME INTO THE LAND AND SHALL HAVE PLANTED ALL MANNER OF TREES FOR FOOD . . . IN THE FOURTH YEAR ALL THE FRUIT THEREOF SHALL BE HOLY, FOR GIVING PRAISE UNTO THE LORD. 'Observe', he said, 'that the tree only produces fruit from the earth, which is its true source, nor does the earth produce the fruit save through another power above it, just as the female only produces issue from the energy of the male. Now, that fruit does not reach its complete state until three years have passed, nor is any power appointed over it above until it has reached its complete state. Then, too, the earth

is established with it, and the establishment of both constitutes completeness. Similarly the progeny of a woman does
not reach completeness till her third delivery, and therefore
Levi was chosen from all the sons of Jacob, being the third
to his mother who was established with him. Thus after
three years a power is appointed over the fruit above, and
in the fourth year "all its fruit is holy for giving praise" to
the Holy One, blessed be He. For in the fourth year [87b]
the Community of Israel becomes united with the Holy One,
blessed be He, and then celestial powers are appointed over
the world, an appropriate one for each object. Thence-
forward all products are blessed and are permitted to be
eaten, since all are in their complete state, in regard both to
heaven and to earth. Till that time it is forbidden to eat
of them; and he who eats of them is like one who has no
share in the Holy One, blessed be He, and in the Community
of Israel, since that fruit is as yet under no holy celestial
control, nor is the strength of the earth established in it, so
that he who eats of it shows that he has no portion either
above or below, and if he makes a blessing over it, it is an
idle blessing.'

R. Jose then said: 'The succeeding verses are to be taken
in their literal meaning, but some remarks may be made on
the verse: THOU SHALT RISE UP BEFORE THE HOARY
HEAD, AND HONOUR THE FACE OF AN OLD MAN. The
"hoary head" refers to the Torah, and a man should rise
before the Scroll of the Torah. When R. Hamnuna the Elder
saw a Scroll of the Law, he used to rise and say, "Thou shalt
rise up before the hoary head". Similarly a man should
rise before a man of learning, because he exhibits the holy
supernal image and is emblematic of the supernal Priest.
Further we may derive from the verse the lesson that we
should rise up to do good deeds before old age comes upon
us; for there is not much credit to a man in doing this when
he is old and cannot do evil any more; but it is an honour
to him if he is good while still in his prime.'

Said R. Eleazar: 'In very truth this way of ours is made
straight before us, and it is the way of the Holy One, blessed
be He. For "God knows the way of the righteous" (Ps. 1, 6),

to benefit them and protect them. Therefore when a man goes forth on the way he should see that that is the way of the Holy One, blessed be He, and should obtain His companionship. [88a] Of such a way it is written: "The path of the righteous is as the shining light that shineth more and more unto the perfect day" (Prov. IV, 18).'

H

EMOR

Leviticus XXI, 1–XXIV, 23

AND THE LORD SAID UNTO MOSES, SPEAK UNTO THE PRIESTS THE SONS OF AARON AND SAY UNTO THEM, THERE SHALL NONE DEFILE HIMSELF FOR THE DEAD AMONG HIS PEOPLE. R. Jose said: 'What is the connection of this with the verse that immediately precedes, "A man also or a woman that hath a familiar spirit or that is a wizard shall be put to death" (Lev. xx, 27) ? It is this: that having admonished the Israelites to sanctify themselves, the Scripture now admonishes the priests to sanctify themselves specially. Later, too, it admonishes the Levites (Num. XVIII, 21 *et seq.*), so that all should become holy and pure. The priests are designated here "the sons of Aaron", to show that they are something more than merely the sons of Levi, Aaron being the starting point of the priesthood because God chose him to make peace in the world, his conduct having entitled him to this distinction, since all his days he strove to promote peace in the world, so that God appointed him to bring peace to the celestial family also.

'THERE SHALL NONE DEFILE HIMSELF FOR THE DEAD AMONG HIS PEOPLE. Observe that when a man is on his deathbed and on the point of departing for the other world, three messengers are sent to him, and he sees what other men cannot see in this world. That day is a day of heavenly judgement on which the King demands back his deposit. Happy the man who can restore the deposit just as it was lodged within him; for if it has been defiled with the impurity of the body, what will he say to the owner of the deposit ? He sees the angel of death standing before him with his sword drawn, and all his limbs are relaxed, nor is anything so hard for the soul as its separation from the body. Before a man dies he beholds the Divine Presence, towards which the soul goes out in great yearning; [88b] and after it has left the body what other soul will cleave to it ? This we have

discussed elsewhere. After the soul has left the body and
the body remains without breath, it is forbidden to keep it
unburied.[1] For a dead body which is left unburied for
twenty-four hours causes a weakness in the limbs of the
Chariot and prevents God's design from being fulfilled;
for perhaps God decreed that he should undergo a transmigration at once on the day that he died, which would
be better for him, but as long as the body is not buried the
soul cannot go into the presence of the Holy One nor be
transferred into another body. For a soul cannot enter a
second body till the first is buried, just as it is not fitting
for a man to take a second wife before the first is buried.
Another reason why the body should be buried on the
same day is that when the soul departs from the body it
cannot enter the other world until it is invested with another
body formed of light. (So Elijah had two bodies, one in
which he appeared on earth, and one in which he appeared
among celestial angels.) So long as the body remains unburied the soul suffers pain and an unclean spirit rests upon
the body, and therefore the body should not be kept over
night, because by night the unclean spirit spreads over the
earth, seeking for a body without a soul to defile it further.
Therefore the priest was warned "not to defile himself for
the dead among his people".' R. Isaac said that the word
"say" here signifies "say quietly", just as all the operations
of the priests were carried out in quietness; and the repetition
"say" and "thou shalt say" is to give emphasis to the injunction that they should not defile themselves, since he
who ministers in a holy place should be holy throughout.
As we have said, the body without the spirit is unclean, and
the desire of unclean spirits is for the bodies of Israel, since
now that the holy spirit has been emptied out of them they
want to be joined to a holy vessel. The priests who are
additionally holy must not defile themselves at all, since
"the oil of the anointment of the Lord is upon him".' [89a]
R. Isaac also said: 'The priest who stands here below is
emblematic of the Priest above, and therefore he must be
in a superior grade of holiness.'

[1] v. T.B. Moed Katon, 28a; Baba Kama, 82b.

AND FOR HIS SISTER A VIRGIN THAT IS NEAR UNTO
HIM. R. Abba quoted here the verse: "Who is this that
cometh from Edom, with dyed garments from Bozrah ?"
(Isa. LXIII, 1). 'God', he said, 'will one day put on garments
of vengeance to chastise Edom for having destroyed His
house and burnt His Temple and driven the Community
of Israel into exile among the nations. He will wreak vengeance on them until all the mountains are full of the slain
of the nations, when he will summon all birds of the air and
the beasts of the field and they shall feast on them, the beasts
twelve months and the birds seven years, and the earth shall
not bear the stench thereof. God shall come from Bozrah,
because from there the world's hosts went forth to war
against Jerusalem, and they began to burn the Temple,
and the children of Edom threw down the walls and destroyed the foundations. God will be "glorious in his apparel",
His robes of vengeance, and "marching in the greatness of his
strength". Said the Israelites to Isaiah: "Who is he that shall
do all this ?" He replied: "I that speak in righteousness,
mighty to save". And why all this ? Because "for his sister
a virgin that is near unto him, which hath had no husband",
to wit, for the Community of Israel who does not belong
to the portion of Esau, for her He may be defiled, to wit,
in those garments of vengeance with which He will stain
himself among all those hosts.'

THEY SHALL NOT MAKE BALDNESS UPON THEIR HEAD.
R. Jose said: 'The reason is that on the head of the supernal
Priest is the holy oil of anointing, the removal of which
would cause baldness; and therefore the priest below must
perform an action symbolical of this.'[1] [89b]

(AND HE THAT IS THE HIGH PRIEST AMONG HIS
BRETHREN, ETC.) R. Abba here quoted the verse: "To
thee, O Lord, belongeth righteousness, but unto us confusion
of face" (Dan. IX, 7). ' "Righteousness" ', he said, 'refers to
the place to which all the shining faces are attached, as it
is attached to them; and "confusion of face" refers to the

---

[1] Here follows in the original a passage expanding this idea in the
highly allusive and untranslatable style of the *Midrash Hareʿelam*.

place from which the shining faces are removed. Therefore
the High Priest should always present a face bright and shining
and more joyful than others, seeing that he symbolizes the
higher grade.

[90*a*] 'HE SHALL NOT PROFANE HIS SEED AMONG HIS
PEOPLE. Whoever discharges his semen without purpose will
never be allowed to behold the divine Presence,[1] and such a
one is called wicked. This is not the case, however, if a man's
wife does not conceive; still, a man should pray that God
should provide him a fitting vessel so that his seed should
not be spoilt. For he who discharges his seed into a vessel
that is not fitting spoils his seed; and if this is the case
with ordinary men, how much more so with the priest who
is the counterpart on earth of the supernal holiness. AMONG
HIS PEOPLE: that is to say, this is a disgrace, a defect
among his people. FOR I AM THE LORD WHICH SANCTIFY
HIM: I am He that sanctifies him every day, and therefore
he must not spoil his seed nor must any blemish be found in
him. He must be holy throughout, so that the Holy One
may be served by a holy one. [90*b*] And because God is
served by the hand of the priest, who is holy, the priest is
served by one who is sanctified by his purity, to wit, the
Levite. The ordinary man, too, is served[2] by one who has
already sanctified himself, and thus Israel are set apart in
holiness to serve the Holy One, blessed be He.'

He further expounded the verse: "Salvation is the Lord's;
thy blessing be upon thy people" (Ps. III, 9). 'We have learnt',
he said, 'that wherever Israel go into exile the Shekinah
goes with them.[3] When, therefore, they will come forth from
captivity, who will be delivered? Israel or God? The answer
is given in the verse, "Salvation is the Lord's". And when
will this be? When "thy blessing is upon thy people, selah",
to take them out of captivity and deal well with them.'

WHOEVER HE BE OF THY SEED THROUGHOUT THEIR
GENERATIONS THAT HATH A BLEMISH. R. Isaac said:
'Whoever has a blemish is not fitted to serve before the

[1] *v.* T.B. Niddah, 13*a*.   [2] i.e. should have water poured over his hands,
v. Shuldan Aruch.   [3] *v.* T.B. Megillah, 29*a*.

Holy One, as we have laid down, that whoever has a blemish
has no true faith, and his blemish bears witness against him.'
R. Eleazar was once sitting in the room of his father-in-law,
and he complained that his eyes were watering. A man
happened to pass by who had lost one eye. 'Let us ask him,'
said the father-in-law. He replied: 'He is blemished, and
therefore not to be trusted.' 'Still let us ask him,' said the
other. So they said to him: 'Who is mightiest in the world ?'
He replied: 'A rich man; and I shall remain with him
through all.' Said R. Eleazar: 'His words show that he has
no religious faith in him.' He then discoursed on the verse:
"For the law and for the testimony; if they speak not
according to this word" (Isa. VIII, 20). ' "Law" here', he said,
'signifies the Written Law, and "testimony" the Oral Law.
The Oral Law does not rest in a blemished place, because
it is fashioned from the Written Law. Hence the text says
"Bind up the testimony" (*Ibid.* 16), because there in the
Oral Law is the bundle of life, and the knot of faith is tied
up with the testimony above, and thence diverse paths
through all the worlds. "Seal the law among my disciples"
(*Ibid.*) Where is the seal of the Written Law ? In "my
disciples", that is, the prophets. The whole is established
only in its completeness, and holiness rests on it only when
it is complete, when part is joined with part and the·e is
no empty place. Hence no man with a blemish must draw
near to serve, nor must a sacrifice with a blemish be o fered.
But surely it may be said, God abides only in a broken place,
a broken vessel, as it is written, "With him that is of a contrite and humble spirit" (Isa. LVII, 15) ? That is so, for this
place is more perfect than all, when a man humbles himself
so that the grandeur of all, the heavenly grandeur may rest
upon him. But it is not written [91*a*] "with the blind and
crippled". If a man humbles himself, God raises him. Therefore the priest must above all others be complete and not
show any blemish, and therefore the Scripture warns the
priests saying, "whoever of thy seed hath a blemish", etc.'
He further quoted the verse: "And when ye offer the blind
for sacrifice, is it no evil ?" etc. (Mal. 1, 8). In those days the
Israelites used to appoint priests with blemishes to serve

at the altar and in the Sanctuary, saying: What does it matter to God if it is this one or another ? It is no evil. And God answered them with their own words: It is no evil ! "Present it now unto thy governor, will he be pleased with thee or will he accept thy person ?" (*Ibid.*) If any one of you wanted to make a present to the king, would he send it by the hand of a man who was deformed ? How then can you set before Me a man with a blemish to present your gift ? Such a gift is given to the dog.' R. Jose said: 'God will one day make Israel whole so that there shall be none with a blemish among them, in order that they may adorn the world as a man's garments adorn his body. Observe that when the dead rise from the dust, they will leave it as they entered; if they went into it lame or blind, they shall rise from it lame or blind, in order that it should not be said that it is another who has risen. Afterwards, however, God will heal them and they will be whole before Him and the world will be whole.[1]

WHEN A BULLOCK OR A SHEEP OR A GOAT IS BROUGHT FORTH, THEN IT SHALL BE SEVEN DAYS UNDER THE DAM. R. Jose said: 'It is written, "Man and beast thou preservest, O Lord" (Ps. XXXVI, 7): that is to say, in mercy God preserves both in equal measure. The law of the beast and the law of the man is the same; man is to be circumcised on the eighth day, and the beast shall be seven days under its dam and from the eighth day it shall be accepted for an offering made by fire unto the Lord.' R. Ḥiya said: 'Israel from the eighth day cleave to God and are impressed with His name and become His, but the other peoples do not cleave to Him nor conform to His rules, and they remove from themselves the holy impress until [91b] they cleave to the other side which is not holy. When God came to give the Law to Israel, before doing so He summoned the children of Esau and said to them: Do you desire to accept the Law ?[2] At that moment the earth quaked and was fain to enter into the cavern of the great deep. She said: Sovereign of the Universe, is that which was a plaything of delight for two

<hr>

[1] Cf. T.B. Sanhedrin, 91a.   [2] v. T.B. Abodah Zara, 2b.

thousand years before the universe was created to be presented to the uncircumcised who are not stamped with thy
covenant ? Whereupon the Holy One, blessed be He, answered: Throne, throne, let a thousand such peoples perish
before the covenant of the Law is presented to them. Hence
it is written, "Lord, when thou wentest forth out of Seir,
when thou marchedst out of the field of Edom, the earth
trembled" (Jud. v, 4), because the Law is not to be given
save to one who bears on himself the holy covenant. And
he who teaches the Torah to one who is not circumcised is
false to two covenants,[1] to the covenant of the *Zaddik* and
the covenant of the Community of Israel, since the Torah
was given to this place and to no other.' R. Abba said that
he is false to three supernal places, the Law, the Prophets,
and the Holy Writings.' R. Ḥiya said: 'When God revealed
himself on Mount Sinai to give the Law to Israel, the earth
reclined and rested at ease, as it says, "the earth feared and
was still" (Ps. LXXVI, 9).

'Observe that when a child is born, a power from above
is not appointed to watch over it until it is circumcised.
When the child is circumcised, some supernal activity is
stirred in connection with it. If he proceeds to the study
of the Torah, the activity is heightened. If he is able to keep
the precepts of the Law, the activity is still further heightened.
If he advances so far as to marry and beget children and
teach them the ways of the Holy King, then he is a complete
man. Contrariwise, the beast from the moment of its birth
is under the same supervision as throughout its life. Therefore it is written, "when a *bullock* or a *sheep* or a *goat* is
born", not "a calf or a lamb or a kid", to show that what it
has at the end it has at the moment of birth. It is to be seven
days under its dam in order that that power may be settled
and firmly established in it. For this it is necessary that one
sabbath should pass over it; and then "it is acceptable for
an offering made by fire unto the Lord".' [92*a*]

AND WHETHER IT BE AN OX OR A SHEEP, YE SHALL NOT
KILL IT AND ITS YOUNG BOTH ON ONE DAY. R. Jose said:

[1] *v.* T.B. Hagigah, 13*a*.

'This must be taken to refer to the mother, since the young goes after the mother and not the father,[1] nor do we know which it is. Why must not both be killed on one day ?' R. Judah said: 'If it is to avoid giving pain to the animal, we could kill one in one place and the other in another, or one somewhat later than the other.' He replied: 'Some actually allow this, but this is not correct; the prohibition relates to the whole of the same day. Observe now that we have learnt that "a fast is as good for a dream as fire for flax",[2] but it must be on the same day, because every day below is controlled by a day above, and therefore if the man fasts, that day does not pass till the adverse decree is annulled, but if he puts it off to another day, then the control belongs to that day. Thus over every day below is appointed a day above, and a man should take heed not to impair that day. Now the act below stimulates a corresponding activity above. [92b] Thus if a man does kindness on earth, he awakens loving-kindness above, and it rests upon that day which is crowned therewith through him. Similarly if he performs a deed of mercy, he crowns that day with mercy and it becomes his protector in the hour of need. So, too, if he performs a cruel action, he has a corresponding effect on that day and impairs it, so that subsequently it becomes cruel to him and tries to destroy him, giving him measure for measure. Israel are withheld from cruelty more than all other peoples, and must not manifest any deed of the kind, since many watchful eyes are upon them.'

R. Simeon said: 'When God resolves to punish the world with famine, He makes the proclamation Himself, and not by the hand of a herald, as in the case of all other punishments.[3] From that moment it is forbidden to a man who still has plenty to make a show of it, since in so doing he defies the word of the King and, as it were, drives the emissaries of the King from their place. Therefore it was that Jacob said to his sons when the famine came, "Do not show yourselves off", as much as to say: Why do you cause blemish both above and below, and belie the word of the

[1] v. T.B. Hullin, 78b, where two views are given.   [2] T.B. Taanith, 12b.
[3] v. T.B. Taanith, 2a.

king and all his emissaries ? For Jacob still had much corn, and yet he only desired to "buy among those that came", so that no blame should attach to his actions. So, too, when Aaron blessed the people he raised his right hand above his left, so that the action below should stimulate a corresponding action above.' [93a]

THE SET FEASTS OF THE LORD WHICH YE SHALL PRO-CLAIM TO BE HOLY CONVOCATIONS. R. Isaac said: 'It is written, "And God called the light day" (Gen. I, 5). Does this mean that the light called day exists by itself ? No, for it says, "and the darkness he called night". Does this mean that each exists separately ? [93b] No, for it says, "And there was evening and there was morning one day". This shows that there is no day without night and no night without day, and on account of their interlocking they are called one. Similarly the Holy One, blessed be He, and the Community of Israel are called one when together, but not when parted; and so now that the Community of Israel is in exile, she is, as it were, not called one, and will only be called one when Israel emerge from captivity. Similarly it says: "These are the appointed feasts of the Lord which ye shall proclaim" (lit. call), that is, invite all to one place so that all shall form one, and Israel below shall be one nation on the earth. And how will they be called one ? Through the earthly Jerusalem, as it is written, "And who is like thy people Israel one nation in the earth" (2 Sam. VII, 23), since they are only called one when wedded to this "earth", after the supernal pattern.'

HOLY CONVOCATIONS. R. Isaac cited here the verse: "Unto thee my heart said, Seek ye my face; thy face, Lord, will I seek" (Ps. XXVII, 8). 'We can explain this verse', he said, by supposing that King David was speaking here on behalf of the Community of Israel, thus: "For Thy sake my heart says to mankind: Seek ye my face, to wit, the Crowns of the King which are one with the King"; and David was more qualified than any other man to speak thus in the name of the Community of Israel because he was closely

attached to Her. We may also interpret the word "face" to
refer to the appointed seasons and festivals, all of which
were invited by David to the place called "holy", in order
to crown each of them on its day and its appointed time,
that all might draw from that most profound source from
which issue streams and fountains. Therefore they are called
"invited to holiness"--invited to that place called "holiness"
to be crowned with it and draw from it that all may be
sanctified together and joy may be found among them.
R. Abba said that "holy convocations" means "invited by
holiness", and when they are invited by this, they are
invited by the Stream that issues forth perennially. We may
compare it to a king who, having invited people to a banquet,
sets before them all manner of dishes and opens for them
casks of well flavoured wine, for he who invites invites to
eat and drink. So the "holy convocations", since they are
invited to the banquet of the King, are invited to partake
of the good wine which has long been kept in store. Israel,
too, are called "holiness", because they are invited by the
holiness above; therefore they should prepare a banquet
and rejoice, since for them it is fitting. [94*a*]

THESE ARE THE SET FEASTS OF THE LORD. R. Simeon
said: 'They are from the Lord (YHVH), because He is the
link between those (grades) above and those below, all
being united through Him. Why ? Because just as the King
inherits the Father and Mother and is attached to their
holiness, so all those that are attached to the King are to be
invited to that supernal place called "holiness" in order
that they may all be united. Hence they are called first "set
feasts of the Lord", and then "holy convocations".

'WHICH YE SHALL PROCLAIM IN THEIR APPOINTED
SEASON. Israel have two portions in them—whether from
the side of the King, since Israel "cleave to the Lord", or
from the side of Holiness, since they are called "men of
holiness". Therefore (says the Scripture), for you it is
fitting to invite them and to prepare a joyful feast before
them and rejoice in them: for one who invites a guest must

show him a smiling face to crown his visit therewith. Imagine a king who invites an honoured guest and says to his court: All other days you are each in his house doing his work there, or in business or in the field, save only on my special day which you devote to rejoicing with me. Now I have invited a very honoured guest, and I desire that you should engage in no work in the house or in business or in the field, but that you should all come together as on my special day and prepare to meet that guest with smiles, with joy and with praises. So God said to Israel: All other days you are engaged in work and in business, save on my special day (the Sabbath). Now I have invited a very honoured guest, and do you therefore receive him with smiles and prepare for him a special table as on my own day. Hence it says: "You shall call (i.e. invite) them in their appointed time". See now. When Israel below rejoice in those festivals and sing praises to the Holy One, blessed be He, and prepare a table and put on their best garments, the angels in heaven ask: What do Israel mean by this, and God answers them: They have a distinguished guest on this day. But, they say, is he not Thy guest, from the place called Holiness ? He replies: And are not Israel holy and called holy, so that it is meet for them to invite My guest—alike from My side, because they cling to Me, and from the side of holiness, since it is written, "Israel are holy to the Lord". Assuredly the guest is theirs. Then they all break forth with the words, "Happy is the people that is in such a case".

'There are three that are invited from Holiness, and no more—the Feast of Unleavened Bread, the Feast of Weeks, and the Feast of Tabernacles.' 'But', said R. Abba to him, 'is not Sabbath also invited from Holiness ?' 'No,' he replied, 'for two reasons. One is that Sabbath is itself called holiness, and the other is that Sabbath has the right of entry by inheritance. Hence all the rest are invited and link themselves with Sabbath and crown themselves with it, but the Sabbath is not invited. It is like a son who enters the house of his father and mother and eats there whenever he desires. A king, we will say, had a son whom he fondly loved, and to whom he assigned a number of companions. One day he said: It would be a good thing to invite my son's companions and to show my affection and esteem for them. So he invited the companions, but the son did not need an invitation, since he could go into his father's house and eat and drink there whenever he wished.' [94b]

It is written here: SIX DAYS SHALL WORK BE DONE. R. Jose said: 'The six Days made the heaven and the earth, each performing its own work, and therefore they are called the six workdays.' Said R. Isaac: 'Why then are they called the six "ordinary" days ?' 'Because now', replied R. Jose, 'the world is carried on by their agent,[1] and therefore they are called "ordinary" or "profane".' R. Ḥiya said 'It is because work may be done on them. For that reason they are not called holy, and what is not called holy is called ordinary. Hence the Companions have laid down that we should say at the close of Sabbath, "who divideth between holy and profane", the separation consisting in the fact that holiness is something apart, and the rest issue from it. Hence these are for work. And there is a time when these too are to be kept, namely, when they are invited, from Holiness'.[2] R. Judah said: 'The joy and the observance of the Sabbath are superior to that of all the others, because this day is crowned with the Father and the Mother, and is invested with an additional holiness; wherefore it is a day of joy for higher and lower, and full of blessings in all worlds. On this day, too, there is rest for higher and lower, and even for the sinners in Gehinnom. Suppose a king made a feast in honour of his only son, during which he placed a crown upon him and invested him with supreme authority. There would be universal joy, so that the governor of a prison who had in his charge men condemned to stripes and execution, would, in honour of the king's celebration, release them, So that day is the day of the King's rejoicing with the Matrona. of the joy of Father and Mother in Him, of the rejoicing of higher and lower. In the joy of the King all must rejoice, and there must be no suffering then. On this day the sons of the King must prepare three meals for their table for the honour of the King, as we have laid down. But if a festival

---

[1] Metatron.   [2] i.e. when the festivals fall on them.

or appointed time occurs on it, a man need not prepare two
tables for each meal, one for Sabbath and one for the guest:
there is sufficient at the King's table for the guest who has
come.' R. Eleazar asked: 'If the guest arrives at the time
of the third Sabbath meal,[1] do we waive it nor not ? If we
waive it, then the guest is debarred from the table of the
King. If we do not waive it, then the banquet of the King
is itself deficient.' R. Simeon his father replied: 'The case
is like that of a king on whom a guest happened to call, so
he took food and put it before him, so that although the
king did not eat with him, yet he ate from the food of the
king. In the household of R. Hamnuna the Elder, however,
they used to pay no attention to the guest at this time, but
later they used to set a table for the guest.' 'But,' said R.
Eleazar, 'how is it possible not to set the king's banquet
before the guest, seeing that if the fourteenth day of Nisan
falls on a Sabbath, the banquet of the king is waived in
favour of the Passover, although it is not yet a guest.' He
replied: [95*a*] 'There are indeed a number of reasons why
the banquet of the King is waived on account of the Passover—one, that a man should come hungry to the unleavened
bread and bitter herbs, and, again, there is no bread after
midday, and a table without bread is not complete. However,
I myself have always been particular not to waive the third
Sabbath meal even when the Sabbath happens to be the
eve of Passover. On this day (of Sabbath) the holy Field of
Apples is blessed, and higher and lower are blessed, and
this day is the link of the (two branches of the) Torah.'
R. Abba said: 'R. Simeon, when the Sabbath meal was
removed, used to arrange his table and meditate on the
Construction of the Chariot,[2] and say, Here is the banquet
of the King, let Him come and partake with me. Therefore
Sabbath is superior to all feasts and appointed seasons, and
is called "holy" and not "holy convocation".' R. Judah
said: 'New Year and the Day of Atonement are not called
"holy convocations", because there is no joy on them, they

---

[1] i.e. if the third meal is prolonged until the evening which commences
a festival.   [2] i.e. the relation of God to the universe, as set forth in the
first chapter of Ezekiel.

being days of judgement. But the three festivals are times
of gladness when Israel have joyous communion with the
Holy One, blessed be He. On the Sabbath all sorrow and
vexation and trouble is forgotten because it is the day of the
espousals of the King, when an additional soul is imparted
(to men) as in the future world. R. Isaac asked R. Judah:
'Why have we learnt that Sabbath is to be remembered
over wine ?' He replied: 'Because wine represents the joy
of the Torah, and the wine of the Torah is the universal joy.'

IN THE FIRST MONTH ON THE FOURTEENTH DAY OF THE
MONTH. R. Ḥiya adduced here the verse: "I was asleep
but my heart waked, it is the voice of my beloved that
knocketh", etc. (S.S. II, 2). 'Says the Community of Israel:
I was asleep in the captivity of Egypt, when my children
were sore oppressed, but my heart was awake to preserve
them so that they should not perish under the oppression.
"The voice of my beloved", the Holy One, blessed be He,
saying, Open to me an opening no bigger than the eye of a
needle, and I will open to thee the supernal gates. "Open
to me, my sister", because thou art the door through which
there is entrance to Me; if thou openest not, I am closed.
Thus it was that when the Holy One, blessed be He, slew
the firstborn in Egypt, at that very time Israel entered into
the covenant of the holy sign, and linked themselves with
the Community of Israel, by means of the blood which
they displayed on the door—the blood of the paschal lamb
and the blood of the circumcision, one on one side and one
on the other, and one between, to show their faith. On the
fourteenth day, too, they removed the leaven and Israel
emerged from the sphere of an alien power and clung to
the unleavened, [95b] which is a holy bond, and later they
became linked to a still higher realm of faith called "heaven".

'AND ON THE FIFTEENTH DAY OF THE SAME MONTH.
At the hour of wedlock, when the moon is in full union with
the sun and the lower crowns are not found in such numbers
in the world (for the evil species abound at new moon and
spread throughout the world, but when the moon enjoys

the full light of the sun they all withdraw to a certain place
and the sanctifications of the King are aroused), of that time
it is written, "a night of vigils for the Lord", for then the
holy wedlock takes place which is protection for all.' R. Abba
said: 'Therefore the adornment of the bride is on that day,
and at night is the visiting of the house. Woe to those that
are not of the household when the two Torahs come to
unite, woe to them that are not present! Therefore holy
Israel prepare for them the house all that day, and through
them the visitors enter, and they rejoice and sing gleefully.'
Said R. Jose: 'The verse says as much distinctly in the word
"vigils", which implies two—the union of the moon with
the sun. It is "for all the children of Israel for their generations", since from that time they were linked to the holy
Name and emerged from the dominion of another power.
Therefore on the fourteenth day they prepare themselves
and remove leaven from among them and enrol themselves
under holy power, and then the bridegroom and the bride
are crowned with the crowns of the Supernal Mother, and
a man should show that he is free.'

R. Jose asked: 'What is the meaning of the four cups of
wine drunk on this night?' R. Abba replied: 'The Companions have explained that they correspond to the four
expressions of deliverance,[1] but a better explanation is given
in the book of R. Jesse the Elder, which says that it is because
the holy wedlock takes place on this night, and this is consummated in four unions. When this wedlock takes place we
partake in the joy of all, and therefore this night is different
from all other nights and it behoves us to form the Name
in all four. Further, we call those four "deliverances",
because this last grade[2] is called "deliverer", and that only
on account of another higher grade which illumines it, and
that one does not do so save through the agency of two more
which are above it, so that in all there are four deliverances.'

R. Judah asked R. Abba: 'Seeing that the seven days of
Passover are all days of joy, why do we not say the complete
Hallel on all of them, as on Tabernacles?' He replied:
'Because at this point Israel were not yet linked with the

[1] In Exodus VI, 2–8, *v.* Shemoth Rabbah, 6.   [2] *Malkuth.*

supernal world to such an extent as they were to be later. Therefore on this night (the first night of Passover) when there is the divine wedlock and universal joy in which Israel participate, we say the whole Hallel as a sign of completeness. But afterwards we do not say the whole, because Israel were not yet linked with those four higher grades, since the holy sign was not yet displayed on their flesh, and they had not yet received the Torah; whereas on Tabernacles all had been completed and the joy was more complete.' [96a] Said R. Judah to him: 'All this is quite correct, and this is the second time I hear it, but I had forgotten. Now I should like to know another thing. Why is it that Passover and Tabernacles consist of seven days, but not the Feast of Weeks, which really ought to more than the others?' He replied: 'It is written: "Who is like thy people Israel one nation in the earth?" (2 Sam. VII, 23). Now why are Israel called "one" here rather than in any other place? It is because the text is here speaking in praise of Israel, because it is the pride of Israel to be one. The reason is that the junction of upper and lower takes place at the spot called "Israel", which is linked with what is above and what is below, and with the Community of Israel: wherefore the whole is called one, and in this spot faith becomes manifest and complete union and supernal holy unity. The Tree of Life is also called one, and its day therefore is one, and therefore we have Passover and Tabernacles and this in the middle, and this is the honour of the Torah that it should have this one day and no more.' R. Isaac said: 'Israel will in the future chant joyful hymns of praise to the Holy One, blessed be He, like those which they chanted on the night of the Passover when the Community of Israel was hallowed with the sanctity of the King, as it is written: "Ye shall have a song as in the night when the holy feast was kept" (Isa. XXX, 29).

'AND ON THE DAY OF THE FIRSTFRUITS WHEN YE BRING A NEW OFFERING TO THE LORD IN YOUR WEEKS, ETC. Up to this time Israel were bringing "the produce of the earth", that is to say, an earthly product (barley),

I

literally, and they occupied themselves therewith and found therein their link (with the divine). God said: I gave you manna in the wilderness from the place which is called "heaven", and now you bring before me barley (for the *Omer*). The truth is that this offering had the same significance as the offering brought by the wife of the jealous husband, which was also of barley, and was to show that the Community of Israel was not unfaithful to the Holy King. [96b] This was brought for seven full weeks, and then the Holy King came to join the Community of Israel and the Torah was given to Israel. [97a]

'AND YE SHALL COUNT TO YOU FROM THE MORROW AFTER THE SABBATH. Observe that when Israel were in Egypt they were under an alien domination and they were trammelled with uncleanness like a woman in the days of her uncleanness. When they were circumcised, they entered into the holy portion which is called "covenant", [97b] and thereupon the uncleanness left them as the blood of uncleanness leaves a woman. Just as a woman then has to count seven days, so now God bade the Israelites count days for purity. They were to count "for themselves", so as to be purified with supernal holy waters, and then to be attached to the King and to receive the Torah. The woman had to count seven days, the people seven weeks. Why seven weeks? That they might be worthy to be cleansed by the waters of that stream which is called "living waters," and from which issue seven Sabbaths. When Israel drew near to Mount Sinai, that dew that descends from the supernal Point came down in its fullness and purified them so that their filth left them and they became attached to the Holy King and the Community of Israel and received the Torah, as we have explained. Observe that any man who does not count those seven complete weeks so as to qualify himself for purity is not called "pure" and is not in the class of "pure", nor is he worthy to have a portion in the Torah. But if a man has reached this day in purity and has not lost count, then it behoves him on this night to study the Torah and to preserve the special purity to which he has attained on this night. We have learnt [98*a*] that the Torah which he ought to study on this night is the Oral Law, and afterwards in daytime the Written Law can come and he can attach himself to it, so that both may be interlocked above. Then proclamation is made concerning him, saying, "And as for me, this is my covenant with them, saith the Lord; my spirit which is upon thee and my words which I have put in thy mouth", etc. (Isa. LIX, 21). Therefore the pious ones of old used not to sleep on this night, but they used to study the Torah and say, Let us acquire a holy inheritance for ourselves and our sons in two worlds. On that night the Community of Israel is crowned above them, and comes to join the Holy King, and both are crowned above the heads of those who are worthy of this. When the Companions gathered round him on this night, R. Simeon used to say: 'Let us go and prepare the ornaments of the Bride, that to-morrow she may appear before the King fitly adorned and bedecked. Happy the portion of the Companions when the King shall inquire of the Matrona who has arranged her adornments and illumined her crowns. For there is none in the world who knows how to arrange the jewels of the Bride like the Companions, happy is their portion in this world and in the world to come ! Now the Companions adorn the Bride, but who prepares the King on this night for his visit to the Matrona ? It is the Holy Stream, the deepest of all streams, the Supernal Mother, as it says, "Go forth, ye daughters of Zion, and behold King Solomon in the crown wherewith his mother hath crowned him in the day of his espousals" (S.S. III, 11). After she has prepared the King and crowned him, she goes to purify the Matrona and those that are with her. Imagine a king who had an only son whom he united in marriage to a noble lady. What did his mother do ? All that night she spent in her storeroom, and she brought forth therefrom a noble crown set with seventy [98*b*] precious stones to crown him with; she brought forth silken garments and clad him therewith and adorned him royally. Then she went to the bride and saw how her maidens were arranging her crown and her garments and her jewels. She said to them: I have prepared a bath with flowing water perfumed with all manner of sweet scents to purify my daughter-in-law. Let my daughter-in-law, the lady of my son, come with all her maidens that they may purify themselves in the place of flowing water which I have prepared for them, and then they can robe her with all her ornaments. To-morrow when my son comes to wed the lady he will prepare a palace for all and his abode shall be among you. So it is with the Holy King and the Matrona and the Companions, whose dwelling shall thus be together inseparably, as it is written, "Lord, who shall sojourn in thy tabernacle ? . . . He that walketh uprightly and worketh righteousness" (Ps. xv, 1, 2); these are they that array the Matrona in her jewels, her raiment and her crowns.

IN THE SEVENTH MONTH IN THE FIRST DAY OF THE MONTH. R.Isaac said: 'Blessed are Israel in that God has drawn them near to Him from a far place, as it says, "And Joshua said unto the people, Thus saith the Lord, the God of Israel, Your fathers dwelt of old beyond the River" (Joshua xxiv, 2), and a little further on it says, "And I took your father Abraham from beyond the River" (*Ibid*. 3). Now these verses require consideration. Did not the Israelites, and still more Joshua, know all this ? [99*a*] Then why did God tell it to them ? The inner meaning, however, is this. Great kindness did God show Israel in choosing the patriarchs and making them a supernal holy chariot for his glory and bringing them forth from the supernal precious holy River, the lamp of all lamps, that he might be crowned with them. Also it says, "I took your father Abraham from beyond the River" (*Ibid*. 4), because Abraham did not cleave to that River as Isaac clave to his side. Now, although this River is not judgement, yet chastisements issue from its side, and when Isaac takes hold of his sons, then higher and lower angels assemble for judgement, and the throne of judgement is set up and the Holy King takes his seat thereon and judges worlds. Then is the time to "blow up the trumpet on the new moon, at the appointed time on our solemn feast day" (Ps. lxxxi, 4): for happy are Israel who know how to remove the throne of judgement and set up the throne of mercy;

and wherewith ? With the *shofar*.' R. Abba, as he was once
studying with R. Simeon, said to him: 'Many times have
I inquired concerning the significance of the *shofar*, but I
have never yet received a satisfactory answer.' R. Simeon
replied: 'The true explanation is this. Why Israel have to
use a ram's horn on this day and not any other is this, that
we know to what place the horn belongs, and we do not
desire to awaken judgement. For, as we have learnt, by word
and deed we have to awaken secret powers. Now when the
supernal *Shofar*, in which is the illumination of all, removes
itself and does not shine upon the sons, then judgement
is awakened and the thrones are set up for judgement, [99b]
and Isaac strengthens and prepares himself for judgement.
But when this *Shofar* rouses itself and men repent of their
sins, it behoves them to blow the *shofar* below, and the
sound thereof ascends on high and awakens another supernal
Shofar, and so mercy is awakened and judgement is removed.
We must produce from this *shofar* below various sounds to
arouse all the voices that are contained in the supernal
Shofar, and therefore we not only use the *shofar* on this day
but arrange the blasts in a number of series.

'With the first blast the voice goes forth and makes its
way upwards to the firmaments, breaking through lofty
mountains till it reaches Abraham, on whose head it rests
so that he awakes and prepares himself for the throne,
where the Father and Mother appoint him to his station.
Then there goes up a second mighty blast to break down
wrath, being itself of broken notes, and all chastisements
that stand in its way as it ascends to Isaac are broken. Then
Isaac awakens and beholds Abraham preparing the throne
and standing before it, and then he also is chastened and
his severity is abated. And on this he who blows the *shofar*
should concentrate his mind, so as to break the strength of
stern judgement. With the third blast the voice issues and
ascends and cleaves the firmaments, till it reaches the head
of Jacob, [100a] who thereupon awakens and sees Abraham
ready on the other side. Then both take hold of Isaac, one
on one side and one on the other, so that his violence cannot
break forth. These three blasts form one series.

'In the next series a voice goes forth and ascends and takes hold of Abraham and brings him down to the place where the harshness of Isaac abides and sets Abraham in the midst thereof. With the second blast goes forth a broken voice, not so powerful as the first; not that it is weaker, but because it does not approach Isaac like the previous one, but only the lower court, which is weaker; and they all see Abraham among them and are humbled. With the third blast a voice issues and rises till it forms a crown on the head of Jacob, whom it brings down to the place where those powers of judgement are, so that Abraham faces them on one side and Jacob on the other, and they being in the middle are rendered more lenient. These form the second series.

'The last series has to take them back to their places and to place Isaac between them as before, since it is necessary to fix him in his place so that he should not leave it in his violent mood. In this way all punishments are kept in check and mercy is awakened. This is the purpose which these blasts should serve, being accompanied by repentance before God. Thus when Israel produce the blasts of the *shofar* with proper devotion, the supernal *Shofar* returns and crowns Jacob so that all is properly arranged. Another throne is set up and joy is universally diffused and God has mercy on the world. Happy are Israel who know how to divert [100b] their Master from justice to mercy and to be the instruments for establishing all worlds. Corresponding to the three series of blasts three books are opened above on this day, and just as mercy is awakened and punishments are restrained and put back in their place above, so below in the same way harsh punishments are kept back and removed from the world. And what are these? These are the irremediably wicked who are inscribed at once for death.' Said R. Abba: 'Assuredly this is the true explanation of the matter. Blessed be God that I asked for and obtained this instruction.' R. Judah said: 'It is written, A MEMORIAL OF BLOWING OF TRUMPETS. We make a memorial by the concentration of our mind and thought. Israel make a memorial below by an appropriate ceremony, so as to arouse a corresponding reaction above.'

R. Eleazar said: 'This day is called "the concealing (*keseh*) for the day of our feast", because the moon is still covered and does not shine.[1] Through what then will it shine ? Through repentance and the sound of the *shofar*, as it is written, "Blessed is the people that know the trumpet sound, because, O Lord, they shall walk in the light of thy countenance" (Ps. LXXXIX, 15). On this day the moon is covered, and it does not shine until the tenth day, when Israel turn with a perfect repentance, so that the supernal Mother gives light to her. Hence this day is called the day of atonements (*kippurim*), because two lights are shedding illumination, since the higher lamp is illumining the lower. For on this day the Moon receives illumination from the supernal Light and not from the light of the Sun.'

R. Abba sent to inquire of R. Simeon: 'When is the union of the Community of Israel with the Holy King ?' He answered him with the verse: "And moreover she is indeed my sister the daughter of my father, but not the daughter of my mother" (Gen. xx, 12). R. Abba lifted up his voice and wept, saying: 'My master, my master, holy lamp, alas for the world when thou shalt depart from it, alas for the generation which shall be orphaned of thee !' R. Ḥiya said to R. Abba: 'What means this answer that he sent you ?' He replied: 'The union of the King with the Matrona is only when she is illumined from the supernal Father, when she is called holy. Then indeed she is "my sister the daughter of my father", but not "of my mother", since it is from the Father that she derives this name.'

R. Abba said: 'On New Year Adam was created and was brought to trial before his Master and [101*a*] repented and was pardoned by the Almighty. He said to him: Adam, thou shalt be a sign to thy descendants for all generations. On this day they are brought to trial, and if they repent I will pardon them and remove from the Throne of Judgement and sit on the Throne of Mercy and have mercy on them.'

HOWBEIT ON THE TENTH DAY OF THIS SEVENTH MONTH IS THE DAY OF ATONEMENT; IT SHALL BE AN HOLY

[1] Cf. T.B. Rosh Hashanah, 8*b*.

CONVOCATION UNTO YOU. R. Ḥiya quoted here the verse:
"A Psalm of David, Maschil. Blessed is he whose transgression is forgiven, whose sin is covered" (Ps. XXXII, 1).
'What', he said, 'is meant by *Maschil?* The waters that
give wisdom to those who seek to find that place which is
called *maschil* (lit. he that giveth heed). And because it is called
so, forgiveness and complete freedom depend on it. What
is meant by "whose sin is covered"? As we have explained,
that sin which he commits before God and, concealing it
from men, confesses to God. Observe that when a man
commits a sin once and twice and three times, and does
not repent, his sins are exposed and are published above and
below, and heralds go before him and proclaim, Keep away
from So-and-so, who is scorned of his Master, scorned above
and scorned below, Woe to him that he has impaired the
likeness of his Master, woe to him that he has not regarded
the honour of his Master. When, however, a man walks in
the way of his Master and occupies himself with His service,
if then he should happen to commit a sin, all screen him,
higher and lower, and he is called "one whose sin is covered".'
Said R. Abba to him: 'All this is quite correct, but you have
not yet got to the root of the matter. There are two recondite
teachings in this expression. One is this. We have learnt
that the good deeds which a man does in this world fashion
for him a precious and noble garment wherewith to cover
himself. Now when a man has laid up a store of good deeds
and then falls into evil ways, if God observes that his bad
deeds outweigh the good and that he is wicked enough to
regret all the good deeds that he did at first,[1] then he is
entirely lost both in this world and in the other. What, then,
does God do with the good deeds which he performed at
first? For though the wicked sinner perishes, the good
deeds that he performed do not perish. If, then, there is a
righteous man who walks in the ways of the King and is
preparing his garment from his works, but before he has
completed it he departs from this world, God completes it
from the deeds which have been lost to that wicked sinner
for him to array himself therewith in the other world, as it

[1] *v.* T.B. Kiddushin, 40*b*.

is written, "He (the wicked man) shall prepare it, but the just shall put it on" (Job XXVII, 17). Hence he may be said to be "covered from sin", that is, from the sins of the wicked. Another lesson is this, that the sin of this righteous man is hidden in what are called "the depths of the sea", just as one who falls into the depths of the sea can never be found, because the waters cover him. [101b] What are these "depths of the sea"? It is a deep mystery, which R. Simeon has explained. All those that come from the violent side and are attached to the "evil species", the lower crowns, like Azazel on the Day of Atonement, are called the "depths (m'zuloth=clarifying region) of the sea", since they draw the impurities off the holy sea in the same way as the fire purifies silver, drawing off its dross. All the sins are thus dropped into it. For this reason it is also called "Sin" (ḥetaah, lit. failure), inasmuch as it takes away, especially on this day, the defilement of the soul and of the body, to wit, the sins committed through the evil prompting which is called filthy and disgusting.'

R. Jose said: 'It is written, "And he shall put on the two he-goats lots". This would seem to be a great honour for Azazel. Have you ever seen a slave cast lots with his master? Usually the servant takes only what his master gives him. The fact, however, is that because Samael is ready on this day with his accusations, and so that he should not have any grievance, he is given a portion in this way. This lot used to come up of itself. For so said R. Judah in the name of R. Isaac: We find a great wonder in the lot. The lot which Joshua cast used of itself to say, This is the portion of Judah, this is the portion of Benjamin, etc. And so here, too, when the priest placed his hands in position, the lots used to leap up and come down in their places, as it is written, "The goat on which *hath gone up* the lot for the Lord".

'Not on this occasion only, but whenever accusation is prepared and permission is given to the accuser it behoves us to set before him something with which he may occupy himself and so leave Israel alone. The Companions have noted in connection with the words of the Satan "from going to and fro in the earth" (Job I, 7), that, when the Israelites

were about to cross the Red Sea, he said, I have gone to and
fro through the Holy Land and I have seen that these are
not worthy to enter it. If Thou wilt here execute judgement
on the Egyptians, how do the Israelites differ from them ?[1]
Either let them all die together, or let them all return to
Egypt. And further, didst Thou not say, "they shall serve
them four hundred years", and only two hundred and ten
of the number are past ? Thereupon God said: 'What am
I to do ? This one must have some sop thrown to him. I
will give him something with which to occupy himself so
as to leave my sons. I have someone for the purpose. Straightway God said to him, "Hast thou considered my servant
Job ?", and straightway the Satan sought to discredit him,
saying, "Does Job fear God for nothing ?". Imagine a shepherd seeking to take his flock across a river, when he sees
a wolf about to fall on them. What shall I do ? he says. While
I am carrying the lambs across, he will fall on the sheep.
Then he catches sight among the flock of a ram from the
fields, strong and powerful. I will throw this one to him,
he says, and while they are struggling I will take all the flock
across and save them. So God said: Here is a strong and
powerful ram, I will throw it to him, and while he is busy
with it my sons shall cross and not be attacked. Thus while
the Satan was busy with Job he left Israel alone and they
were not accused. So on the Day of Atonement also the
informer is ready to spy out the land, and we must send him
something with which he may occupy himself. So there is
a saying, Give some wine to the menial of the king's palace
and he will praise thee to the king, and if not he will malign
thee to him, and it may be that the officers of the king will
take up his words and the king will execute judgement.'
R. [102*a*] Isaac said: 'Give the fool who stands before the
king some wine and tell him all the faults and errors thou
hast committed and he will come and praise thee and say
that there is not another in the world like thee. So here the
informer is ever before the king, and Israel present him a
gift along with a list of all the faults and wrongs which they
have done, and he comes and praises Israel and becomes

---

[1] *v.* Yalkut Reubeni on Beshalaḥ.

their defender, and God puts all on the head of the wicked of his own people.' Said R. Jose: 'Woe to the people of Esau at the time when Israel send that he-goat to the Informer who is their Chieftain, since for its sake he comes and praises Israel and God diverts all those sins on to the head of his people.' Said R. Judah: 'If the heathen knew of that he-goat, they would not leave Israel alive a single day. All that day Satan is occupied with that goat, and therefore God makes atonement for Israel and purifies them from all their sins and they are not accused before Him. Afterwards the Satan comes and praises Israel and the accuser becomes defender and departs. Then God says to the seventy Chiefs that surround His throne, Do you see how this Informer is always seeking to attack my sons? A certain goat has been sent to him with a tablet recording all their sins and errors which they have committed before me, and he has accepted it. Then they all agree that those sins should be discharged on the head of his own people.' R. Abba said: 'At first all those sins cleave to him, and afterwards they are discharged upon the head of his people.

'On this day the priest is crowned with superior crowns and stands between heavenly and earthly beings and makes atonement for himself and his house and the priests and the sanctuary and all Israel. We have learnt that at the moment when he enters with the blood of the bullock he concentrates his thoughts on the highest principle of faith and sprinkles with his finger, as it is written, "and he shall sprinkle it upon the mercy-seat and before the mercy-seat". He used to dip the top of his finger in the blood and sprinkle, going lower and lower each time, at the side of the mercy-seat. He began to count one[1]—the first "one" by itself, one being the sum of all, the glory of all, the goal of all, the beginning of all. Then "one and one", joined together in love and friendship inseparable. When he had passed this "and one" which is the mother of all, he began to count in pairs, saying, "one and two", "one and three", "one and four", "one and five", "one and six", "one and seven", so as to draw down this "one" which is the supernal Mother

[1] v. T.B. Yoma, 53b.

by certain grades to the crown of the lower Mother[1] and to draw deep rivers from their place to the Community of Israel. Hence on this day two luminaries diffuse light together, the supernal Mother giving light to the lower Mother.' R. Isaac said: 'A cord was tied to the feet of the High Priest before he entered the Holy of Holies, so that if he died suddenly within they should be able to draw him out. They used to know by a certain thread of scarlet if the priest had been successful in his intercessions. If its colour did not change, they knew that the priest within was not free from sin, but if he was to issue in peace, it was known by the thread changing its colour to white, when there was rejoicing above and below. If it did not, however, all were distressed, knowing that their prayer had not been accepted.'[2] R. Judah said: 'When he went in and closed his eyes so as not to see what he had no right to see, and heard the voice of the Cherubim chanting praises, he knew that all was in joy and that he would come out in peace, and another sign was if his words came forth joyfully, so as to be accepted and blessed.' [102b]

R. Eleazar asked R. Simeon: 'Why is this day attached only to this grade ? Surely it should more than any other day be in the grade where the King abides ?' He replied: 'Eleazar, my son, you have asked a good question. The reason is this. The Holy King has left his temple and house in the hands of the Matrona and has left his sons with her that she may guide them and chastise them and abide in their midst, so that if they are virtuous the Matrona enters with joy and honour into the presence of the King. If, however, they are not deserving, She and they are sent into exile according to our interpretation of the text, "and through your transgression your mother is sent away" (Isa. L, 1). Hence one day is appointed in the year for examining them. When this day comes the supernal Mother, in whose hand is all freedom, comes to examine Israel, and Israel prepare themselves on this day with many prayers and services and fastings to make themselves worthy. Then is freedom granted to them from the place where all freedom abides, through

---

[1] Al. "to illumine the lower Mother".   [2] v. T.B. Yoma, 39a.

the hand of the Matrona. And when she sees the sons of the King, her sons who are entrusted to her hands, all virtuous without sin or guilt, She joins the King with smiles, with gladness, and with perfect love, because she has trained up fitting sons for the supreme King. But if they are not found as they should be on this day, woe to them and woe to their emissaries, for the Matrona is removed from the King and the supreme Mother departs and no freedom proceeds from her to any world. Happy are Israel whom the Holy One, blessed be He, has taught His ways that they may be delivered from judgement and found deserving before Him. Hence it is written: "For on that day he shall make atonement for you" (Lev. XVI, 30), and "I shall sprinkle on you purifying waters" (Ezek. XXXVI, 25).'

HOWBEIT ON THE FIFTEENTH DAY OF THE SEVENTH MONTH. R. Jose asked R. Abba: 'What is the meaning of these fifteen days ?' He replied: 'Assuredly they contain a deep mystery. Observe that both above and below each day proceeds on its own path and remains in its own place and performs its own function. The first group of ten belongs to the Community of Israel, while the five are of the King, because in the fifth grade (from the Matrona) the King sits upon his throne. Then the Father shines upon the Mother and fifty gates are illumined from Her to shed light upon the fifth. And should you say that the Matrona is the seventh, this is because the King completes the Patriarchs. Therefore the seventh is the day on which the King is fully crowned and inherits from the Father and Mother, who are joined together. Hence both come to the same thing.'

R. Judah discoursed here on the verse: "And the Canaanite the king of Arad heard" (Num. XXI, 1). 'We have learnt',[1] he said, 'that three notable gifts were conferred upon Israel through the three brethren, Moses, Aaron, and Miriam. The manna was given to them for the merit of Moses, the clouds of glory for the merit of Aaron, and the well for the merit of Miriam. [103a] When Miriam died the well was taken from them, as it is written, "And Miriam died, and there

---

[1] v. T.B. Taanith, 9a.

was no water for the congregation" (Num. xx, 1, 2). Another
well which was with Israel also desired to depart, but when
it saw six clouds that hovered over them it remained attached
to them. When Aaron died the clouds departed and the
cloud of the well with them, until Moses came and brought
them back.' R. Isaac said: 'Why was this honour conferred
upon Aaron ? Because he was linked with clouds and he linked
them all together, so that they were all blessed through him.
For in addition to all the lovingkindness that God did with
Israel, He linked with them seven precious clouds which
He also linked with the Community of Israel, whose cloud
was linked with seven others, and Israel traversed the wilderness protected by all of them. They all form a bond of faith,
and therefore Israel were bidden to dwell in booths seven
days, so that the Israelite may show that he is dwelling in
the shadow of faith. As long as Aaron was alive, Israel were
in the shadow of faith under those clouds. When Aaron
died, a cloud on the right departed and the rest departed
with it, and the weakness of Israel was exposed, and straightway the king of Arad heard that the clouds had departed[1]
and the great explorer to whom they were all linked was
dead.' R. Isaac observed that the King of Arad dwelt in the
south, and the spies also brought back word that Amalek
dwelt in the south (Num. xiii, 20), to awe the people, because
Amalek had struck the first blow at them. R. Abba said:
Why is the Canaanite mentioned here ? Because Canaan
was a slave of slaves (Gen. ix, 25), and this shows that he
who withdraws himself from the shadow of faith deserves
to be a slave to the slave of slaves. Hence "all that are home-
born in Israel shall dwell in booths"; everyone who is of the
holy root and stock of Israel shall dwell in a booth under
the shadow of faith. Shall he that is not of the holy stock
withdraw himself from the shadow of faith ? We are told
that Eleazar the servant of Abraham was a Canaanite, but
because he served Abraham, who sat under the shadow of
faith, he was delivered from the curse of Canaan and was
even called "blessed", as it is written, "Come in, thou blessed
of the Lord" (Gen. xxiv, 31). Thus whoever abides under

[1] Cf. T.B. Taanith, *ibid.*

the shadow of faith acquires freedom for himself and his descendants in perpetuity, and is blessed with a noble blessing, but he who withdraws from the shadow of faith brings captivity upon himself and for his children, as it is written, "And he took some of them captive". [103b]

YE SHALL DWELL IN BOOTHS. The word *succoth* (booths) is written without a *vau*, to show that there is one cloud to which all the others are linked. R. Eleazar cited here the verse: "Thus saith the Lord, I remember for thee the kindness of thy youth", etc. (Jer. II, 2). 'This verse', he said, 'refers to the Community of Israel at the time when She went in the wilderness with Israel. The "kindness" (*ḥesed*) is the cloud of Aaron which carried along with it five others which were linked with thee and shone for thee. "The love of thine espousals": when they adorned and perfected thee like a bird. And all this for what ? That thou mightest "go after me in the wilderness, in a land not sown". Observe that when a man sits in this abode of the shadow of faith, the Shekinah spreads her wings over him from above and Abraham and five other righteous ones make their abode with him.' R. Abba said: 'Abraham and five righteous ones and David with them. Hence it is written, "In booths ye shall dwell seven days", as much as to say, "Ye seven days shall dwell in booths", and a man should rejoice each day of the festival with these guests who abide with him.' R. Abba further pointed out that first it says "*ye* shall dwell" and then "*they* shall dwell". The first refers to the guests, and therefore Rab Hamnuna the Elder, when he entered the booth, used to stand at the door inside and say, Let us invite the guests and prepare a table, and he used to stand up and greet them, saying, In booths ye shall dwell, O seven days. Sit, most exalted guests, sit; sit, guests of faith, sit. He would then raise his hands in joy and say, Happy is our portion, happy is the portion of Israel, as it is written, "For the portion of the Lord is his people", and then he took his seat. The second "dwell" refers to human beings; for he [104a] who has a portion in the holy land and people sits in the shadow of faith to receive the guests so as to rejoice in

this world and the next. He must also gladden the poor,
because the portion of those guests whom he invites must
go to the poor. And if a man sits in the shadow of faith and
invites these guests and does not give them their portion,
they all hold aloof from him, saying "Eat thou not the bread
of him that hath an evil eye" (Prov. XXIII, 6). That table
which he prepares is his own and not God's. Alas for him
when those guests leave his table.' R. Abba further said:
'Abraham always used to stand at the cross roads to invite
guests to his table.[1] Now when a man invites him and all
the righteous and King David and does not give them their
portion, Abraham rises from the table and exclaims, "Depart,
I pray you, from the tents of these wicked men" (Num. XVI,
26), and all rise and follow him. Isaac says, "The belly of
the wicked shall want" (Prov. XIII, 26). Jacob says, "The
morsel thou hast eaten thou shalt vomit up" (*Ibid*. XXIII, 8).
The other righteous ones say,"For all tables are full of
vomit and uncleanness" (Isa. XXVIII, 8). David says. . . .[2]
In those ten days during which David judges the world, that
man is judged who has treated him more ungratefully than
Nabal.' R. Eleazar said: 'The Torah does not demand of a
man more than he can perform, as it says, "Each one man
shall give as he is able" (Deut. XVI, 7). A man should not
say, I will first satisfy myself with food and drink, and what
is left I shall give to the poor, but the first of everything
must be for the guests. And if he gladdens the guests and
satisfies them, God rejoices with him and Abraham proclaims
over him, "Then shalt thou delight thyself in the Lord", etc.
(Isa. LVIII, 14). Isaac proclaims, "No weapon that is formed
against thee shall prosper" (*Ibid*. LIV. 17).' R. Simeon said:
'This verse is said by King David, because all royal weapons
of war have been handed to David. What Isaac says is, "His
seed shall be mighty on the earth" (Ps. CXII, 2). Jacob
proclaims, "Then shall thy light break forth as the morning"
(Isa. LVIII, 8). The other righteous say, "The Lord shall
guide thee continually and satisfy thy soul in dry places"
(*Ibid*. 11). Happy the lot of the man who attains to
all this !'

---

[1] *v*. T.B. Sotah, 10*b*.   [2] There is here a lacuna in the text.

AND YE SHALL TAKE YOU ON THE FIRST DAY THE
FRUIT OF GOODLY TREES. R. Simeon quoted here the
verse: "Every one that is called by my name, for my glory
I have created him, I have formed him, yea I have made
him" (Isa. LXIII, 7). ' "Every one that is called by my
name": this is man whom God has created in His likeness
and whom He calls by His own name when he does truth
and justice, as it is written, "Thou shalt not revile the
judges" (*Elohim*, Ex. XXII, 28). "I have formed him, yea
I have made him": as has been explained, the words "Let
us make man in our image, after our likeness" refer to the
time of wedlock, namely, the union of "image" and "likeness", so that man issued from Male and Female. In the
Book of King Solomon it is written that at the hour of wedded
union [104b] on earth, God sends a certain form with the
figure of a human being which hovers over the union, and
if a man's eye were capable of such a thing it would see such
a form over his head. The child is created in that form, and
before that form stands over a man's head the child is not
created, that form being prepared for it before it issues into
the world. In that form it grows up, in that form it goes
about, as it is written, "Surely every man walketh in a form"
(*zelem*, Ps. XXXIX, 9). This form is from on high. When the
spirits go forth from their places, each one stands before
the Holy King with its adornments, with the countenance
which it is to wear in this world; and from that adornment
comes forth this form (*zelem*). Thus it is the third from the
spirit, and it comes down first to this world at the time of
wedded union, from which it is never absent. In the case
of Israel, who are holy, this *zelem* is holy and from a holy
place. But for the heathens it comes from the "evil species",
from the side of uncleanness. Therefore a man should not
mix his form with that of a heathen, because the one is holy
and the other unclean.[1] This explains why the dead body
of an Israelite defiles while the dead body of a heathen does
not defile. For when an Israelite dies, all the sanctifications
of his Master depart from him, and that holy form and holy

[1] From here to the end of the paragraph is inserted from Zohar,
Genesis, 220a, whither it has been transposed in the text.

spirit leave him and his body is left unclean. But the contrary
is the case with the heathen: his form and spirit are unclean
in him when he is alive, but when he dies they leave him,
and his body, though unclean itself, does not propagate
uncleanness. Observe that when judgement is aroused, and
God sits upon the throne of judgement to judge the world,
a man should betake himself to repentance and amend his
ways, since on this day the sentences are written. If a man
repents in time, his sentence is torn up. If not, he still has
a chance on the Day of Atonement. If still his repentance
is not perfect, his sentence is suspended till the last day, the
eighth of the Feast of Tabernacles, after which the sentences
are no more returned to the court of the King. The sign is
that a man's shadows depart from him.'

ON THE EIGHTH DAY SHALL BE AN HOLY CONVO-
CATION UNTO YOU. This is because this day is from the
King alone, it is his day of rejoicing in Israel. A king invites
some guests, and while they are there all the household
attend on them. When they depart the king says to his
household, Till now I and you have all of us been attending
to the guests; now I and you will rejoice together for one
day. So God said: Up to now you have been bringing sacrifices for the other peoples, now bring one for yourselves.
The guests of faith are with the King continually and all
assemble before him on the day of the King's rejoicing.
On this day Jacob is at the head of the rejoicing. Therefore
it is written: "Happy art thou, O Israel, who is like unto
thee?" (Deut. XXXIII, 29).

THAT THEY BRING UNTO THEE PURE OLIVE OIL BEATEN
FOR THE LIGHT. Why does this section follow the section
of the festivals? Because there are lamps above in which
burns the supernal oil, and through Israel both higher and
lower are blessed and the lamps are lit. [105*a*] R. Abba quoted
here the verse: "Be glad in the Lord and rejoice, ye righteous"
(Ps. XXII, 11). ' "Be glad in the Lord", when judgement is
repressed and mercy is aroused. Then "the righteous",
that is, *Ẓaddik* and *Ẓedek*, bless and rejoice all worlds. Then

"Exult, ye upright of heart": these are the sons of faith who are linked with them. In all things some action is required below to arouse the activity above. For observe: he who says that no action is needed or no audible utterance, a curse light on such a one ! This section confutes him, of the lighting of the lights, for through this act there is a kindling above and a rejoicing above and below and a proper linking of both.' R. Judah said: 'The altar below rouses another altar, above, the priest below rouses another Priest, above.'

R. Jose and R. Isaac were once walking together when the former said: 'It is written, "Thou shalt call the Sabbath a delight and the holy of the Lord honourable, and shalt honour it, not doing thine own ways" (Isa. LVIII, 13). So far I understand. But what is the meaning of the next words: "Nor finding thine own pleasure, nor speaking thine own words" ? What derogation is there in this for the Sabbath ?' He replied: 'Truly it is derogatory. For there is no word which issues from the mouth of a man but has a voice which rises aloft and awakens something else, namely that which is called "ordinary" above, belonging to the ordinary days. Now if the ordinary is awakened on the holy day, it is counted something derogatory above, and the Holy One and the Community of Israel ask: Who is this that seeks to break up our union, who is it that seeks the ordinary here ? The Ancient Holy One appears not and rests not on the ordinary. For this reason it is permitted on Sabbath to think about ordinary things, because mere thinking produces no effect, but if a word issues from a man's mouth it becomes a voice and rises aloft and breaks through ethers and firmaments and arouses something else. Therefore it says, "Not to find thine own pleasure nor speaking thine own word". But if a man utters a holy word of the Torah, it rises aloft and arouses the saints of the King, who set a crown on its head, so that there is rejoicing above and below.' 'Assuredly it is so,' said R. Jose, 'and so I have already heard. But tell me, if a man fasts on Sabbath, does he do anything derogatory to the Sabbath or not ? How can you say he does not, seeing that he neglects the repasts of faith, and his punishment must be great, since he does away with the joy of the Sabbath.' He replied: 'I have heard that on the contrary this is he who is more remarked above than any other. For this day is one of supreme joy above and below, joy of all joys, the joy of faith, on which even sinners in Gehinnom have respite. Now when this man is seen to be without joy and without rest, different from all others above and below, they all ask, What is the cause of So-and-so being in sorrow ? And when the Ancient Holy One is revealed on this day and the prayer of this sorrowful one rises and stands before Him, then all the punishments decreed against him are cancelled, even if the Court of the King has concurred in the sentence, because when the Ancient One is revealed all freedom and all joy is present. Hence, as we have learnt, the sentence of "seventy years" is annulled, the "seventy years" being the seventy crowns of the king in which He is revealed. All this, however, is only [105b] when a man is warned in a dream on the night of Sabbath. Imagine a king who makes a wedding feast for his son and orders all to rejoice. All therefore rejoice, but one man is in sorrow because he is chained for execution. When the king comes he sees all rejoicing as he ordained, but he lifts up his eyes and sees one man chained and sorrowing. Why, he says, should all rejoice in the espousals of my son and this one be chained for execution ? And straightway he orders him to be released. So with him who fasts on Sabbath when all the world is rejoicing: when the Holy Ancient One is disclosed, even though all those "seventy years" have concurred in his sentence, it is wholly annulled. If on other days it is possible to procure annulment, how much more on Sabbath ? For every day has its own power, and if a man fasts on account of a dream, before the day ends his sentence is annulled; not, however, if it is of the "seventy years", unless on Sabbath. Hence he has to fast on that day and not on another, for one day has no power over the next, each being responsible only for what happens in itself. Hence a man should not postpone his fast from one day to another. Observe, too, that a man is not warned in a dream without reason. Woe to him who has no warning dreams; he is called "evil", as it is written: "He that is not visited (in a dream) is evil" (Prov. XIX, 23).'

AND THE SON OF AN ISRAELITISH WOMAN WHOSE
FATHER WAS AN EGYPTIAN WENT OUT. R. Judah said:
'He went out from the sphere of the portion of Israel, from
the sphere of the whole, from the sphere of faith. AND
THEY STROVE TOGETHER: From this we learn that he
who comes from a polluted seed is ultimately exposed before
all. What is the cause ? The defilement of the evil portion
in him, since he has no portion in the whole body of
Israel.'

(AND THE SON OF THE ISRAELITISH WOMAN BLAS-
PHEMED THE NAME.) R. Ḥiya quoted here the verse:
"It is the glory of God to conceal a thing" (Prov. xxv, 2).
'This means', he said, 'that it is not permitted to a man to
disclose mysteries which are not meant to be disclosed, and
which the Ancient of Days has hidden, as it is written, "To
eat sufficiently, but to conceal the Ancient One" (Isa. xxiii,
18). "To eat sufficiently"—until that place which is permitted, but no further. Or we may also take the words to
refer to R. Simeon and his generation, the Companions
who know how to walk in the path of faith, like the generation
of R. Simeon and his colleagues, but such things are to be
concealed from other generations which are not fitted to
"eat a sufficiency". In the days of R. Simeon a man would
say to his companion, Open thy mouth and let thy words
give light, but after his death they said, "Let not thy mouth
cause thy flesh to sin" (Eccl. v, 6). [106*a*]

'AND HIS MOTHER'S NAME, ETC. Up to this point his
mother's name was concealed, but now that he had uttered
blasphemy his mother's name is mentioned.' Said R. Abba:
'Were it not that the Sacred Lamp is still alive, I would not
reveal this, since it is not meant to be revealed save to those
who are among the reapers of the field: a curse light on
those who want to reveal to those who should not know ! The
Israelitish man mentioned here was the son of another
woman, and his father was the husband of Shelomith. When
an Egyptian came to her in the middle of the night and he
returned home and became aware of it, he separated from

her and took another wife. Hence one is called "the Israelitish man" and the other "the son of the Israelitish woman".
Now if they quarrelled, how came the Holy Name to be involved ? The reason was that the Israelitish man reviled
the other's mother, and the latter took the *Hé* from the
Holy Name and cursed with it to defend his mother; hence
the word *nakab* (lit. hollowed) is used, to show that he separated the letters of the Holy Name. But all this is only for
"the reapers of the field".'

(AND THEY PUT HIM IN WARD.) R. Isaac said: 'Besides
insulting his mother, he mentioned that his father was the
man whom Moses had slain with the Holy Name, and therefore it was that "they brought him to Moses", since Moses
was concerned in the matter. When Moses perceived who it
was, straightway "they put him in ward", and so both
father and son fell by the hand of Moses.'

WHOEVER CURSETH HIS GOD SHALL BEAR HIS SIN.
R. Isaac quoted here the verse: "There shall no strange
god be in thee, neither shalt thou worship any strange god"
(Ps. LXXXI, 9). 'The "strange god" ', he said, [106b] 'mentioned in the first clause refers to the evil prompting, for
if a man links himself with this, a "strange god" enters
into him, for straightway he breaks the commandments of
the Torah, and so he comes to abandon the faith in the Holy
Name and to bow down to false gods. Hence the verse tells
us that "if there is no strange god in thee, through the evil
prompting, then thou shalt not come to bow down to a
strange god". Hence if a man only "curses his god", in
which case he may plead that he is referring only to that
evil prompting which abides in him, and we do not know
whether he is speaking truly or not, he shall merely "bear
his iniquity"; but "he that uttereth the name of the Lord
shall be put to death".' Said R. Judah: 'If that is so, it
should say, "his sin shall be forgiven", not "he shall bear
his sin".' He replied: 'We must suppose him to say "my
god", without specifying.' Said R. Ḥiya: 'Certainly in that
case he shall bear his iniquity, but if he pronounces the

name of the Lord he shall be put to death, because on this all faith depends and he can make no excuse.' R. Jose said: 'Assuredly it is so, that this name is the basis of the faith of higher and lower, and all worlds are established on it. On one tiny letter are suspended thousands of thousands and myriads of myriads of delectable worlds, as we have learnt that these letters are linked with one another, and thousands and myriads of celestials depend on each one, and there is wrapped in them that which is not grasped by higher or lower.'

R. Hizkiah cited the verse: "No hand shall touch it, for he shall surely be stoned or shot through", etc. (Ex. XIX, 13). 'Now if', he said, 'this was to be the penalty for touching a mere mountain like Sinai because the glory of the Holy King was revealed on it, what must happen to one who touches the King ? And if this was to happen to one who touched the mountain, even respectfully, what must happen to one who touches the King insultingly ?' R. Jesse cited the verse: "Draw not nigh hither, put off thy shoes from off thy feet", etc. (Ex. III, 5). 'If', he said, 'this could be said to Moses, from whom the holy halo never departed from the day that he was born, and who drew near in reverence and holiness, what would be said to one who draws near to the King insultingly ?'

R. Abba said: 'When Israel were in Egypt, they were acquainted with the Chieftains who are appointed over the various nations of the world, and each of them feared one or other of them. When they were linked with the bond of faith and God brought them near to His service, they abandoned those powers for the higher faith. Therefore they were commanded, "Whoever curseth his god", etc., as much as to say: Although the service of these is strange worship, yet I have appointed them to control the world, and therefore whoever curses or insults them must bear his iniquity. But "he that blasphemeth the name of the Lord shall be put to death".'

R. Simeon was once going along accompanied by R. Eleazar, R. Abba, R. Ḥiya, R. Jose, and R. Judah. They came to a certain watercourse, and R. Jose slipped down in his clothes into the water. He said: [107a] 'I wish this water channel had never been here.' Said R. Simeon to him: 'You must not say that. This is for the service of the world, and it is forbidden to revile a ministrant of the Holy One, blessed be He, especially those loyal servants of his. They are appointed by Providence. It is written that "God saw all that he had made, and behold it was very good" (Gen. I, 31), even serpents and scorpions and fleas and all things that appear to be pests—all these are for the service of the world, though men know it not.'[1] As they went along, they saw a snake crawling in front of them. Said R. Simeon: Assuredly this creature is there to perform some miracle for us. The snake quickly crept in front of them and wound itself round a basilisk in the middle of the path. They then struggled together until both were killed. When they came up to them they found them lying dead in the road and R. Simeon said: 'Blessed be God for performing for us this miracle, for if anyone had looked upon this creature while it was alive, or had been looked upon by it, he would not have escaped harm, much less if he had approached it. Thus God makes all things His agents and we must not revile anything that He has made.'

R. Simeon discoursed on the verse: "I am a rose of Sharon, a lily of the valleys" (S.S. II, 1). 'How beloved', he said, 'is the Community of Israel to the Holy One, blessed be He, so that He continually praises Her and She continually praises Him, having many chants and hymns in store for the King. The Community of Israel is called the rose of Sharon because she flowers beautifully in the Garden of Eden, and the lily of the valleys because she desires to be watered from the deep stream, the source of rivers, as it is said, "Sharon is like an Arabah" (dry land). She is also called the lily of the valleys because she is at the lowest point of all. At first she is a rose with yellowish leaves, afterwards a lily with two colours, white and red, a lily with six leaves, a lily which changes from one colour to another. When she seeks to unite with the King she is called "rose", but after she has joined him with her kisses she is called "lily".

'Observe that when God created man and invested him with high honour, He required of him to cleave to Him in

[1] v. T.B. Shabbath, 77b.

order that he might be unique and single-hearted, cleaving to the One by the bond of single-minded faith wherewith all is linked together. Afterwards they turned aside from the way of faith and abandoned the unique tree which is high above all trees and clung to the place which is ever changing from colour to colour, from good to bad and bad to good, and came down from on high and clung below to the ever changeable and abandoned the supreme and changeless One. Hence their hearts alternated between good and bad: sometimes they deserved mercy and sometimes punishment, [107b] according to that to which they clave. Said the Holy One, blessed be He: Man, thou hast abandoned life and clung to death; verily death is before thee. Therefore death was decreed for him and for all the world. Now if Adam sinned, what was the sin of the rest of the world? For it cannot be said that all creatures came and ate of the forbidden tree. No. What happened was that when man stood upright, all creatures saw him and feared him and followed him like slaves. So when he said to them, "Come, let us bow down to the Lord who made us", they all went after him. And when they saw man bowing down to the other place and cleaving to it, they again followed him, and thus he brought death on himself and all the world. Thus Adam alternated between various colours, good and bad, commotion and rest, judgement and mercy, life and death: never constant in one, through the influence of that place, which is therefore called "the flame of a sword which turns every way", from this side to that, from good to evil, from mercy to judgement, from peace to war. The Supreme King, however, in compassion on the works of his hands, warned them saying, "From the tree of knowledge of good and evil ye shall not eat". Man, however, did not listen, and followed his wife and was banished for ever, for woman can attain to this place but no further, and woman brought death on all. But in days to come "the days of my people shall be as the days of the tree" (Isa. LXV, 22)—like that tree of which we know. Of that time it is written, "He hath swallowed up death for ever, and the Lord God hath wiped away tears from all faces" (*Ibid.* XXV, 8).'

BEHAR

Leviticus XXV, 1–XXVI, 2

AND THE LORD SPAKE UNTO MOSES . . . THEN SHALL
THE LAND KEEP A SABBATH UNTO THE LORD. R. Eleazar
introduced this portion with a discourse on the verse: "This
is the law of the burnt-offering, the burnt-offering shall be",
etc. (Lev. VI, 2). 'We have explained this verse', he said,
'to refer to the Community of Israel when she ascends to
join the Holy King in perfect union. When night enters
and the gates are closed, the lower judgements are aroused
in the world, and asses, she-asses and dogs wander about;
that is to say, the asses of their own accord, but the she-asses
and dogs only if human beings practise sorceries with them.
Then all men sleep, and a fire is kindled on the lower altar
without [the curtain]. At midnight the north wind awakes,
and from the lower altar there goes forth a flame of fire, and
the gates are opened and the lower judgements shrink back
into their holes. The flame of fire in its passage parts and
travels in many directions and enters [108a] under the
wings of the cock, which thereupon crows. Then the Holy
One, blessed be He, enters the company of the righteous,
and the Community of Israel utters His praises until morning,
when they are found to be discoursing on a certain secret.
The daybreak is a time for flames and judgements, but then
Abraham awakens and there is rest for all. Now when Israel
entered the promised land, there were no lower judgements
in it, and the Community of Israel was at ease in it upon the
wings of the Cherubim, for Israel did not go to rest until
they had brought the evening sacrifice and so caused judgements to depart. When the burnt-offering burnt on the
altar, there was ease and comfort throughout, and the Spouse
was with her Husband. Hence it is written, "and the earth
shall rest a sabbath for the Lord"; for such it was literally.'

R. Eleazar further quoted here the verse: "If thou buy
an Hebrew servant, six years shall he serve" (Ex. XXI, 2).
'Every Israelite', he said, 'who is circumcised and bears

on him the holy impress has relief in the sabbatical year, because it belongs of right to him to find rest therein: and this is called "the Sabbath of the land". Truly there is freedom and rest in it; as the Sabbath is rest for all, so the sabbatical year is rest for all, for the spirit and the body. Observe that the *Hé* denotes rest for higher and lower—the higher *Hé* for the higher and the lower for the lower. The higher *Hé* is seven years seven times, the lower *Hé* is seven years only; the one is a sabbatical year, the other a Jubilee; and when closely scrutinized, both are found to be one.

'In this rest of the land slaves are also required to partake. Hence it is written, "In the seventh year he shall go out free for nothing" (Ex. xxi, 2). What is meant by "for nothing"? The words have the same inner meaning as in the verse, "We remember the fish which we did eat in Egypt for nought" (Num. xi, 5)—that is to say, without pronouncing a blessing; for in Egypt the yoke of heaven was not upon them. What is the yoke of the kingdom of heaven? Just as an ox is put under a yoke in order that it may be of use, and otherwise it never does any work, so a man must first accept the yoke and then perform religious service: and without it he will not be able to serve God. This yoke will not rest upon one who is subject to another, and therefore slaves are exempt from the yoke of the kingdom of heaven. And if they are exempt from this yoke, they are exempt from all the rest of the religion, and therefore Israel ate in Egypt "for nothing". Here, too, the slave shall go forth to freedom, although so far all that he did was "for nothing", without the yoke of heaven, and he shall have rest. Later when he is free and has rest, he receives a yoke from the place which brought him forth to freedom. And if a man refuses to go forth to freedom, he impairs that place, since he leaves the yoke of the kingdom of heaven and accepts the yoke of a master. Therefore "his master shall bring him to *Elohim*"— to the place which he impairs, "and bring him to the door or the doorpost", [108b] since this place is the gateway to the higher world. And since he was minded to impair that place, a blemish is left in his body, as it is written, "And his master shall bore his ear through". And since Israel at

Mount Sinai placed "doing" before "hearing", therefore "hearing" is attached to this sabbatical year.

'It is written: "Six years thou shalt sow thy land and in the seventh year thou shalt let it rest", etc. Why so ? "That the poor of thy people may eat" (*Ibid.*). For the poor are attached to that place, and therefore let them eat. Hence he that loves the poor brings peace to the Community of Israel and increases blessing in the world, and brings joy and strength to the place which is called Righteousness that it may pour down blessing on the Community of Israel.' [110b]

AND IF YE SAY, WHAT SHALL WE EAT, ETC. R. Judah cited here the verse: "Trust in the Lord and do good, dwell in the land and follow after faithfulness" (Ps. XXXVII, 3). 'Observe', he said, 'that, as we have learnt, the deed below arouses the activity above, as it says, "and ye shall do (lit. make) them", as much as to say, by your action below you *make* those above. Hence it says here, "Do (i.e. make) good", "good" being a reference to the *Zaddik*. When you do this, then that "good" is aroused, and then you may "dwell in the land and follow after faithfulness". The "earth" referred to here is the supernal earth, with which none can abide save he first arouse this "good"; but if he does that he may dwell in its midst and eat its fruit and delight in it. And the same meaning is in the words "follow after faithfulness". We may also take these words to mean, "Concentrate all thy thought upon Her". For if thou arousest not this good to meet Her, bestirrest thyself not to meet Her, this good departs from Her and thou canst not approach Her, as thou canst not approach a burning furnace, and if thou dost approach it will be in fear, like one who is afraid of death, for then a fire burns to consume the world. But if this "good" advances to meet Her and abides in Her, then thou needest not to fear, and then "thou shalt decree a thing and it shall be established unto thee and light shall shine upon thy ways" (Job XXII, 28). For the sons of faith bend Her to their will every day. Who are the sons of faith ? Those who arouse this "good" to meet Her, and do not spare their substance, knowing that the Holy One, blessed be He, will

give them more, because they set in motion blessings before
Him. Hence "if ye say, What shall we eat in the seventh
year ?" the answer is, "I will command my blessing upon
you in the sixth year"; just as it is written elsewhere: "See
that the Lord . . . giveth you on the sixth day the bread of
two days" (Ex. XVI, 29).'

As R. Jose and R. Ḥiya were once travelling together,
they saw in front of them two other men going along. They
saw a man come up to them and say, I beg of you, give me
some food, if only a piece of bread, because for two days
I have been wandering in the wilderness without tasting
anything. One of the two men thereupon took out the food
which he had brought with him for the journey and gave
him to eat and drink. Said his companion to him: 'What
will you do for food, for I am going to eat my own ?' He
replied: 'Do I want to eat yours ?' The poor man ate up all
that he had save some bread, and this he gave him for the
road. Said R. Ḥiya: 'God did not desire that this good deed
should be done by us.' R. Jose replied: 'Perhaps that man
was doomed to some punishment, and God sent this man
to him so as to deliver him.' They resumed their journey,
and soon after the man who had given his food became faint.
Said his companion to him: 'Did I not [111*a*] tell you not
to give your bread away ?' R. Ḥiya then said to R. Jose: 'We
have bread, let us give him some.' Said R. Jose to him: 'Do
you want to undo the merit of his good deed ? Let us watch
a little, for assuredly the pallor of death is on this man's face,
and God prepared some merit for him in order to deliver
him.' Meanwhile the man fell asleep under a tree and his
companion left him. R. Jose and R. Ḥiya then saw a fiery
adder by him. 'Alas for that man,' said R. Ḥiya; 'surely he
will now be killed.' R. Jose replied: 'He deserves that a
miracle should be done on his behalf.' At that point a snake
came down from the tree with intent to kill the man, but
the adder attacked and killed it, and then turned its head
and departed. Said R. Jose: 'Did I not tell you that God
desired to perform a miracle for him, and that you should
not exhaust his merit ?' The man then woke up and began
to go. R. Ḥiya and R. Jose came up to him and gave him

food. When he had eaten they informed him of the miracle which God had performed for him. R. Jose then quoted the verse: "Trust in the Lord and do good, dwell in the land and follow after faithfulness" (Ps. xxxvii, 3). 'Happy', he said, 'is the man who does good with what he hath, because he arouseth good for the Community of Israel, to wit, with righteousness.[1] Hence it is written, "Righteousness delivereth from death" (Prov. x, 2). Why so? Because righteousness is the tree of life, and it rouses itself against the tree of death and takes those who are attached to it and delivers them from death. And what rouses it to do so? You must say, the charity which that man does; as it were, he performs it above also.'

---

[1] *Zedakah*, i.e. charity.

BEḤUKOTHAI

Leviticus XXVI, 3–XXVII, 34

IF YE WALK IN MY STATUTES, ETC. R. Ḥiya introduced this section with a discourse on the verse: "O my people, remember what Balak king of Moab consulted, and what Balaam the son of Beor answered him" (Micah VI, 5). 'Happy', he said, 'is the people whose Master exhorts them thus, as though to say, Although you go astray from the ways of My people, My ways, yet ye are My people, and I do not desire to requite you according to your deeds.' R. Isaac said: 'Happy the portion of the people whose Master says to them, "O my people, what have I done to thee and wherein have I wearied thee?" (*Ibid.* 3).' R. Jose said: 'God said to Israel, "Remember now (I pray you)". We cry every day with tears and wailing, "Remember, O Lord, what is come upon us" (Lam. V, 1), "Remember, O Lord, against the children of Edom" (Ps. CXXXVII, 7), and He says to us, "I pray you, remember now", and we pay no heed; therefore when we cry He pays no heed to us.' R. Judah said: 'In truth God does heed us and remember us, otherwise Israel would not be able to stand a single day in captivity, for so it is written, "And yet for all that when they be in the land of their enemies", etc. (Lev. XXVI, 44). [112b] God does not requite us according to our deeds.

'Balak was a greater master of magic arts than Balaam. For just as the celestial holiness can be aroused both by act and by word on our part, so can they that come from the side of uncleanness. Balaam was the greatest of sorcerers, but Balak was still greater. Balaam was greater in divination, but Balak in sorcery. For sorcery depends on actions, but divination on utterances and observations. Not so holy Israel, whose whole endeavour is to draw upon themselves the spirit of holiness, wherefore it is written, "For there is no divination against Israel nor enchantment against Jacob" (Num. XXIII, 23). Because Balaam was more powerful with his mouth than all diviners and in the observation of the great Serpent, therefore Balak wished to combine his own sorcery with his divination. Said God to him: Wretch, my sons have anticipated you. They have something which prevents all evil sides and species and sorceries from coming near them, to wit, the tent of assembly and the holy vessels and the utensils of the Sanctuary and the incense of spices, which allays all wrath and anger, both above and below, and the daily sacrifices and the two altars and the table and the shew-bread and the laver and its base, and many utensils to serve the utterance of the mouth, the ark and the two tablets of the Law and Aaron to make atonement for the people with his prayer every day. When the wicked Balaam saw all this he said: "For there is no divination against Israel nor sorcery against Israel". Why ? Because "the Lord his God is with him, and the pleasure of the King is in him". Therefore, "My people, I beseech you to remember the time when Balak and Balaam joined forces to destroy you, but did not succeed because I took hold of you as a father takes hold of his son, not letting him fall into the hand of another." The verse continues, "From Shittim to Gilgal". Why are these places mentioned ? As much as to say: Remember that when you let go your hold upon me, then in Shittim "the people ate and bowed down to their gods" (Num. xxv, 2), and in Gilgal "they sacrificed bullocks" (Hos. xii, 11), and then your enemies prevailed over you. Why all this ? "That you might know the righteous deeds of the Lord", all those kindnesses that I did to you when you kept hold on Me, and I allowed nothing in the world to dominate you and neither the higher nor lower wrath nor the evil species were able to touch you. "And he said to them: Tarry here this night, and I will bring you word again as the Lord shall speak unto me." Observe that when the sun goes down and all the gates are closed and night falls and it grows dark, many dogs are loosened from their chains and go wandering about the world. There are many Chieftains who guide them and one supreme Chieftain from the side of the Left. That wicked Balaam gained access to this supreme Chieftain by his sorceries, which he practised in the night when he was at the head of all his company, and then he made known his requests to him. [113a] The word *Elohim* is used in connection with Balaam as with Laban and with Abimelech, because this is a name of general application, being used of idols under the title of "other gods", which includes these Chieftains also. So this wicked Balaam summoned the Chieftain to him and he came to him. It may be said that he was with him by day (when he was with Balak). The truth is, however, that at that hour he only made observations by means of his divinations to fix the right hour, and when it says, "he went not as at other times to meet with enchantments" (*Ibid.* XXIV, 1), this signifies that he tried to fix the hour, but was not able as on other days, because he saw that there was no great wrath in the world and knew that "it was good in the eyes of the Lord to bless Israel" (*Ibid.*). For when burning wrath is rife the Left is aroused, and the wicked Balaam knew how to take hold of the left side so as to curse; but on this occasion he looked and saw that the wrath was not there.

'IF YE WALK IN MY STATUTES. This is the place from which depend the decrees of the Law, whereas "judgements" signifies another and higher place to which this statute is attached; and the two, "statute" and "judgement", are connected both on the higher and the lower plane. All the commandments and decrees and sanctifications of the Torah are attached to these, because one is the Written Torah and the other the Oral Torah. Both are intertwined and form one entity, and this is the sum of the Holy Name, so that he who transgresses against the commandments of the law in effect impairs the Holy Name.

'AND YE SHALL DO (MAKE) THEM. After "walk" and "keep" have been mentioned, why does it also say "do"? Because he who "keeps" the precepts of the Law and "walks" in God's ways, if one may say so, "makes" Him who is above. Also it says, "You shall make them", because the two aspects (of statute and judgement) are both aroused through you and join together so that the Holy Name is consummated.' Similarly, R. Simeon commented on the

verse, "And David made him a name" (2 Sam. VIII, 13).
'Did, then, David really *make* it ?' he asked. 'What it means
is that because David walked in the way of the Torah and
carried out the precepts of the Torah and exercised his
royal power in the fitting manner, he, as it were, "made"
a Name on high. No other king was so worthy to accomplish
[113b] this as David, because he used to rise at midnight
and praise the Holy One, blessed be He, until the Holy
Name ascended on its throne at the hour when the light
of day appeared. In the same sense it is written here, "and
ye shall make them"; and if ye strive to stablish thus the
Holy Name, all those blessings from above shall abide firmly
with you. Similarly it is written: "And they shall keep the
way of the Lord to do justice and judgement" (Gen. XVIII,
19), to signify that he who keeps the ways of the Torah, as
it were, "makes" justice and judgement. And who are these ?
The Holy One, blessed be He.' R. Simeon here wept and
exclaimed: 'Alas for mankind that they know not and heed
not the honour of their Master ! Who is it that "makes"
the Holy Name every day ? You must say, he that gives charity
to the poor. As we know, the poor man takes hold of judgement and all his food is judgement, the place that is called
Ẓedek (righteousness). Hence he that gives charity (*ẓedakah*)
to the poor makes the Holy Name complete as it should be
above, since *ẓedakah* is the tree of life, and when it gives
to *Ẓedek* the Holy Name becomes complete. Hence he who
sets this activity in motion from below, as it were, fully
makes the Holy Name. It has been stated elsewhere which
is the place of the poor man.[1] Why is it so ? Because the poor
man has not anything of his own, save what is given him,
and the moon has no light save what is given her by the sun.
Why is a poor man counted as dead ? Because he is found
in the place of death.[2] Therefore, if one has pity on him and
gives him charity, the tree of life rests upon him, as it says,
"*Ẓedakah* (charity) delivereth from death" (Prov. x, 2). This
applies only to charity done for its own sake, for then the doer
links together *ẓedakah* with *ẓedek* so that the whole forms the
Holy Name, since *ẓedek* is not established without *ẓedakah*.'

[1] Viz. the Shekinah. [2] The Shekinah being called "the tree of death".

AND I SHALL GIVE PEACE IN THE LAND, AND YE SHALL
LIE DOWN AND NONE SHALL MAKE YOU AFRAID. R. Jose
cited here the verse: "Stand in awe and sin not", etc. (Ps. IV, 5).
'When night has fallen', he said, 'and men have gone to
bed, many emissaries of the law arise and go about the
world, and it behoves men to tremble in awe before the
Holy One, blessed be He, in order that they may be delivered
from them. And a man should be careful not to make any
reference to them with his lips so as not to draw their
attention to him. Hence it is written, "Commune with your
own heart upon your bed" (*Ibid.*) Hence, when Israel are
virtuous it is written of them, "I shall give peace in the
land". This means peace above, where the Holy One,
blessed be He, comes to join the Community of Israel. Then
"ye shall lie down and none shall make you afraid". Why
so ? Because "I shall cause evil beasts to cease out of the
land". [114a] These beasts are the evil species below, namely
Iggereth bath Mahalath with all her company. She it is by
night, but in the day the men who come from her side, in
reference to whom it is written, "neither shall the sword go
through your land".' R. Abba said: 'We have explained
that this includes even a sword of peace, like that of Pharaoh
Necho. King Josiah interpreted the verse thus, but as we
have learnt, he was made to suffer for the sins of Israel.
Here a difficulty arises, since we have learnt that if the head
of the people is good, they are all delivered for his sake, and
if the head is not good the whole people is made to suffer
for his sake. Now seeing that Josiah was a good king and
acted rightly, why had he to suffer for the sins of Israel ?
The reason was because he did not exercise control over
Israel, since he thought that they were all virtuous like
himself, and though Jeremiah told him that they were not,
he did not believe him. Another reason was that the Moon's
light was fading and it was seeking to disappear.

'AND I WILL SET MY TABERNACLE AMONG YOU. "My
tabernacle" (*mishcani*) means the Shekinah; the word can
also be rendered "my pledge", which was taken back for the
sins of Israel. Once a man was very fond of a friend of his

and said to him: I am so fond of you that I am going to
stay with you. Said the other: How do I know that you will
stay with me ? So he took all his most precious belongings
and brought them to him, saying: Here is a pledge to you
that I shall never leave you. So God sought to abide with
Israel, and He therefore took his most desirable possession
and sent it down to Israel, saying: Here is my pledge to you
that I shall never leave you. And although the Holy One,
blessed be He, has departed from us, He has left his pledge
in our hands, and we keep that treasure of His, so that if He
wants His pledge He must come and abide with us.

'AND MY SOUL SHALL NOT ABHOR YOU. Suppose now
the man is so fond of his friend that he wants to live with
him, then he takes his bed to his house, saying: Here is my
bed in thy house so that I shall have no need to leave thee.
So the Holy One, blessed be He, said: Here is my bed in
your house, and therefore you shall know that I shall not
leave you.

'AND I WILL WALK AMONG YOU AND BE YOUR GOD.
Since my pledge is with you, of a surety you will know that
I walk with you, as it is written, "For the Lord thy God
walketh in the midst of thy camp to deliver thee and to give
up thine enemies before thee" (Deut. XXIII, 14).' Once, when
R. Isaac and R. Judah were in a village near the Lake of
Tiberias, they rose at midnight and R. Isaac said to R. Judah:
'Let us discourse on the Torah, for though we are in such
a place as this, we ought not to go away from the Tree of
Life.' R. Judah then expounded the verse: "Now Moses
took the tent and pitched it without the camp" (Ex. XXIII, 7).
Why did he do so ? Said Moses: Since Israel have denied
the Holy One, blessed be He, and have exchanged His glory
for another, let His pledge here be in the hands of a faithful
keeper until we see with whom it will be left. He said to
Joshua: Thou shalt be the man of trust between God and
Israel, and the pledge shall be entrusted to thee, until we
see [114b] with whom it shall be left. Why to Joshua ?
Because he stood to Moses in the relation of the moon to

the sun,[1] and he was a fitting person to hold the pledge, and therefore it is written, "Joshua the son of Nun, a young man, departed not out of the camp" (*Ibid.* 11). Said the Holy One, blessed be He, to Moses: Moses, this is not right. I have given my pledge to them, and even though they have sinned against me, it must remain with them. Therefore return my pledge to them, and for its sake I will not abandon them wherever they are. Therefore wherever Israel go into exile the Shekinah is with them, and therefore it is written, "And I will set my tabernacle among you".'

R. Isaac adduced the verse: "My beloved is like a doe or a young hart, behold he standeth behind our wall", etc. (S.S. II, 9). 'Happy', he said, 'are Israel to whom it has been granted that this pledge should be with them from the supreme King, for though they are in exile, the Holy One, blessed be He, comes at the beginning of every month and on every Sabbath and festival to take note of them and to look at his pledge which is with them, his most precious possession. He is like a king whose queen has offended him so that he has expelled her from the palace. What does she do ? She takes the king's son, his pride and his darling; and because the king is still fond of her he leaves him with her. When the king yearns for the queen and her son, he climbs up roofs and goes down steps to peep at them through chinks in walls, and when he obtains a glimpse of them he weeps behind the wall and then departs. So Israel, though they have gone forth from the king's palace, have not lost that pledge, which the King has left with them because He still loves them, and when He yearns for them He goes up on roofs and steps to gain a sight of them through the chinks of the wall, as it says, "He looketh in at the windows, he glanceth through the lattice", in the synagogues and houses of learning. Therefore Israel should rejoice on the day on which they know this, and say, "This is the day on which the Lord hath wrought, we will rejoice and be glad in it" (Ps. CXVIII, 24).'

AND IF YE SHALL REJECT MY STATUTES, ETC. R. Jose adduced here the verse: "My son, despise not the chastening

[1] Cf. T.B. Baba Bathra, 75*a*.

of the Lord, neither be weary of his reproof" (Prov. III, 11).
'Israel', he said, 'are beloved to God, and therefore God is
fain to reprove them and to lead them in the right path as
a loving father leads his son, and because of his love he
always has the rod in his hand to keep him in the right path
and to prevent him from straying to the right or the left.
But from him whom He loves not and hates God withdraws
His reproof and His rod; and so we interpret the verse,
"I have loved you, saith the Lord . . . but Esau I hated" (Mal. I,
2). The word *takuz* (be weary) in the above-quoted verse
may be connected with *koẓin* (thorns), for the reproof is like
a thorn in a man's flesh, and yet he should not flee from it.
When righteousness arises with its judgements, many are
the shining emissaries who bestir themselves on the right
hand and on the left, with many rods of fire, coal and flame,
with which they traverse the world and smite the sons of
men. Under them are many other emissaries, lords of the
thirty-nine strokes, who come down and smite and ascend
and receive authorization, who enter [115*a*] into the hollow
of the great deep where they become painted with flames
and a burning fire is attached to them and they issue forth
like burning coals. Hence it is written, "I shall chastise you
still more (lit. I will add to chastise you) seven times for
your sins", that is to say, I will give additional power to the
chastisers to chastise, up to seven times for your sins. It
may be asked: How can this be, seeing that if God were to
collect His due, the world could not endure for an instant ?
The truth is that this "seven" refers to the Sabbatical Year
which is so called: "seven" will chastise you.'

AND I ALSO WILL CHASTISE YOU SEVEN TIMES FOR
YOUR SINS. R. Abba said: 'This means that I will rouse
this Seven against you. Observe the deep love of the Holy
One, blessed be He, for Israel. We may compare Him to a
king who had a dearly beloved son who repeatedly offended
against him. At length one day the king said: All these days
I have chastised thee and thou hast not hearkened. What
shall I do to thee ? If I banish thee from the land and depose
thee from the kingdom, perhaps bears or wolves or robbers

will attack thee and destroy thee. Therefore I and thou together will leave the land. So God said to Israel: What shall
I do to you ? Behold I have smitten you and ye have not
inclined your ears. I have sent against you smiters and
burners and ye have not hearkened. If I send you out of the
land alone, I fear for the many bears and wolves who may
rise against you and drive you from the earth. What, then,
shall I do ? I and you will leave the land and go in exile: yet
think not that I shall abandon you, for "I also" shall be
with you. For "Seven" shall be banished with you: the
Matrona shall leave her temple with you, and all will be
desolate, both my temple and yours. Hence I too will be
with you, and therefore when Israel emerge from captivity,
God will return with them.'

As R. Ḥiya and R. Jose were journeying together, they
came to a cave in a field and R. Ḥiya asked R. Jose: 'Why is
it written "These are the words of the covenant which the
Lord commanded Moses to make with the children of Israel,
besides the covenant which he made with them in Horeb"
(Deut. xxviii, 69) ? It should be: These are the words of the
adjuration, should it not ?' He replied: 'Both were words of
a covenant, for [115b] although the later ones were not from
the mouth of God (but of Moses), yet they were words of a
covenant, since both good and evil are foreshadowed in them,
good from the side of *Ẓaddik* and evil from the side of judgement, which is *Ẓedek*, and *Ẓaddik* and *Ẓedek* are called
"Covenant". Hence these words are words of a covenant.'

AND YET FOR ALL THAT, WHEN THEY BE IN THE LAND
OF THEIR ENEMIES I WILL NOT REJECT THEM, NEITHER
WILL I ABHOR THEM TO DESTROY THEM UTTERLY
AND TO BREAK MY COVENANT WITH THEM. R. Jose said:
' "When they be" means when they are all together. "I
will not reject them, neither will I abhor them", so as not
to be associated with them. "To break my covenant with
them": for if I shall not redeem them, my covenant will be
divided.' Said R. Ḥiya: 'I have heard the following from
R. Eleazar. The expression "I will not reject them or abhor
them to destroy them" is somewhat strange: we should

expect, "I will not smite them or slay them". What it means, however, is this. One who is hated of another is abhorred and rejected of him, but God will not reject Israel, because the beloved of His soul is among them, and for her sake all of them are beloved of Him. If a man loves a woman who lives in a street of tanners, if she were not there he would never go into it, but because she is there it seems to him like a street of spice makers where all the sweet scents of the world are to be found. So "even when they are in the land of their enemies", which is the street of tanners, "I will not abhor or reject them", because of that bride in their midst, the beloved of my soul who abides there.'

Said R. Jose: 'If I had only come to hear this, it would have been worth my while. It is written,' he continued, ' "A son honoureth his father" (Mal. 1, 6). We have learnt that when the father is alive it is the son's duty to honour him with food and drink. Is he free from the obligation of honouring him after his death ? Not so, since it is written, "Honour thy father" (Ex. xx, 12). If the son walks in the crooked path, of a surety he brings dishonour and shame on his father. But if he walks in the straight path and his deeds are upright, then he confers honour on him both in this world among men and in the next world with God, who gives him a special throne of honour. An example is R. Eleazar, who honoured his father in his lifetime and now has made him more honoured in the next world after his death as the progenitor of holy sons and a holy stock.'

NUMBERS

BEMIDBAR

Numbers I, 1–IV, 20

AND THE LORD SPAKE UNTO MOSES IN THE WILDER-
NESS OF SINAI, IN THE TENT OF MEETING, ETC. R. Abba
cited here the verse: "And God created man in his own
image, in the image of God created he him", etc. (Gen. I, 27).
'We have already explained', he said, 'that when the Holy
One, blessed be He, created man, He made him in the image
of the higher and the lower grades, so that he epitomised
the whole, and his light shone forth from one end of the
world to the other, and the whole of creation feared him.
It is necessary, however, to look deeper into this verse. For
since Scripture says "And God created man in his own
image", why repeat "in the image of God created he him" ?
But what it signifies is a two-foldness of grades, of male and
female comprised within the man, which made him a duality
of *prosopa*, so that he was complete in all respects, and he
contemplated in wisdom both what was above and what was
below. But once he sinned his *prosopa* diminished, wisdom
departed from him, and he could survey only the affairs
of his body. He then begat offspring partaking both of the
higher and of the lower nature, but the world was not settled
by either of them until Adam begat a son called Seth,[1] by
whom the world was made complete.[2] Yet was not the lower
world finally completed, nor was it firmly established until
Abraham appeared, until Abraham took hold of it by the
right hand as one upholds with his right hand one who is
falling. Then came Isaac, who seized the world by the left
hand, establishing it still more firmly. When Jacob came, he
held the world by the centre of the body, uniting the two
sides, whereby the world became firm and immovable.
With all that it did not take deep root until there were born
the twelve tribes and their offspring, numbering seventy
souls. Nor yet was the world finally completed until Israel

[1] Sheth = foundation.   [2] Al. with whom the world was planted. *v.* Mid.
R. Num. XIV, 12; Cant. VIII, 9.

received the Torah on Mount Sinai and the Tabernacle
was set up. All worlds were then finally established and
perfected, and higher and lower creatures were properly
based. The Torah and the Tabernacle thus having been
established, the Holy One, blessed be He, desired to take
a muster, as it were, [117b] of the forces of the Torah and
the forces of the Tabernacle. For a thing cannot be finally
settled in its place until its name has been called and it has
been assigned there. We thus see here that the Holy One,
blessed be He, decided on an enumeration of the forces of the
Torah and of those of the Tabernacle, these two being in
essence one and inseparable on the celestial model. Their
forces were thus enumerated and noted, excepting some
who did not enter into the count. Therefore it is written
that "the Lord spake unto Moses *in the wilderness of Sinai,
in the tent of meeting*", the two corresponding one to the
Torah and the other to the Tabernacle. Both were "in the
first day of the second month", the two being one. That
month, besides, is called Ziv (=brightness, splendour), in
allusion to the brightness of the moon of that month in that
year, by reason that then the worlds altogether found themselves in completion.

'AFTER THEY HAD COME OUT OF THE LAND OF EGYPT:
this emphasizes the fact that Israel's exodus from Egypt
took place in the first month.' R. Isaac cited here the verses:
"The Lord hath been mindful of us, he will bless . . . the
house of Israel . . . the house of Aaron . . . them that fear
the Lord, both small and great. The Lord increase you"
(Ps. cxv, 12-14). 'The first "he will bless",' he said, 'refers
to the men who were numbered, and whom the Lord blesses
and "increases more and more". Observe this. Whoever
speaks in praise of his companion or of his children or his
substance, should also bless him and shower blessings on
him. We learn this from Moses, who, after saying "And,
behold, ye are this day as the stars of the heaven for multitude" (Deut. I, 10), continued, "The Lord, the God of your
fathers, make you a thousand so many more as ye are" (*Ibid.*
11), and then confirmed his words by adding "and bless

you, as he hath promised you" (*Ibid.*). But he who, recounting his neighbour's good points, omits to bless him, will be the first to incur heavenly displeasure. Whereas he who does so bless will receive blessings from above. The man's blessing, moreover, must be given not grudgingly, but generously and with a good heart, as God above all desires man's good heart.[1] How much more so must this be the case when a man offers praise to the Holy One, blessed be He ! So Scripture says: "And thou shalt love the Lord thy God with all thy heart", etc. (*Ibid.* vi, 5). Now it has been laid down that the heavenly blessing does not rest on anything enumerated. How, then, is it that the Israelites were enumerated ? Because the enumeration was by means of a ransom taken from them. The Israelites were thus first blessed, then their ransoms were counted, and that was followed again by a blessing given to them. The blessings, before and after, were a shield against death, which is ready to attack wherever there is enumeration. Should the blessing be removed, the "other side" may swoop down and inflict harm. The text continues: "He will bless the house of Israel", indicating the women who were not included in the enumeration, "He will bless the house of Aaron", who pronounce the blessing on Israel generously and out of goodness of heart and love. "The house of Aaron": again including their women. "He will bless them that fear the Lord", alluding to the Levites, all of whom are blessed, because they fear the Lord. "Both small and great": that is, even those who were not included in the enumeration. Observe that at no other enumeration were the Israelites blessed as at this one, which was intended in especial to be attended by a blessing and to put the finishing touch to all worlds.' [118*a*]

R. Judah used to be much in the company of R. Simeon. Once he asked him: 'Which region is it whence blessings go forth to Israel ?' R. Simeon replied: 'Woe to the world in that its people do not ponder or reflect on the glory of the Most High King. Observe this. When Israel are found worthy before the Holy One, blessed be He, and are with Him in a certain sacred celestial tree which contains the

---

[1] *v.* T.B. Sanhedrin, 107*a*.

food of the whole world, then He is blessed from the repository of all the blessings, and Israel below are blessed from the place from which all blessings come, as it says: "Then Lord bless thee out of Zion" (Ps. cxxxiv, 3), also, "Like the dew of Hermon that cometh down upon the mountains of Zion; for there the Lord commanded the blessing, even life for ever" (*Ibid.* cxxxiii, 3). This same is, too, the shining light of the world of which Scripture says: "Out of Zion the perfection of beauty, God hath shined forth" (*Ibid.* l, 2). It is the light which, when once it shines, will shine for all the worlds. When that light will awaken, the whole will be one common fellowship, under the reign of universal love and universal peace. There will be peace in heaven and peace on earth. So Scripture says: "Peace be within thy walls, and prosperity within thy palaces" (Ps. cxxii, 7).'

EVERY MAN WITH HIS OWN STANDARD, ACCORDING TO THE ENSIGNS, BY THEIR FATHER'S HOUSES, SHALL THE CHILDREN OF ISRAEL PITCH. R. Eleazar began a discourse, citing the verse: "Rejoice ye with Jerusalem, and be glad in her, all ye that love her", etc. (Isa. lxvi, 10). 'How beloved', he said, 'is the Torah before the Holy One, blessed be He, inasmuch as wherever words of the Torah are heard the Holy One, blessed be He, listens together with all His hosts. Indeed, He comes to lodge with the one that gives utterance to those words, as Scripture says: "In every place where I cause my name to be mentioned", etc. (Ex. xx, 21). Moreover, the enemies of such a man fall down before him, as said elsewhere. Observe this', he continued. 'The precepts of the Torah are exalted essences on high. Whenever a man fulfils one of the precepts, that precept presents itself, all adorned, before the Holy One, blessed be He, saying: So-and-so fulfilled me and I proceed from him. That man, thus, as he roused that precept below, caused a stirring on high, and brought about peace on high and below. Of this Scripture says: "Or else let him take hold of my strength, that he make peace with me; yea, let him make peace with me" (Isa. xxvii, 5); twice "peace", to

wit, peace on high and peace below. Happy is the portion
of the man who observes the precepts of the Torah. The
text cited above says: "Rejoice ye with Jerusalem", etc.,
inasmuch as at no time is there joy save when Israel is
established in the Holy Land, where the Wife is joined to
her Spouse, diffusing thereby world-embracing joy, both
on high and below. But when Israel is not in the Holy Land,
a man is forbidden to display joy or gladness, as Scripture
says: "Rejoice ye with Jerusalem, and be glad *in her*", to
wit, only when within her.' R. Abba once saw a man making
merry in the house of some Babylonian officers. R. Abba
struck at him, citing the words: "Rejoice ye with Jerusalem",
etc., which teaches us that only when Jerusalem is in joy is
it permissible for us to rejoice. In harmony with this idea,
R. Eleazar reconciled the two seemingly contradictory
verses, one of which says "Serve the Lord with gladness"
(Ps. c, 2), whilst the other says, "Serve the Lord with fear,
and rejoice with trembling" (*Ibid.* II, 11). 'The former', he
explained, 'speaks of the time when Israel dwells in the
Holy Land, whilst the latter refers to the time of their
dwelling in a strange land. Or we may also say that "serve
the Lord in fear" speaks to the Community of Israel at a
time when She is in exile among the nations.' R. Judah
adduced in opposition to this the verse, "For ye shall go
out with joy" (Isa. LV, 12), which seems to show that the
Community of Israel will be in joy whilst still in exile.
R. Eleazar, in reply, said: 'The truth is that so long as She
is in exile and lies in the dust there will be no real gladness.
But only when the Holy One, blessed be He, will raise Her
from the dust, saying, "Shake thyself from the dust", etc.
(Isa. LII, 2), "Arise, shine", etc. (*Ibid.* LX, 1), and the people
will assemble together, then there will be gladness indeed—
gladness for all. Then indeed "ye shall go out with joy";
then indeed numerous hosts will go forth to meet the
Matrona, sharing in the joy of her espousals with the King.
Scripture thus says: "The mountains and the hills shall
break forth", etc. (*Ibid.* LV, 12); also, "For the Lord will go
before you, and the God of Israel will be your rearward"
(*Ibid.* LII, 12). [118b]

'EVERY MAN WITH HIS OWN STANDARD, ACCORDING
TO THE ENSIGNS. . . .'[1] This signifies the four camps of
the Community of Israel, comprising the twelve tribes,
forming twelve boundaries enclosing Her, all on the celestial
model. Of this Scripture says: "Whither the tribes went
up" (Ps. cxxii, 4), to wit, the twelve tribes, the twelve
lower boundaries: "even the tribes of *YH*, as a testimony
unto Israel" (*Ibid.*), inasmuch as of a truth *YH* is the
attestor of Israel. This we see in their names, as *H*areuben *Y*
(the Reubenite), *H*ashimeon *Y* (the Simeonite), and so on.
Assuredly it is so, inasmuch as a sacred celestial Tree traced
out its boundaries through them, as expounded elsewhere.
We find Scripture saying: "As for the likeness of their
faces, they had the face of a man; and they four had the
face of a lion on the right side", etc. (Ezek. i, 10). The
image of man, that is, was combined with all of them. The
faces turned toward the four cardinal points, each with its
own likeness, but all combined with the likeness of man.
Michael was on the right, Gabriel on the left, Uriel in
front, and Raphael behind, while the Shekinah was hovering
over them all. Thus there were two on each side with the
Shekinah in the centre. This model was followed here
below, namely, two on either side with YH in the centre;
for as soon as two standards had commenced to march, then
"the tent of meeting, the camp of the Levites, journeyed",
and then two others set forth. First "the standard of the
camp of the children of Judah set forward" (Num. x, 14),
corresponding to the camp of Uriel; the camp of Reuben
corresponded to the camp of Michael; the one was toward
the south, the other toward the east, symbolic of the south-
east of the altar. Then the camp of Dan toward the north,
corresponding to the camp of Gabriel, and the camp of
Ephraim to the west, corresponding to the camp of Raphael.
This is symbolic of the north-west of the altar. The whole
was linked together and was unified in the Divine Name,
which is both the starting-point and the consummation of
all existence. Thus the *Yod*, symbolic of the east, is the
starting-point of light which moves on toward the south;

[1] There is here a lacuna in the text.

the *Hé* is symbolic of the south and the north. Thus, YH
(the *Yod* and the *Hé*) is the upholder of the south and the
north; whilst the *Vau* is the centre, and is significant of the
male child. Hence the dictum, "Whoever places his bed
between north and south will have male children born to
him".[1] Then the last *Hé* denotes the west. The south is
thus interlinked with the east, which constitutes the starting-
point of the sun. Hence we have learnt that it is the side
of the Father to which is attached the supernal *Ḥesed*
(Mercy), and the side of the Mother from which depends
Geburah (Might). So are the corners of the altar circled (by
the priest when sprinkling the blood), beginning with south-
east, as the strength of the south resides in the east, the
starting-point of the sun; followed by the east-north, since
the south in its turn gives its light to the north, the north
being enfolded in the south, as the left hand is clasped in
the right; there follows north-west, the west, symbolised
by the last *Hé*, deriving from the north; finally, west-south,
the west thus proceeding to be embraced, as it were, by the
south; in the same way as the south depends on the east,
from which it derives its strength, so the west is embraced
by the south, as it says: "Let his left hand be under my
head, and his right hand embrace me" (S.S. II, 6). The right
signifies the south, and the left the north. This mystery we
are taught by the Holy One, blessed be He, who thus places
His bed between the north and the south, and so has man
to do—as my father taught me—in order that he may have
male children born to him. In all his deeds [119a] it behoves
a man to imitate the celestial model, and to realize that
according to the nature of a deed below there is a responsive
stirring on high.' R. Phineas, having heard this discourse,
kissed R. Eleazar. He wept and laughed, saying: 'Happy is
my portion in this world and in the world to come.' The
same R. Phineas then quoted the verse: "The Lord is my
light and my salvation, whom shall I fear?", etc. (Ps. XXVII, 1).
'When a man', he said, 'turns his eyes to the heavenly
light, he will be illumined by the light that God will cause
to shine upon him, and he will fear no one, either in the upper

[1] T.B. Berachoth, 5b.

worlds or the lower. So Scripture says: "But upon thee the
Lord will arise, and his glory shall be upon thee" (Isa. LX, 2);
"The Lord is the stronghold of my life" (Ps. XXVII, 1),
for when the Almighty takes hold on a man he will have
no fear in the other world of any of the executors of judgement. So I,' said R. Phineas, 'having taken hold of thee and
of thy father, have no fear of anything in this world or in
the other world. It is concerning such a one as thou that it
is written: "Let thy father and thy mother be glad, and let
her that bore thee rejoice" (Prov. XXIII, 25). "Thy father"
is the Holy One, blessed be He, and "thy mother" is an
allusion to the Community of Israel, while "her that bore
thee" refers to thy mother here below. As for thy father,
R. Simeon, where is his joy referred to ? In a separate verse,
saying: "The father of the righteous will greatly rejoice,
and he that begetteth a wise child will have joy of him"
(*Ibid.* 24), where by "the father of the righteous" is meant
the Holy One, blessed be He, and "the begetter of a wise
child" refers to thy father here below.' R. Eleazar cited the
verse: "In thy hand I commit my spirit; thou hast redeemed
me, O Lord, thou God of truth" (Ps. XXXI, 6). 'This statement', he said, 'is somewhat surprising; for have you ever
seen a man committing anything into the hand of the
King ? But, assuredly, happy is the man who walks in the
paths of the Most Holy King and does not sin before Him.
For as soon as night falls the Tree of Death dominates the
world and the Tree of Life ascends to the height of heights.
And since the Tree of Death has sole rule of the world, all
the people in it have a foretaste of death. It is therefore
incumbent upon man to make haste and meet the Tree of
Death and deposit his soul with it, as a man deposits a
pledge with his creditor. For, although the debt exceeds the
value of the pledge, yet the creditor does not distrain on
him because he has the pledge, but otherwise he will exact
his debt. So all the souls of man are taken by the Tree of
Death in deposit, and all have a taste of death. Now although
their sins are excessive, and they do not deserve to receive back
their souls, and the Tree has really no right to give them back,[1]

---

[1] Being the attribute of Judgement.

yet they are returned to men at the moment the Tree of Life awakens in the world, to wit, the moment when dawn breaks. The Tree of Death then departs, and people come to life again by reason of the Tree of Life. It is true that many men wake during the night, but this, too, is the work of the Tree of Life. This happens in accordance with what is written, "to see if there were any man of understanding that did seek after God" (*Ibid.* XIV, 2); for thereby is removed any excuse that man might plead, saying: "Had I been in control of my soul in the night, I would have laboured in the study of the Law".' Said R. Judah: 'This is rightly explained in regard to Israel; but what about the other nations to whom we see the same thing happens ?' R. Eleazar replied: 'That is a good remark.' He then discoursed (concerning the other nations), citing the verse: "How shall I curse, whom *EL* (God) hath not cursed, and how shall I execrate, whom the Lord hath not execrated ?" (Num. XXIII, 8). 'Observe', he said, 'that the lower world is modelled on the upper world. On high there is a Right and a Left; so below there are Israel and the idolatrous nations, the former on the right, attached to the holiness of the Holy King, the latter on the left, on the side of the unclean spirit. The grades are linked one with another, [119b] all depending finally on the one at the head, and the tail has to move in accordance with the head. Balaam could avail himself of all the lower grades, but he saw that even the lowest was still guided by the head. Hence his declaration: "How shall I curse, whom *EL* hath not cursed ?", because the superior Head did not exercise rigour in those days. It is true that *El* denotes Goodness and Mercy, but it also expresses Rigour, as it says, "and *El* (God) hath indignation every day" (Ps. VII, 12). As for the compound "El-Shaddai", this signifies the God who put a limit to the universe.[1] Hence "How shall I curse, whom El hath not cursed ?". For, as the Head moves, so does the Tail.'[2] R. Eleazar wept.

[1] SHaDaY (*Shaddai*)=He who . . . enough; i.e. He who, at the proper moment, put a limit to the expanding universe at the Creation by the word of command: "Enough !", *v.* T.B., Hagigah, 12a.   [2] This is in reply to the question of R. Judah as to how men of other nations awake during the night.

He discoursed on the verse: "The sound thereof shall go like the serpents", etc. (Jer. XLVI, 22). 'At the present time,' he said, 'when Israel is in exile, he is assuredly as the serpent. For when the serpent presses its head into the sand its tail flies upwards, being master, as it were, and lashing out at anyone near him; so Israel in exile has his head bowed down into the dust whilst the tail obtains the mastery. But although the head is bowed down into the sand, it is the same head, and that directs and rules the movements of the tail; and so at the present time it is indeed the other nations, who are attached to the tail, that rise on high, have the mastery and are lashing out, whilst the head is bowed down into the dust, as it says, "The virgin of Israel is fallen, she shall no more rise" (Amos V, 2); yet it is the head that directs the tail in its motions, as it says: "They made me keeper of the vineyards" (S.S. I, 6), to wit, of the idolatrous nations, which are the tail.' R. Judah then came and kissed the hands of R. Eleazar, saying: 'Had I never asked you any other question but only this, my gain would already be great in that now I know how the sway of the idolatrous nations is being directed. Happy is the portion of Israel, in regard to whom it is written: "For the Lord hath chosen Jacob unto himself, and Israel for his own treasure" (Ps. CXXXV, 4).' R. Eleazar asked him what was meant by "for his own treasure". R. Judah replied: 'The three patriarchs are called "treasure", both on high and here below; so are the priests, the Levites, and the Israelites; it is all one, and this is indicated in the words, "Then ye shall be mine own treasure from among all peoples" (Ex. XIX, 5).'

THEN THE TENT OF MEETING, WITH THE CAMP OF THE LEVITES. . . . THE STANDARD OF THE CAMP OF EPHRAIM, ACCORDING TO THEIR HOSTS, SHALL BE ON THE WEST SIDE. This was because the Shekinah is in the west.[1] In this regard it is written: "And he blessed them that day, saying, By thee shall Israel bless, saying. . . . And he set Ephraim before Manasseh" (Gen. XLVIII, 20). It is not written "shall be blessed", but "shall bless", as much as to

[1] *v.* T.B. Baba Bathra, 25*a*.

say: Holy Israel will not bless the world save by invoking
Thee,[1] who art in the west. This shows that Jacob then saw
the Shekinah. It is true that it is written, "the eyes of Israel
were dim for age, so that he could not see" (*Ibid.* 10), but it
also says, "putting his hands crosswise" (*Ibid.* 14). That is,
he first raised up his right hand, but the Shekinah turned it
toward Ephraim, and having caught the scent of the Shekinah, as it were, over his head, he said: By Thee will Israel
bless. He saw then that the Shekinah is in the west. The
reason for this, as has been explained, is that She may be
between north and south, in an attitude of nuptial union,
with the north supporting Her beneath Her head and the
south embracing Her. So says Scripture: "Let his left hand
be under my head, and his right hand embrace me". There
is a dictum: "Whoever recites the Psalm *Praise of David*
(Ps. CXLV) thrice daily may be assured that he is destined
for the world to come".[2] [120*a*] This is because thereby we
symbolize daily the union that is effected between north
and south. Thus in the morning a man takes upon himself
the yoke of heaven by reciting the Psalm headed "Praise of
David", followed by ten "Hallelujahs", to wit, the five
Psalms each commencing with "Hallelujah" and ending
with "Hallelujah", with the very last of them containing
ten times the expression "praise ye" (*Ibid.* CL). Then
follows the Song of Moses, which contains all praises, and
whereby a man takes upon himself the yoke of the Holy
Kingdom. Then at the end of the Service he places Her in
Ḥesed at the end of the prayer proper, to be sanctified
therewith. Then the same Psalm is repeated at *Minḥa*
(Afternoon Prayer), when Vigour is in the ascendant and
Rigour prevails alongside the south. Thus unification is
effected all along between north and south; and whoever
co-ordinates daily his prayers in this way is assuredly destined
for the world to come. Thus ON THE WEST SIDE SHALL
BE THE STANDARD OF THE CAMP OF EPHRAIM, that is,
lying between north and south; with the standard of the
camp of Reuben on the south, and the standard of the camp
of Dan on the north, Ephraim is found on the west between

[1] Referring to the Shekinah.   [2] T.B. Berakoth, 4*b*.

the two, between north and south, all on the heavenly pattern. The following is a mystery known to those who inhabit the south, and has been sent to us by our "brethren who arrange the lamps". 'That ye may effect unification by means of the intertwined mysteries that are of the shape of the celestial intertwining, accept upon yourselves the first thing every day the yoke of the Holy Kingdom; thereby will ye enter into the holy intertwining of the south. These encircle the sides of the world until they become bound up in one knot, but keep firm hold of the south and there abide.' R. Eleazar then asked his father, R. Simeon, for a mnemonic suggestive of this method of effecting unification. In reply his father mentioned the manner in which the priest goes round the altar, regarding which the Mishnah-Code says: "And [the priest] came to the south-eastern, then to the north-eastern, the north-western, and the south-western horn".[1] R. Eleazar then asked: 'How could one come to the south before taking upon oneself the yoke of the Kingdom of Heaven?' R. Simeon, in reply, said: 'Just so. It says [literally] "and he came to the horn of south-east", that is, first to the horn, symbolic of the yoke of the Kingdom of Heaven, and then to the south-east, symbolic of the Tree of Life. . . . And whoever accomplishes [120b] unification in the proper way as just indicated, happy is his portion in this world and in the world to come, and, moreover, in such a one the Holy One, blessed be He, glorifies Himself. Concerning such a one, Scripture says: "And he said unto me, Thou art my servant, Israel, in whom I will be glorified" (Isa. XLIX, 3).'

R. Simeon began a discourse, citing the verse: "[A Psalm] of David. Unto thee, O Lord, do I lift my soul. O my God, in thee have I trusted", etc. (Ps. XXV, 1–22). 'Why did David', he asked, 'compose this Psalm in an alphabetic acrostic, and besides, why is the letter *Vau* absent therefrom? Why, again, has this Psalm been prescribed as the "falling-on-one's-face prayer"?[2] Now the solution of all

---

[1] Mishnah Zebaḥim v, 3. [2] This in accordance with the Sephardi ritual. *v.* Common Prayer Book, ed. Gaster. The Ashkenazi ritual prescribes Psalm VI.

this is based on an esoteric doctrine known to the Companions, which is as follows. When night falls the Nether-tree, from which death issues, spreads its branches so as to cover the whole of the universe. And so darkness prevails, and all the people of the world have a foretaste of death. And every man hastens to surrender his soul into His Hand as a trust. And inasmuch as He takes them in trust He returns each one to her owner in the morning. Thus, as each morning arrives, man, having received back his deposit, ought to render blessings to the Holy One, blessed be He, who is trustworthy above all. Then, having risen, a man goes to Synagogue, adorns himself with phylacteries and enwraps himself in a garment provided with fringes, then he first purifies himself by the [recital of the regulations concerning the] sacrifices, then follows the recital of the hymns of David by which he accepts upon himself the yoke of the Kingdom of Heaven. After that comes the prayer said sitting, followed by the prayer said standing, the two being knit together into one. Observe the inwardness of the matter, to wit, that although prayer is performed by speech and verbal utterance, its efficacy springs primarily from the preparatory actions performed. First action, then prayer—utterance corresponding to that action. Thus a man has in the first place to cleanse himself [by ablution], then accepts upon himself the Heavenly Yoke symbolized in the act of spreading over his head the fringed robe. Then he makes tight on himself the knot expressive of unification, to wit, the phylacteries, consisting of the phylactery of the head and that of the hand, the latter on the left hand over against the heart, in consonance with the Scriptural verses, saying: "Let his left hand be under my head", etc. (S.S. ii, 6), and "Set me as a seal upon thy heart, as a seal upon thy arm" (*Ibid*. viii, 6). So far the preparatory actions. Then corresponding to these, man, in entering Synagogue, first cleanses himself by the [recital of the regulations concerning the] sacrifices; then he accepts upon himself the Heavenly Yoke by the recital of the hymns of King David. Then comes the prayer said sitting, which corresponds to the arm-phylactery, followed by the prayer said standing, which corresponds to the head-phylactery. So prayer is made up of both action and speech, and when the action is faulty speech does not find a spot to rest in; such prayer is not prayer, and the man offering it is defective in the upper world and the lower. The main thing is to perform the act and to give utterance to words in co-ordination with it; this is perfect prayer. Woe to him who spoils his prayer, the worship of his Master. Of such a one Scripture says: "When ye come to appear before me . . . yea, when ye make many prayers, I will not hear" (Isa. I, 12–15). Observe this. Both upper and lower worlds are blessed through the man who performs his prayer in a union of action and word, and thus effects a unification. And so with the conclusion of the prayer said standing, a man has to assume the appearance of one who has departed this world in that he has separated himself from the Tree of Life. Now he has to be gathered towards that Tree of Death and fall on his face and say: "Unto thee, O Lord, do I lift up my soul. . . ." As much as to say: "Before, [121*a*] I gave Thee my soul in trust, now that I have effected unification and performed act and word in befitting manner and have confessed my sins, behold, here is my soul which I surrender to Thee completely." A man must then look upon himself as having departed this world, his soul having been surrendered to the region of death. This is the reason that that Psalm does not contain the letter *Vau*, since that letter is symbolic of the Tree of Life, whereas that Psalm is concerned with the Tree of Death. For there are sins which are beyond forgiveness until a man departs this world, of which Scripture says: "Surely this iniquity shall not be expiated by you till ye die" (Isa. XXII, 14), so that man has given himself over, as it were, to death, and delivered his soul into that region, not merely in trust as during the night, but as though he had actually departed this world. This service must be performed by the man with full devotion of heart, and then the Holy One, blessed be He, will take pity on him and forgive his sins. Happy is the man who knows how to persuade, as it were, and how to offer worship to his Master with devotion of will and heart. Woe to him who comes to persuade his Master with an absent heart and without true intent in the way described in the words: "But they beguiled him with their mouth, and lied unto him with their tongue. For their heart was not steadfast with him" (Isa. LXXVIII, 36–37). Such a one may recite: "Unto Thee, O Lord, do I lift up my soul . . .", but all his words proceed from an absent heart; and this causes him to be removed from the world before his allotted days, at a moment when that Tree bestirs itself in the world to execute judgement. Hence it is incumbent on man to cleave heart and soul to his Master, and not to come to Him with deceitfulness. Of such a one Scripture says: "He that speaketh falsehood shall not be established before mine eyes" (*Ibid.* CI, 7). Being interpreted, this means that when a man prepares himself for this, but with a heart remote from the Holy One, blessed be He, a Voice proclaims, saying: He will not be established before Mine eyes. All the more is this so when a man comes to effect unification of the Divine Name, but does not do so in the proper manner. Happy is the portion of the righteous in this world and in the world to come. Of them it is written, "and they shall come, and shall see my glory", etc. (Isa. LXVI, 18); and again, "Surely the righteous shall give thanks unto thy name", etc. (Ps. CXL, 14).' R. Eleazar then approached and kissed his father's hand, saying: 'Had I not come into the world for aught else but to hear these words it would have sufficed me.' Said R. Judah: 'Happy is our portion and the portion of Israel who cleave to the Holy One, blessed be He. So Scripture says: "But ye that did cleave", etc. (Deut. IV, 4); and again, "Thy people also shall be all righteous", etc. (Isa. LX, 21).'

NASO

Numbers IV, 21–VII, 89

AND THE LORD SPAKE UNTO MOSES, SAYING: TAKE THE SUM OF THE SONS OF GERSHON, ETC. R. Abba began a discourse on the verse: "Happy is the man unto whom the Lord counteth not iniquity, and in whose spirit there is no guile" (Ps. XXXII, 2). 'The two halves of this verse', he said, 'do not seem to hang together,[1] but it has been explained thus. At the time of the Afternoon Prayer (*Minḥa*) Rigour prevails over the world. For it was Isaac who instituted Afternoon Prayer, and so supreme Force prevails then and the Left aspect is diffused. This continues until night bestirs itself. Then all the keepers of the outer gates of the universe bestir themselves and spread about, and all mankind have a foretaste of death. At the precise moment of midnight the Left aspect bestirs itself again as before, the Divine Rose[2] diffuses a sweet odour, and breaks forth into loud praise-giving, then ascends and rests Her head on the Left Arm, [121*b*] which is extended to receive Her. Then proclamation goes forth into the world, announcing that it is the time for awakening and chanting praises to the King. A chorus of praises then breaks forth, accompanied by a sweet odour permeating the whole. Happy is the portion of whoever awakens then to effect this espousal. When morning comes round and the Right aspect awakens and embraces Her, then the wedlock is complete. Observe that when mankind lie asleep and experience a foretaste of death, the soul of each ascends on high and to an assigned region. There she is examined concerning all the actions she performed during the day. These are recorded on a tablet. Indeed, the soul then gives evidence concerning man's works, and concerning each word that issued from his mouth. Should that word be an appropriate word, a holy word of Torah study or of prayer, it will cleave its way

[1] The first half implies that there is iniquity in him, the second that there is not. [2] i.e. the Shekinah.

through the heavens until it reaches an assigned place. There it halts until night falls, when the soul ascends, seizes that word and presents it to the King. An improper word, however, a word uttered by an evil tongue, goes up to its assigned spot, where it is put on record, charging the man with the commission of a sin. Of this Scripture says: "Keep the doors of thy mouth from her that lieth in thy bosom"[1] (Micah VII, 5). Hence the Psalm says: "Happy is the man unto whom the Lord counteth not iniquity", to wit, the man "in whose spirit there is no guile".' [122a]

R. Isaac and R. Judah were walking together on the road leading from Usha to Lud. Said R. Judah: 'Let us discourse on the Torah whilst walking.' R. Judah then cited the verse: "And if a man shall open a pit, or if a man shall dig a pit . . . the owner of the pit shall make it good", etc. (Ex. XXI, 33-34). 'If that man', he said, 'has to make good, how much more so he who brings the whole world into disfavour by his sins. And I do, indeed, find it strange, that having brought the world into disfavour a man can make restitution by penitence, as Scripture says: WHEN A MAN OR WOMAN SHALL COMMIT ANY SIN . . . THEN THEY SHALL CONFESS THEIR . . . AND HE SHALL MAKE RESTITUTION, ETC. The truth, however, is that through man's penitence the Almighty Himself, as it were, rectifies on high the wrong committed, and thus the world is put right again.' R. Isaac then cited the verse: "In thy distress, when all these things are come upon thee, in the end of days, thou wilt return. . . . For the Lord thy God is a merciful God", etc. (Deut. IV, 30–31). 'We learn from here', he said, 'that penitence is of most effect before Rigour lights upon the world. For once it does so it strongly entrenches itself, and who can remove it ? Indeed, [122b] it will not depart until restitution is made, followed by penitence; and then only is the world again put right. Now the phrase "in the end of days" points to the Community of Israel who is in exile and shares Israel's distress. For this reason, the Holy One, blessed be He, although he has sent Rigour into the world, desires that Israel should repent so that

[1] i.e. the soul.

He may do good to them in this world and in the world to come. For nothing can withstand the power of repentance. Proper repentance is only effected by a surrender of one's soul, so that she is taken away in a state of repentance. One sinner in the world brings about the destruction of many. Woe to the sinner, woe to his neighbour! We see this in the case of Jonah. Through his refusing to carry the message of his Master, how many people would have been destroyed on his account in the sea! So they all turned on him and carried out on him the sentence of sea-drowning, whereby they were all saved. The Holy One, blessed be He, however, had mercy on him and so brought about the deliverance of multitudes of people. This happened after Jonah returned to his Master out of the midst of his affliction, as we read: "I called out of my affliction unto the Lord, and he answered me" (Jonah II, 3).' [124a]

IF ANY MAN'S WIFE (lit. man, man, if his wife) GO ASIDE, AND COMMIT A TRESPASS (lit. trespass a trespass) AGAINST HIM, ETC. R. Eleazar said: 'Why twice "man, man"? It speaks of a man who has behaved as a man should, following the admonition: "Drink waters out of thy own cistern", etc. (Prov. v, 15). Why, again, the double expression "trespass a trespass"? It points, on the one hand, to the Community of Israel, and, on the other, to her Spouse. We thus read further: THEN SHALL THE MAN BRING HIS WIFE UNTO THE PRIEST, for the reason that the priest is the "best man", so to speak, of the Matrona. Again, she has to be brought to the priest, although in regard to any sacrifice we read: "And he shall kill the bullock before the Lord" (Lev. I, 5), signifying that a layman ought to kill it and not a priest, he being forbidden[1] to execute judgement so as not to impair the region to which he belongs. Here, however, the priest alone is the fit person for the performance, he being the "best man" of the Matrona, and all the women of Israel are blessed by the medium of the Community of Israel. Therefore it is that the woman here on

[1] This is contrary to the Mishnah, which does not forbid, but makes it optional for the priest.

earth at her marriage has conferred upon her seven bene-
dictions, in that she is bound up with the Community of
Israel. It is the priest alone, and no outsider, who arranges
all the service of the Matrona and attends closely to all that
is needed. Hence the priest functions here, and no other.
And, in fact, it is not judgement that the priest executes in
this matter, but, on the contrary, he promotes peace in the
world and increases lovingkindness. For should the woman
be found innocent, the priest will have promoted peace
between them, and, moreover, she will conceive a male
child,[1] which is also a means of bringing peace. Should she,
however, not be found innocent, it is not the priest that
will have doomed her, but it will be the Divine Name
which she invoked falsely that will have probed and doomed
her. Observe that the priest does not obtrude himself into
the affair, but when she presents herself before him to clear
herself [124*b*] he questions her once and twice, and then
performs a ceremony in order to restore peace. The priest
writes the Divine Name once in a straightforward way and
then upside down,[2] symbolic of Mercy and Rigour intertwined. If she be proved innocent the letters signifying
Mercy remain, and those pointing to Rigour disappear. But
if she be not as she should be, Mercy departs and Rigour is
left, and judgement is executed.' R. Eleazar adduced here
the verse: "And when they came to Marah, they could not
drink the waters of Marah, for they were bitter. . . . There
he made for them a statute and an ordinance, and there he
proved them" (Ex. xv, 23–25). 'I wonder', he said, 'how
it is that people take so little trouble to understand the
words of the Torah. Here, for example, one should really
inquire what is the point of the words "There he made for
them . . . and there he proved them". But the inward significance of the water mentioned here is this. The Egyptians
claimed to be the parents of the children of Israel, and
many among the Israelites suspected their wives in the
matter. So the Holy One, blessed be He, brought them to
that place, where He desired to put them to the test. Thus

[1] Cf. T.B. Sotah, 26*a*.   [2] $\overline{\text{ΛΗΛΗ}}$
$\overline{\text{YHVH}}$

when Moses cried to the Lord he was told: Write down the
Divine Name, cast it into the water, and let all of them,
women and men, be tested, so that no evil report should
remain in regard to My children; and until they all be
probed I will not cause My Name to rest upon them.
Straightway "the Lord shewed him a tree, and he cast it
into the waters", the tree being thus identical with the
Divine Name the priest has to write for the testing of the
wife of an Israelite. Thus "There he made for them a statute
and an ordinance, and there he proved them". Now it may
be asked: This was properly done for the women, but why
include the men ? But, indeed, the men also had to be
probed to show that they had not contaminated themselves
with Egyptian women, in the same way as the women had
to be probed to show that they had kept themselves uncon-
taminated by Egyptian men, all the time they were among
them. And all, male and female, were proved to be pure,
were found to be the seed of Israel, holy and pure. Then [125*a*]
the Holy One, blessed be He, caused His Name to dwell
among them. Hence assuredly it was by the waters "there
that he . . . proved them". Similarly here it is through water
that the priest proves the woman, and through the Divine
Name.'

'AND OF THE DUST THAT IS ON THE FLOOR OF THE
TABERNACLE. We find it written: "all are of the dust, and
all return to dust" (Eccl. III, 20). There is a teaching concerning this, saying that even the orb of the sun is of the
dust, all the more so then the sons of men.' Said R. Jose:
'If it were written here "and of the dust" and no more, this
remark would be relevant; but since it says, "and of the
dust that is on the floor of the tabernacle", it seems to
point to something else. Indeed, it points to the verse,
saying: "He makes his sword in the form of dust" (Isa. XLI,
2). This verse speaks of the archers and catapult throwers,
symbolic of rigorous judgement. Similarly here "the floor
of the tabernacle", which is connected with elements underneath. The priest then puts it into the water, "the water
of bitterness that causes the curse". This refers to the

Divine Name when it is in Rigour, and for this reason the waters of the sea are bitter. For the Sacred Sea has many sweet rivers flowing into it, yet since it presents the world's judgement its waters are bitter, since universal death is attached to it. Yet when these waters flow outwards they are sweet. The sea, besides, exhibits a variety of colours. Now it is when the Serpent injects into it its venom that its waters become bitter and accursed; and therefore the priest has to go through his performance below, and recite an adjuration, so that judgement may be executed. If the woman is proved pure, these waters enter her body, [125b] turn into sweet waters, act as a cleansing force, and remain there until she becomes pregnant. Their effect is that a male child is born, one comely and pure and without any blemish. But if not, these waters enter her, causing her to smell the odour of the venom, and are transmuted into a serpent. Her punishment is thus of the same nature as her sin, and her shame is openly revealed. Happy is the portion of Israel in whom the Holy One, blessed be He, delights and whom He desires to purify.'

R. Hizkiah discoursed on the verse: "Thy wife shall be as a fruitful vine in the innermost parts of thy house" (Ps. cxxviii, 3). 'As a vine cannot receive any graft but of its own kind, so a woman in Israel, after the example of the turtle dove, only accepts her own spouse. She is thus fruitful, spreading her branches on all sides. And where ? "In the innermost parts of thy house", and not abroad, in the market place, so as not to be false to the supreme covenant. Of the false wife Solomon says: "She forsaketh the lord of her youth, and forgetteth the covenant of her God" (Prov. ii, 17), indicating the place called "covenant" to which she is attached. This is the meaning of "the innermost parts of thy house".' R. Hizkiah further said: 'Cursed be the man who allows his wife to let the hair of her head be seen. This is one of the rules of modesty in the house. A woman who exposes her hair for self-adornment brings poverty on her household, renders her children of no account in their generation, and causes an evil spirit to abide on her house. If this is so when the woman does this in the house, how

much more is it when in the open road; and ever so much more so does all this result from another kind of shamelessness.'
Said R. Judah: 'The hair of the head [126a] of a woman being exposed leads to Hair of another kind being exposed and impaired. Hence a woman should not let her hair be seen, even by the beams of her house, much less in the open. Observe that as the rule is most strict in the case of a man's hair,[1] so is it with a woman's. Consider the harm a woman's hair brings about. It brings a curse on her husband, it causes poverty, it causes something besides to happen to her household, it causes the inferiority of her children. May the Merciful One deliver us from their impudence! A woman thus should cover her hair in the four corners of her house. When she does this, then "thy children like olive plants" (Ps. *ibid.*). As the olive does not shed its leaves either in winter or summer, but ever retains its superiority over other trees, so her children will excel all other children; her husband, moreover, will receive blessings from above and from below, will be blessed with riches, with children and children's children. So the Psalm continues: "Behold, surely, thus shall the man be blessed. . . . And see thy children's children. Peace be upon Israel" (*Ibid.* 4–6).'

WHEN EITHER MAN OR WOMAN SHALL CLEARLY UTTER A VOW, ETC. R. Eleazar began a discourse on the verse: "Wherefore, when I came, was there no man?" etc. (Isa. L, 2). 'How beloved', he said, 'are Israel before the Holy One, blessed be He, in that wherever they dwell He is found among them, for He never withdraws His love from them. We find it written: "And let them make me a sanctuary, that I may dwell among them" (Ex. xxv, 8). That is, any sanctuary whatever, inasmuch as any Synagogue, wherever situated, is called sanctuary, and the Shekinah hastens to the Synagogue (before the worshippers). Happy is the man who is of the first ten to enter Synagogue, since they form something complete, and are the first to be sanctified by the Shekinah. But it is necessary that the ten should come together at the same time and not in sections, so as

---

[1] The reference apparently is to the Nazirite.

not to delay the completion of the body in its members. So did the Holy One, blessed be He, make man all at one time, and establish all his members in one act. So we read: "Hath he not made thee and established thee ?" (Deut. XXXII, 6). So when the Shekinah goes early to the Synagogue she desires ten to be there at the same time so that a completed body should be formed with every member in its place. Those that come later are the mere "adornments of the body". But when the people do not arrive together the Holy One, blessed be He, exclaims: "Wherefore, when I came, was there no man ?"[1] For inasmuch as the single members are not together there is no complete body, and so that is "no man". Observe that the moment the body is made complete here below a supernal holiness comes and enters that body, and so the lower world is in truth transformed after the pattern of the upper world. Thus it is incumbent on all not to open their mouths to talk of worldly matters, seeing that Israel then are at their completest and holiest. Happy is their portion !

'WHEN A MAN SHALL CLEARLY UTTER (*yaflee*=shall separate) A VOW; that is, when a man shall place himself apart from the rest of the world, to sanctify himself on the pattern on high and thus to be found perfect. For whoever sets out to purify himself is assisted from above.[2] When one wishes to sanctify himself, they spread on him a sanctity derived from that of the Holy One, blessed be He. . . .'[3]

R. Abba discoursed on the verse: "[A Psalm] of David bless the Lord, O my soul, and all that is within me, bless his holy name" (Ps. CIII, 1). 'How much', he said, 'it behoves a man to study and reflect on the service of his Master ! For every day a proclamation goes forth, saying: "How long, ye thoughtless, will ye love thoughtlessness ?' etc. (Prov. I, 22); "Return, ye backsliding children, I will heal your backslidings" (Jer. III, 22), but there is no one who inclines his ear; the Torah makes proclamation before the people and none pay regard. Observe this. A man walks

[1] *v.* T.B. Berachoth, 6b. [2] *v.* T.B. Yoma, 38b. [3] There is here a lacuna in the text.

N

about in the world thinking that it is his perpetual possession and that he will abide therein from generation to generation. But even while he walks he is being put in chains; while he sits he is being tried in the conclave among the other prisoners. If there be an advocate on his side he is delivered from punishment. So Scripture says: "If there be for him an angel, an intercessor, one among a thousand, to vouch for man's uprightness; then he is gracious unto him, and saith", etc. (Job XXXIII, 23). Who [126b] is his advocate ? It is man's good works that stand by him at the moment of need. Should no advocate be found for him, he is declared guilty and is sentenced to be removed from the world. At that moment, whilst lying bound in the chains of the King, lifting his eyes he sees two beings near him who write down all that he did in this world and every word that ever went forth from his mouth. Of all this he has to give an account, as it is written: "For, lo, he that formeth the mountains, and createth the wind, and declareth unto man what is his thought (*siho*=speech)".[1] He admits all this, since the works which he did are there present to testify against him and to be inscribed in his presence; they do not leave him until the time that he is adjudged guilty on their account in the other world. Observe that all a man's works in this world are ready to testify against him: they do not vanish. And when he is led to his grave they all go before him; and three heralds, one in front, one to his right, and one to his left, proclaim: "Behold So-and-so who rebelled against his Master, who rebelled on high and here below, who rebelled against the Torah and against its commandments. Behold his actions, behold his utterances. It were better he had not been created !" When he arrives at his burial place, all the dead quake in their places on account of him, saying: "Woe, woe, that this man is buried among us !" His deeds and words precede him, enter the grave and stand over the body, whilst his spirit hovers to and fro mourning over the body. So soon as the man is hidden away in the tomb, [the angel] Dumah advances accompanied by three judges who are appointed to sit in judgement over the newly-buried; these

[1] *v.* T.B. Hagigah, 5*b*.

hold in their hands fiery rods and submit to examination the
spirit and the body together. Woe to [the victim of] that
judgement ! Woe for his deeds at the time when he is caught
in the fetters of the King, if no advocate is found on his
behalf ! The King's officer advances towards his feet holding
in his hand a sharp sword. The man lifts up his eyes, and
sees the walls of his house in a blaze of fire, kindled by
himself. Presently he sees before him one full of eyes all
over,[1] and clothed in fiery garments. (This may indeed be
so, inasmuch as many a man meets an angel in the road,
whilst other passers-by do not see him.) You may ask, since
it is written, "Who maketh spirits (winds)[2] his angels"
(Ps. CIV), how can an angel be visible ? It has, however, been
explained that when an angel descends to earth he assumes
the guise of man, and in this guise he makes himself visible
to this man or the other. Otherwise mankind could not
endure any sight of him. All the more does this apply to
this one, to whom all the world must come. He instils three
drops with his sword, and so on, as the Companions have
expounded elsewhere. At the sight of him the man's body
falls a-trembling, and his heart throbs, this being the
king of the whole body, and the spirit passes along through
the members of the body, taking leave of each one in turn,
like a man taking leave of his neighbour when departing for
another place. Woe, it exclaims, for the man's deeds ! There
is no remedy for such a man unless he repents in time. Until
the last moment the man is in fear, attempts to hide himself,
but is not able. Seeing his helplessness he opens his eyes and
gazes at the Angel of Death with open eyes, and surrenders
himself, body and soul. It is the moment of the Great Judgement to which man is subjected to in this world. As the
spirit makes its journey through the body and takes leave of
each separate member and parts from it, that member
immediately dies. When the spirit is about to depart, having
thus taken leave of the whole body, the Shekinah stands
over the body and the spirit straightway flies off. Happy is
the portion of whoever cleaves to Her ! Woe to the sinners

[1] i.e. the Angel of Death, v. T.B. Abodah Zaroh, 20b.   [2] *Ruḥoth* =
winds or spirits.

who keep afar from Her ! Indeed, what a number of ordeals
man has to undergo in passing out of this world ! First
comes the ordeal from on high, at the moment when the
spirit leaves the body, just mentioned. Then comes his ordeal
when his actions and utterances precede him and make
proclamation concerning him. Another ordeal is when he
enters the tomb. [127a] One more is in the tomb itself. He
afterwards undergoes an ordeal at the hands of the worms.
There is then the ordeal of Gehinnom. And finally there is
the ordeal undergone by the spirit when it roams to and fro
through the world, finding no resting-place until its tasks
are accomplished. Man has thus to pass through seven ordeals.
Hence it behoves man while in this world to fear his Master
and minutely to examine daily his works and to repent of
any misdeeds before his Maker. So King David, in reflecting
on the ordeals man has to undergo on departing this world,
made haste to exclaim, "Bless the Lord, O my soul" (Ps.
CIII, 1); to wit: Do it before thou leavest this world, and
whilst thou art in the body; "and all that is within me, bless
his holy name" (*Ibid.*), in other words: Ye bodily members
who are associated with the spirit, whilst that spirit is with
you, make haste to bless the Divine Name in advance of
the time when ye will be unable to bless Him and offer up
thanks. Observe then the words: *When a man shall separate
himself by uttering a vow, the vow of a Nazirite*, etc., referring
to him who makes haste whilst in this world, to consecrate
himself to his Master. *He shall abstain from wine and strong
drink . . . nor eat fresh grapes*, etc. The question here arises,
why should the Nazirite, in addition to wine, be forbidden
also grapes, seeing that the priest, who is also enjoined to
"drink no wine nor strong drink" (Lev. x, 9), is yet permitted
to eat grapes. There is, however, a recondite idea involved
in this. It is a known thing that the tree of Adam's transgression was a vine, the fruits of which, wine, strong drink
and grapes, belong together to the side of the left. Hence the
Nazirite has to keep altogether away from them. The Book of
Rab Hamnuna the Elder supports this exposition. There we
read in reference to the injunction, *he shall let the locks of hair
of his head grow long*, that the letting of the hair of his head and

beard grow long and the abstention from wine and strong drink and grapes is for the reason that all these belong to the left side and they are, moreover, unhairy: the wine is the Superior Mother, the strong drink is a product of the wine and is unhairy. It belongs to the region of the Levites, and hence the Levites were enjoined to "cause a razor to pass over all their flesh" (Num. viii, 7). The grapes are the Lower Mother, which gathers in herself both the wine and the strong drink. The Nazirite therefore has to abstain from the whole of the left side, so that none of their works should be seen in him. And the grapes grow no hair nor beard, symbolic, as it were, of the female, who has to remove her hair before having relations with the male, and who is by nature beardless. Hence the Nazirite has to let grow his hair, including his beard. Now Samson, although a Nazirite of God, was punished because he married the daughter of a strange god, so that instead of associating himself with his own he debased his holiness by mingling with the daughter of a strange god. It is held by some that he will have no portion in the world to come, for the reason that he said: "Let me die with the Philistines" (Jud. xvi, 30), and thus placed his portion among those of the Philistines. [127b] Now in regard to the Levites it says: "And thus shalt thou do unto them to *cleanse* them: sprinkle the water of purification upon them, and let them cause a razor to pass over all their flesh" (Num. viii, 7). After the hair has been removed and all the details performed, the Levite is designated "pure", but not "holy". But the Nazirite, having abstained from the side of rigour, is designated "holy" and not simply "pure". So Scripture says: *All the days of his vow of Naziriteship . . . in which he consecrateth himself unto the Lord, he shall be holy, he shall let the locks of the hair of his head grow long.* This is explained by the passage, "and the hair of his head [was] like pure wool"[1] (Dan. vii, 9), inasmuch as the Nazirite in this regard resembles the celestial pattern.' R. Judah said: 'It is indeed by his hair that the Nazirite is distinguished as holy. This is in allusion to "his locks are curled" (S.S. v, 11).' A teaching of R. Simeon says: 'Did men but understand

---

[1] i.e. white, the symbol of mercy.

the inner significance of the Scriptural passages regarding
the hair, they would acquire a knowledge of their Master
by means of the Superior Wisdom.'[1] [145a]

SPEAK UNTO AARON AND UNTO HIS SONS, SAYING:
ON THIS WISE YE SHALL BLESS, ETC. R. Isaac quoted
here the verse: "But the grace (ḥesed) of the Lord is from
everlasting to everlasting upon them that fear him, and his
righteousness unto children's children" (Ps. CII, 17). 'How
great', he said, 'is the virtue of fear in the esteem of the
Almighty, inasmuch as fear embraces humility, and humility
embraces a state of grace (ḥ'siduth)! Hence, whoever is
possessed of fear of sin is possessed of all those virtues;
but whoever does not fear Heaven possesses neither humility
nor the state of grace. There is a teaching: Whoever emerges
from the stage of fear and robes himself in humility, attains
thereby a higher degree, as it says, "The fear of the Lord is
the heel of humility"[2] (Prov. XXII, 4). Whoever is possessed
of the fear of Heaven is rewarded with humility, and he who
is possessed of humility is rewarded with the state of grace;
so that fear of the Heaven leads to both of these. We have
been taught: Whoever has attained the degree of grace is
designated "angel" [145b] of the Lord of hosts, as we read:
"For the priest's lips should keep knowledge, and they
should seek the law at his mouth; for he is the angel of the
Lord of hosts" (Malachi II, 7). Wherewith did the priest
merit to be called "angel of the Lord of hosts"?' Said R.
Judah: 'As the angel of the Lord of hosts is a priest on high,
so is the priest below an angel of the Lord of hosts. The
angel of the Lord of hosts on high is Michael the great
prince who issues from the celestial Grace (ḥesed) and is the
celestial High-priest. So the High-priest on earth is called
"angel of the Lord of hosts" by reason that he belongs to
the side of Grace. He has attained that degree through fear
of God. Scripture thus says: "And the grace of the Lord is
from everlasting to everlasting (lit. world to world) upon
them that fear him". What means "from world to world"?

[1] Here follows in the text the *Idra Rabba* ; v. Appendix. [2] E.V. "The
reward of humility and the fear of the Lord is . . ."

Said R. Isaac: 'As it has been established in the exposition of the Holy Assembly;[1] it alludes to the two worlds.' R. Ḥiya objected: 'If so, it should have been written "from *the* world to *the* world".' Said R. Eleazar: 'It is an allusion to the celestial Adam and the earthly Adam. "Upon those who fear Him", inasmuch as whoever fears sin is called "Adam" (Man).' Said R. Judah: 'But there is a teaching that the term "Adam" signifies the conjunction of male and female ?' R. Eleazar in reply said: 'Assuredly so. He who achieves for himself the union of male and female is called Adam, and in this way has the fear of sin. He attains, moreover, to the virtue of humility, and even the degree of grace. Contrariwise, he who remains without that union possesses neither fear nor humility nor the state of grace. So Scripture says: "For I have said: The world is built by Grace" (*Ibid.* LXXXIX, 3), to wit, by Adam, who denotes the union of male and female. Again: "And the grace of the Lord is from world to world" is an allusion to the priests who proceed from the side of Grace and have obtained this inheritance that descends from the upper world to the lower. "Upon those who fear him", to wit, the priests here below, regarding whom it is written, "and [he shall] make atonement for himself, and for his house" (Lev. XVI, 6), by means of which house (i.e. wife) he falls within the category of Adam. The Psalmist continues: "and his righteousness unto children's children", in allusion to the priest who was rewarded with children's children. Hence the teaching: A priest who has no wife is forbidden to perform the service, as it is written, "and he shall make atonement for himself and for his *house*".' R. Isaac said that the reason is because the Shekinah does not abide with one who is not married, and the priest in especial must be one with whom the Shekinah abides. Along with the Shekinah there rests on the priests *Ḥesed* (Grace), and they are called *ḥasidim* (grace-endowed), and as such it behoves them to bless the people. So Scripture says: "And thy saints (*ḥesidim*) shall bless thee" (Ps. CXLV, 10); also, "Thy Thummim and thy Urim be with thy saintly one (*ḥasid*)".

[1] The *Idra Rabba*.

' "On this wise ye shall bless", to wit, in the holy tongue; "on this wise", to wit, in fear and in humility.' R. Abba said: 'We have learned that *KoH* (on this wise) is the name of the Power whence all judgements come into action. [146a] But when *Ḥesed* (Grace) is joined to *Koh* the latter is sweetened. Hence the priest, who is derived from *Ḥesed*, is entrusted with *Koh* to have it blessed and sweetened. Thus the command was "On this wise (*KoH*) ye shall bless", that is, by the influence of *Ḥesed* ye shall fill with blessing and make sweet the power of *Koh* in its relation to Israel, so that Rigour should not prevail.

'It says: "On this wise ye shall bless the children of Israel, saying (*amor*) unto them". It is not written "ye shall say unto them", parallel to "ye shall bless".' R. Judah taught that we have therefore to construe it thus: If they will be worthy, then [the blessing is] *to them*, but if not, then there is merely *saying*.

R. Isaac discoursed on the verse: "And I Daniel alone saw the vision; for the men that were with me saw not the vision", etc. (Dan. x, 7). 'There is a tradition', he said, 'that those men were prophets, to wit, Haggai, Zechariah and Malachi, whereas Daniel himself was not a prophet. There was thus a reversal of the relation of holy and common. For they, the holy men, were seized with fear and were not able to see the vision, whereas he, a common man, did see without fear. This is explained, however, by the verse: "Though a host should encamp against me, my heart shall not fear; though war should rise up against me, in this (*zoth*) I will be confident" (Ps. xxvi, 3). The word "this" (*zoth*) is an allusion to the Providence presiding over David's inheritance that will ensure it for him and will execute vengeance on his behalf. There is a teaching that the Holy One, blessed be He, prepared for David a Holy Chariot, adorned with the holy superior crowns of the Patriarchs. That remained an inheritance for David, and his kingdom was reserved in perpetuity for his descendants. This kingdom had its counterpart on high, and fortified by that heavenly kingdom the rulership of the House of David will never depart from it throughout all generations. So that whenever the crown of Kingship in any way bestirs itself for a descendant of David there is no one who can stand up against him. The reason thus why "Daniel alone saw the vision" was because he was a descendant of David, as we read: "Now among these were, of the children of Judah, Daniel, Hananiah", etc. (*Ibid.* 1, 6); he saw the vision and rejoiced in that it was of the side of the inherited possession which was the lot and portion of his fathers; it was his own, and thus he could endure it, whereas others could not.'

R. Simeon said: 'When *KoH* bestirs itself in its rigour, mankind cannot stand against it. But when the priests spread out their hands, which are derived from *Ḥesed* (Grace), celestial Grace bestirs itself in response and allies itself to *KoH*, whereby the latter is sweetened, as it were, and in this way the priests, with shining faces, pronounce the blessing on Israel, so that judgement of Rigour is removed from them.

'To the children of Israel, and not the other nations. Only the priest is empowered to pronounce the blessing, and no other, since he is under *Ḥesed* (Grace) and is called *Ḥasid* (grace-endowed), and it is said, "and Thy *ḥasidim* shall bless thee (*yevareku-Koh*)" (Ps. CXLIX, 10), to wit, they will cause *KoH* to join in the blessing. On this wise ye shall bless: to wit, by the ineffable Name and in the holy tongue.' R. Judah said: 'When the priest below stands up and spreads out his hands, all the celestial sacred Crowns bestir themselves and make ready to receive blessings, and draw sustenance unto themselves from the depth of the Well, the never-ceasing Well whence blessings ever flow forth for all worlds; these Crowns drink in, as it were, all the blessings. At that moment there is a whisper followed by silence throughout the universe. So when a king is about to join his queen, all his attendants are agog and a whisper runs through them: Behold, the King is about to meet his Matrona. Here the Matrona is the Community of Israel.' R. Isaac said: 'The priest [in pronouncing the benediction] has to raise his right hand higher than his left hand, for the reason that the right is higher in estimation than the left.

'There is a teaching: The priest who is about to spread forth his hands [for the benediction] needs an inflow of holiness [146b] in addition to his own; he must therefore have his hands washed by one who is himself holy, to wit, a Levite, of whose order it is written: "And thou shalt sanctify the Levites".[1] Thus the priest may not receive the sanctification of the washing of hands from any commoner who is not himself sanctified. It may be asked, why only a Levite? Why should not the priest be sanctified by the hands of another priest? The answer is, because the other priest would not be complete, but the Levite is complete, being qualified for his own service, and he is also designated "cleansed", as it says, "and cleanse them" (Num. VIII, 6). Tradition, again, teaches us that the priest, in the spreading forth of his hands, should not have his fingers joined close together, for it is requisite that the sacred Crowns should receive the blessing each one apart in a manner proper to each, because the letters of the Divine Name require also to be kept distinct and not to run into each other.' R. Isaac said: 'The Holy One, blessed be He, desired that the upper beings should be blessed, in order that the lower beings should draw down the blessing from above, and, on the other hand, that the most holy beings above should reciprocally draw to themselves the blessings through the lower beings who are the most holy here below, as we read, "and thy godly ones shall bless thee" (Ps. CXLV, 10).' R. Judah said: 'If a priest is ignorant of this inward significance of the blessing and does not know whom he blesses or what his blessing connotes, his blessing is naught. So Scripture says: "For the priest's lips should keep knowledge, and they should seek the law at his mouth; for he is the messenger of the Lord of hosts" (Mal. II, 17). That is, the upper beings should seek at his mouth the Torah, to wit, the Written Law and the Oral Law, which are bound up with the two celestial Crowns called by the same names; they do so because he is "the messenger of the Lord of hosts". So the priest, as tradition tells us, needs to think with devotion on the inward and elevated significance of the words uttered

---

[1] These words are not to be found in our texts.

whereby the unification of the Divine Name is achieved.'

R. Simeon cited the following from the Book of Mystery. 'The Divine Name has both a revealed and an undisclosed form. In its revealed form it is written *YHVH*, but in its undisclosed form it is written in other letters, this undisclosed form representing the most Recondite of all.' R. Judah said: 'Even the revealed form of the Name is hidden under other letters,[1] in order to screen more effectively the most Recondite of all. For it behoves the priest to concentrate on the various permutations of the Divine Name, and to call down the mercies of all the Attributes through the two Crowns of mercy.[2] In these letters of this Name are concealed twenty-two attributes of Mercy, viz. thirteen of the Ancient One, Most Recondite of all, and nine of the *Mikroprosopus* (Lesser Figure); but they all combine in one composite Name, on which the priest concentrated his mind when he spread forth his hands, a name containing twenty-two engraven letters. We have learnt that when reverence was prevalent among mankind, the ineffable Name was openly enunciated in the hearing of all, but after irreverence became widespread it was concealed under other letters. Therefore at the time when the Name was disclosed, the priest would concentrate his mind on its deep and inner meaning, and he would utter the Name in such a way as to accord with that meaning. But when irreverence became common in the world he would conceal all within the written letters. Observe that the twenty-two letters [147*a*] were uttered by Moses in two sections. The first time[3] he uttered thirteen attributes of the Ancient of Ancients, the Most Undisclosed, so as to bring them down to the region where Rigour rules and subdue it. The second time[4] he uttered nine attributes of Mercy which are inherent in the *Mikroprosopus* (Lesser Figure) and which are radiated from the light of the Ancient and Undisclosed One. All this the priest combined together when he spread forth his hands to bless the people, so that all the worlds received the blessings from the side of the mercies which are drawn from the Ancient and Most Undisclosed One. It is for this

[1] i.e. ADNY (*ADoNaY*). [2] Viz. *Mah, Adonay.* [3] Ex. xxxiv, 6. [4] Num. xiv, 18.

reason that in the command it says simply "saying" (*amor*), instead of the definite form "say" (*imru*), this being a reference to the hidden letters within the words of blessing. Again, the word *AMoR* has in its letters the numerical value of two hundred and forty-eight less one, equal to the number of the bodily members of man, excepting the one member on which all the rest depend. All these members thus receive the priestly blessing as expressed in the three verses.'

R. Jose said: 'One day I was sitting in the presence of R. Eleazar, the son of R. Simeon, when I asked him the import of David's words, saying: "Man and beast thou preservest, O Lord" (Ps. xxxvi, 7). "Man" is plain enough, I said, but why associate with him "beast" ? He replied: It is as much as to say: If they are worthy they are of the category of man, if not they are of that of beast. I said to him: Rabbi, I would like a deeper exposition. He then said: Observe that the Holy One, blessed be He, called Israel "Adam" (Man), in virtue of their being of the celestial pattern, and He also called them "beast". So we read in one and the same verse, "And ye my sheep, the sheep of my pasture, are men (Adam)" (Ezek. xxxiv, 31): thus Israel is called both sheep, which is beast, and man (Adam). Hence "man and beast the Lord preserveth". Furthermore, when they are virtuous they are "Adam", of the celestial pattern, otherwise they are called "beast", but both receive the blessing at one and the same time, the celestial Adam and the earthly beast. Observe that no blessing is found here below until it comes into existence on high. But so soon as it comes into existence on high it is found below. The same correspondence exists whether for good or for ill. In regard to good, Scripture says: "I will respond to the heavens, and they shall respond to the earth" (Hos. II, 23); in regard to ill, we read: "the Lord will punish the host of the high heaven on high, and the kings of the earth upon the earth" (Isa. xxiv, 21).'

R. Judah remarked: 'It is for this reason that it is written "say to them", without specification, implying that the blessing embraces the upper world and the lower together; and similarly it first says "thus" (*Koh*), and then "the children of Israel". THE LORD BLESS THEE, to wit, on high, AND KEEP THEE, here below; THE LORD MAKE HIS FACE TO SHINE UPON THEE, to wit, on high, AND BE GRACIOUS UNTO THEE, here below; THE LORD SHOW FAVOUR UNTO THEE, on high, AND GIVE THEE PEACE, below.' R. Abba said: 'They all are blessed together by the twenty-two engraven letters of the Divine Name that are embraced within the priestly blessing. They symbolize, moreover, Mercy within Mercy, with the entire absence of Rigour. As for the words "*yisa . . . panav*" (the Lord lift up His countenance), it may also be translated, "the Lord remove and put away His anger", so that Rigour will be entirely absent. There is a teaching in the name of R. Jose, saying: When the priest spreads forth his hands it is forbidden to look at them,[1] for the reason that the Shekinah is hovering over his hands. R. Isaac remarked: 'Inasmuch as one is unable to see the Shekinah, as it says, "for man shall not see me and live" (Ex. XXXIII, 2), to wit, not whilst alive but only in death, what matters it then if one looks at the priest's hands ?' Said R. Jose: 'It matters because the Divine Name is reflected in the fingers of the priest's hands, so that although people cannot see the Shekinah they ought not to look towards the hands of the priests, as that would indicate irreverence towards the Shekinah. We have learnt that when the priests hold their hands outspread [in blessing], the congregation should be in fear and awe, and realize that it is a time of favour in all the worlds when the upper and lower worlds are being blessed, and there is everywhere an absence of Rigour. It is a moment when the undisclosed aspect of the Ancient of Ancients is being revealed as *Microprosopus* (Lesser-Figure), and thus peace prevails then everywhere. [147b] A teacher taught in the presence of R. Simeon: Whoever is in distress on account of a dream should recite during the time the priests spread forth their hands the following:[2] "O Master of the world, I am Thine and my dreams are Thine. . . ." For that is a propitious moment, and if one then offers up prayer in his distress, Rigour is turned for him into Mercy.'

[1] *v.* T.B. Hagigah, 16a.   [2] T.B. Berachoth, 55a.

So they shall put my name upon the children
of Israel. R. Judah said that the term *samu* (put) conveys
the idea of orderly arrangement, as the priests are therein
bidden to arrange by their blessing the Crowns of the right
to the right, and the Crowns of the left to the left, without
confusing them, so that the upper world and the lower will
receive the blessing. If they follow this, then I will bless
them, a blessing extended to the priests themselves, as we
read: "And blessed be every one that blesseth thee" (Gen.
xxvii, 29), also, "And I will bless them that bless thee"
(*Ibid.* xii, 3). We are told that a priest not beloved by the
people ought not to take part in blessing the people. On one
occasion, when a priest went up and spread forth his hands,
before he completed the blessing he turned into a heap of
bones. This happened to him because there was no love
between him and the people. Then another priest went up
and pronounced the blessing, and so the day passed without
harm. A priest who loves not the people, or whom they love
not, may not pronounce the blessing. So Scripture says:
"He that hath a bountiful eye shall be blessed" (Prov. xxii,
9), where the word *YeBoRaKH* (shall be blessed) can also
be read *YeBaReKH* (shall bless).' R. Isaac said: 'Note that
the wicked Balaam, when he was entrusted with the task
of blessing Israel, fixed on them an evil eye so as to prevent
the blessing from being fulfilled. So Scripture says: "The
saying of Balaam the son of Beor" (Num. xxiv, 3), that is,
the son of the most hateful enemy of Israel; "and the saying
of the man whose eye is closed"[1] (*Ibid.*): that means that
he closed his benevolent eye so that the blessing should be
of no effect.' R. Judah remarked: 'This is assuredly so, as
indeed we find that a real blessing is associated with the
opening of the eye. Thus it is written, "Open thine eyes"
(Dan. ix, 18), that is, in order to bless. So R. Hamnuna the
Elder's blessing for anyone took the form of "May the Holy
One, blessed be He, keep His eyes open on thee".' R.
Isaac continued: 'Thus the blessing pronounced by the
priest with a benevolent eye is effective, but if it is not given

[1] By a change from right to left of the diacritical point, the word
shethum (opened) is read *sethum* (closed).

with a benevolent eye, of such it is written: "Eat thou not
the bread of him that hath an evil eye, neither desire thou
his dainties" (Prov. XXIII, 6), to wit, in no wise seek any
blessing from such a man.' Said R. Jose: 'Observe the
verse: "Nevertheless the Lord thy God would not hearken
unto Balaam" (Deut. XXIII, 6). Now we should have expected
rather "to hearken unto Balak" instead of "unto Balaam",
seeing that Balak was the instigator of the whole attempt. But
the reason why Balaam is mentioned is because he closed
his eye in order to make his blessing of no effect.' R. Jose said:
'The Holy One, blessed be He, said in effect to Balaam:
"Wretch! Thou hast closed thine eye in order that My children should not receive any blessing. I, however, will open
thine eyes and so I will turn all thy utterances into blessings."
So we read: "But the Lord thy God turned the curse into a
blessing unto thee, because the Lord thy God loved thee"
(*Ibid.*). It has been taught: How beloved are Israel before
the Holy One, blessed be He, in that the upper beings are
only blessed for the sake of Israel. Thus R. Judah said in the
name of R. Ḥiya, who had it from R. Jose: 'The Holy One,
blessed be He, swore that he would not enter the heavenly
Jerusalem save after Israel had entered the earthly Jerusalem,
as it is said: "[I am] the holy one in the midst of thee, and
I will not come into the city" (Hos. XI, 9). That means that
so long as the Shekinah is here in exile the Name on high
is not complete, the arrangements [of the Divine Powers]
are not properly effected,[1] and, if it were possible to say so,
[148*a*] the Holy Name is left impaired.' R. Abba was once
going toward Lud when he met R. Zeira, the son of Rab.
Said R. Zeira: 'Now do I behold the presence of the Shekinah, and whoever beholds the presence of the Shekinah
ought to quicken his pace and follow Her. So we read: "And
let us know and pursue to know the Lord" (*Ibid.* VI, 3);
also, "And many peoples shall go and say: Come ye and
let us go up to the mountain of the Lord . . . for out of Zion
shall go forth the law" (Isa. II, 3). I thus desire to follow
thee and taste of some of the good things that ye learn daily

[1] i.e. there is friction between the Grades, *v.* Appendix.

in the Holy Assembly.[1] Now,' he asked, 'it is written: "And he believed in the Lord, and he counted it to him for righteousness" (Gen. xv, 6). Does it mean that the Holy One counted it to Abraham, or that Abraham counted it to the Holy One ? I myself', he said, 'heard that it means that the Holy One counted it to Abraham, but this does not satisfy me.' Said R. Abba: 'It is indeed not so. Observe that it is written, "and he counted it" (*vayahsh'veha*), but not "and he counted to him" (*vayahshov lo*). This assuredly means that Abraham counted it to the Holy One, blessed be He. It has been taught on this point as follows. It is written: "And he brought him forth abroad" (*Ibid.* 5), to wit, the Holy One, blessed be He, said to Abraham in effect:[2] Give up thy astrological speculations; this is not the way to acquire a knowledge of My Name. Thou seest, but I see also. Abram, it is true, is not to beget children, but Abraham will beget children. Henceforth follow another direction. "So (*KoH*) shall thy seed be" (*Ibid.*). The word *KoH* is expressive of the tenth sacred Crown of the King by which His Name may be known; it is the Crown through which rigorous judgements are set in motion. At that moment Abraham became filled with joy, inasmuch as the good tidings came to him through the medium of *KoH*, for although rigorous judgements are stirred up thence, yet "Abraham counted it", —to wit, the Crown, source of Rigour—"for righteousness": that is, he realized that the very Rigour was turned for him into Mercy. Now, in the command "On this wise (*KoH*) shall ye bless", it is signified that for the sake of Israel the very *KoH* is to be blessed by the priest, so that Israel will be blessed below, and thus blessing will be diffused through the universe. As for the time to come, it is written, "The Lord bless thee out of Zion . . ." (Ps. cxxxiv, 3); as well as, "Blessed be the Lord out of Zion, who dwelleth at Jerusalem" (*Ibid.* cxxxv, 21).'

AND IT CAME TO PASS ON THE DAY THAT MOSES HAD MADE AN END (*Khalloth*), ETC. R. Jose taught: 'This

---

[1] i.e. the full assembly of R. Simeon and the Companions. [2] *v.* T.B. Shabbath, 156a.

was the day when the bride[1] entered under the canopy, and
it was by the hands of Moses that she entered there.' R.
Judah remarked: 'And did She then delay until that time
to enter into Her place ? Is it not written: "And Moses was
not able to enter the tent of meeting", etc. (Ex. XL, 35) ?'
Said R. Isaac: 'The Torah is not written in chronological
order.[2] Again, "*Khalloth*" (making an end) is the same as
"*Khallath*" (the bride of) Moses. Assuredly she was the
"*khallah*", bride of Moses. So we learn that R. Simeon
explained the verse: "Thou hast ascended on high; thou
hast led captivity captive", etc. (Ps. LXVIII, 19), as follows.
When the Holy One, blessed be He, said to Moses, "Put
off thy shoes from off thy feet" (Ex. III, 5), the mountain
shook. Said Michael to the Holy One, blessed be He: Lord
of the Universe ! Art Thou about to annihilate man ? Is it
not written, "Male and female created he them, and blessed
them" (Gen. V, 2), so that blessing is only found in the
association of male and female ? But now Thou biddest him
to separate from his wife. The Holy One replied: Indeed,
Moses has already fulfilled the command of bearing children.
Now I desire him to espouse, as it were, the Shekinah, and
thus for his sake the Shekinah will descend to dwell with
him. This is what is meant by "Thou hast ascended on
high; Thou hast led captivity captive", to wit, the Shekinah,
who was, as it were, espoused to thee. In regard to Joshua,
whose face shone as the face of the moon,[3] it is written:
"Put off thy *shoe* (singular) from off thy *foot*" (Jos. V, 15),
for the reason that he separated himself from his wife only
at certain times, inasmuch as the Shekinah was not espoused
to him in the same degree, he not being so much deserving
of her. So it is written: "And Joshua fell on his face to the
earth" (*Ibid.* V, 14). But here we read of her being the bride
of (*KHLLTH*) Moses in all truth. Happy was the portion
of Moses, whose Master delighted in his glory above all the
rest of mankind.'

AND THE LORD SAID UNTO MOSES: EACH PRINCE ON

---

[1] *Khalloth* (=ending) suggests *Khallah* (=bride=Shekinah). [2] *v.* T.B.
Pesaḥim, 6b, *et passim.* [3] Cf. T.B. Baba Bathra, 75a.

HIS DAY. 'The word *layom* (=to the day)', said R. Judah,
'is an allusion to the celestial Days which were dedicated
[148b] to be blessed by the twelve delimited areas;[1] and
each one was put right and dedicated by means of a blessing
through the days here below. We have learnt that all are
blessed through the celestial altar. All are blessed, even the
lower world, even the other nations of the world.' R. Simeon
said: 'If not for the sacrifices offered by these twelve princes,
the world could not stand against the twelve princes of
Ishmael, of whom it is written, "twelve princes according
to their nations" (Gen. xxv, 16). Hence "each prince on *the*
day"; and whatever he offered was after the celestial
pattern, so that all should receive the blessing. THE RAMS
SIXTY, THE HE-GOATS SIXTY, representing the "threescore mighty men about it" (S.S. iii, 7), which belong to
the side of Strength. ONE GOLDEN SPOON OF TEN
GOLDEN SHEKELS, etc. Based on this, it was declared:
Happy is the portion of the righteous on whom the Holy
One, blessed be He, pours blessings, and unto whose prayer
He hearkens. Regarding them it is written: "When he hath
regarded the prayer of the destitute, and hath not despised
their prayer" (Ps. cii, 18).'

---

[1] The twelve permutations of the Tetragrammaton.

BEHA‘ALOTHEKHA

Numbers VIII, 1–XII, 16

AND THE LORD SPOKE UNTO MOSES, SAYING: SPEAK
UNTO AARON, AND SAY UNTO HIM: WHEN THOU
LIGHTEST THE LAMPS. . . . R. Judah discoursed here on
the verse: "Which is as a bridegroom coming out of his
chamber", etc. (Ps. XIX, 6). 'Happy is the portion of Israel',
he said, 'in whom the Holy One, blessed be He, delights
and to whom He gave the Torah of truth, the Tree of Life,
whoever takes hold of which achieves life in this world and
in the world to come. Now the Tree of Life extends from
above downward, and it is the Sun which illumines all.
Its radiance commences at the top and extends through
the whole trunk in a straight line. It is composed of two
sides, one to the north, one to the south, one to the right,
and one to the left. When the trunk shines, first the right
arm of the tree is illumined, and from its intensity the left
side catches the light. The "chamber" from which he goes
forth is the starting-point of light, referred to also in the
words of the next verse, "from the end of the heaven",
which is, indeed, the starting-point of all. From that point
he goes forth veritably as a bridegroom to meet his bride,
the beloved of his soul, whom he receives with outstretched
arm. The sun proceeds and makes his way toward the west;
when the west is approached the north side bestirs itself
to come forward to meet it, and joins it. Then "he rejoices
as a strong man to run his course" (Ps. *ibid.*), so as to shed
his light on the moon. Now the words WHEN THOU LIGHT-
EST THE LAMPS contain an allusion to the celestial lamps,
all of which are lit up together from the radiance of the sun.'[1]

R. Abba began a discourse with the verse: "Happy is the
people that know the joyful shout; they walk, O Lord, in
the light of thy countenance" (Ps. LXXXIX, 16). 'Happy', he
said, 'are Israel to whom the Holy One, blessed be He,
gave the Holy Law [149a] and whom He taught His ways,

[1] There seems to be a lacuna here in the text.

how to cleave unto Him and observe the precepts of the
Torah whereby to merit the world to come; and whom He
brought near to Himself at the time when they went forth
from Egypt. For then He took them away from a strange
dominion and caused them to be united to His Name. Then
they were called "the children of Israel", to wit, free men
entirely emancipated from any strange power, and united
to His Name that is supreme over all, that rules over the
upper beings and the lower; and out of His love for them
He designated them "Israel my firstborn" (Ex. IV, 22), on the
celestial pattern. Then He slew every firstborn on high and
below, set free the bondmen and prisoners, the upper and
the lower ones, so as to free Israel completely. Hence the
Holy One, blessed be He, did not send an angel or a seraph,
but performed the deed Himself. Furthermore, He alone,
being all-knowing, could distinguish and discern and set
free the bondmen, things not within the power of any
messenger but only within His own. Now on that night
when the Holy One, blessed be He, was about to slay all
those firstborn, the angels came forward to sing their song
of praise before Him. He said to them: "This is not the time
for it, as another song my children on earth are about to
sing." Then at the division of the night the north wind
bestirred itself, and the Holy One, blessed be He, executed
judgement and Israel broke forth in loud songs of praise.
Then He made them free men, freed from every bondage;
and the angels and all the celestial hosts hearkened unto the
voice of Israel. After Israel had circumcised themselves
they marked their houses with that blood and with the
blood of the paschal lamb in three spots, to wit, "the lintel
and the two side-posts" (Ibid. XII, 22). For when the destroying angel went forth and saw the mark of the holy sign on
that door he had compassion on Israel, as it is written:
"the Lord will compassionately pass over the door" (Ibid.
23). There is a certain difficulty here. For since the Holy
One Himself was to come and slay in the land of Egypt,
what need was there for a sign on the door, seeing that all
is revealed before Him? Further, what signifies "and [He]
will not suffer the destroyer" (Ibid.)? We should have

expected "and [He] will not destroy". But the truth is as
follows. It is written, and "the Lord smote all the firstborn
in the land of Egypt" (*Ibid.* 29). Now "and the Lord"
(V–YHVH) everywhere denotes "He together with His
tribunal", and on any such occasion it behoves man to
exhibit some visible act in order to be saved. It is thus of
importance to have sacrifices offered on the altar so as to
keep at a distance the Destroyer during a service. The same
applies to the New-Year Day, the Day of Judgement, when
the lords of the evil tongue rise up against Israel; it is then
that we need prayer and supplication, and, in addition,
some outward and visible act. This act consists in blowing
the trumpet, the sound of which wakes into action another
trumpet. We thereby bring about the working of Mercy and
Rigour at one and the same time, like the celestial trumpet
that emits a combined sound. Our object is to awaken
Mercy and to bring about the subjection of the Masters of
Rigour so that they may be impotent on that day. And so
when the powers of Mercy are awakened, all the celestial
lamps are lit on both sides, and then "In the light of the
King's countenance is life" (Prov. xvi, 15). So at the
moment when the priest is about to kindle the lamps here
below and offers up the perfumed incense, the celestial
lights are kindled and all is linked together so that joy and
gladness pervade all the worlds. So Scripture says: "Ointment and perfume rejoice the heart" (Prov. xxvii, 9). This,
then, is the full import of "When thou lightest the lamps".'

R. Eleazar, R. Jose and R. Isaac once on their travels
came to the mountains of Kurdistan. As they approached
them R. Eleazar raised his eyes and saw some tall and
forbidding cliffs, and they were all filled with fear. Said
R. Eleazar to his Companions: 'Had my father been here
I should not have feared, but all the same, as we are three
and are discussing words of the Torah, there is no place
here for the divine Rigour.' R. Eleazar then quoted the
verse: "And the ark rested in the seventh month, on the
seventeenth day of the month, on the mountains of Ararat"
etc. (Gen. viii, 4). 'How precious', he said, 'are the words
of the Torah, seeing that each particular word contains

sublime mystical teachings, the Torah itself being designated the sublime general rule. Now, one of the thirteen exegetical principles by which the Law is expounded reads: "If anything is included in a general proposition and is then made the subject of a special statement, that which is predicated of it is not to be understood as limited to itself alone, but is to be applied to the whole of the general proposition." So it is with the Torah itself. It [149b] is itself the supernal all-comprehensive Rule, yet in addition does each particular narrative, seemingly a mere story or fact, standing outside the all-comprehensive Rule of the Torah, teach us not only its own limited lesson, but supernal ideas and recondite doctrines applicable to the whole of the all-comprehensive Rule of the Torah. Thus when we read that "the ark rested in the seventh month, on the seventeenth day of the month, upon the mountains of Ararat", we assuredly find here a particular statement, apparently a superfluous detail; for what matters it to us whether the ark rested in this or in the other place so long as it rested somewhere ? Yet does it contain teaching applicable to the whole principle of the Torah. And happy are Israel to whom was given the sublime Torah, the Torah of truth. Perdition take anyone who maintains that any narrative in the Torah comes merely to tell us a piece of history and nothing more ! If that were so, the Torah would not be what it assuredly is, to wit, the supernal Law, the Law of truth. Now if it is not dignified for a king of flesh and blood to engage in common talk, much less to write it down, is it conceivable that the most high King, the Holy One, blessed be He, was short of sacred subjects with which to fill the Torah, so that He had to collect such commonplace topics as the anecdotes of Esau, and Hagar, Laban's talks to Jacob, the words of Balaam and his ass, those of Balak, and of Zimri, and suchlike, and make of them a Torah ? If so, why is it called the "Law of truth" ? Why do we read "The law of the Lord is perfect. . . . The testimony of the Lord is sure. . . . The ordinances of the Lord are true. . . . More to be desired are they than gold, yea, than much fine gold" (Ps. XIX, 8–11) ? But assuredly each word of the Torah signifies sublime things, so that this or that narrative, besides its meaning in and for itself, throws light on the all-comprehensive Rule of the Torah. See now what the resting of the ark comes to teach us. At the time when Rigour impends over the world and the Holy One, blessed be He, sits on His throne of Judgement to judge the world, within that Throne, in the King's chest, there are deposited ever so many records, notes and books, so that nothing is forgotten by the King. That Throne attains its full significance only in the seventh month, on the Day of Judgement, when all the people of the world pass before it for scrutiny. "The Ark" thus "rested in the seventh month", on the world's Day of Judgement, "on the mountains of Ararat", that is, attended by the lords of Rigour, the lords of the hostile shout. Many are the executioners who bestir themselves on that day and place themselves underneath the Throne to take part in the world's judgement. Israel on that day offer up prayer and supplication before Him, they blow the trumpet, and the Holy One, blessed be He, takes compassion on them and changes Rigour into Mercy. Then all the upper and the lower beings proclaim: "Happy is the people that know the joyful shout" (Ps. LXXXIX, 16). Hence, on that day, whoever blows the trumpet should know the root of the matter, so as to concentrate his mind on the meaning of the blowing and to perform it with understanding. Thus, "happy is the people that *know* the joyful shout", and not merely "that *sound* the joyful shout".'

The Companions then proceeded on their journey the whole day. When night fell they ascended to a spot where they found a cave. Said R. Eleazar: 'Let one of us enter inside the cave if haply he find there a more convenient spot.' R. Jose entered and noticed therein an inner cave lit by a lamp, and he heard a voice speaking thus: "When thou lightest the lamps the seven lamps shall give light in front of the candlestick". Here (said the voice) the Community of Israel receives the light whilst the supernal Mother [150*a*] is crowned, and all the lamps are illumined from Her. In Her are two small flames, companions of the King, as it were, which kindle all the lights on high and

below.' R. Jose, on hearing this, rejoiced, and reported it
to R. Eleazar, who said to him: 'Let us enter therein, for
the Holy One, blessed be He, seems to have appointed for
us this day as one on which a miracle should happen to us.'
When they entered their eyes met there two men engaged
in the study of the Torah. R. Eleazar proclaimed: ' "How
precious is thy lovingkindness, O God ! and the children
of men take refuge in the shadow of thy wings" (Ps. xxxvi, 8).'
The two men stood up, then they all sat down in joyful
mood. Said R. Eleazar: 'The Holy One, blessed be He, has
shown us lovingkindness in letting us find you in this spot.
Now, light the lamps !'

R. Jose then began the following discourse: *When thou
lightest the lamps.* 'The term *beha'alothekha* (when thou lightest) has here its literal meaning [to wit, when thou makest
ascend], inasmuch as the verse speaks here of the services
performed by the priest, the two which form a unity, to
wit, those of the oil and the incense, so that "Oil and perfume rejoice the heart" (Prov. xxvii, 9). So Scripture says:
"And Aaron shall burn thereon incense . . . when he dresseth
the lamps. . . . And when Aaron lighteth the lamps at dusk
he shall burn it" (Ex. xxx, 7–8). Why the term *b'hetivo*
(when he dresseth, lit.=when he maketh good) ?' R. Judah
said that this points to the idea contained in "but he that is
of a merry (lit. good) heart hath a continual feast" (Prov.
xv, 15), whilst the expression "when he maketh ascend"
(*b'ha'aloth*) points to the exaltation of the supernal beings
after having drunk their fill of the waters of the River, so
that blessings and joy are diffused throughout.' Said R. Aḥa:
'When the Most Profound illumes the River, and the River
so illumined flows on in a straight path—of such a moment
it is written, "when he makes ascend", in that from the Most
Profound there issue the causes that come from the supernal
side of the Most Profound which is called Thought. The
two terms ["make ascend" and "make good"] thus signify
one and the same thing. At that moment the Community of
Israel is blessed and blessings are diffused throughout the
worlds.' [151a]

R. Eleazar said: 'This section, dealing with the ceremonies

of the candlestick, is a repetition of another section dealing
with the same. The reason for the repetition is as follows.
Having recorded the offerings brought on the altar by the
Princes, and all the ceremony of its dedication, Scripture
records the service of the candlestick, which was a finishing
touch ministered by Aaron, inasmuch as it was through Aaron
that the supernal candlestick with all its lamps was lighted.
Observe that the altar had to be dedicated and perfected by
the twelve Princes, representing the twelve tribes, who were
ranged on four sides carrying four standards. It was all
on the supernal pattern, to wit, the candlestick [151b] with
its seven lamps to be lighted by the hand of the priest.
Candlestick and the inner altar together minister to the joy
of the whole of existence, as Scripture says: "Ointment and
perfume rejoice the heart" (Prov. xxvii, 9). For of the two
altars, the inner one [on which the incense was offered]
radiated its force to the outer one, the one assigned for other
offerings; and it is by meditating on the inner altar that
one obtains a knowledge of the Supernal Wisdom, which is
concealed within the words ADoNaY YHVH. Hence the
incense had to be offered up only when the oil had been
poured in the lamps. The following is found in the Book of
King Solomon. The incense has the virtue of diffusing
joy and putting away death. For whereas Judgement
prevails on the exterior, joy and illumination, on the other
hand, proceed from the interior, the seat of all happiness.
So when this bestirs itself all Judgement is removed and is
powerless. The incense thus has the virtue of annulling
death and binds all together, and was therefore offered on
the interior altar. *Take the Levites. . . .* This indicates that
it was needful to cleanse them and draw them on that they
might be linked to their own proper place. For they symbolize the Left Arm, identical with the side of Judgement, and
whoever proceeds from the side of Judgement ought not to
let his hair grow, as he thereby strengthens Judgement in
the world. For the same reason a woman may not have her
hair exposed to view, but it behoves her to cover her head
and keep her hair concealed. When this is done, all those
who proceed from the side of Judgement are blessed; and

thus is explained the significance of the command saying: *And thus shalt thou do unto them to cleanse them . . . and let them cause a razor to pass over all their flesh. . . .* Furthermore, the Levites could not take up their post until the priest had offered them up for a wave-offering, inasmuch as it is the right that has to lead the left.' Said R. Simeon: The Levites, on entering into their assigned places, had to bring as an offering two bullocks, symbolic of the left side, as they themselves were of the left side. On the other hand, power and adjustment are vested in the priest, inasmuch as the power of the body is chiefly displayed in the right arm. The priest was therefore the right arm of all Israel, charged to set right Israel and all the world. Nevertheless he, together with the left side, was part of the body, the body being the all-in-all.

'THIS IS THAT WHICH PERTAINETH UNTO THE LEVITES, ETC. Observe that the Levite enters on his service when twenty-five years old, and remains in his service for twenty-five years until he reaches the age of fifty. When he reaches the fifty-year grade the strong fire within him is cooled down, and in such a state he cannot but impair the spot to which he is attached. Besides, his singing voice no longer serves him so well, whereas that voice ought not to be impaired, but should constantly gain in vigour; and since the Levite stands in the region of Strength (*Geburah*), no feebleness whatever can be permitted to attach to him.'

AND THE LORD SPOKE TO MOSES IN THE WILDERNESS OF SINAI, ETC. Said R. Abba: 'Why was the command regarding the paschal lamb repeated here after it had been given them once whilst they were still in Egypt ? The reason is that the Israelites thought that that command was intended only for the one year in Egypt and not for future years. Hence, [152*a*] "in the wilderness of Sinai . . . of the second year": the command was renewed to indicate that it was to be kept throughout the generations. "In the first month of the second year" contains a sublime mystery. The month signifies the Moon,[1] and the year points to the Sun[2] that sheds

[1] *Malkuth.*   [2] *Tifereth.*

his rays on the Moon. Thus it happened at the time when
all the precepts of the Torah were delivered to Israel.'
Said R. Simeon: 'Alas for the man who regards the Torah
as a book of mere tales and everyday matters ! If that were
so, we, even we could compose a torah dealing with everyday
affairs, and of even greater excellence. Nay, even the princes
of the world possess books of greater worth which we could
use as a model for composing some such torah. The Torah,
however, contains in all its words supernal truths and sublime mysteries. Observe the perfect balancing of the upper
and the lower worlds. Israel here below is balanced by the
angels on high, of whom it says: "who makest thy angels
into winds" (Ps. CIV, 4). For the angels in descending on
earth put on themselves earthly garments, as otherwise they
could not stay in this world, nor could the world endure them.
Now, if thus it is with the angels, how much more so must
it be with the Torah—the Torah that created them, that
created all the worlds and is the means by which these are
sustained. Thus had the Torah not clothed herself in garments of this world the world could not endure it. The
stories of the Torah are thus only her outer garments, and
whoever looks upon that garment as being the Torah itself,
woe to that man—such a one will have no portion in the
next world. David thus said: "Open thou mine eyes, that
I may behold wondrous things out of thy law" (Ps. CXIX, 18),
to wit, the things that are beneath the garment. Observe this.
The garments worn by a man are the most visible part of
him, and senseless people looking at the man do not seem to
see more in him than the garments. But in truth the pride
of the garments is the body of the man, and the pride of the
body is the soul. Similarly the Torah has a body made up
of the precepts of the Torah, called *gufe torah* (bodies, main
principles of the Torah), and that body is enveloped in
garments made up of worldly narrations. The senseless
people only see the garment, the mere narrations; those
who are somewhat wiser penetrate as far as the body. But
the really wise, the servants of the most high King, those who
stood on Mount Sinai, penetrate right through to the soul,
the root principle of all, namely, to the real Torah. In the

future the same are destined to penetrate even to the super-soul (soul of the soul) of the Torah. Observe that in a similar way in the supernal world there is garment, body, soul and super-soul. The heavens and their hosts are the outer garment, the Community of Israel is the body which receives the soul, to wit, the "Glory of Israel"; and the super-soul is the Ancient Holy One. All these are interlocked within each other. Woe to the sinners who consider the Torah as mere worldly tales, who only see its outer garment; happy are the righteous who fix their gaze on the Torah proper. Wine cannot be kept save in a jar; so the Torah needs an outer garment. These are the stories and narratives, but it behoves us to penetrate beneath them. [152b]

'IF ANY MAN (lit. a man, a man) OF YOU . . . SHALL BE UNCLEAN, ETC. What signifies the repetition of the term "a man"? It signifies "a man who is a man", that is, who is otherwise worthy of the name "man", and fit to receive the supernal soul, but who has allowed himself to be blemished and defiled so that the Shekinah cannot abide with him. We read further: OR BE IN A JOURNEY AFAR OFF. There is a dot over the *resh* of the word *reḥokah* (afar off) to indicate that if a man sullies himself here, they sully him on high. He is thus "in a journey afar off", far away from the region and the path which the seed of Israel have chosen.' R. Isaac remarked: 'Is it not written, "If a man . . . shall be unclean . . . *or* be in a journey afar off", thus signifying two different cases?' Said R. Jose: 'Just so. The former speaks of a man not yet defiled on high, whilst the latter refers to one who has been thus defiled. Neither upon the one nor upon the other, Scripture implies, can holiness rest, and so neither may offer up the paschal lamb at the time when the rest of Israel offer it up. As for the secondary paschal lamb, the man is only permitted to offer it after he has purified himself and repaired his defect. Israel, however, who offered the passover in its proper time, stand in a higher degree in that they receive the beneficences of the Moon and the Sun[1] together.' [153b]

[1] *Malkuth* and *Tifereth*.

AND ON THE DAY THAT THE TABERNACLE WAS REARED
UP. R. Ḥiya cited here the verse: "He hath scattered abroad,
he hath given to the needy, his righteousness stands for ever"
(Ps. CXII, 9). 'The term "scattered" here', he said, 'is to
be interpreted in the light of the saying: "There is that
scattereth, and increaseth all the more" (Prov. XI, 24), that
is, increaseth in riches, increases in life. Besides, the term
nosaf (increaseth) has the secondary meaning of "gathering
in", thus pointing to the region of death. The verse thus
says that such a man draws to himself, where death would
otherwise have been, an increase of life from on high.' R.
Judah said, in the name of R. Ḥiya: 'This verse testifies that
whoever gives to the poor induces the Tree of Life to add
of itself to the Tree of Death,[1] so that life and joy prevail
on high, and so that that man, whenever in need, has the
Tree of Life to stand by him and the Tree of Death to
shield him. The verse continues, "and his charity[2] standeth
for ever", that is, it stands by him to provide him with life
and strength; as he has awakened life, so will the two Trees
stand by him to shield him and grant him an increase of
life.' R. Abba said: 'Every time the tabernacle was set up
by the hands of men there was a day of universal joy, and
the sacred Oil was poured into the lamps, and these all shed
their light abroad, and those who brought this about won
redemption for themselves in this world and life in the next.
Thus "righteousness delivereth from death".' [154*a*]

MAKE UNTO THEE TWO TRUMPETS OF SILVER, ETC.
R. Simeon adduced here the verse: "And when the *Ḥayoth*
(living creatures) went, the wheels went hard by them; and
when the *Ḥayoth* were lifted up from the bottom the wheels
were lifted up" (Ezek. I, 19). 'The *Ḥayoth*', he said, 'are borne
along by the supernal power; and so were the movements of
the tribes below who bore on their standards the likenesses
of the *Ḥayoth*, that of Lion, Eagle, Ox, Man. Angels attended
each of the standards. The first standard bore the likeness of
Lion and was attended by Michael, who had under him two
chieftains, Zophiel and Zadkiel. When these set out numerous armed hosts moved in unison on the right-hand side

[1] The Shekinah. [2] *ẓidkatho*=his righteousness; in later Hebrew=his charity.

whilst the sun on the left illumined them. The Lion put forth his right hand and summoned to himself all his hosts, to wit, three hundred and seventy thousand lions, and they all assembled round him. When this Lion roars all the firmaments and all their hosts and legions quiver and shake. The Fiery River blazes forth and sinks a thousand and five hundred stages to the lower Gehinnom. Then all the sinners in the Gehinnom shake and tremble and burn in the fire. So Scripture says: "The lion hath roared, who will not fear?" (Amos III, 8). A second roar he emits, which is taken up by his entourage of three hundred and seventy thousand lions. Then he puts forth his left hand, when all the "masters of Rigour" here below are seized with fear and are bowed down underneath that hand. So we read: "Thy hand shall be on the neck of thy enemies" (Gen. XLIX, 8). Each of the Hayoth had four wings formed of white flaming fire, as well as four faces turned towards the four cardinal points, all illumined by the white light of the sun; the one turned to the east was illumined with a joyous light, the one towards the west with a concentrated light, the one towards the north was within the penumbra of the sun. These contained three groups.[1] One numbered seventy-four thousand and six hundred. These were of the higher grades. There were, besides, a long succession of lower grades. These were innumerable. The second group contained fifty-four thousand and four hundred besides [154b] those of the lower grades, who were innumerable. The third group, which followed behind, contained fifty-seven thousand and four hundred. So soon as the first standard began to march *the tabernacle was taken down*, and all the Levites chanted hymns, and the lords of praise were all ranged there "for the spirit of the Hayoth was in the Ophanim (Wheels)". The second standard bore on it the Eagle, symbolic of the angel Uriel, and was ranged on the south. Two chieftains accompanied him, namely, Shamshiel and Ḥasdiel. When the Eagle arose all the winged forces went in front, accompanied by innumerable hosts on all sides. When he set off he put forth his right pinion, and gathered unto him all his hosts to the number

[1] Corresponding to the three tribes under each standard.

of three hundred and fifty thousand. Three groups belonged to that standard; the first contained forty-six thousand and five hundred, the second fifty-nine thousand and three hundred, and the third fifty-four thousand six hundred and fifty. Two heralds, emerging out of these two flanks, marched in front of all these hosts. At their proclamation there assembled all hosts and legions, living creatures, small and large. All the firmaments indeed moved forward along with these hosts in front of the tabernacle. We thus read: "And when the *Hayoth* went, the *Ophanim* went hard by them". Then follows the third standard to the north. It had for its ensign Ox and was accompanied by the angel Gabriel and his two chieftains, Kafẓiel and Ḥizkiel. The Ox, being of the left side, has horns between his two eyes, which flame as it were with burning fire; he gores and tramples with his feet ruthlessly. When he moos there emerge out of the hollow of the great abyss numerous spirits of wrath who proceed in front in a chorus of shrieking. Seven fiery rivers flow in front of him, and when thirsty he draws up a whole riverful at one gulp. Yet this river is straightway filled again as before, unfailingly. And were it not for a stream of water from the region of the lion quenching the fiery coals, the world could not endure. It is a region where the sun never rises, and where numberless spirits roam about in the darkness, and the fire of the burning river is itself dark and black. You may wonder that there should be such things as fire of various hues, white, black, red and of double hue, but indeed it is so. Thus we have learnt that the Torah was written with black fire on white fire. [155*a*] Now the third standard also had under it three divisions. One contained sixty-two thousand and seven hundred; the second forty-one thousand and five hundred; whilst the third contained fifty-three thousand and four hundred. All this besides all the other grades scattered all around them, grades upon grades innumerable, as well as lower grades, executioners, who have the impudence of a dog and bite like an ass. Woe to whoever finds himself near them and under their judgement! On the fourth side the fourth standard, on the west, had for its symbol Man, the angel

Raphael,[1] with whom there is healing. Blessed are Israel in whose glory the Holy One, blessed be He, delights, and to whom He assigned a portion above all other nations and in whose praise He glorifies Himself, as we read: "And he said unto me, Thou art my servant", etc. (Isa. XLIX, 3).'

AND IT CAME TO PASS WHEN THE ARK SET FORWARD....
R. Eleazar said: 'What is the meaning of the inverted letter *Nun* introduced here twice?[2] We explain it thus. We read a little before: "And the ark of the covenant of the Lord went before them three days' journey, to seek a resting-place for them". Now, as soon as the ark set off the *Nun*[3] accompanied it, with its face turned towards Israel. The Shekinah ever hovered over the ark, but the love of the Holy One, blessed be He, towards Israel was such that even though they strayed from the straight path He would not forsake them, but always turned His countenance towards them, for otherwise they could not endure in the world. So that whilst "the ark . . . went before them three days' journey", the *Nun* (symbol of the Shekinah) remained inseparable from it, and accompanied it, yet turned her face away from the ark and towards Israel, like a young hart that, whilst going, turns its face towards its starting-point. Thus when Moses said, "Rise, O Lord . . .", implying "do not forsake us, turn Thy face towards us", the *Nun* turned round facing Israel in the manner of one turning his face towards his beloved friend. "And when it rested" the *Nun* turned its face again towards the ark.' Said R. Simeon: 'O Eleazar, assuredly it is as you said, saving that when the ark rested the Shekinah did *not* turn her countenance away from Israel. This is clearly shown by the second *Nun*, which is also of an inverted shape. The truth is that when Moses said "Return, O Lord", and the ark rested, the Shekinah turned back and stood on the other side of the ark,[4] but her countenance turned both

[1] Whose chief function, as his name (RaFA=to cure) denotes, was the healing of men. [2] In the Massoretic text there are inserted here two isolated *Nuns*, turned upside down and sideways, one preceding and the other following the two verses beginning with our text. [3] i.e. the Shekinah, symbolized by this letter. [4] i.e. instead of between the ark and Israel, as during the journey.

[155*b*] towards Israel and towards the ark. Israel, however, caused afterwards the turning away of the Shekinah from them. So we read: *And the people were as murmurers* [*K'mithonnim*).[1] Said R. Eleazar: 'What I said I found in the Book of R. Yeba the Elder.' R. Simeon replied: 'What he said is rightly said, but you will find my exposition in the book of R. Hamnuna the Elder, and this is assuredly the right exposition.'

NOW THE MANNA WAS LIKE CORIANDER (*gad*) SEED. Said R. Jose: 'The term *gad* (lit. troops) signifies that the manna had the virtue of inducing propagation. It implies further that in the same way as the seed of Gad took their portion in another land,[2] so the manna hovered over Israel outside the Holy Land. We may also explain the words to mean that it was white in appearance, like coriander seed, and coagulated when it reached the atmosphere, and was transmuted into material substance[3] inside the body.[4] AND THE APPEARANCE THEREOF AS THE APPEARANCE OF BDELLIUM, to wit, it was white in colour like bdellium, this being the colour of the Right in the supernal sphere.'

AND IF THOU (*at*) DEAL THUS WITH ME. R. Isaac asked: 'For what reason did Moses make use of the feminine form *at* (thou) instead of the masculine *atta*? The reason is', he explained, 'that Moses directed his words towards the realm of death, the realm associated with the female principle. Therefore he said "Kill me, I pray thee, out of hand', an invocation to the Tree of Death. Hence the feminine *at*.

'AND THE LORD SAID UNTO MOSES: GATHER UNTO ME SEVENTY MEN . . . . The Holy One, blessed be He, in effect said to him: On every such occasion you wish to die,[5] so "I

---

[1] A play upon the Hebrew word, which contains two *Nuns* of ordinary shape, their faces, as it were, being away from Israel. [2] i.e. outside the border of the Holy Land proper, in Transjordania. [3] i.e. out of its ethereal state. [4] Al. "it was absorbed by the body", i.e. without leaving any waste, as with material food. *v.* T.B. Yoma, 75*b*. [5] Allusion to "blot me, I pray thee out of thy book . . ." (Ex. XXXII, 32), in connection with the Golden Calf.

will take of the spirit which is upon thee, and will put it upon them". Observe that Moses was here made to know that he would die [in the wilderness] and not enter into the Land, as, in fact, Eldad and Medad announced.[1] This is a lesson that in time of wrath a man ought not to utter anything in the nature of a curse against himself, inasmuch as ever so many malignant powers are standing by, ready to take up that utterance. On the other occasion, when Moses prayed for death to himself[2] his request was not taken up, for the reason that Moses meant it all for the benefit of Israel. Here, on the other hand, Moses only gave vent to his anger and anguish of heart; his words, therefore, were taken up, and Eldad and Medad, who remained in the camp, announced, "Moses will be gathered in and Joshua will bring Israel into the Land". This made Joshua jealous for the sake of Moses, and so he came to him and said, "My lord Moses, restrain them", or, as we might also render, "withhold from them these words". But Moses, regardless of his own glory, did not consent. Observe the meekness evinced in the reply of Moses: "Art thou jealous for my sake?" Happy is the portion of Moses, who rose high above the highest prophets (al. the prophets of the world).' R. Judah remarked: 'All the prophets were to Moses like the moon to the sun.'

One night R. Abba was sitting and studying the Torah, R. Jose and R. Hizkiah being with him. Said R. Jose: 'How obtuse are mankind that they have no regard whatever for the things of the other world.' Said R. Abba: 'This is caused by the badness of their heart, which spreads through all the members of the body.' He then cited the verse: "There is an evil which I have seen under the sun, and it is heavy upon man" (Eccl. VI, I). 'The evil here referred to', he said, 'is the evil residing in the hardened heart that longs to obtain dominion in affairs of this world, but is altogether regardless of the other world. Scripture continues: "a man to whom God giveth riches, wealth and honour . . ." (*Ibid.* 2). There is here an apparent contradiction, since it first says, "so that he wanteth nothing for his soul of all that he desireth", and then goes on, "yet God giveth him not

[1] *v.* T.B. Sanhedrin, 17*a*. [2] Viz., in connection with the Golden Calf.

power to eat thereof". If he is in want of nothing for himself, how can we say that God gives him not power to eat thereof ? There is, however, an inner meaning here as in all the words of Solomon, and although we have to take note also of the outer garb, we must look deeper into the meaning of this verse, which is as follows. There is a man to whom [156*a*] the Holy One, blessed be He, gives a certain riches which he may enjoy in the next world and which may remain with him as a capital, to wit, the ever-enduring capital, which consists of the realm of the bundle of souls. It is thus incumbent on man to reserve and leave behind him that capital, which he will receive after he has left this world. This capital is indeed the Tree of Life belonging to the other world, the fruit of which alone has any place or room in this world. The good man thus enjoys its fruit in this world whilst the capital remains for him for the other world, where he obtains the superior celestial life. But if a man has sullied himself and followed his selfish desires, and "wanted nothing", that is, abstained from gratifying no desire, then that Tree remains apart and will not acknowledge him on high, for "God giveth him not power to eat thereof" and to have the reward of that riches, "but a stranger eateth it", as we read elsewhere: "He may prepare it, but the just shall put it on" (Job XXVII, 17). It thus behoves man to use what the Holy One, blessed be He, has given him so as thereby to merit the next world. He will thus enjoy of it in this world and have the capital left for the next world to be bound up in the bundle of life.' Said R. Jose: 'Assuredly it is so.' R. Jose further said: 'It is written: AND IF THOU DEAL THUS WITH ME, KILL ME, I PRAY THEE, OUT OF HAND. . . . Is it likely', he asked, 'that Moses, the meekest of men, should have wished death for himself just because the Israelites asked him for food ?' R. Abba said in reply: 'There is a deep mystery here which I have learnt. Moses did no evil in His sight, and his asking for death was not by reason of Israel's asking for food. Mark now, that Moses was attached to a high grade to which no other prophet attained. And so when the Holy One, blessed be He, said to him, "Behold, I will cause to rain bread from heaven for you" (Ex. XVI, 4), he rejoiced, saying: Verily, there is completeness found in me, seeing that it is for my sake that the manna is now provided for Israel. But when Moses saw that they lowered themselves again to the other grade, and asked for flesh, "If so", he said, "my own grade must be blemished, since it was for my sake that the Israelites have the manna in the wilderness." He therefore besought death for himself rather than fall from his high grade. So the Lord said unto him: GATHER UNTO ME SEVENTY MEN, reassuring him thereby that his grade was not blemished, adding thus, AND I WILL TAKE OF THE SPIRIT THAT IS UPON THEE, AND WILL PUT IT UPON THEM, inasmuch as they all are of the degree of the Moon, and so need the Sun[1] to illumine them; and so this food would not descend for the sake of Moses. Happy the portion of Moses, whom the Holy One, blessed be He, desires to honour, and whom He loves above all other prophets, communicating with him without an intermediary, as it says, "With him do I speak mouth to mouth".

'AND MOSES CRIED UNTO THE LORD SAYING: HEAL HER NOW, O GOD, I BESEECH THEE. In this prayer is involved the mystery of the Divine Name formed of eleven letters, and Moses did not wish to lengthen his prayer further, for the reason that, since it concerned his own,[2] he was unwilling [156b] to trouble the King, as it were, over-much. Therefore God was solicitous for the honour of Moses; and, indeed, everywhere He is more solicitous for the honour of the righteous than for His own.'

---

[1] i.e. Moses.   [2] i.e. his own sister.

SHELAḤ LECHA

Numbers XIII, 1–XV, 41

AND THE LORD SPAKE UNTO MOSES SAYING, SEND
THEE MEN TO SPY OUT THE LAND OF CANAAN, ETC.
R. Ḥiya here cited the verse: "Hast thou caused the day-
spring to know his place", etc. (Job XXXVIII, 12). 'Note', he
said, 'that Moses was the sun, and when he desired to enter
the land, God said to him, Moses, when the light of the sun
arrives, the moon [157a] is embraced in it, but the sun and
the moon cannot shine together; the moon cannot shine
till the sun is gathered in. Now thou art not permitted to
enter, but if thou wouldst fain know of the land, send thee
men who will inform thee. For Moses already knew at this
time that he was not to enter the land, and since he wanted
to know of it before he departed, he sent the spies. When
they failed to bring him back a proper report, he did not
send again, but waited till God showed him the land.

'The first instruction that Moses gave to the spies was
to inquire "whether there were trees in it or no". Moses in
fact knew already, and what he really referred to was the
Tree of Life, of which the proper place is the terrestrial
Garden of Eden. He said: If this tree is in it, I shall enter,
but if not, I shall not be able to enter. Observe that there
are two Trees,[1] one higher and one lower, in the one of
which is life and in the other death, and he who confuses
them brings death upon himself in this world and has no
portion in the world to come.' Said R. Isaac: 'Moses took
to himself the Tree of Life, and therefore he wished to
know whether it was in the land or not.'

SEND THEE MEN. R. Judah quoted here the verse:
"Like the coolness of snow in the day of harvest, so is a
faithful messenger to one who sends him, he refresheth the
soul of his master" (Prov. XXV, 13). ' "The faithful messenger"
is exemplified in Caleb and Phineas, who were sent by

---

[1] *Tifereth* and *Malkuth*.

Joshua and brought back the Shekinah to abide in Israel. But those whom Moses sent were a source of weeping to future generations, and caused many thousands to perish from Israel.'

As R. Hizkiah and R. Jesse were once walking together, the latter said: 'I see from your looks that some thought is troubling you.' He replied: 'I am pondering on the verse: "For that which befalleth the sons of man befalleth beasts, even one thing befalleth them" (Eccl. III, 19). This saying of the wise Solomon troubles me, because it seems to give an opening to the unbelievers.' [157b] 'That is assuredly so,' he replied. At that moment a man came up to them and asked them for water, as he was thirsty and weary from the heat of the sun. They asked him who he was. He replied that he was a Jew. 'Have you studied the Torah?' they asked. He replied: 'Instead of talking with you, I can go up to that hill and find water there and drink.' R. Jesse thereupon brought out a flask full of water and gave it to him. When he had drunk, they said: 'We will go up there with you for water.' So they went up to the rock and found there a trickling stream from which they filled a bottle. They then sat down, and the man said to them: 'You just now asked me if I had studied the Torah. I have done so through a son of mine whom I have put under a teacher, and from whom I have gained some knowledge of the Torah.' R. Hizkiah said to him: 'If it is through your son, well and good; but I see that for the solution of our problem we shall have to look somewhere else.' The man said: 'Let me hear it, since sometimes in the beggar's wallet one finds a pearl.' They then quoted to him the verse of Solomon. He said to them: 'Wherein are you different from all other men who also do not know?' They replied: 'Wherein then?' He then said: 'That is the way in which Solomon meant this verse. He was not saying it in his own name like the rest of the book, but was repeating what is said by worldly fools, that "the hap of man and the hap of the beast", etc.; that is to say, that this world is the sport of chance, and there is no Providence, but "the hap of man and the hap of beast is the same". When Solomon observed this, he called those fools themselves "cattle", as it says in the next verse, "I said in my heart concerning this saying of the sons of men that God should put them on one side and that (the faithful) should see that they are cattle for themselves". A curse on those cattle, on those fools, on those faithless unbelievers ! Better they had never come into the world ! What did Solomon ánswer them ? "Who knows the spirit of the sons of man which goeth upwards and the spirit of the beast which goeth downwards to the earth ?" Who of those fools that wot not of the honour of the supreme King knows that the spirit of the sons of man goes upwards to a supernal, precious and holy place to be nourished by the supernal brightness of the Holy King and to be included in the "bundle of the living", while the spirit of the beast goes downwards to the earth, and not to that place where is every man of those of whom it is written, "In the image of God he made man" ? How can those foolish unbelievers say that there is one spirit to all ? They shall be like chaff before the wind, and will be left in Gehinnom and not ascend for all generations.'

R. Hizkiah and R. Jesse thereupon came and kissed him on his head, saying: 'All this you knew and we were not aware ! Blessed the hour in which we met thee !' [158*a*] He then proceeded: 'This is not the only instance of such a usage. There is, for instance, the verse: "This is evil in all that is done under the sun, for there is one hap to all" (*Ibid.* IX, 3): as much as to say, "What the evil man says is, There is one hap to all". And he goes on: "For he who chooses (the *future* world) does naught,[1] for we are well assured that for all the living there is trust", and also that a live dog is better than a dead lion.' They said to him: 'Would you mind if we join you, and you should accompany us ?' He replied: 'Were I to do so, the Torah would call me a fool, and, moreover, I should render my life forfeit.' 'Why so', they asked. 'Because', he said, 'I am a messenger, and King Solomon said, "He cutteth short his own legs, and drinketh in damage who sendeth words by the hand of a fool" (Prov. XXVI, 6). For the spies, because they did not prove trusty and faithful messengers forfeited their lives both in

[1] Translating the Kethib of Eccl. IX, 4.

this world and the next.' He then embraced them and departed. R. Hizkiah and R. Jose also went their way, and meeting some men they inquired about the stranger. They were told that he was R. Haggai and one of the leading Companions, and that the Companions in Babylon had sent him to make some inquiries of R. Simeon and the other Companions. Said R. Jesse: 'Assuredly this is the R. Haggai who was always unwilling to let it be known that he is a scholar, and therefore it was that he told us that he learnt the Torah through his son. Verily he is a faithful messenger, and happy is the man who has committed his message to him. So, too, Eleazar, the servant of Abraham, was accursed in virtue of being a Canaanite, but because he was a faithful messenger he escaped from his curse and was blessed in the name of the Lord (Gen. XXIV, 31).

'ALL OF THEM MEN. They were all virtuous, but they were misled by a false reasoning. They said: If Israel enter the land, we will be superseded, since it is only in the wilderness that we are accounted worthy to be leaders, and this was what caused their death and the death of all who followed them. [158b]

'AND MOSES CALLED HOSHEA THE SON OF NUN JOSHUA: As much as to say: May Jah save thee from them !' R. Abba said: 'As he was being sent for the purpose of entering the land, it was requisite that he should be perfect, to wit, through the Shekinah, for up to that time he had been called "a lad", and therefore Moses joined the Shekinah with him. And though we find the name Joshua before this in the text (e.g. Ex. XVII, 9; XXXIII, 11), it is there used in anticipation.'

WHETHER THERE ARE TREES (lit. tree) IN IT OR NOT (ayin). Said R. Ḥiya: 'Did not Moses know that there were trees in it, seeing that God had told him that it was a land flowing with milk and honey ?' R. Simeon said: 'What he said was this: "If you see that the produce of the land is like that of other lands, then the Tree of Life is in it, but it does not derive from a still higher place. But if you see that its produce is superior to that of all the rest of the world, then you will know that that difference originates from the Ancient Holy One who is called *ayin* (nothing), and you will know the answer to the question once asked by the Israelites, "whether the Lord is in our midst or *ayin*" (Ex. XVII, 7).'

AND THEY WENT UP IN THE SOUTH AND (HE) CAME TO HEBRON. It should surely be "*they* came" ?' R. Jose said: 'The reference is to Caleb, who went to pray over the graves of the patriarchs. Caleb said: Joshua has been blessed by Moses with support from heaven, and can therefore be delivered from these. What shall I do ? He therefore conceived the idea of praying on the graves of the patriarchs in order to keep clear of the evil counsel of the other spies.' R. Isaac said: 'That which was more distinguished than all of them went in within him; [159a] the Shekinah entered the land in Caleb in order to bring tidings to the patriarchs that the time had arrived for their descendants to come into the land which God had sworn to give them.

'AND THERE WERE AHIMAN, ETC. We have learnt that Ahiman, Sheshai and Talmai were of the descendants of the giants whom God cast down upon the earth and who begat children from the daughters of men.'

AND THEY CAME TO THE BROOK OF ESHCOL. As R. Judah was once walking along with R. Abba, he said to him: 'I should like to ask you one question. Seeing that God knew that man was destined to sin and to be condemned to death, why did He create him ? That He knew this is proved by the fact that in the Torah, which existed two thousand years before the universe, we find it already written, "When a man shall die in a tent", and so forth. Why does God want man in this world, seeing that if he studies the Torah he dies, and if he does not study he also dies, all going one way.' He replied: 'What business have you with the ways and the decrees of your Master ? What you are permitted to know and to inquire into, that you may ask, and as for what you are not permitted to know, it is written: "Suffer not thy mouth to cause thy flesh to sin" (Eccl. v, 6).' He said to him: 'If that is the case, all the Torah is secret and recondite, since it is the Holy Name, and if so we have no permission to ask and inquire ?' He replied: 'The Torah is both hidden and revealed, and the Holy Name is also hidden and revealed, as it is written, "The hidden things belong to the Lord our God, and the revealed things are for us and for our children" (Deut. XXIX, 29). The revealed things we may inquire into, but the hidden things are for the Lord alone. Hence men are not permitted to utter secret things and divulge them, save only the Holy Lamp, R. Simeon, since the Holy One, blessed be He, has concurred with him, and because his generation is distinguished both on high and below, and therefore things are divulged through him, and there shall be no such another generation till the Messiah comes. Now, as for your question. The Holy One, blessed be He, has three words in which He is enshrouded. The first[1] is a supernal recondite one which is known only to Him who is concealed therein. The second[2] one is linked with the first and is the one from which the Holy One, blessed be He, is known. The third[3] is a lower one in which is found separation, and in this abide the celestial angels, and the Holy One, blessed be He, is both in it and not in it, so that all ask, "Where is the place of his glory ?" Similarly man has [159*b*] three worlds. The first is the one which is called "the world of separation", in which man both is and is not; as we look at him he departs and vanishes. The second is the world which is linked with the higher world, being the terrestrial Garden of Eden, while the third is a hidden recondite and unknowable world. Now the first world is a stepping-stone to the others, and did not man sin he would not have a taste of death when he is about to enter those other worlds and when the spirit is divested of the body. But as it is, the spirit has to be cleansed in the "stream of fire" to receive its punishment, and then it enters the terrestrial Garden of Eden, and it is furnished with a robe of light resembling its appearance in this world, and therewith

[1] *Aziluth.*   [2] *Beriah.*   [3] *Yeẓirah.*

it is equipped, and then its abode is there continually, and on New Moons and Sabbaths it attaches itself to the super-soul and ascends aloft. This is the essence of the matter, and so it is with all save the sinners who are cut off from all worlds if they do not effect repentance.' Said R. Judah: 'Blessed be God that I put this question and gained this knowledge.'

R. Simeon said: 'All this section (Num. XIII) can be expounded esoterically. God praises the Torah and says: "Walk in My ways and devote yourselves to My service, and I will bring you in to good and noble worlds." To men who will not believe this God says: "Go and spy out that good and desirable land." They say: "How are we to spy it out and to find out all this ?" Therefore it is written: "Go up here in the south": study the Torah, and from it you will know that the land is before you. "And ye shall see the land what it is": from it you shall see the world of that inheritance into which I am bringing you. "And the people that dwell in it": those are the righteous in the Garden of Eden who stand in rows in the celestial glory. "Whether he is strong or weak": through this you shall see whether they attained to all this when they conquered their evil inclination or no, or when they clung fast to the Torah to study it night and day, or if they relaxed their hold on it and still attained to all this. "Whether they be many or few": whether they be many that devote themselves to my service and cling to the Torah in order to attain to all this or not. "And what is the land, whether it is fat or lean": from the Torah ye shall discover what is the nature of that other world, whether it confers in abundance heavenly bliss on those that dwell there or withholds from them anything. "Whether there are in it trees or no": whether the Tree of Life is therein for all eternity, and whether the "bundle of the living" is there or not. [160a] "And they went up by the south": men go up therein halfheartedly, like one working for nothing, since they think it brings no reward and they see that the riches of this world are lost through it, until "he comes to Hebron", that is, he comes to read and re-read it. "And there were Ahiman, Sheshai and Talmai": there they see great contrasts, unclean and clean, forbidden and permitted, punishments and rewards. "And they came to the brook of Eshcol": these are the words of Agadah which strengthen faith. "And they cut from there a branch": they teach from there general principles which rejoice the true believers and show them how all is reduced to one principle without deviation. But the sceptical and those who do not learn the Torah for its own sake find deviation, as it says, "and they carried it on upon a pole between two". Then, "they returned from spying out the land": they turn from the way of truth and return to the evil side, saying: What use is this ? Till this day we have derived no benefit; we have laboured for nothing. We have made ourselves laughing-stocks, and as for the other world, who can make himself worthy to enter it ? We have laboured and toiled to find out what is the portion of that world, and "indeed it is flowing with milk and honey"; that other world is indeed good. "Howbeit the people are fierce": he that would study must be strong-minded so as to disregard this world, and therefore he should be well provided with money, and also a strong body, since the study of the Torah weakens a man's strength. And should a man say that with all this he will still manage, "Amalek dwells in the south land": the evil inclination, the seducer of man, is always in his body, "and the Hivite and the Amorite": many are the accusers there to prevent a man entering into that world; so who can attain it ? Thus "they spread an evil report of the land". What say then the faithful ? "If the Lord delight in us, he will give it to us": if a man seeks with all his heart to serve God, only the heart is required; [160b] only "rebel not against the Lord": he should not rebel against the Torah, for the Torah demands not wealth nor vessels of gold or silver. "Neither fear ye the people of the land": for if a broken body will study the Torah, it will find healing therein. "For they are bread for us": those accusers themselves provide every day food for those who study the Torah.'

AND THEY CAME UNTO THE VALLEY OF ESHCOL. R. Abba said: 'They cut off the cluster, and when they came to raise it they were not able, nor even to move it, but Caleb and Joshua came and lifted it. While joined to the tree it was called a "branch", but afterwards a "staff". Through this Joshua and Caleb knew that they were destined to enter into the land and obtain a portion in it. On the way the others plotted against them, so Caleb addressed the branch, saying: Fruit, fruit, if for thee we are to be killed, why should we have thee ? Straightway it lightened itself and they gave it to them.' R. Eleazar said: 'They did not give it to any other, but when they came back to the Israelites they gave it to them, and withdrew into the background.' R. Isaac said: 'When they came into the presence of the Anakim they displayed before them the staff of Moses and so were delivered.' R. Judah said: 'We have a tradition that Moses transmitted to them the Holy Name, and through this they were delivered.' R. Ḥiya said: 'The giants were called by three names: *Nefilim, Anakim, Refaim*. Their original name was Nefilim, and when they associated with the daughters of men they were called Anakim, and then when they went about the world and neglected the Heavenly One they were called Refaim. They lived to a great age until at last half their body became paralysed while the other half remained vigorous. They would then take a certain herb and throw it into their mouths and die, and because they thus killed themselves they were called Refaim.' R. Isaac said that they used to drown themselves in the sea, as it is written, "The Refaim are slain beneath the waters" (Job XXVI, 5). R. Simeon said: 'Had Israel entered the land under the sign of [161a] the evil tongue, they would not have endured an instant. Observe how much evil was wrought by the evil tongue: it called forth the decree that our ancestors should not enter the land, those that uttered it died, and weeping was decreed for succeeding generations. Their calumny of the Holy Land was, as it were, a calumny of the Almighty, and therefore God was indignant on account of this, and all Israel would have been destroyed but for the prayer of Moses.

AND THEY TOLD HIM: the word "told" (*sapper*) means

"explaining in detail". WE CAME: as much as to say, "We entered into that land of which you were always singing the praises". AND SURELY IT FLOWETH WITH MILK AND HONEY: R. Isaac said that if a man wants to deceive he should first say something true so that he may be believed. R. Ḥiya, however, said that what they meant was, "We came into the land which you praised so much and which you said was flowing with milk and honey, and this is its fruit! If this is the inheritance which God is giving to Israel and for which they have endured such sufferings, there is fruit in Egypt twice as good". HOWBEIT THE PEOPLE THAT DWELL IN THE LAND ARE FIERCE: as a rule the best warriors are stationed outside the towns to protect the roads, but here even those who dwell in the cities are mighty men. AND THE CITES ARE FORTIFIED: even if all the kings of the world were to assemble against them, they could make no impression on them. R. Jose said: 'The worst of their calumnies was that AMALEK DWELLS IN THE LAND OF THE SOUTH: so when a man has been bitten by a snake, if people want to frighten him they say, There is a snake here. So they said: That one that made war on you before is here, and where? In the land of the south, by which you have to enter. Straightway ALL THE CONGREGATION LIFTED UP THEIR VOICE AND CRIED: they doomed that night to be one of weeping for all generations.

'AND NOW, I PRAY THEE, LET THE POWER OF THE LORD BE GREAT. Observe that when God created man, He formed him on the supernal pattern, and placed his strength and power in the middle of the body where the heart is. Now the heart [161b] is closely attached to a place above it, to wit, the brain. In a similar way did God fashion the world. He placed the ocean round about the inhabited world, and the habitation of the seventy nations round about Jerusalem. Jerusalem itself is round about the Temple Mount, and the Temple Mount round about the courts of the Israelites, and the courts of the Israelites round about the Chamber of Hewn Stone where the Great Sanhedrin used to sit, and this again was round the place of the altar, and the place of the altar round the court, and the court round the Temple proper, and the Temple round the Holy of Holies, where the Shekinah used to abide, and there was the heart of the whole world, and the whole world was nourished from there, while this heart itself was nourished from the brain and the two were linked together. Similarly in a higher sphere, in the mystery of the supernal King. The Stream of Fire is round about many camps, which again are round certain Ministers, who in turn surround the four Chariots, which again surround the Holy City, which rests upon them. Thus ultimately it is found that all is nourished from the supernal hidden Brain, and when examined all are found to be linked together. Now when the Hidden Ancient One illumines the Brain, and the Brain the Heart by the way of "the pleasantness of the Lord", then this is the "power of the Lord"; and Moses now prayed that it might be magnified and ascend higher and higher, and then be drawn down below. As THOU HAST SPOKEN: as we have explained. SAYING: that is, that all future generations should learn to use this address in the time of trouble, namely, THE LORD IS SLOW TO ANGER, ETC.' R. Isaac asked: 'Why is "truth" not mentioned here (among the attributes)?' R. Ḥiya answered: 'Because they caused it to depart through having spoken falsely; they were thus punished with measure for measure.'

[1] . . . with one another things that they had not been able to discuss previously. They went out through that door and sat down in a garden under some trees. They said: 'Now that we are here and see all this, if we die here we shall certainly enter the future world.' So they sat there and fell asleep, until the guardian came [162*a*] and woke them, saying: 'Rise and go forth into the outer garden'. So they went out and found the Masters of Holy Writ expounding the verse, IN THIS WILDERNESS THEY SHALL BE CONSUMED: but not (they said) in any other place. AND THERE THEY SHALL DIE: but not in any other place. This speaks of the

[1] There is here a lacuna in the text.

bodies, but in regard to their souls they shall be like the denizens of the Garden.

The guardian then told them to leave the garden, and they went out with him. He said to them: 'Did you hear anything from that grade ?' They replied: 'We heard a voice say, "He who interrupts shall be interrupted, he who shortens shall be shortened, he who shortens shall be lengthened".' 'Did you understand what it meant,' he asked, and they answered, 'No'. He said to them: 'Did you observe a mighty eagle, and a boy who gathered herbs ? R. Ilai of Nisibis and his son once came here and saw this cave, and when they went into it they could not endure the darkness and died. The boy stands every day before Bezalel when he comes down from the heavenly Academy and says three things. "He who interrupts shall be interrupted": that is, if one interrupts his study of the Torah to speak of idle matters, his life shall be interrupted in this world and his judgement awaits him in the other world. "He who shortens shall be shortened": if one shortens his "Amen", and does not draw it out, his life shall be shortened. "He who shortens shall be lengthened": the first syllable of *ehad* (one)[1] should be uttered very rapidly and not dwelt on at all; and if one does so, his life will be prolonged.' They said to him: 'He also said: "They are two, and one is joined to them, making three, and when they are three they are one".' He said to them: 'These are the two names "Lord" in the *Shema* ;[2] "our God" is, as it were, the signature, and when they are joined they form one.' They said to him: 'He also said: "They are two and have become one; when he has sway he flies on the wings of the wind and traverses two hundred thousand and hides himself".' He said to them: 'These are the two cherubim on which the Holy One, blessed be He, used to ride, but from the day that Joseph has been hidden from his brethren one has been hidden away in two hundred thousand worlds, and He who was wont to ride upon it has hidden himself. Now go forth from here.'

They went forth and the guardian gave them a rose, and the mouth of the cave closed, leaving nothing visible. They

[1] In the *Shema*.　[2] "Hear, O Israel, the Lord our God, the Lord is one."

saw the eagle come down from a tree and enter another
cave. They smelt the rose and entered there, and the eagle
said to them: 'Enter, ye truly virtuous, for yours is the
first society I have enjoyed since I came here.' They went
in and came to another garden along with the eagle. When
they came to the Masters of the Mishnah the eagle took the
form of a man in a resplendent robe like theirs and sat down
with them. He said to them: 'Pay honour to the scholars
of the Mishnah who have come here, since their teacher
showed us many wonderful things here.' One of them said
to them: 'Have you a token ?' They said: 'Yes', and brought
out the two roses. They smelt them and said to them: 'Sit,
members of the Academy, sit, ye truly virtuous.' Then they
took hold of them and they sat down and learnt thirty rules that
they did not know before, and other mysteries of the Torah.

They then went back to the Masters of Holy Writ and
found them expounding the verse: "I said, Ye are gods,
and all of you sons of the Most High" (Ps. LXXXII, 6). 'This',
they said, 'is what God said when Israel at Mount Sinai
said "we will do" before "we will hear",[1] but when they
followed their evil imagination He said, "Verily like Adam
ye shall die"; like Adam, that is, whose death drew him
down to the dust in order that the evil imagination in him
might be wiped out; for it is that evil imagination which
died and was consumed within him.' [162b] An old man who
was at their head said: 'Here, too, it is written: AND
YOUR CARCASES SHALL FALL IN THIS WILDERNESS.
What is meant by "carcases" ? The evil imagination. "In
this wilderness they shall be consumed" (v. 35), to wit,
these carcases, and there they shall die, because it is the will
of the Holy One, blessed be He, to destroy those carcases
from the world.'

R. Ilai said to them: 'Ye truly virtuous, enter and see,
for permission is given you to enter as far as the place where
the curtain is hung, happy is your lot !' So they arose and
went to a place where there were Masters of the Agadah,[2]
their faces shining like the sun. 'Who are these,' they asked.
He replied: 'These are the Masters of the Agadah who

---

[1] v. Ex. XXIV, 7.　　[2] i.e. the Cabbalah.

every day see the true splendour of the Torah. They stood there and heard many new expositions of the Torah, but they were not permitted to join with them. R. Ilai said to them: 'Come into another place and you will see.' They went into another garden and saw there people digging graves and dying immediately, and coming to life again with holy, luminous bodies. 'What does this mean?' they asked. He replied: 'They do this every day. As soon as they lie in the dust the evil taint which they received at first is consumed and they rise at once with new and luminous bodies, those in which they stood at Mount Sinai. As you see them, so they stood at Mount Sinai, with bodies free from all taint; but when they drew upon themselves the evil imagination, they were changed into other bodies.'

A voice then came forth saying: 'Go, assemble, since Aholiab is in his place and all the thrones before him.' So the others all flew away and they were left alone under the trees of the garden. They saw a door and went in through it, and they then saw a temple, in which they went and sat down. Two young men were there. They lifted up their eyes and saw a tent embroidered with all sorts of figures in various colours, and over it a curtain of flashing light too dazzling to behold. They also heard a voice saying: 'Bezalel is the fourth of the supernal lights. . . .'[1] When the voice ceased the two youths said to them: 'Have you a token?' They said 'Yes', and brought out the two roses. They smelt them and said: 'Sit here till you shall hear two profound mysteries from the head of the Academy, which you must always keep secret.' They promised to do so. (Said R. Simeon: 'They wrote down all that they had seen, but when they came to this point they said, "I will take heed to my ways that I sin not with my tongue" (Ps. xxxix, 2): I asked my father about those two words and he said to me: I swear to you, my son, those two words could build worlds and destroy worlds in the hands of one who knew how to use them.') When they had heard those two words the two youths said: 'Go out, go out, you are not permitted to hear any more.' One of them brought out an apple and said: 'Smell

---

[1] Here follow in the text a number of similar enigmatic utterances.

this'. They did so and went out, and forgot nothing of all they had seen.

Another guardian then came and said to them: 'Companions, R. Ilai has sent me to bid you wait here at the entrance of the cave till he comes and tells you notable things which you have not heard before; for he has asked [163a] permission from the Academy to reveal to you certain things.' So they went out and waited at the entrance of the cave, discussing with one another what they had seen and heard there. At last R. Ilai came, resplendent like the sun. They said to him: 'Have you heard any new exposition ?' He said: 'Assuredly so, and permission has been given to me to tell you.' So they gathered together at the mouth of the cave and sat down. He said to them: 'Happy are you to have been shown by your Master the like of the other world. Are you not afraid ?' They said: 'Assuredly, we can no longer feel like other human beings, being so amazed at all we have seen in this mountain.' He said to them: 'Do you see those rocks ? They are the Heads of the Academies of this people in the wilderness, and they enjoy now privileges which they did not enjoy when they were alive. On New Moons and Sabbaths and festivals these Heads of Academies gather to the rock of Aaron the priest and throng round him and enter into his academy, and there they are renewed with the purity of the holy dew which descends upon his head and the oil of anointment which flows upon him, and along with him they are all renewed with the rejuvenation of the beloved of the Holy King, so that this is called the Academy of Love, and He sustains the whole Academy secretly[1] . . . flashing like eagles' wings in the Academy of light, and this is the Academy of Moses. All stand without and no one enters save Aaron alone, but occasionally one or other of them is called by name. No one can see Moses, because a veil overspreads his face and seven clouds of glory surround him. Aaron stands within the curtain below Moses, the curtain half separating them, and all the Heads of the Academies remain outside of this curtain. All the rest remain outside of the clouds. The more illuminating the

---

[1] The text seems here to be imperfect.

exposition given of the Torah, the more those clouds are lit
up, and they become more and more transparent until the veil
becomes visible, and from the midst of that veil they see a
light brighter than that of all other lights, and this is the
face of Moses. No one actually sees his face, but only the
light which proceeds from the veil behind all the clouds.
Moses makes a remark to Aaron, and Aaron explains it to
the Heads of the Academies. How does he explain it ? With
all those founts of wisdom which were closed to him when
the time of Joshua came. Now he restores them with wonderful streams that flow from each word. Similarly all the
virtuous women of that generation come to Miriam. Then
they all ascend like pillars of smoke in this wilderness. That
day is called the day of the marriage celebration. The women
on the eves of Sabbaths and festivals all come to Miriam
to gain knowledge of the Sovereign of the Universe. Happy
is that generation above all other generations. When they
emerge from the Academy of Moses they fly to the Academy
of the firmament, and those who are qualified fly to the
highest Academy. Of that generation it is written: "Happy
is the people that is in such a case, yea, happy is the people
whose God is the Lord" (Ps. CXLIV, 15).[1] [174*a*]

AND THE LORD SAID TO MOSES, SPEAK UNTO THE
CHILDREN OF ISRAEL . . . THAT THEY MAKE THEM-
SELVES FRINGES ON THE CORNERS OF THEIR GARMENTS,
ETC. R. Hizkiah adduced here the verse: "And he showed
me Joshua the high priest", etc. (Zech. III, 1). [174*b*] 'What
did he see ? He saw him standing before the angel.' R. Isaac
said: 'What does this tell us ? That every man who in this
world does not wrap himself in the ceremonial garb and
clothe himself therewith, when he enters the other world
is covered with a filthy garment and is brought up for trial.
Many are the garments prepared for man in this world, and
he who does not acquire the garment of religious observance
is in the next world clad in a garment which is known to
the masters of Gehinnom, and woe to the man who is clad

[1] From here to p. 174*a* the text is fragmentary, and it is not easy to
find a connecting thread.

therein, for he is seized by [175*a*] many officers of judgement and dragged down to Gehinnom, and therefore King Solomon cried aloud, "At all times let thy garments be white".' [175*b*]

R. Judah said: 'God has appointed many witnesses to give man warning. When he rises in the morning and begins to move, the witnesses stand before him and say: "He shall keep the feet of his saints" (1 Sam. 11, 9), and "keep thy feet when thou goest" (Eccl. IV, 17). When he opens his eyes to observe the world, the witnesses say: "Thine eyes shall look right on" (Prov. IV, 25). When he begins to speak the witnesses say: "Keep thy tongue from evil" (Ps. XXXIV, 14). When he begins to transact business they say: "Depart from evil and do good" (*Ibid.* 15). If he listens to them, well and good, but if not, then they all testify against him above. But if he desires to labour in the service of the Almighty, they all become his advocates in the hour of need. When, therefore, he rises in the morning, he should recite a number of blessings. He then puts the phylactery on his head and he knows he has the Holy Name impressed on his head. When he stretches out his arm he sees it bound with the knot of the Holy Name. When he puts on the ceremonial garment he sees in the four corners four kings issuing to meet four. Four true witnesses of the King are suspended from the four corners like grapes from a cluster. Like seven couriers are the seven windings of blue round each one, which may be increased up to thirteen, but not more.' R. Isaac said that if there are seven, they are symbolical of the Shekinah, and if thirteen, of the thirteen attributes. R. Isaac said that the threads indicate how the four sides of the world are suspended from that special place which controls all as the heart the body. R. Judah said: 'The Holy One, blessed be He, thus signifies that whoever wishes to walk in the fear of Him should follow after this heart and after the eyes that are above it, but "ye shall not go astray after *your* heart and *your* eyes".' [176*a*] R. Ḥiya said: 'Why is the exodus from Egypt mentioned in this passage ? Because when they went forth from Egypt God brought them into this portion (of the commandments), and therefore He admonished them thus.'

KORAH

Numbers XVI, 1–XVIII, 32

NOW KORAH THE SON OF IZHAR THE SON OF KEHATH THE SON OF LEVI, ETC. He who makes the right left and the left right, as it were, lays waste the world. Now Aaron represented the right and the Levites the left, and Korah sought to make the right and the left change places, and therefore he was punished. Further, the evil tongue was also found in him, and for that also he was punished. R. Judah said: 'The left should always be embraced in the right. Korah sought to change the order fixed both above and below, and therefore he perished both above and below.

'TOOK. What did he take ? He took an evil counsel for himself. If one runs after that which is not his, it flies from him, and what is more, he loses his own as well. So Korah pursued that which was not his, and he lost his own without obtaining the other. Korah quarrelled with peace, and he who quarrels with peace quarrels with the Holy Name, [176*b*] because the Holy Name is called peace.' R. Jose said: 'The Torah is also peace, as it is written: "And all her paths are peace" (Prov. III, 17). Korah tried to upset peace on high and below, and therefore he was punished both on high and below.'

AND THEY ROSE UP BEFORE MOSES, ETC. R. Simeon said: 'The earthly kingdom is on the pattern of the heavenly kingdom. All those supernal Crowns to which the Holy Name is attached are summoned from a place called Holiness, and just as the higher Holiness summons them, so the lower Holiness summons its hosts to be crowned and exalted therewith. And just as its hosts are above, so are the rulers of the people below. Hence they are described here as "called to the assembly". They are also called here "men of name", but not "men of the Lord", because they came from the side of Geburah, but they arrogated more to themselves and banded together in contention.

'IN THE MORNING THE LORD WILL SHOW WHO ARE HIS
AND WHO ARE HOLY. Why "morning", and why "holy",
rather than "pure" ? Moses meant this: In the morning
the Crown of Priest is active, and if you are priests, then
in the morning perform the service of the morning and the
Lord will make known who is His—that is to say, the Levite
—and who is the holy one—that is to say, the priest—
and he shall bring near to Himself. The test will only be
made by "Morning". If it is meet for you to remain on the
side of Judgement, then Morning will not endure you, for
it is not the time of Judgement. But if it is meet for you
to remain on the side of Grace, then as it is the time thereof,
you shall remain with it and it will accept you. In virtue of
what ? Of the incense, since the incense requires the "best
man" to form the link and union; and the "best man" is
the priest. Therefore the man whom the Lord shall choose,
he shall be "holy", and not only "pure".

'AND THEY FELL ON THEIR FACES AND SAID, O GOD,
THE GOD OF THE SPIRITS OF ALL FLESH. Moses and
Aaron at this point risked their lives, since "falling on one's
face" always means a supplication to the place of the Tree
of Death,[1] the place where is the bundle of all souls, to
which they ascend and from which they issue.' [177a]

AND MOSES SAID UNTO AARON, TAKE THY CENSER,
ETC. R. Ḥiya adduced here the verse: "The wrath of the
king is as messengers of death, but a wise man will pacify
it" (Prov. XVI, 14). 'How careful men should be', he said,
'to abstain from sin and to watch their actions, for at many
periods the world is judged and every day deeds are placed
in the balance and examined on high and recorded before
the Almighty; and when the deeds of men are not approved
before the King, wrath arises and judgement is awakened.
But if when the executioners of judgement are ready to
strike and wrath impends, there is found in the generation a
righteous man who is inscribed above, then God looks upon
him and His wrath is mollified. He is like a king who is

[1] The Shekinah.

angry with his servants and sends for the executioner to punish them, but meanwhile the king's friend enters and stands before him, and when the king sees him his face lights up, and when he begins to speak he is glad. So when the executioner comes and sees the king all smiling, he goes away and does not execute judgement, and then the king's friend intercedes for his servants and procures forgiveness for them. So here, when Moses saw wrath [177b] impending he at once told Aaron, who was the "friend" of the Matrona, to take the incense, which increases peace in the world and binds the knot of faith, which is the joy of higher and lower and effects the removal of wrath.'

R. Eleazar said: 'It is written "Cut ye not off the tribe of the families of the Kohathites from among the Levites" (Num. IV, 18), because they are the main stock of the Levites, and further, "This do unto them that they may live". This means that the priest had to regulate them, since although they were near to the holiness they were not to enter save with the regulation of the priest, who knew exactly how far they could go in, and when the holy vessels began to be covered another covering also began, and it was forbidden them to see. For things done quietly are the province of the priests and not of the Levites, whose function it was to raise the voice in song. Hence, when judgements begin to assail the world from the side of the Left, the Right Hand must bring appeasement with the incense, which makes no sound. Observe that when that other altar commences to grow restive because there are no righteous, the inner altar intervenes with it and judgements are allayed. Hence AARON TOOK AS MOSES SPAKE, AND RAN INTO THE MIDST OF THE ASSEMBLY, AND HE PUT ON THE INCENSE, which belongs to the inner precinct symbolizing the Priest, and so HE MADE ATONEMENT FOR THE PEOPLE AND HE STOOD BETWEEN THE DEAD AND THE LIVING, between the Tree of Life and the Tree of Death. Then the Right Hand drew them near one to another and the plague was stayed. Happy the lot of the priest who has power above and below and brings peace above and below !'

As R. Eleazar was once standing before his father, R.

Simeon, he quoted to him the verse: "See life with the wife whom thou lovest all the days of the life of thy vanity" (Eccl. IX, 9). 'This', he said, 'is a hint to a man that he should unite Life with this place,[1] the measure of day with the measure of night. All Solomon's words', he went on, 'are written in wisdom, yet it would seem that here he is giving the rein to worldliness, and equally in the words that follow: "Whatsoever thy hand findeth to do, do with thy might, for there is no work nor device", etc. How could the wise Solomon [178a] speak thus? But, indeed, all the words of Solomon have a deep inner significance. What is indicated here is that a man should always merge the left in the right, and all his actions should be controlled by the right. Thus we interpret, "all that thy hand findeth to do" of the left, and "that do with thy might" of the right. When a man is careful that all his acts should be towards the right side, and that he should include the left in the right, then God dwells within him in this world and brings him into the next world. A man should not say, When I reach that world I will seek mercy of the King and repent before him, for "there is no work or device or knowledge or wisdom" after a man departs from this world, but if a man desires that the Holy King should illumine him for that world and give him a share in the world to come, he should strive in this world to place his actions in the sphere of the right. Or we may also explain that there is no work nor device nor knowledge nor wisdom in Sheol. There are storeys in Gehinnom, one above another; there is Sheol and below it Abadon. From Sheol it is possible to come up again, but not from Abadon. Now those who have good works in this world, or reckoning or knowledge or wisdom, when they pass by to observe the sinners in Gehinnom and hear them crying out from the grade of Sheol, are not left there, but ascend aloft to the place of illumination and delight where God comes to have converse with the righteous in the Garden of Eden.

'BUT THE LEVITES SHALL DO THE SERVICE OF THE TENT OF MEETING. At the time of the Creation the world was

---

[1] i.e. *Tifereth* with *Malkuth*.

not completed and established until man emerged in his complete form as the consummation of all and the (seventh) day was sanctified and the holy throne was set for the King. At the moment when the day was about to be sanctified the spirits of the demons issued forth, but the day was sanctified before their bodies were created, and so the world was left deficient. [178b] When Israel were sanctified and all their grades completed with the Levites on the left side, then this deficiency of the world on the left side was made good, and all was then subordinated to the right and the world was freed from defect. Hence it says "the Levite shall do", i.e. "make" or "complete". We may also translate, "And the Levite shall serve *hu* (him)", the reference being to the Ancient One, and the Levite typifying Judgement, but for which men would not rise to the higher faith, nor study the Torah, nor carry out the precepts of the Torah for the service of the Holy King.'

HUKKATH

Numbers XIX, 1–XXII, 1

AND THE LORD SPAKE UNTO MOSES AND UNTO AARON
SAYING, THIS (*zoth*) IS THE STATUTE OF THE LAW
WHICH THE LORD HATH COMMANDED, SAYING. R. Jose
said: 'This passage commences simply, "*This* is the statute
of the law", but in another passage we find, "*Now this
(ve-zoth)* is the law which Moses set before the children of
Israel" (Deut. IV. 44). Why this difference? As we have
learnt, because the addition of the *vau* (now) indicates the
complete union of all, of the Community of Israel with the
Holy One, blessed be He; and such is the essence of the
Torah. But where this *vau* is absent, there we have only
the "statute of the Law" and not the Law itself.'

When R. Simeon and R. Eleazar and R. Abba and R.
Isaac were once in the house of R. Phineas ben Jair, the
latter asked R. Simeon to give some new exposition of the
section commencing: "This is the statute of the law".
R. Simeon, however, [180a] called on R. Eleazar. The latter
thereupon discoursed on the text: "Now this was the custom
in former time in Israel concerning redeeming and concerning exchanging, to confirm all things", etc. (Ruth IV, 7).
'This verse', he said, 'raises a problem. If the ancients
adopted this custom on the basis of the Torah, and later
generations abolished it, how could they do so, seeing that
to abolish a thing laid down in the Torah is like laying waste
the whole world? If, again, it was not an injunction of the
Torah, but a mere custom, why was a shoe chosen for the
purpose? The truth is that this was enjoined originally
by the Torah, and because the ancients were pious and
virtuous this thing was revealed to them, but when sinners
multiplied the thing was done in a different way, in order
to conceal matters which have a high mystic significance.
Now when God said to Moses, "Draw not nigh hither"
(Ex. III, 5), He also said, "Put off thy shoes from off thy
feet"; and it has been explained that by these words He

enjoined him to part from his wife and attach himself to another wife of holy supernal radiance, to wit the Shekinah, and the drawing off of the shoe removed him from this world and placed him in another world. Similarly with a dead man who has departed from the world without children. The Shekinah does not gather him in, and he is driven to and fro about the world, but God has pity on him and bids his brother redeem him so that he may be set right by means of other dust. Now if that redeemer is not willing to establish seed for his brother in this world, he must tie a shoe on his foot and the wife must loosen it and take it to herself. Why was a shoe chosen for this purpose ? Because the shoe was the support of the dead man in this world, and the woman, by taking it, signifies that the dead man who was wandering about among the living will now through that shoe no longer wander about among them. She must dash the shoe on the ground to show that she has laid to rest the body of the dead, and God then, or after a time, has pity on him and receives him into the future world. Therefore it was that whoever desired to confirm an undertaking took off his shoe and gave it to his neighbour. This was beforetime in Israel when they were pious and holy, but when sinners multiplied they concealed the matter under another form, using the corner of a garment. [180b]

'A RED HEIFER, ETC. The heifer receives from Ox, who is on the left, and is therefore used to purify. "Red" symbolizes the sentence of judgement. "Without spot" symbolizes lenient judgement. "Wherein is no blemish" indicates the Shekinah.

'AND YE SHALL GIVE HER UNTO ELEAZAR THE PRIEST. Why to him and not to Aaron ? Because Aaron was the friend of the Matrona, and also because Aaron came not from the side of Pure, but from the side of Holy; for only he is called pure who emerges out of impurity. The key to the whole passage is in the words, "for a water of impurity, it is a sin-offering" (v. 9). For all the lower judgements, and all that come from the side of uncleanness, when it sucks from the "other side" sitting in judgement bestir themselves and haunt the world, but when all this ceremony of the heifer is performed on earth, and cedar wood, etc., is thrown into it, [181a] then their strength is enfeebled and wherever they are they are crushed and weakened, since their power also appears to them in this form (of an ox), and they no longer stay with a man, and he is purified.'

AND THE CHILDREN OF ISRAEL, EVEN THE WHOLE CONGREGATION, CAME INTO THE WILDERNESS OF ZIN. R. Judah said: 'Why is the section of the red heifer followed immediately by the statement of the death of Miriam ? To show that just as judgement was executed on this heifer to purify the unclean, so judgement was executed on Miriam to purify the world. When Miriam departed, the well which accompanied Israel in the wilderness also departed. Therefore THERE WAS NO WATER FOR THE CONGREGATION, because the well had departed both above and below. Then the right hand was broken, as it says, "Let Aaron be gathered to his people", and finally the sun was darkened, when God said to Moses, "And die in the mountain", etc. There never was a generation like that in which Moses was present along with Aaron and Miriam. And think not that there was the like in the days of Solomon, for in the days of Solomon the Moon held sway but the Sun was gathered in, whereas in the days of Moses the Moon was gathered in but the Sun held sway. It is written: "And the sun ariseth and the sun goeth down" (Eccl. 1, 5). This signifies, as we have explained, that when the Israelites came forth from Egypt the Sun[1] shone for them and not the Moon, but it went down in the wilderness. To where, then, was it gathered in ? "Unto its place", in order to give light to the Moon. So it was with Moses, and that is the point of the verse, "What profit is there to a man from all his labour", etc. (*Ibid.* 3). The "man" here is Joshua, who laboured to give Israel possession of the land and yet did not succeed in bringing the Moon to fullness, because he laboured for Israel "under the sun", that is, on a lower plane than the sun of Moses, and he did

[1] *Tifereth.*

not really take his place. That being so, what was his glory, seeing that he did not reach perfection on either side (either of the sun or of the moon) ? [182a] R. Simeon said: 'What is "under the sun" ? This is the moon; and whoever attaches himself to the moon without the sun, his labour is "under the sun" assuredly; and this was the original sin of the world; and hence it says, "What profit is there to man in all his labour, to wit, to the first Adam and all who have followed him.'

LET AARON BE GATHERED UNTO HIS PEOPLE, ETC. R. Ḥiya adduced here the verse: "Wherefore I praised the dead which are already dead", etc. (Eccl. IV, 2). [182b] 'How could King Solomon praise the dead more than the living, seeing that only he is called "living" who walks in the way of truth in this world, while the wicked man who does not walk in the way of truth is called "dead" ? We must, however, look at the words which follow, "which are already dead". This refers to one who has already died but who has the opportunity to return to this world in order that he may rectify (his previous life); verily this one is more to be praised than the other dead, because he has received his punishment, and he is more to be praised than the living who have not yet received their punishment. Such a one is called "dead" because he has had a taste of death, and although he is in this world he is dead and has returned from the dead; whereas "the living who are still alive" have not yet had a taste of death, and have not received their punishment and do not know if they will be worthy of the other world or not. Observe, further, that the virtuous who are thought worthy to be "bound up in the bundle of the living" are privileged to see the glory of the supernal holy King, and their abode is higher than that of all the holy angels, while those who have not merited to ascend so high are assigned a lower place according to their deserts. They are stationed in the lower Eden, which is called "lower Wisdom", and between which and the higher Eden there is a difference as between darkness and light. These, then, are they whom Solomon called "the living who are still alive", but the

others "who have already died" and who have received
their punishment once and twice are in a higher grade than
they, and are called refined silver which has been purified
of its dross. "And better than both is he which hath not
yet been"; this refers to the spirit, which remains above
and which delays to come down to earth, since it has not
to receive any punishment, and it is nurtured with that
supernal food above. [183a] [Or, again, we may explain that]
best of all is he that has not separated from God and is
concealed in obscurity, the pious saintly ones that keep the
precepts of the Law and study the Torah day and night:
such a one reaches a higher grade than all other men, and
all envy his canopy. Now when God said to Moses, "Let
Aaron be gathered to his people", he was greatly distressed,
as he knew that his right hand was being broken, and he
trembled greatly, until God said to him, "Take Aaron and
Eleazar his son", as if to say: "Moses, see, I have prepared
for thee another right hand". And for all that, Eleazar did
not completely fill the place of his father, since the clouds
of glory departed on Aaron's death and did not return save
for the merit of Moses, and not of Eleazar.

'AND MOSES DID AS THE LORD COMMANDED, ETC. Why
did they go up "in the sight of all the congregation"?
Aaron was most dearly beloved of all the people, and therefore, so that they should not say that he was laid out by
Moses, they all saw when he stripped Aaron of the garments
and put them on Eleazar. Why was Moses chosen for this
task? Because Moses had put them on Aaron when he was
invested with the priesthood; so now he stripped him of
what he had given him, while God stripped him of what *He*
had given him, Moses stripping without and God within.
God prepared for Aaron a bed and a candlestick of gold
with a light, taken from the candlestick which he used to
light twice a day, and He closed the mouth of the cave and
they descended.' R. Judah said: 'The mouth of the cave
was left open and all Israel saw Aaron lying there and the
light burning before him and his bed being taken out and
in, with a cloud resting on it, and then they knew that

Aaron was dead, besides which they saw that the clouds of glory had departed. Therefore all the house of Israel, men, women and children, wept for Aaron because he was most beloved of all.' R. Simeon said: 'Why were not these three holy brethren buried in one place ? Some say that each was buried in a place where Israel was destined to be in danger, so as to protect them, but in truth each died in the fitting place, Miriam in Kadesh, between the north and the south, Aaron on the right side, and Moses in his fitting place, which was connected [by underground passages] both with the mountain where Aaron died and with the grave of Miriam. [183b]

'AND THE PEOPLE SPAKE AGAINST GOD AND AGAINST MOSES. That is to say, they spoke against God and wrangled with Moses. WHEREFORE HAVE YE BROUGHT US UP: they put all faces [i.e. God and Moses] on the same level. Therefore there were sent among them serpents that burnt them like fire, and the fire entered their bodies and they fell dead.

'THAT IS THE WELL WHEREOF THE LORD SAID UNTO MOSES, GATHER THE PEOPLE, ETC. This well never left them. It may be asked, How could they all draw from it ? It issued into twelve streams and a channel went forth in every direction, and when Israel encamped and required water they used to stand by it and recite this song: "Ascend, O well, bring up thy waters to provide water for all, so that they may be watered from thee". So, too, they sang the praises of the well: "The well which the princes digged", etc. All that they said in its praise was true, and from this we learn that if one wishes to set in motion the powers above, whether through action or words, he produces no effect if that action or word is not as it should be. All people go to synagogue to influence the powers above, but few know how to do it. God is near to all who know how to call upon Him and to set powers in motion in the proper manner, but if they do not know how to call upon Him He is not near. So here, the Israelites spoke words of truth so as to set in motion [184*a*] this well, and before they did this it would not move. So also with magicians who get the "evil species" to serve them, if they do not employ the right formulas to draw them, they do not stir. So it says, "They called on the name of Baal", etc. (1 Kings XVIII, 26), yet they availed nothing, for one thing because it was not permitted to them to bring fire down from heaven, and for another because they did not use the right invocation, since God confused them, as it says, "Thou didst turn their heart backwards" (*Ibid.* 37).' R. Simeon said: 'Here I must tell you something. Whoever knows how to perform the correct ceremony and recite the proper words can certainly influence the Holy One, blessed be He. If so, it may be asked, what is the superiority of the righteous who know the root of the matter and can concentrate their minds and thoughts more than the others who do not know this? The truth is that those who do not know the basis of the ceremony, and perform it only as a matter of rote, draw down to themselves an influence from behind the shoulders of the Holy One, blessed be He, which is only called "Providence", but those who do know draw forth blessings from the place which is called "Thought" until upper and lower beings are blessed and the Holy Name is blessed through them. Happy are they in that God is near them and ready to answer them when they call.

'AND THE LORD SAID TO MOSES, DO NOT FEAR HIM. Og was one of those who clave to Abraham and were circumcised with him. Hence Moses was afraid that he would not be able to overcome the sign which Abraham had impressed upon him. Therefore God said to him, "Do not fear him (*otho*)", as much as to say, Do not fear that sign (*oth*) which is upon him, because he has impaired that sign of his, and whoever impairs his sign deserves to be annihilated. [184*b*] Therefore Israel destroyed him entirely, with his sons and all his people, as it is written: "And they smote him and his sons and all his people".'

BALAK

Numbers XXII, I–XXV, 9

AND BALAK THE SON OF ZIPPOR SAW, ETC. What did he see? He saw both through the window of wisdom and with his physical eyes. The tails of the skirts of the stars are the windows of wisdom, and there is one window through which the very essence of wisdom can be seen. So Balak saw with his own particular wisdom. He was the "son of a bird",[1] for he used birds for all his magic arts. He used to mark a bird plucking a herb or flying through the air, and on his performing certain rites and incantations that bird would come to him with grass in its mouth and he would put it in a cage. He would tie knots before it and it would tell him certain things. He would perform his magic arts and the bird would chirp and fly away to the "open of eye" and tell him, and then return. One day he performed his arts and took the bird, and it flew away but did not return. He was greatly distressed, until he saw it coming with a fiery flame following it and burning its wings. Then he saw strange things and became afraid of Israel. The name of that bird is known, but none can make use of it for magic arts with the same effect as Balak. All his wisdom was through that bird. He covered his head and crawled before it, saying "The people", and the bird answered "Israel". He said "exceedingly" and the bird answered "numerous". Seventy times they thus chirped to one another, with the result that he was seized with fear, as it says: "And Moab was sore afraid of the people, for they were many". In the descriptions of the magic of the ancient Kasdiel we find that they used to make a bird of this kind at stated times out of silver mingled with gold. Its head was of gold, its mouth of silver; its wings of polished brass mixed with silver; its body of gold, the dots on its wings of silver, and its legs of gold. They used to place in its mouth a tongue of that known bird and set it in a

[1] *Zippor* means, in Hebrew, "bird".

window which they used to open to face the sun, or at night to face the moon, and then they used to tie knots and do magical rites and adjure the sun, or at night the moon; [185*a*] and so they used to do for seven days. From that time the tongue used to quiver in the bird's mouth, and they used to prick it with a needle, when it would utter wonderful things of itself. Balak knew all things through this bird, and therefore he was called "son of the Bird".

It is written: "The Lord said, I will bring again from Bashan, I will bring again from the depths of the sea" (Ps. LXVIII, 23). God's words are true and can be relied upon, for what He says is done. In time to come God will arouse and bring back from Bashan all those who were killed and devoured by the wild beasts of prey. For there is in the world an abode of all great beasts, and lofty mountains where they hide. The mighty Og was among the wild asses of the wilderness, and his strength was there because he was the king of Bashan. No king could make war against him, till Moses came and did so. Sihon was the colt of the wilderness, and the reliance of Moab was upon him. When Israel destroyed the city of Sihon, a herald traversed the kingdom of heaven saying: "Assemble, ye rulers of all the peoples, and see how the kingdom of the Amorite has been laid waste". At that time all the Governors of the seven nations (of Canaan) gathered together and sought to restore the kingdom to its former condition. But when they saw the power of Moses they turned back. Hence it is written: "Therefore the rulers said, Come ye to Heshbon, let the city of Sihon be built and established" (Num. XXI, 27). But when they saw the might of Moses they said: "A fire has gone out of Heshbon, a flame from the city of Sihon". Why did they use both names ? They said: All paths and ways are closed by the power of their leader. If we should say, Let Heshbon be rebuilt, behold, a fire has gone out of Heshbon; and if we say merely "the city of Sihon", behold, a flame has issued from the city of Sihon. Since that flame of fire is there, none can prevail against it to restore the place to its former condition; on every side we are prohibited. Therefore, "Woe is thee, Moab"; he that was thy shield has been crushed. Seeing this, "Moab was sore afraid of the people"—more than of death, because they saw that Israel prevailed above and below, over their Chieftains and Rulers above, and over their chieftains and rulers below. Israel, in fact, was the "great one", the elder and the holy one, and not Esau. [185b]

AND MOAB SAID UNTO THE ELDERS OF MIDIAN, ETC. R. Ḥiya spoke on the verse: "And he showed me Joshua the high priest standing before the angel of the Lord" (Zech. III, 1). 'How careful', he said, 'should a man be of his ways in this world, to walk in the way of truth, because all his actions are recorded in writing before the King ! The gatekeepers are ready, the witnesses are at hand, the prosecutors are well prepared, the judge is waiting to receive the evidence, and those who have charges to bring are bestirring themselves, and it is not known whether they will come from the right or the left. For when the spirits of men leave this world many are the accusers who stand up against them, and heralds to proclaim the result of the trial, whether good or bad, as it has been taught: Man is sentenced many times in this world, both during his lifetime and after, but God's mercies are over all and He does not desire to judge men according to their works, as David said: "If thou, Jah, shouldst mark iniquities, Lord, who should stand ?" (Ps. cxxx, 3). In this verse David mentioned three degrees of mercy. If one's sins are so numerous that they are marked by *Jah*, then there is "the Lord", who stands for mercy: and if even this name which stands for mercy arises to chastise, and all grades are sealed in judgement, there is still one grade to which we can turn, since all healing comes from it, and this will have pity on us: this is *MI* (Who). Therefore it says here, "*Who* shall stand ?", since all the ways of mercy and repentance open out from it. Now Joshua the son of Jehozedek was a perfectly righteous man, a man who penetrated to the innermost shrine, who was admitted to the Heavenly Academy. All the members of the Academy assembled to consider his case. For it is the rule there that when one is brought to be tried a herald proclaims: All members of the Academy enter the secret chamber. Then the Court assembles and the spirit of the man to be tried is brought up by two officers, and placed near a pillar of flashing flame which stands there and which is kept in shape by a current of air blowing on it. Now if any have on earth studied the Torah and given original explanations, their words have been immediately reported to the members of the Academy. They all now come to see him. If his word was a fitting one, happy is he, for he is crowned with many radiant crowns by all the members of the Academy. If, however, his word was of another kind, alas for his disgrace. They thrust him outside, and he stands within the pillar until he is taken to his punishment. Heaven preserve us ! Others there are who are taken up there when the Holy One, blessed be He, is arguing with the members of the Academy and says: Who shall decide ? Here is So-and-so, who will decide. And so they take him up there and he decides that matter in dispute between God and the members of the Academy. Others are taken up there to be chastised in order to become cleansed and purified.' Said R. Jose to him: 'If so, then a man departs this world without judgement; and if he departs after judgement, why is he judged a second time ?' He replied: 'What I have learnt is that a man does indeed depart this world in judgement, but before he enters the place set aside for the righteous he is taken up to be tried (again) before the Heavenly Academy, the official of Gehinnom standing there in order to pervert the judgement, if possible. Happy is he who emerges from the trial successfully; otherwise the officer of Gehinnom seizes him so soon as he is delivered into his power, and hurls him down to nether regions like a stone [186a] from a sling, and there he receives his punishment according to his sentence. Similarly Joshua the high priest was taken up for trial to that Heavenly Academy when he departed this world. He was "standing before the angel of the Lord": this is the "youth",[1] the head of the Academy, who pronounces sentence on all. The "Satan" is he who has charge of the souls in Gehinnom, who ever craves for more and says

[1] Metatron.

"give, give", more souls to Gehinnom. Then, "The Lord said unto Satan, The Lord rebuke thee, Satan, and the Lord rebuke thee. . . ." Why two rebukes here? One for Dumah and one for him who comes out of Gehinnom to lead astray. That higher Satan, as we have stated elsewhere, goes down to earth in the form of an ox, and all those wicked spirits which have been condemned to Gehinnom he licks up in one moment and hands over to Dumah after he has swallowed them. Therefore it was that Moab said to the elders of Midian, "Now shall this multitude lick up all that is round about us as the ox licketh up the grass of the field", since it is known that the ox is there to do evil to all mankind.' Said R. Jose: 'If so, Balak was clever?' He replied: 'Certainly; and he had to know all the ways of that ox, as otherwise he would not have been able to practise his magic arts.'

Once, when R. Isaac and R. Judah were on a journey, they came to a place called Kfar Sachnin, where Rab Hamnuna the Elder used to live. They put up at the house of his wife. She had a young son who was still at school, and when he came from school and saw the strangers his mother said to him: 'Go up to these distinguished gentlemen that you may obtain a blessing from them'. He began to approach, but suddenly turned back, saying to his mother: 'I don't want to go near them, because they have not recited the Shema this day, and I have been taught that if one does not recite the Shema at the proper time, he is under a ban the whole of that day.' When the others heard him they were amazed, and they lifted up their hands and blessed him. They said: 'Indeed this is so; to-day we were busy looking after an engaged couple who had no means of their own, and were therefore delaying their marriage. There was no one to provide for them, so we did so, and so omitted to say the Shema at the proper time, since if a man is engaged on one *mizvah* (religious precept) he is exempt from performing another (which might interfere with it).' They then asked him how he knew. He replied: 'I knew by the smell of your clothes when I came near you.' In great surprise they sat down, washed their hands and broke bread. R. Judah's hands were dirty, but he commenced to say the blessing before he had poured water on them. Said the boy to them: 'If you are the disciples of R. Shemaya the Saint, you ought not to say a blessing with dirty hands, as this renders one liable to death.' He then began a discourse on the verse: "When they go in to the tent of meeting they shall wash with water, that they die not" (Ex. xxx, 20). 'We learn from this text', he said, 'that one who is not careful on this point and appears before the King with soiled hands is liable to the death penalty. The reason is that a man's hands are stationed in the highest heights. It is written: "And thou shalt make bars of acacia wood, five for the boards of the one side of the tabernacle, and five for the boards of the other side" (*Ibid.* xxvi, 26), and it is further written, "And the middle bar in the midst of the boards shall pass from end to end" (*Ibid.* 27). Now it must not be thought that this middle bar is not included in the five mentioned previously; it was one of the five, being the middle one with two on each side, symbolical of Moses, [186b] the most important of all, as the rest depended on it. To these the five fingers of the hand correspond, and therefore all the blessings of the priest are made with separated fingers. If so much significance is attached to them is it not right that they should be clean when a blessing of God is said over them, seeing that through them and what they stand for the Holy Name is blessed ? Seeing, therefore, that you are so wise, why did you not take heed of this and listen to R. Shemaya the Saint, who said that all dirt and all stains betake themselves to the "other side", which derives sustenance from them, and therefore it is a religious duty to wash the hands after a meal ?'

They were dumbfounded, and could say nothing. R. Judah asked the boy what was the name of his father. The boy was silent for a moment, then went to his mother and kissed her saying: 'Mother, these wise men have asked me the name of my father; shall I tell them ?' His mother said: 'Have you tested them ?' He replied: 'I have tested them and not found them satisfactory.' His mother then whispered something to him, and he went back to them and said: 'You asked about my father. He has departed this world, but

whenever holy saints travel on the road he follows them in
the form of a pedlar. If you are sainted holy ones, how is
it that you did not find him following you ? The truth is that
I saw through you before, and now I see through you again,
since my father never observes a wise man on the road without following him with his ass in order to carry the yoke of
the Torah. Since my father did not deign to follow you,
I will not tell you who was my father.' Said R. Judah to
R. Isaac: 'Methinks that this child is no son of man.'

They ate their meal, while the boy gave expositions of the
Torah. Having finished they said: 'Come, let us say grace.'
He said to them: 'You have spoken well, since the Holy
Name is not to be blessed with this blessing unless permission is asked.' He then cited the verse: "I will bless the
Lord at all times" (Ps. xxxiv, 2). He said: 'The permissive
form *abarechah* (let me bless) is used, because when a man
sits at table the Shekinah is there and the "other side" is
there. If a man invites the company to bless the Holy One
the Shekinah takes her place above to receive the blessings,
and the "other side" is kept down. But if a man does not
invite the company to bless, the "other side" hears and
pushes in that he may have a share in that blessing. It may
be asked, why is not such an invitation necessary in the
case of other blessings (over food) ? The fact is that the
character of the thing over which the grace is said is itself
an invitation. For instance, if one says grace over fruit, that
fruit is itself an invitation, and the "other side" has no
share in it. For previously (in the three years of "uncircum-
cision") it was in the power of the "other side", and no
blessing could be said over it. But when it has emerged
from the power of the "other side" it may be eaten and a
blessing is said over it, and this is itself the invitation to the
blessing. You may still ask, Seeing that similarly for the
grace after meals the cup of benediction is the invitation,
why should one have to say, Come, let us say grace ? The
reason is that when one drank earlier in the meal he said
the blessing "Creator of the fruit of the vine", which was
an invitation, and now for the grace after meals we require
a change for another invitation, since this cup is for God and

not for food.' Said R. Judah: 'Happy is our lot, for [187*a*] never till this moment have I heard these things. Assuredly I say that this is no son of man.'

He said to him: 'My son, messenger of the Lord and His beloved, in regard to what you said before about the bars, there are many bars but only two hands.' He replied: 'This bears out the saying: From a man's mouth one can tell who he is. However, since you did not pay attention, I will explain. It says: "the wise man's eyes are in his head" (Eccl. II, 14). Where, it may be asked, should they be if not in his head ? What it means, however, is this. We have learnt that a man should not go four cubits with his head un-covered, the reason being that the Shekinah rests on the head. Now a wise man's eyes are directed to his head, to that which rests on his head, and then he knows that the light which is kindled on his head requires oil, which consists in good deeds, and therefore the eyes of a wise man are towards his head, and no other place. You being wise men, on whose head certainly the Shekinah rests, why did you not mark what is written, "Thou shalt make bars for the boards of one side . . . and thou shalt make bars for the boards of the second side", but there is no mention of a third and fourth side, since the first and the second are the important ones ?' They came and kissed him again. R. Judah wept and said: 'R. Simeon, happy is thy portion, happy is thy genera-tion, since for thy sake even schoolchildren are like lofty and mighty mountains.' His mother came and said to them: 'I beg of you, sirs, look not on my son save with a benignant eye.' They said to her: 'Happy is thy portion ! Thou art a goodly woman, a woman selected from all others, for the Holy One, blessed be He, has selected thy portion and raised thy standard above that of all other women.' The boy said: 'I am not afraid of any evil eye, since I am the son of a great and precious fish,[1] and fishes are not susceptible to the evil eye.' They said: 'My son, messenger of the Lord, there is no evil eye in us, nor are we from the side of the evil eye. May the Holy One protect thee with his wings !'

He then began to discourse on the verse: "The angel

[1] A play on the name Hamnuna and the word *nuna*, the Aramaic for "fish".

which hath redeemed me from all evil bless the lads" (Gen. XLVIII, 16). 'These words', he said, 'were uttered by Jacob in the spirit of holiness, and therefore they must contain some mystery of wisdom."Angel" is here one of the names of the Shekinah, applied to her when she is a messenger from on high and receives radiance from the supernal mirror, for then she is blessed by the Father and Mother, who say to her: Daughter, go, mind thy house, attend to thy house; go and feed them, go to the lower world where thy household wait for sustenance from thee; here is all which they require. Then she is "angel". True, she is in many places called "angel" when she does not come to give sustenance to worlds, and further she gives sustenance not in this name but in that of "the Lord". She is, however, called "angel" when she is sent by the Father and Mother, and "Lord" when she rests on the two Cherubim. When she first appeared to Moses she was called "angel", but to Jacob she appeared only under the figure of Rachel, as it is written, "And Rachel came with the sheep". [187b] To Abraham again she appeared as "*Adonay*", as it is written, "And *Adonay* appeared to him in the plains of Mamre" (Gen. XVIII, 1), because at that time he had accepted the covenant, and what had been concealed from him till then was now revealed. Jacob called her "angel" when he was about to depart from the world, because at that moment he was about to inherit her. "Who redeemed me from all evil": because he never drew near the side of evil, and evil never had dominion over him. "Bless the lads": Jacob was speaking like a man who goes into a new house and gives his orders for furnishing and decorating it, "the lads" referring to those who are appointed to be the channels of blessing to the world, to wit, the two Cherubim. "And let my name be named on them": with these words he set his house in order and rose to his proper grade to be united with the supernal Jacob. When those "lads" are duly blessed, then "they swarm like fishes in the midst of the earth". Fishes multiply in the sea and die as soon as they are brought to dry land, but these, although they come from the Great Sea, have their increase in the midst of the earth.'

They came and kissed him again and said: 'Come, let us say grace.' He said: 'I will say grace, because all that you have heard so far has been from me, so I will fulfil in myself the verse, "He that hath a bountiful eye shall be blessed" (Prov. XXII, 9), which we may also read as "shall bless". Why? "Because he hath given of his bread to the poor". Of the bread and food of my Torah have ye eaten.' Said R. Judah: 'Son beloved of the Lord, we have learnt that the host breaks bread and the guest says grace.' He replied: 'Neither am I host nor you guests, but I have found a text which I will carry out. For, indeed, I am "bountiful of eye", seeing that without being asked I have spoken till now, and you have eaten my bread and food'. He then took the cup of benediction and said grace. His hands shook as he held the cup, and when he came to "for the earth and for the food", he exclaimed, "I will lift up the cup of salvation and call on the name of the Lord", and he placed the cup down and took it up again in his right hand and resumed. When he finished he said: 'May it please God that the life of one of these may be prolonged from the Tree of Life, on which all life depends, and may the Holy One, blessed be He, be surety for him, and may he find an additional surety for himself below.' He then closed his eyes an instant, and then opening them, said: 'Companions, peace to you from the Lord of good, to whom belongs the whole world.'

In great wonder they wept and blessed him. They stayed there overnight, and in the morning [188a] rose early and departed. When they came to R. Simeon they told him all that had happened. R. Simeon wondered greatly and said: 'He is a mighty rock, and is worthy of this and even of more than one can imagine. He is the son of R. Hamnuna the Elder.' R. Eleazar was greatly excited and said: 'I must go to see that bright lamp.' Said R. Simeon: 'His name will not be known in the world, because there is something very exceptional about him. It is the light of the anointing of his father which shines on him, and this secret is not divulged among the Companions.'

One day the Companions were sitting arguing with one another—R. Eleazar and R. Abba, and R. Ḥiya and R. Jose, and the other Companions. They said: 'It is written, "Vex not Moab neither contend with him", etc., Moab and Ammon being spared because of Ruth and Naama, who were destined to issue from them. Now,' they asked, 'seeing that Zipporah, the wife of Moses, was from Midian, and Jethro and his sons, who were most virtuous, came from Midian, and Moses lived in Midian, was not Midian in fairness even more deserving to be spared than Moab and Ammon?' R. Simeon replied: 'A tree from which figs have still to be gathered is not like one from which they have been already gathered.' Said R. Eleazar: 'But even if the figs have been gathered, credit is due to the tree?' He replied: 'If a man has not yet gathered figs from a tree, he watches it so that no harm should come to it on account of the figs which it is still to bear. But once he has gathered the figs, he leaves it and no longer watches it. So God protected Moab, which had still to yield its figs, but not Midian, which had already yielded them: and this in spite of the fact that here it was Moab who took the first step, as it says: "And Moab said to the elders of Midian".'

R. Eleazar once went to see R. Jose b. R. Simeon b. R. Lakunia, his father-in-law. He was accompanied by R. Abba and R. Jose, and on the way they discussed points of Torah. Said R. Abba: 'Why did the Israelites treat the Moabites differently from the Ammonites, for, as we have learnt, in the presence of the former they brandished their weapons as if they meant to attack them, whereas against the Ammonites they made no display of military force?' R. Eleazar gave the answer that the younger daughter of Lot, from whom Ammon came, was more modest than the elder from whom Moab came. As they were going along, R. Eleazar suddenly remembered that boy, so they went three parasangs out of their way to get to that spot. They arranged to lodge in the house, and when they went in they found the boy sitting there and a table being laid before him. When he saw them he came up to them and said: 'Enter, holy saints, enter, ye shoots of the world to come, who are praised above and below, to meet whom even the fishes of the sea come up on the dry land.' R. Eleazar went to him and kissed him on his head. Then he again kissed him on his mouth. He said: 'The first kiss is for the fishes that leave the sea and come up on the dry land. The second was for the spawn of the fishes which produce good increase in the world.' Said the boy: 'From the smell of your garments I can see that Ammon and Moab have been attacking you; how did you escape them ? You had no weapons, and yet you went in confidence without fear.' [188b] R. Eleazar and R. Abba and the Companions were in amazement. Said R. Abba: 'Blessed is this journey and happy is our lot that we have been privileged to see this.' They went on preparing the table, and the boy said: 'Holy sages, do you desire the bread of ease without warfare, or the bread of warfare ?' R. Eleazar replied: 'Beloved son, dear and holy, so we desire. We are practised in all weapons of war, and we know how to use the sword and the bow and the lance and the sling, but thou art young and hast not yet seen how mighty warriors contend in battle.' The boy rejoiced and said: 'In truth I have not seen, but it is written: "Let not him that girdeth on boast like him that putteth off".' They then laid the table with all requirements. Said R. Eleazar: 'How I rejoice over this youngster, and how many new points will be brought out at this table ! Therefore I said that I knew that his heart was being agitated by the holy spirit like a bell.' Said the boy: 'He that desires bread at the point of the sword, let him eat.' R. Eleazar drew him near to him and said: 'Because you boasted, you must commence the fight.' 'But', said the boy, 'I said at first that the fighting would be after the meal. Now, however, whoever wants fine flour must bring his weapons in his hands.' R. Eleazar replied: 'It is most fitting for you to give us a taste of your weapons.'

The boy then took the text: "It shall be that when ye eat of the bread of the land, ye shall offer up an heave offering unto the Lord" (Num. xv, 19). 'This verse refers to the Omer of waving (*tenufah*). What is *tenufah* ? We may read it *Tenu feh*, "Give a mouth", the mouth being symbolic of the honour which we have to give to the Holy One, blessed be He. Hence the Omer had to be lifted up to show that we give to God this "mouth", since the chief praise of the

Supreme King is when Israel prepare for him this honour
and give glory to the King. Why was the Omer from barley
and not from wheat ? Because barley ripens first, whereas
wheat is the more perfect food, being symbolical of the
elimination of sin by the substitution of *hittah* (wheat) for
het (sin). You, Companions, who have not attended on
R. [189a] Shemaya the Saint, say that in the five kinds of
corn there is no share for the "other side", but in truth in
whatever rots in the ground there is a share for the other
side, namely the chaff and the straw. These are represented
by the *heth* and the *teth* of *hittah*, and so wheat, in virtue
of the *hé*, is the most perfect of plants, and wheat is the
plant with which Adam sinned.' Said R. Eleazar: 'Assuredly,
it is so.' The boy proceeded: 'The Holy Land is under the
control of the Holy One, blessed be He, and no other power
can enter there. How was the land tested to see whether it
remained faithful and did not attach itself to any other
power ? By the bringing of an offering of barley, like the
suspected wife.'[1] Said R. Abba: 'Of a surety thy sword is
sharp.' The boy replied: 'I am prepared with shield and
buckler to protect myself.' He said: 'There is no other power
that can enter the Holy Land. Whence, then, come chaff and
straw there ?' The boy replied: 'It is written, "And God
created man in his image . . . and God said to them, Be
fruitful and multiply", etc. (Gen. I, 27, 28). Shall we say
that if the serpent had not had intercourse with Eve there
would have been no generations in the world, or if Israel
had not sinned with the calf they would have had no posterity ?
The fact is that had not the serpent had intercourse with
Eve, Adam would have produced progeny at once, in accordance with the verse just quoted, and that progeny would
have been perfectly pure without any defilement. So here,
the Holy Land, into which no alien power can enter, produces
straw and chaff, but not from that side, but outside the
Land the straw and chaff are from the "other side", which
dogs holiness as a monkey dogs a man.' R. Eleazar and the
Companions thereupon went and kissed him, and he said:
'I fancy that I have made good use of the weapons of war,

[1] Num. v.

the bread of the table.' Said R. Eleazar: 'Indeed it is so, and all weapons of war prosper in thy hands.'

He then discoursed on the verse: "And in the vine were three branches", etc. (Gen. XL, 10). 'We have learnt', he said, 'that there are seven firmaments which are six and also five. All issue from the ancient holy supernal Wine, which Jacob presses from a certain Vine. Therefore it was that Jacob presented to Isaac the wine which was fitting for him. That wine proceeds from grade to grade up to Joseph the Righteous, who is David the Faithful. [189*b*] This Vine is the one that is recognized as holy, in contrast to another which is called the "strange vine", the grapes of which are hard and bitter. But this is the vine from which all the holy ones drew the taste of old and good wine, the wine in which Jacob poured water so that all who knew the taste of wine could drink it with relish. When this vine came near the Shekinah it put forth three branches. Then it "was as though it budded", like a bride bedecking herself, and it entered in the love and the joy of that wine to the place where joy abides. Then "its blossoms shot forth": its love went out to its beloved and it began to sing in love. Then were those tender grapes ripened and filled with the good old wine into which Jacob had poured water. Therefore one who blesses over wine should pour some water into it, since the blessing, "Have mercy, O Lord, upon thy people Israel", should not be said save with water in the wine.' R. Eleazar and R. Abba were amazed. They said: 'Holy angel, messenger from above, thy wine has conquered in the mystery of the holy spirit.' They all came and kissed him, and R. Eleazar said: 'Blessed be God for sending me here.' The boy then said: 'Bread and wine are the essence of the meal, all the rest being subsidiary. The Torah is begging of you, saying: "Come, eat ye of my bread and drink of the wine I have mingled" (Prov. IX, 5). Since the Torah calls you, you must obey her behest.' They said: 'That is assuredly so.' So they sat and ate and rejoiced with him.

After they had finished eating they still lingered at the table, and the boy discoursed further, on the verse: "And Moab said to the elders of Midian". 'It does not say, "the elders of Moab'',' he said, 'but simply ''Moab'': the younger took counsel of the elders. What counsel did they give them ? They gave a counsel which redounded to their own hurt. They said to Moab: We have reared a curse among us, namely Moses their chief, through a certain priest who was among us, who brought him up in his house and gave him his daughter to wife. Nay more, he gave him money and sent him to Egypt to destroy all the land, and he and all his household followed him. If we can uproot that chief of theirs, all his people will be immediately uprooted. All the nefarious plan of Peor was from Midian. On their advice they hired Balaam, and when they saw that Balaam could not prevail, they adopted another plan and prostituted their daughters and wives more than Moab. They planned [190a] with their prince that he should prostitute his daughter, thinking to catch Moses in their net. They invested her with all kinds of magic in order to catch their chief, but God ''turns the wise backwards''. They foresaw that a chief of the Israelites would be caught in their net, but they did not understand what they foresaw. They enjoined her not to unite herself with any man save Moses. She said to them: How shall I know him ? They said: Join the man before whom you see all others rise, but no other. When Zimri, son of Salu, came, fifty-nine thousand of the tribe of Simeon rose before him, as he was their prince. She thought he was Moses and joined him. When all the rest saw this they did likewise, with the consequences that we know. Thus all was from Midian, and therefore Midian was punished. God said to Moses, ''Avenge the children of Israel of the Midianites'' (Num. XXXI, 1), as though to say: For thee this is fitting and proper. Moab I leave until two pearls shall have issued from them. David the son of Jesse shall punish Moab and wash the pot clean of the filth of Peor, as it says, ''Moab is my washpot'' (Ps. LX, 9). With all this the sinners of Moab did not desist from their wickedness. In a later generation, when they saw that Joshua and all the elders for whom miracles might have been performed were dead, they said: Now we have a chance, and so they went and joined Amalek, saying, Remember what the children of Israel and Moses their chief, and Joshua their disciple did to you, trying to destroy you. Now is the time when they have no one to shield them, and we will join you. So it is written, "The Midianites came up and the Amalekites and the children of the East" (Judges VI, 3), and again, "Because of Midian the children of Israel made themselves the dens", etc. (*Ibid.* 2). No one did them as much harm as Midian. Hence Moses told the Israelites: "God said to me, Vex not Moab" (Deut. II, 9); that is to say, this injunction was laid upon Moses but not on any other, on David, for instance. In fact, Joshua and the elders who survived him were also forbidden to attack Moab because they were all members of the Beth Din of Moses, and what was forbidden to Moses was forbidden to them, and also because the precious pearls had not yet issued from them. For Ruth was in the days of the Judges. She was the daughter of Eglon, King of Moab, and when Eglon was killed by Ehud they appointed another king, and his daughter was left in charge of a guardian. When Elimelech came to the field of Moab she married his son. She was not made a Jewess by Elimelech, but she learnt all the ways of his house and the rules about food, and when she went with Naomi, then she was converted. Naamah came from the children of Ammon in the days of David. Then the holy spirit rested on David, saying: David, when I measured out all the earth and cast lots, then "Israel was the lot of his inheritance", and I remember what Moab did to them. Hence it is written that David "measured them with the line"; All who were of that tribe and deserving of death the line seized. Midian was destroyed by Gideon, so that none were left of the seed which harmed Israel with counsel or in any other way. God cherishes enmity against all who harm Israel and takes vengeance on them, but if anything good for the world is destined to issue from them, He [190b] bears with them until that good has come forth, and then He punishes them.' Said R. Eleazar: 'This is indeed so, and all this is correct.' Said the boy: 'Now do you Companions prepare your weapons and join combat.'

R. Eleazar then discoursed on the verse: "Bless the Lord, ye angels, ye mighty of his", etc. (Ps. CIII, 20). 'King David', he said, 'here invited the hosts of heaven which are the stars and constellations to bless the Holy One, joining his own soul with them, wherefore he concluded the Psalm with the words, "Bless the Lord, O my soul". Before Israel came, the heavenly angels used to serve with the performance of ceremonies. When Israel at Mount Sinai said, "We will do and we will hearken", performance was taken from the ministering angels and confined to the land of Israel alone. Hence it says, first, "Mighty in strength that fulfil his words", and then, "To hearken". Happy are Israel who took performance from them and carried it out themselves.' Said the boy to him: 'Be on your guard and have your weapon ready. Did Israel take this honour and no other ?' He replied: 'I have found this and no other.' Said the boy to him: 'Your sword is of no avail, or you do not wield it properly. Leave the sword to one who knows how to use it. The highest term of praise which has been entrusted to the ministering angels—not by themselves, but only in conjunction with Israel—is "Holy", but benediction is committed to them when alone, as also to Israel. Not so "holy", for they say the sanctification only in conjunction with Israel. Before Israel sanctify below they cannot sanctify above; hence the great honour of Israel is that they say the sanctification below by themselves.' Said R. Eleazar: 'This is indeed so, and all this has been established. We have also explained that three sanctifications were entrusted to Israel below, from the verse: "And ye shall sanctify yourselves and be holy, for I the Lord am holy" (Lev. xi, 44, and xx, 26).' Said the boy: 'Quite so, but you did not remember your lance till I took it from your shoulder and put it in your hand. Now remember that the lance is in your hand. Return to where you left off.' R. Eleazar then resumed: 'We were speaking of benediction. What is the meaning of "bless ye" ? The drawing of blessings from the place from which all blessings issue until they become a blessing through the abundance of the drawing, and from the abundance of waters in that blessing straightway they swarm with fishes of all kinds. The angels who dwell in the heavenly abodes say simply "Bless the Lord", but we who dwell below

say "Bless *eth* the Lord", because we need to draw this *eth*[1]
down upon us, and through it we enter the presence of the
King. And since we draw this *eth* down upon us, we have
at the same time to say prayers and praises, and therefore
it is forbidden to greet any man until one has said his
prayers, and if he does so he draws a "high place" down
upon himself instead of this *eth*.' Said the boy to him: 'Of
a truth I see that your weapons are good; be mindful of
them and do not forget them. Assuredly the might of a
warrior lies [191a] in his lance and sword. But what is the
meaning of "mighty in strength that fulfil his word, hearkening unto the voice of his word" ?' Said R. Eleazar: 'I have
already explained.' Said the boy: 'I see that your arm has
become faint. Now it is time not to hold back, but to sling
from the catapult stone after stone.'

He then cited the verse: "I am black but comely, O ye
daughters of Jerusalem" (S.S. 1, 5). 'This means that when
she (the Moon) is very lovesick for her Beloved, she shrinks
to nothing until only a dot is left of her, and she is hidden
from all her hosts and camps. Then she says, I am black,
like the letter *yod*, in which there is no white space, and I
have no room to shelter you under my wings; therefore
"do not look at me", for ye cannot see me at all. What then
do her mighty warriors do ? They roar like lions, until their
voice is heard by the Beloved above, and He knows that
his Beloved is lovesick like himself, so that none of her
beauty can be seen, and so through the voices of those
warriors of hers her Beloved comes forth from his palace
with many gifts and presents, with spices and incense, and
comes to her and finds her black and shrunken, without form
or beauty. He then draws near to her and embraces and
kisses her until she gradually revives from the scents and
spices, and her joy in having her Beloved with her, and she
is built up and recovers her full form and beauty. And this
was brought about by the might and power of her doughty
warriors. Hence it is written, "Mighty in strength that
fulfil his word". And then when they have restored her to
her form and beauty they and all the other hosts wait

[1] The Shekinah.

attentively for her words, and she is like a king in the midst
of his army. In the same way below, when there are sinners
in the generation, she hides herself and diminishes herself
till only a dot is left, until the mighty ones, the truly virtuous,
come and as it were restore her, so that she gradually
brightens and recovers her form and beauty and becomes
as before.' The Companions came and kissed him, saying:
'Had even the prophet Ezekiel said this, the world would
have wondered.' The boy then said: 'I will say the grace.'
They said: 'Do so, for to you it is fitting.' He said: 'How
holy you are, how many blessings await you from the holy
Mother because ye have not refused to let me say the grace !
We have learnt that it is the duty of every one to say grace.
If he cannot himself, his wife or his sons can say it for him,
but a curse light on the man who does not know how to say
grace himself and has to ask his wife or children. If he knows,
he must train his son and give him the cup of benediction.
And if he does not, then we say of him, "He that withholds
his son shall be cursed to the holy Mother" (Prov. XI, 26),
but as I am the only son of my mother, give me the cup and
I will bless the Holy King who has brought to my mother's
house men of worth before whom I can utter powerful
discourse. Before I say grace, however, I will expound
properly the verse [191b] I have quoted. The word *yikbuhu*
(curse him) means properly "pronounce distinctly": that is,
they will set forth his sins distinctly to the holy Mother.
We may also translate, "he who withholds blessings from
the Son", whom the Father and Mother have crowned and
blessed with many blessings, and concerning whom they
commanded, "Kiss the son lest he be angry" (Ps. II, 12),
since he is invested both with judgement and with mercy.
The last part of the verse we may translate, "He who gives
blessing to the Head breaks the power of the "other side".
Now, Companions, let us say grace.' They handed him the
cup and he said grace, and the Companions rejoiced more
than they had ever done since the wedding of R. Eleazar.
They blessed the boy with all their hearts, and he said to
them: 'You should not depart save with words of the
Torah.' He then expounded for them the verse: "And the

Lord went before them by day in a pillar of cloud" (Ex. XIII, 21). 'We should', he said, 'render thus: And the Lord, that is, the Shekinah, was there, but day, that is Abraham (*ḥesed*) went before them by day, while the Bride went before them by night, as it is written, "and by night in a pillar of fire to give light to them"—each one at the fitting time. And as for you, Companions, may night and day ever be before you.'

They kissed and blessed him as before and went their way. When they came to R. Simeon they told him what had happened. He was greatly astonished, and said: 'This is indeed excellent, but he will not make a name. When a thin stick burns it burns only for a little time. It is written, "His seed shall be mighty upon earth, the generation of the upright shall be blessed" (Ps. CXII, 2). When a man is mighty on the earth, mighty in the Torah and in control of his passions, then his light goes forth and is continued through many generations.' 'But', said R. Abba, 'we see children who say wonderful things and afterwards become very eminent.' He replied: 'When a child says one or two wonderful things by accident, then we may be confident that he will one day teach the Torah in Israel. But the same cannot be said of this one whose light is already complete. And besides, the Holy One, blessed be He, desires to smell this apple. [192*a*] Happy are the righteous, of whom it is written "And the remnant that is escaped of the house of Judah shall again take root downwards and bear fruit upward" (2 Kings XIX, 30). His father who has departed this world is a root below in the Academy of the firmament, and he shall bear fruit above in the highest Academy. Were it not that I would fain not oppose the Holy One, blessed be He, whose desire is to savour him, none should have dominion over him. As it is, may it be God's will that his mother should have no trouble from him'. And so it came to pass.

'AND HE SENT MESSENGERS UNTO BALAAM THE SON OF BEOR. There are here twenty-eight words corresponding to the twenty-eight degrees of the sorceries of the bird. It may be asked, Why did Balak commence with Balaam so abruptly? He should have first ingratiated himself with him and then told him what he wanted. The truth is', said R. Jose, 'that we see from here that Balak knew the disposition of that bad man, that he was always craving for honour and had no pleasure save in doing evil. Balak, through his sorceries, knew that the grades of Moses were very high, and he knew by the same means that the grades of Balaam corresponded. Pethor, to which he sent, was the town of Balaam; it was so called because Balaam used to prepare a table (*pethor*) there with food and drink for the evil sides, as is the custom of those who practise magic, in order to bring together the evil spirits to answer their inquiries.'

He then cited the verse: "And thou shalt make a table of acacia wood" (Ex. xxv, 23), and again, "Thou shalt put upon the table shew bread", etc. 'God desired all those holy vessels to be made in order that the holy spirit might be drawn down from heaven to earth. Similarly the wicked Balaam prepared one for the other side, with bread which is called "abominable bread".

'It is written, "Lord, when thou wentest forth out of Seir, when thou marchedst out of the field of Edom, the earth trembled", etc. (Jud. v, 4). This refers to the fact that before God gave the Law to Israel He offered it to the children of Esau and the children of Ishmael, and they would not accept it. The question may be asked—and there is no sin in scrutinising the language of the Law minutely—when God went to Seir, to what prophet of the children of Esau did He reveal himself? And similarly when He went to Paran, to what prophet of them did He reveal himself? We cannot say that He was revealed to all of them, for we find no such thing save in the case of Israel, and that by the hand of Moses. Further, in the verse, "The Lord came from Sinai and shone forth from Mount Seir", etc. (Deut. xxxiii, 2), it should be "came *to* Sinai", "shone *to* Seir", etc.' When R. Simeon came, he asked him. He said: 'This question has been answered as follows. "God came from Sinai" to reveal Himself to the Israelites. "He shone forth [192b] from Seir", that is, from the refusal of the children of Esau to receive the Law; from this Israel derived additional light and love. So, too, with Mount Paran, from the refusal of

the children of Ishmael. As for your question, through whom
was He revealed to Esau and Ishmael, this is a profound
mystery which is to be revealed through you. The Torah
issued from the mystic Head of the King. When it came
to the Left Arm the Holy One, blessed be He, saw some
vicious blood that had collected there. He said: I must cleanse
and purify this arm, since if this vicious blood is not lessened
it will damage all. He therefore summoned Samael and said
to him: Dost thou desire my Law ? What is written in it,
he asked ? He replied, taking a test passage: "Thou shalt not
kill". Whereupon Samael said: Heaven save us. This Torah is
thine, and let it remain thine. I do not want it. He then
besought Him, saying: Master of the Universe, if Thou
givest it to me, all dominion will vanish, for it is based upon
slaughter, on the star of Mars, and if there are no wars it
will pass away from the world. Master of the Universe, take
Thy Law, and let me have no portion in it. But, if it please
Thee, there is the people of the sons of Jacob, for them it is
fitting. He thought to do them a mischief: If they receive
this, he said, assuredly they will vanish from the world and
will never have dominion. God said to him: Thou art the
firstborn and for thee it is fitting. He replied: He has my
birthright, as it was sold to him and I consented. Then God
said: Since thou desirest no portion in it, leave it entirely.
He replied: Good. He then said: This being so, give me
an advice how I shall induce the children of Jacob to accept
it. He said: Master of the Universe, it is necessary to offer
some inducement to them. Take some light from the light
of the powers of the heavens and put it upon them, and for
this they will receive it, and give them some of mine first.
He then took off some of the light with which he was covered
and gave it to Him to give to Israel. Hence it says, "He
shone forth to them from Seir", Seir being a name of
Samael. Having thus cleared away the bad blood from the
Left Arm, God turned to the Right Arm and saw it in the
same state. So He called Rahab and said: Dost thou desire
my Law ? He asked what was written in it. God again
selected a crucial passage and said: "Thou shalt not commit
adultery". He exclaimed: Alas for me, if God shall give

me this inheritance, since it will destroy all my dominion, for I have received the blessing of the waters, of the fishes of the sea, to whom it was said: Be fruitful and multiply, etc. He began to beseech the Almighty, saying: Master of the Universe, two sons came forth from Abraham, there are the sons of Isaac, give to them, for them it beseems. He said: I cannot, for thou art the firstborn, and to thee it belongs. He commenced to implore Him, saying: Master of the Universe, let my birthright be his, and this extra light which I inherit on this account take and give to them. And God did so; wherefore it is written, "He shined forth from Mount Paran". When He had taken these gifts for Israel from those great Chiefs, He summoned all [193*a*] the myriads of holiness who are appointed to rule the other nations and they gave Him the same reply, and from all of them He received gifts to give to Israel. He was like a physician who had a phial full of some elixir of life which he desired to keep for his son. He was a clever man, and he said to himself: I have bad servants in my house; if they know that I intend to give to my son this present, they will be jealous of him and seek to kill him. What did he do therefore ? He took a little poison and smeared it round the edge of the phial. He then called his servants and said to them: You are faithful servants, do you want to try that drug ? They said: Let us see what it is. They just took a taste, and they had scarcely smelt it when they came near dying. They said to themselves: If he gives this poison to his son, he will certainly die, and we shall inherit our master. They said to him: Master, this medicine is fitted only for your son. We remit to you the reward of our labour, which you can give to him as a present so that he may take the medicine. So God, being a wise physician, knew that if He gave the Torah to Israel without telling them they would every day pursue them and kill them for it, but in this way He made them give presents and gifts so that Israel should accept it, and Moses received all of them to give to Israel, as it is written: "Thou hast ascended on high, thou hast taken captives" (Ps. LXVIII, 19), and in this way Israel inherited the Torah without any opposition or challenge. These gifts and presents which they received are their ornament, and therefore death and the other side had no dominion over them till they sinned, when, as it says, "they took off their ornaments from Mount Sinai" (Ex. xxxiii, 6). Whenever Israel return to their father in heaven those ornaments are restored to them and they are invested with them, and in the time to come all will be returned.'

R. Jose said: 'It says, "Lord, when thou didst go forth from Seir the earth shook". Why did it shake ? Because it desired to return to chaos when it saw that God had offered the Torah to all peoples and they had not accepted it and only Israel was left, and it was thought that Israel would refuse like the other nations. When, however, they said, "We will do and we will hearken", it became calm again. Observe that because Israel said "we will do", they are not afraid of anything that magicians may do with their arts. One reason is this, and another is because when God brought them out of Egypt He broke before them all kinds of magic and divination so they cannot prevail against them. When Balak came he knew this, and therefore he sent messengers to Balaam that he might prepare a table and seek counsel therefrom.'

R. Eleazar and R. Abba were once going to see R. Jose, son of R. Simeon b. Lakunia, the father-in-law of R. Eleazar. They rose at midnight and sat down to study the Torah. Said R. Eleazar: 'Now is the hour when the Holy One, blessed be He, goes into the Garden of Eden to have joyous converse with the righteous there.' Said R. Abba: 'What is this joyous converse ?' R. Eleazar replied: 'This is a profound mystery, [193b] concealed with the Unknown.' Said R. Abba: 'Were, then, the great ones of former days relying on an empty fantasy, and did they not try to find out on what they were established in this world, and what they were to expect in the next ?' R. Eleazar then commenced to discourse on the verse: "O Lord, thou art my God, I will exalt thee, I will praise thy name, for thou hast done wonderful things" (Isa. xxv, 1). 'This verse', he said, 'contains the mystery of faith. "Lord" is the supreme mystery, the beginning of the supernal Point, the recondite and unknowable. "My God"

refers to the still small Voice which is the first subject of
interrogation, and is also the supernal Priest. We have further
laid down that there are three places each of which is called
"thou". "I will exalt thee": all together. "I will praise
thy name": in fitting manner, this being the known Name.
"For thou hast done wonderful things": this is the secondary
light with which is invested the hidden ancient primordial
light, the supreme grade, the primordial Adam. Rab Ham-
numa the Elder said that "wonderful things" is a grade of
the wonders of wisdom, to wit, "a path which no bird of
prey knoweth" (Job XXVIII, 7). The "counsels of old" are
the two willow twigs[1] whence comes all the counsel of the
prophets. "Faithfulness and truth" are two things which
are one, the river and the garden; the one issues from Eden
and the other is watered from it. Thus we have here the
whole mystery of faith.'

R. Eleazar said: 'Who killed the wicked Balaam, and
how was he killed ?' R. Isaac replied: 'Phineas and his comrades killed him, as it says, "they slew on their slain". For
we have learnt that through his magic arts in the city of
Midian he became able to fly in the air, he and the kings
of Midian, and it was the holy frontlet and the prayer of
Phineas that brought them down on their slain.' Said R.
Eleazar: 'I know all this.' R. Simeon then said: 'Eleazar,
Balaam was a powerful adversary, as it says, "There arose
not a prophet in Israel like Moses", but—so we explain—
there did arise among the Gentiles, to wit, Balaam, who was
supreme among the lower Crowns as Moses among the
upper Crowns. How, then, were they able to kill him ? The
answer is to be gathered from a remark of the Book of the
Wisdom of King Solomon. There are three signs in a man:
paleness is a sign of anger, talking is a sign of folly, and self-
praise is a sign of ignorance. It is true that it says, "Let a
stranger praise thee and not thy own mouth" (Prov. XXVII, 2),
and we alter this to "Let a stranger praise thee, and if not,
thine own mouth", but that only means that if thou art
not known, discourse on the Torah so that through the
opening of thy mouth in the Torah men should know who

---

[1] *Nezaḥ* and *Hod*.

thou art and praise thee. But the wicked Balaam praised himself in everything, and deceived people as well. He made much of little; for all that he said of himself referred only to the unclean grades, and though it was true, it did not mean much, though whoever heard it imagined that he surpassed all the prophets of the world. When, for instance, he said, "Which heareth the words of God and knoweth [194a] the knowledge of the Almighty", who that heard would not think that there was no true prophet like him ? Certainly it was true; but only with reference to the grades to which he was attached. He heard the words of a god—the one who is called "another god", and he knew the knowledge of the most high, that is, the highest of the grades of uncleanness, those who direct the boat and the tempest. There are forty-nine of them, and the steersman is the highest of them all. Thus he praised himself vaguely, and while speaking truthfully he yet misled people. So when he said, "Who seeth the vision of the Almighty", the hearers thought that he saw something which no other could see, but what he saw was only one of the branches that issue from Shaddai. What was that vision ? Uzza and Azael, who were "falling down and having eyes open".

'Now where was Balaam at that time ? Seeing that he said, "Now I am going to my people", how can he have been in Midian ? The truth is, however, that when he saw that twenty-two thousand of Israel fell through his counsel, he stayed there and demanded his reward; and while he was staying there Phineas and his captains of the host came there. When he saw Phineas he flew up into the air with his two sons, Yunus and Yamburus. But these, you will say, died at the time when the golden calf was made ? (We learn this from the words of the text, "there died of the people about three thousand" (Ex. XXXII, 28), the word "about" indicating that these two were reckoned as equal to three thousand men.) That wretch, however, being acquainted with every kind of enchantment, took also those of his sons, and with them commenced to fly away. When Phineas saw a man in the air flying away, he shouted to his soldiers: Is anyone able to fly after him, for it is Balaam ? Then Zilya, of the tribe of Dan, arose and seized the Domination that rules over enchantments and flew after him. When Balaam saw him he changed his direction in the air and broke through five ethers [194b] and vanished from view. Zilya was then sorely vexed, not knowing what to do. Phineas thereupon called out: Shade of the dragons which overshadow all serpents, turn thy tresses. Straightway he revealed his path and Zilya approached him and both came down in front of Phineas. This is referred to in the blessing of Jacob (Gen. XLIX, 17): "Dan shall be a serpent in the way"—this is Samson: "an adder in the path"—this is Zilya; "that biteth the horses' heels"—this is Ira the companion of David; "so that his rider falleth backward"—this is Shiryah, who is destined to come with the Messiah of Ephraim, and who will wreak vengeance on other nations; and then it will be time to expect the deliverance of Israel, as it says, "For thy salvation I hope, O Lord". When Balaam came down in front of Phineas, he said to him: Wretch, how many evil haps hast thou brought upon the holy people! He then said to Zilya: Kill him, but not with the Name, for it is not meet that the divine sanctity should be mentioned over him, so that his soul in leaving him should not be united with matters of holy grades, and his prayer be fulfilled: "May my soul die the death of the righteous" (Num. XXIII, 10). He then tried to kill him in many ways, but did not succeed, until he took a sword on which was engraved a snake on each side. Said Phineas: Kill him with his own weapon. And then he did kill him; for such is the way of that side, he who follows it is killed by it and it is with his soul when it departs from him, and he is punished in the other world and never finds burial, and his bones rot and become noxious serpents, and even the worms that eat his body become serpents. We have found in the Book of Asmodai which he gave to King Solomon, that anyone who desires to make powerful enchantments, if he knows the rock where Balaam fell, will find there snakes formed from the bones of that wicked one, and if he kills one he can make certain enchantments with its head and others with its body, and others again with its tail, there being three kinds in each one. One of the questions

which the Queen of Sheba asked Solomon was how to take
hold of the bone of the serpent of three enchantments. From
that point, Eleazar my son, God did other things with that
sinner, and these are secret mysteries which should not be
revealed, only in order that the Companions here should
know the hidden ways of the world I have revealed them.'
[195*a*]

COME NOW, THEREFORE, I PRAY THEE, CURSE ME THIS
PEOPLE, ETC. R. Abba discoursed on the verse: "A prayer
of the afflicted when he is overwhelmed" (Ps. CII, 1). He
said: 'There are three to whom prayers are ascribed in the
Scripture, viz., Moses and David and the afflicted one.
We also find, it is true, "A prayer of Habakkuk the prophet",
but when we examine this we find that it is a praisegiving
to the Almighty for having revived him and performed
miracles for him. The "prayer of Moses" is one such as no
other man ever offered. The "prayer of David" (Ps. LXXXVI)
is one such as no other king ever offered. Yet the prayer of
the poor man is the most excellent of all, and takes precedence
of the prayer of Moses or of David, or of any other man.
The reason is that the poor man is broken of heart, and it
is written, "God is near to the broken of heart" (Ps. XXIV, 19).
The poor man always expostulates with God, yet God
listens and hears his words. When he prays He opens all the
windows of the firmament, and all other prayers which
ascend aloft have to make way for that of the broken-hearted
poor man. God says, as it were: Let all other prayers wait,
and let this one enter before me. I require here no court to
judge between us, let his complaint come before Me and I
and he will be alone. And so God alone attends to those
complaints, as it is written, "and poureth out his complaint
before the Lord". Truly, "before the Lord". All the hosts
of heaven ask one another: With what is the Holy One, blessed
be He, engaged ? They answer: He is engaged eagerly with
His own vessels. None of them know what is done with that
prayer of the poor man and with all his complaints. But when
he pours out his tears with expostulation before the Almighty,
God desires nothing so much as to receive them. Now David

saw that all the windows and all the gates of heaven were
opened to the poor man, and there was no other to whose
prayer God gave ear so readily, so he made himself a poor
man and a beggar, he stripped himself of his royal garment
and sat on the ground like a beggar and uttered his prayer.
Hence it says, "A prayer of David. Bow down thine ear,
O Lord, and answer me"; why? "for I am poor and needy"
(Ps. LXXXVI, 1). Said the Almighty to him: David, art thou
not a king, the ruler over mighty kings, and thou makest
thyself a pauper and a beggar? Straightway he gave his
prayer another turn, and leaving the pose of a pauper he
said: "Preserve my soul, for I am pious"; and in truth, all
these features were in David.' Said R. Eleazar to him:
'What you have said is quite right; and withal[1] a man in
praying should make himself poor and needy in order that
his prayer may enter along with that of the rest of the poor,
for the doorkeepers allow none to enter so readily as the
poor, since they can even enter without asking permission.
So if a man puts himself in the position of the poor, his
prayer ascends and meets the other prayers of the poor
and ascends with them and enters as one of them and is
favourably received before the King.

'King David placed himself in four categories. He placed
himself among the poor; he placed himself among the
pious; he placed himself among the servants; and he placed
himself among those who are ready to sacrifice themselves
and their lives for the sanctification of God's Name. He
placed himself among the poor, as it is written, "For I am
poor and needy". He placed himself among the pious, as it
is written, "Preserve my soul, for I am pious". For a man
should not consider himself wicked; nor can it be objected
that if so he will never tell of his sins, for when he makes
confession of his sins then he is pious, since he comes to
make repentance; he removes himself from the evil side in
the uncleanness of which he abode until now, and cleaves to the
right hand which is outstretched to receive him. Nor should
you think that God does not receive him till he makes full
confession of all the sins that he has committed since he was

[1] Al. therefore.

born, for if so, what of those [195b] that are concealed from him ? The truth is that he need only recount those that he remembers, and if he concentrates his attention on these, all the others follow them, just as in searching for leaven we do not peer into every nook and cranny, but if we have searched as far as the eye can see, the rest is reckoned as cleared away along with this. So also the priest declared the leper clean if he could observe no mark on him without peering too closely. So a man need not recount all his sins since the day he was born, or those which are concealed from him. Hence David placed himself among the saints. He placed himself among the servants, as it is written, "Save thy servant, O thou my God". He placed himself among those who are ready to sacrifice themselves for the sanctification of God's Name, as it is written, "Rejoice the soul of thy servant, for unto thee, O Lord, do I lift up my soul" (*Ibid.* 4). All these four characters did King David assume before his Master.'

R. Eleazar said: 'I lift up my hand in prayer before the Holy King, for we have learnt that it is forbidden for a man to raise his hand above him save in prayer and blessing and supplication, since the fingers of man have an important significance—and so I do now, and say that if any man shall arrange his service thus before his Master and sincerely carry out this purpose, his prayer shall not return un-answered. At first he must make himself a servant to arrange a service of praise and song before Him. Again he becomes a servant to recite the standing-up prayer, and once more after saying his prayer. Therefore David called himself "servant" three times in this psalm, as it says, "Save thy servant, thou my God", "Rejoice the soul of thy servant", and "Give strength to thy servant". Next a man should place himself among those who are ready to sacrifice them-selves for the sanctification of God's Name, by reciting with proper devotion the formula of the unity, "Hear, O Israel". Then he must make himself poor, when he knocks at the doors of the highest heights in saying the prayer "true and certain", and proceed thus to the *Amidah* prayer, so that he, in saying it, should feel himself broken-hearted, poor and

needy. Then he should place himself among the saints by
recounting his sins in the prayer "hearkening to prayer",
for so the individual should do in order to cling to the right
hand which is stretched forth to receive sinners who repent.
We have learnt that when a man has sincerely prayed in
these four styles, God is pleased and stretches forth His right
hand over him when he comes to the third servant, and says
of him, "Thou art my servant". Assuredly the prayer [196*a*]
of such a man shall never return unanswered.' R. Abba
came and kissed him. He said: 'This is what we call "more
desirable than gold and much fine gold" (Ps. XIX, 10). How
sweet are the time-honoured words which the ancients have
strung together ! When we taste them we are unable to eat
any other food. Assuredly it is so, and the Scripture proves
that there are three servants who are mentioned in one place
—two as you have said, and the third for the Holy One,
blessed be He, to crown Himself withal.'

R. Eleazar then discoursed on the verse: "Who is among
you that feareth the Lord, that hearkeneth to the voice of his
servant" (Isa. L, 10). 'This verse', he said, 'has been explained by the Companions to refer to one who is accustomed
to go to synagogue to pray and one day does not come. Then
God inquires of him, saying: "Who is among you that feareth
the Lord, that hearkeneth to the voice (of) his servant":
that is to say, who is wont to hear himself called servant,
the name given in honour by the Almighty, the "voice" being
heard in all the firmaments that this is the servant of the
Holy King. "He that walketh in darkness and hath no light":
before Israel gather in their synagogues for prayer, the
"other side" closes up all the supernal lights and prevents
them from diffusing themselves over the worlds. Three times
in the day, however, the other sides, male and female, go
and wander over the world, and that is the time which is
fitting for prayer, because then there is no accuser there at
all. And while they are wandering over "mountains of
darkness", the windows of the upper lights are opened and
they come forth and rest in the synagogues upon the heads
of those who are praying there, and God inquires of him
who is not there and says: Alas for So-and-so who was wont

to be here and is now going in darkness and has moved away from the light—"he hath no light"; how many good things he has lost ! But if he were there "he would trust in the name of the Lord", in the circle of the first Servant, "and stay upon his God", in the mystery of the second Servant.' Said R. Simeon: 'Eleazar, my son, of a surety the spirit of prophecy rests upon thee.' R. Abba said: 'Lion, son of lion, who can stand before them when they roar to take prey ? All lions are strong, but these above all. But from other lions it is hard to rescue prey, whereas from these it is easy, for when they snatch they give to all.' [196b]

R. Eleazar said: 'Of a truth there is a hidden reference in the name Zippor. It is written, "Yea the sparrow (*zippor*) hath found her a house, and the swallow a nest for herself" (Ps. LXXXIV, 4). Would King David have said this of a mere sparrow ? The reference, however, is to what we have learnt: How beloved are souls (*neshamoth*) before the Holy One, blessed be He. This does not mean all souls, but the souls of the righteous whose abode is there with Him. We have learnt that there are three walls to the Garden of Eden, and between each pair many souls and spirits walk about and enjoy the perfumes from within, though they are not permitted to enter. On certain days in the year, in the months of Nisan and Tishri, those spirits assemble in a certain place on the walls of the garden, where they look like chirping birds every morning. This chirping is praise given to the Almighty, and prayer for the life of human beings, because in those days Israel are all busy with performing the commandments and precepts of the Lord of the universe.' Said R. Simeon: 'Eleazar, so far very good, since in truth those spirits are there, but what will you make of "and the swallow a nest for herself" ?' He replied: 'What I have learnt is that this is the holy super-soul that goes aloft to a hidden place which no eye but God's has seen.' Said R. Simeon: 'Eleazar, truly all this is correct, and so it is in the lower Garden of Eden as you have said. The "sparrows" are the holy spirits that are privileged to enter and then come out again, and these "find a house", each one its appropriate chamber, and nevertheless they are all jealous

T

of the canopy of their comrades, those that have freedom
from all. God shows them a certain hidden palace, "which
no eye has seen but thine, O God", and which is called "the
bird's nest". From there are woven crowns for the Messiah
in the time to come, and three times a year God holds converse with those righteous and shows them that hidden
palace which is not known even to all the righteous there.
"Who hath put her young with thine altars": these are the
righteous whose merit has been perfected with holy sons
learned in both Torahs in this world, and who are called
two altars crowned before the Holy King, since the merit
of their sons in this world shields them and crowns them
there. Now continue thy discourse, since we did not mean
to shame thee.' R. Eleazar then proceeded: 'The "bird"
is Jethro and the "swallow" indicates his sons, who used to
be in the Chamber of hewn stone (in the Temple) teaching
the Torah and giving decisions on religious matters. At first
they left the comfort of their homes in Midian to dwell in
the wilderness, but when God saw that their yearning was
for the Torah, He drew them from there and made them a
"house" in the Chamber of hewn stone. The "swallow" here
is the same as the "bird". This is why the name of Balak's
father, Zippor, is mentioned here, though we do not find
this with other (heathen) kings. Jethro abandoned idolatry
and came to join Israel, and for this he was banished and
[197a] persecuted. Balak, who was of his descendants, abandoned his path. When the elders of Moab and the elders of
Midian, who were brothers in idolatry, saw that whereas
Jethro and his son had clung to the Shekinah, this one had
abandoned it, they came and made him king over them, as
it is written, "And Balak son of Zippor was king of Moab
at that time". Hence he is specially mentioned as being the
son of Zippor, as if to say that this was not worthy of him.
It says that "he saw". We should have expected "he heard".
What did he see ? He saw that he was destined to fall into
the hands of the Israelites, after Israel had first fallen into
his hands.'

R. Abba discoursed on the passage beginning: "If thou
know not, O thou fairest among women", etc. (S.S. 1, 8).

'The Community of Israel', he said, 'is she that gathers in
from all the camps above, and holds in all that she gathers,
letting it escape only by drops like dew, because there is
not sufficient faith below. For if She were to find faith as it
is found in her, She would pour the light on every side
without restraint, and they would give to her also gifts and
presents without stint. But it is those of the lower world
who restrain them and restrain her, and therefore she is
called *Azereth* (the restrainer). Nevertheless, as a mother
gives to her sons in secret and unbeknown, so she does with
her children, Israel. We have learnt from the Sacred Lamp
that when She ascends to receive delights and dainties, if
then there is a blemish in Israel She is separated from her
Spouse a fixed number of days. Then it is known above
that there is a blemish in Israel and the Left awakens and
lets down a thread below. Then Samael quickly rouses himself
to assail the world, as it says, "And he called Esau his elder
(lit. great) son" (Gen. XXVII, 1). He is indeed great with the
camps of the "other side" and he steers all the ships of the
sea of accusations with the evil breeze to sink them in the
depths of the sea. Now when the Holy One, blessed be He,
is in merciful mood, He gives to him all the sins of Israel
and he casts them into the depths of the sea—for so his
camps are called—and they take them and flow with them
to all other peoples. Are, then, the sins and guilt of Israel
scattered among their people ? The truth is that they wait
for gifts from above like a dog at a table, and when God takes
all the sins of Israel and throws them to them, they think
that He is diverting from Israel the gifts which He intended
to give them, and giving to them instead, and they straightway rejoice and throw them to the other peoples. Observe
now. The Community of Israel says first, "Black am I and
comely", humbling herself before the Holy King. Then
She inquires of Him, saying: "Where feedest thou thy flock,
where makest thou it to rest at noon ?" The two "where"s
hint at the two destructions of the Temple. The word
"feed" refers to the captivity of Babylon, which lasted but
a short time, and the word "causest to lie down" to the
captivity of Edom, which is long drawn out. We might also

translate, "where does *she* feed and cause to lie down", making Her refer to Herself as if to say: How can she cause dew to drop upon them from the heat of midday? Also when Israel cry out because of their oppression [197b] and the taunts of their enemies and yet they praise and bless God for all their tribulations, (She says) I "sit as one that is veiled" and cannot work wonders for them or avenge them. Then He answers Her: "If thou knowest not, O thou fairest among women", how to gather strength in captivity and to defend thy children, "go thy way forth by the footsteps of the flock": these are the school children who learn the Torah, "and feed thy kids": these are the infants who are snatched away from this world to the Academy on high which is "beside the shepherds' tents". This is the Academy of Metatron where are all the mighty of the world and all those who guide men in the laws of permitted and forbidden.' R. Eleazar interrupted, saying: 'The "footsteps of the sheep" are the students who have come later into the world and find the Torah clearly expounded, and yet manage to find new expositions every day, and the Shekinah rests on them and listens to their words.' R. Abba said: 'That is indeed so, but it comes to the same thing. Why does it say here, "O thou fairest among women", seeing that she called herself "black"? He says to Her: "Thou art the fairest of women", the fairest of all the grades. Or it may mean that He approves of the kindnesses which she did for her sons in secret, just as a father is glad when a mother is secretly merciful to his children, even though their conduct has not been good.'

R. Abba here broke off to say: 'I find rather surprising the words of the Scripture, "If a man have a stubborn and rebellious son . . . then shall his father and his mother lay hold of him", etc. (Deut. XXI, 19), concerning which we have learnt that when God told Moses to write this, Moses said: Sovereign of the Universe, omit this; is there any father that would do so to his son? Now Moses saw in wisdom what God would later do to Israel, and therefore he said, Omit this. God, however, said to him, Write and receive thy reward; though thou knowest I know more; what thou seest I will attend to; examine the Scripture and

thou wilt find. God then nodded to Yofiel, the teacher of the
Law, who said to Moses, I will expound this verse: "When
a man shall have": this is the Holy One, blessed be He, who
is called "a man of war". "A son": this is Israel. "Stubborn
and rebellious", as it is written, "For Israel hath behaved
himself stubbornly like a stubborn heifer" (Hos. IV, 16).
"Which will not obey the voice of his father nor the voice
of his mother": these are the Holy One, blessed be He, and
the Community of Israel. "Though they chasten him", as
it says, "Yet the Lord testified unto Israel and unto Judah
by the hand of every prophet" (2 Kings XVII, 13). "Then
shall his father and mother take hold of him", with one
accord, "and bring him out unto the elders of his city and
unto the gate of his place": "the elders of his city" are the
ancient and primeval Days. [198*a*] "And they shall say,
This our son": assuredly our son, and not the son of other
peoples. "He is a riotous liver and a drunkard". Why are
these last words added now? Because what caused Israel
to be rebellious against their Father in heaven was because
they were riotous and drunken among other nations, as it
is written, "They mingled themselves with the nations
and learnt their works" (Ps. CVI, 35). Therefore, "the men
of his city shall stone him with stones": these are the other
peoples who hurled stones at them and cast down their
walls and towers and did not help them at all. When Moses
heard this, he wrote this section. And with all this, "thou
fairest of women, go thy way forth by the footsteps of the
flock": these are the synagogues and houses of study; "and
feed thy kids": these are the young school children who
know not the taste of sin; "beside the shepherds' tents":
these are the teachers of children and the heads of academies.
We may also refer this to the kings of the Amorites whose
land the Israelites took for pasture for their cattle. When
Balak heard that so valuable a land had been turned by the
Israelites into pasture, he began to take active steps and
associated with himself Balaam.'

COME NOW, THEREFORE, I PRAY THEE, AND CURSE ME
THIS PEOPLE. R. Eleazar said: 'That villain said to himself:

In truth, now is the propitious hour for me to do what I desire. He saw, but he did not see properly. He saw that many thousands of Israel would through him fall in a short time, and therefore he said "now". He said, Till now there was no one in the world who could prevail against them, because of the protector who was with them, but now that the time is propitious, let us make war against them. FOR THEY ARE TOO MIGHTY FOR ME. In what battle had he up to now tested their might [198b] that he could say this? The truth is that he was far-sighted, and saw King David, the descendant of Ruth the Moabitess, mighty as a lion, fighting many battles and conquering Moab, and placing them under his feet. Hence he said, "He is mighty", meaning a certain king who will issue from them. He went on: "Perhaps I shall be able to smite him", or, as we might translate, "Perhaps I might prevail on thee so that we should diminish him", depriving the mighty lion of this limb before that king comes into the world, so that he should not drive Moab out of his territory.'

CURSE (*arah*) FOR ME. R. Abba said: 'Balak used two expressions to Balaam, *arah* (curse) and *kaboh* (imprecate). What is the difference? The word *arah* means cursing by the use of herbs and snakes' heads. When he saw that Balaam had more power in his mouth, he said *kaboh*. Yet all the same Balak did not neglect enchantments, but took all manner of herbs and snakes' heads and put them in a pot, which he buried under the ground fifteen hundred cubits down. When David came he dug down fifteen hundred cubits and brought up water from the depths and poured it on the altar. That was when he said, "Moab is my washpot" (Ps. LX, 10), that is, I have washed clean the pot of Moab. He went on: "Over Edom I cast my shoe". This also had reference to a much earlier event, when Esau said to Jacob, "Make me swallow, I pray thee, some of that red stuff", and David now said, "I will stuff my shoe down his throat". He also said: "Over Philistia I will blow the trumpet", because Philistines were from the "other side", and for the "other side" the blowing of the trumpet was required, as it is written, "And when ye go to war in your land ye shall sound an alarm with the trumpet" (Num. x, 9).'

R. Hizkiah cited here the verse: "And righteousness shall be the girdle of his loins and faithfulness the girdle of his reins" (Isa. XI, 5). 'The second part of this verse', he said, 'seems at first to be a mere repetition of the first, but this is not so. Though "righteousness" and "faithfulness" are much the same, and represent the same grade, yet there is a distinction between the two. When this grade wields stern judgement and receives power from the left side, then it is called "righteousness". It is "faithfulness" when truth is joined with it, and then there is joy and all faces smile. Then there is pardon for all, and the souls even of sinners, since they are given in trust, are restored in mercy. Similarly, there is a distinction between "loins" and "reins", the former being the upper and the latter the lower part. Hence for valour and for war "righteousness" is the girdle of his "loins", while for mercy and for kindness "faithfulness" is the girdle of his "reins". Thus with one and the same grade he will judge in two directions, one being mercy [199a] for Israel and the other chastisement for the other nations. Also when Israel went forth from Egypt they were girt with these two girdles, one for war and one for peace.

'THAT I MAY DRIVE THEM FROM THE EARTH. When Balak took counsel of Balaam', he said, 'That grade to which they are attached is assuredly from the earth. Therefore if I drive them from this earth, I shall be able to do all that I desire. Wherein does their strength lie ? In deeds and words. You have words and I have deeds.

'FOR I KNOW THAT HE WHOM THOU BLESSEST, ETC. From where did he know ? As has been explained, from the help he gave to Sihon. But in truth, he knew it from his own wisdom.

'WHOM THOU BLESSEST IS BLESSED. Why should he mention blessing, seeing that he wanted him for cursing ? This is a question which I could not solve till R. Eleazar came and expounded the verse: "I will bless *eth* the Lord" (Ps. xxxiv, 2). Who is it that requires blessings from those on earth ? *Eth*, because it is connected with them as the flame with the wick. Said that sinner: That grade of theirs is attached to them because of the blessings which they address to it every day. You have power to bless that grade and so detach it from them, and by this we shall prevail against them.'

He then discoursed on the verse: "Therefore fear thou not, O Jacob my servant, saith the Lord, neither be dismayed, O Israel . . . for I am with thee", etc. (Jer. xxx, 10, 11). 'The word "thou" here', he said, 'contains a reference to the Ark of the Covenant, which is the grade that went into captivity with her sons, the holy people. As has been pointed out, it does not say here, "for thou art with me", but "for I am with thee". The word *kalah* (full end) occurs twice here. The first time it is written hard (for I will make *kalah* with all the nations), and the second soft (I will not make *khalah* of thee). From this', said R. Hamnuna the ancient, 'we can learn that the oppression of Israel brings benefit to them, and that the ease of the other nations brings evil to them. For the word *kalah* can be read [199b] *kallah* (bride) while *khalah* can only mean destruction and annihilation. The verse continues: "But I will correct thee with judgement" (lit. for judgement). God provides remedies for Israel before they appear for judgement. What are these remedies ? On every occasion God punishes Israel little by little in each generation, so that when they come to the great day of judgement when the dead shall arise, judgement shall have no power over them. "And will in no wise leave thee unpunished". What is the meaning of this ? When Israel are by themselves and do not come up for judgement with the other peoples, God is lenient with them and makes atonement for them. But when they come up with the other peoples, God knows that Samael, the guardian of Esau, will come to call to mind their sins, and therefore He provides a remedy for them and for each sin He smites them and purifies them with chastisements little by little, but does not clear them out of the world. When they come up for judgement Samael brings up many records against them, but God brings forth the records of the sufferings which they have endured for each sin, so that they are all wiped off without any indulgence. Then Samael has no more power and can do nothing to them and he vanishes from the world with all his followers and peoples. Similarly the words of King David: "For lo, the wicked bend the bow, they make ready their arrow upon the string" (Ps. xi, 2), although explained as referring to Shebna and Joach, the officers of Hezekiah, can also be applied to this Samael and his company, whose whole object is to harm Israel. Balak and Balaam chose that path, and, as we have said, made an evil partnership.' R. Simeon said: 'Let Balak and Balaam rot in hell. They took evil counsel together against the Protector, whom they thought to remove by means of deed and word. Said that wicked one: The ancients tried and did not succeed. The generation of the Tower of Babel tried but could not, because though they had deeds the word of the mouth was lacking, as their tongues were confused. But thy mouth is sharp and thy tongue is ready for either course. That side which thou desirest to remove is removed by thy mouth and tongue, and that side which thou desirest to curse by the power of thy mouth is cursed. [*200a*] Therefore I will do the enchantments, and do thou complete all with thy mouth. He, however, did not know that God "removeth the speech of the trusty and taketh away the understanding of the elders" (Job xii, 20). "He removeth the speech of the trusty", as from the generation of the Tower of Babel, whose speech He confused, "and taketh away the understanding of the elders", to wit, of Balak and Balaam. Observe that all the acts of the wicked Balaam were dictated by pride and arrogance. Both offered sacrifices, as it says, "And Balak and Balaam offered" (xxiii, 2), and it was Balak who prepared all the altars, yet Balaam said, "*I* have prepared the seven altars, and *I* have offered a bullock and a ram on every altar" (*Ibid.* 4). Said God to him: Villain, I know all, but return to Balak, and thou needest not to speak with him, but thus shalt thou say. Hence it says, "He taketh away the understanding of the wise".

'AND HE SAID TO THEM, LODGE HERE THIS NIGHT. Because night is the time of the "other side" for enchanters, when the evil sides are at large in the world. AS THE LORD SHALL SPEAK UNTO ME. He made a boast of the Name of the Lord. AND THE PRINCES OF MOAB ABODE WITH BALAAM. Those of Midian, however, left and would not stay with him; and they would have done well to separate from him altogether, as then they would not have been smitten at the end; for it was through his advice that they sent their women to the Israelites. Or, again, we may say that the princes of Moab did better by staying, for they thereby showed respect for the word of the Lord, and for this they were rewarded afterwards, whereas the princes of Midian showed that they had no desire to hear the word of the Lord, and for this they were punished afterwards.

'In that night he used enchantments and divinations until he called down to himself a spirit from above, as it says, AND AN ELOHIM CAME TO BALAAM: this was his grade from the "other side", of the Left. AND SAID, WHAT MEN ARE THESE WITH THEE? Being of the other side, of the Left, he needed to ask. The Companions, however, say that God made trial of him by thus speaking to him. There were three who were thus tried: Hezekiah, Ezekiel, and Balaam, and only Ezekiel gave the right answer, for when God asked him, "Shall these bones live?" he replied, "O Lord God, thou knowest" (Ezek. XXXVII, 3). Hezekiah, however, when God said to him, "Whence come these men?" replied, "They have come to me from a far land, from Babylon" (2 Kings XX, 14). And so Balaam now answered, "Balak son of Zippor King of Moab sent to me", as much as to say: I am highly esteemed in the eyes of kings and rulers. A certain Kuthean said to R. Eleazar: I discern a superiority in Balaam over Moses, for of Moses it says, "And the Lord called unto Moses", but of Balaam it says, [200b] "And God met Balaam, And God came to Balaam'. He replied: A king was once sitting on his throne in his palace when a leper came to the gate. Who is knocking at the gate? he asked. They said: A certain leper. He said: He must not enter here and defile the palace. I know that

if I tell this to a messenger he will take no notice, and my
son will come in and be defiled by contact with him. I will
therefore go and threaten him so that he shall go away from
the abode of my son and not defile him. So the king got up
and went to him and threatened him, saying: Leper, leper,
keep away from the path of my son, and if not I will tell
the sons of my handmaidens to cut you in pieces. Then the
friend of the king called at the door. Who is it ? said the king.
They replied: Your friend, So-and-so. He said: It is my
friend, the beloved of my soul; no other voice shall call him
in save mine. The king then cried out saying: Enter, beloved
of my soul, my own friend; prepare the palace that I may
converse with him. So when Balaam, who was rejected of
men like a leper, called at the gate of the King, the latter,
on hearing, said: The unclean leper shall not enter and
defile my palace. It is necessary for me to go and threaten
him so that he shall not approach the gate of my son and not
defile him. Therefore it says, "God came to Balaam". He
said to him: Leper, leper, "thou shalt not go with them,
thou shalt not curse the people for he is blessed". You shall
not come near my people either for good or for evil, being
wholly unclean. But of Moses it is written, "He called unto
Moses", with the voice of the King and not through a
messenger, "from the tent of meeting", from the holy
palace which higher and lower angels desire to approach
but are not allowed.

'BALAK SON OF ZIPPOR KING OF MOAB. Above (v. 4)
Balak was called "king *to* Moab", to show that he was
only appointed king for the emergency, not like "the first
king of Moab" (Num. XXI, 26), who was an hereditary
monarch. Balaam, however, out of his pride called him
"king *of* Moab", as if to say: See how great a king sends
to me !'

R. Phineas was once going to see his daughter, the wife
of R. Simeon, who was ill. He was accompanied by the
Companions, and was riding on his ass. On his way he met
two Arabs, and said to them: 'Has a voice ever been heard
in this field ?' They replied: 'About former times we cannot

say, but we know that in our own time there used to be
robbers who waylaid men in this field and they once fell
on some Jews with intent to cut them down, when there was
heard from a distance in this field the voice of an ass braying
twice, and a flame of fire came into the field and burnt them,
so that the Jews escaped.' He said to them: 'Arabs, Arabs,
for the sake of this information that you have given me
you shall be delivered this day from other robbers who are
lying in wait for you on the way.' R. Phineas wept, and said:
'Sovereign of the Universe, thou hast caused this miracle
to befall on my behalf, and those Jews were delivered and I
knew it not. It is written, "To him who alone doeth great
wonders, for his mercy endureth for ever" (Ps.cxxxvi, 4).
How much kindness does God do for men, and how many
miracles does He cause to befall for them, and no one knows
save He ! A man will rise in the morning and a snake comes
to kill him and he treads on the snake and kills it without
knowing, but God alone knows. A man goes on the road
and robbers are in wait for him, and another comes and
takes his place and he is delivered, and does not know the
kindness that God has wrought with him or the miracle He
has done on his behalf. God alone does it and knows it.' He
then said to the Companions: 'Companions, [201*a*] what
I really wanted to learn from the Arabs who frequent this
field was whether they have heard the voice of the Companions who study the Torah, for R. Simeon and R. Eleazar
and the rest of the Companions are in front of us without
knowing of us, and I was asking those Arabs about them,
because I know that the voice of R. Simeon shakes the
field and the rocks; they, however, have told me something
I did not know.'

As they were going along the Arabs returned to him and
said: 'Old man, old man, you asked us concerning bygone
days but not concerning this day in which we have seen
wonder on wonder. We have seen five men sitting together
and one old man among them, and we saw the birds collecting
and spreading their wings over his head, some going and
others coming, so that there was always a shade over their
heads, and as the old man raised his voice they were listening.

He said: 'That was what I wanted to know; Arabs, Arabs, may you have all the good fortune on this journey that you desire. You have told me two things which have given me joy.' They then proceeded on their way. Said the Companions to him: 'How are we to find the place where R. Simeon is ?' He replied: 'Leave it to the Master of the steps of my beast, who will guide its steps thither.' He then gave the rein to his ass, which thereupon turned aside from the road two miles, after which it commenced to bray three times. R. Phineas dismounted and said: 'Let us prepare ourselves to meet the presence of the day, for now great faces and small faces will come out to us.' R. Simeon heard the braying of the ass and said to the Companions: 'Let us rise, for the voice of the ass of the pious elder has reached us.' R. Simeon thereupon rose and the Companions also.

R. Simeon cited the verse: "A psalm. O sing unto the Lord a new song, for he hath done marvellous things" (Ps. XCVII, 1). 'The tonal accent on the word *mizmor* (psalm) here', he said, 'shows that this psalm has some special distinction. Who was it that uttered this song ? It was the kine (that bore the ark from the house of Obed Edom) in their lowing. Whom did they call upon to "sing" ? All the Chariots, all the Chieftains, all the grades (of angels) who had come thither to meet the Ark. The word for "song" here is the masculine form, *shir*, whereas Moses designated his song by the feminine form, *shirah* (Deut. XXXI, 32). The reason is that in the time of Moses only the Ark itself was coming forth from captivity, but here the Ark was coming forth with what was deposited in it. "For he hath done marvellous things": this refers to what was done to the Philistines and their idols. "His right hand hath wrought salvation for him": that is, for the psalm itself and the holy spirit concealed in it. His right hand takes hold of this psalm and does not leave it in the hand of another. In the words "taking hold with the right hand" the comparison is to a father who draws his son to his breast in front of him so as to protect him, as though to say: Who shall touch my son ? But when the son does wrong the father takes hold of the son by the shoulders and pushes him away, and so it is written, "He hath drawn back his right hand before the enemy" (Lam. II, 3). Here, however, it says, "His right hand and his holy arm hath wrought salvation for him"—he being held fast in two arms. Now if those kine for which miracles were an unusual thing, being vouchsafed to them only on that occasion, uttered this song in their lowing, how much more must we say that the braying of the ass of the pious elder signifies a song of praise! Nor think, Companions, that this has not been the manner of this ass from the time the world was created. For if this was the case with the ass of the wicked Balaam, how much more must it be so with the ass of R. [201*b*] Phineas ben Jair! Now it is time, Companions, to reveal something. When you are told that the mouth of the ass was created on the eve of Sabbath at twilight,[1] do you think that its mouth was open from that time, or that God made stipulation with it from that time? Not so; there is here a mystery which has been transmitted to the wise who pay not heed to folly. The mouth of the ass is the grade of the asses, that supernal one from the side of the females who rested on that ass and spoke over it. When God created that grade called "the mouth of the ass" He enclosed it in the hollow of the great deep and kept it there till that day, and when the time came He opened the hollow and it came forth and rested on the ass and spoke. So when it says that "the earth opened its mouth" (Num. XVI, 32), this refers to Dumah. The mouth of the ass was called Kadriel and the mouth of the well was called Yahadriel. These three "mouths" were created on the eve of the Sabbath. But at the hour when God sanctified the day there came up a Mouth which is superior to all other mouths, namely, that day which was exalted and sanctified in all, and was called "the mouth of the Lord".'

They now caught sight of R. Phineas coming towards them. When he came up he kissed R. Simeon, saying: 'I kiss the mouth of the Lord, I catch the perfume of His Garden.' They all rejoiced and sat down. Thereupon all the birds that were making a shadow over them flew away in all directions. R. Simeon turned his head and called after

[1] *v.* T.B. Aboth v.

them, saying: 'Birds of heaven, have ye no respect for your master who is here ?' They thereupon remained still, not moving from their place, but not drawing nearer. Said R. Phineas: 'Tell them to go their ways, since they are not permitted to return to us.' Said R. Simeon: 'I know that God desires to perform a miracle for us. Birds, birds, go your ways, and tell him who is in control of you that at first he was his own master, but now he is not his own master, but we are leaving him for the day of the rock when enmity will arise between two mighty ones and they will not unite.' The birds then scattered and went. Meanwhile they found three trees spreading their branches over them in three directions and a stream of water flowing in front of them. All the Companions rejoiced at this, as did also R. Phineas and R. Simeon. Said R. Phineas: 'It was a great trouble for those birds at first, and we do not desire to give pain to living creatures, since it is written, "and his mercies are on all his works" (Ps. CXLV, 9).' R. Simeon replied: 'I did not trouble them, but if God was kind to us, we cannot reject His gifts.' They then sat down under the tree and drank of the water and refreshed themselves.

R. Phineas then discoursed on the verse: "A fountain of gardens, a well of living waters and flowing streams from Lebanon" (S.S. IV, 15). 'Are there not then', he said, 'other fountains besides those of the gardens ? There is, however, a difference in the benefit they confer. If a fountain gushes forth in the wilderness, in a dry place, it is serviceable to one who sits by it and drinks from it. But how good and precious is a fountain of gardens, for it benefits herbs and plants, and he who draws near to it derives benefit not only from the water but also from the herbs and plants. That fountain is bedecked in all ways, having many fragrant flowers around it, so that it is truly a "well of living waters". Now it has been explained that it is the Community of Israel who is called "a fountain of gardens". The Holy One, blessed be He, has five gardens in which He delights himself, and there is one hidden and secret fountain which waters all of them, and all produce fruit and flowers. There is one garden below them which is guarded on all sides, and below this are other gardens which produce fruit and flowers after their kinds. This garden transforms itself and becomes according to need either a fountain or a well to water them; for there is a difference between waters flowing [202*a*] of themselves and waters drawn by irrigation. And just as drops of water gradually become a fountain, so those five sources that issue from Lebanon drip gradually into this fountain. What is meant by "flowing streams from Lebanon"? Those five sources that issue from Lebanon above become "streams", for when they become a fountain water issues from it, drop by drop, sweet water that refreshes the soul. So God has wrought for us a miracle in this place, and I apply this verse to this fountain.'

He then discoursed on the verse: "When thou shalt besiege a city a long time in making war against it to take it", etc. (Deut. xx, 19). 'How goodly', he said, 'are the ways and paths of the Torah, since it is full of good counsel for man, and every word of it radiates light in many directions. This verse can be taken literally, and it can be expounded homiletically, and it contains also a lesson of the higher wisdom. He who constantly occupies himself with the Torah is compared by the Psalmist to "a tree planted by streams of water" (Ps. 1, 3). Just as a tree has roots, bark, sap, branches, leaves, flowers and fruit, seven kinds in all, so the Torah has the literal meaning, the homiletical meaning, the mystery of wisdom, numerical values, hidden mysteries, still deeper mysteries, and the laws of fit and unfit, forbidden and permitted, and clean and unclean. From this point branches spread out in all directions, and to one who knows it in this way it is indeed like a tree, and if not he is not truly wise. Observe how beloved are those who study the Torah before the Holy One, blessed be He, for even when chastisement impends over the world and permission is given to the destroyer to destroy, the Holy One, blessed be He, charges him concerning them, saying: "When thou shalt besiege a city", because of their numerous sins against Me, for which they have been adjudged guilty, "for many days", that is to say, three successive days, so that the thing is known in the town, then I will charge thee concerning the sons of My house, "Thou shalt not destroy the tree thereof": this is the learned man in the town, who is a tree of life, a tree that produces fruit. Or, again, we may explain it of one who gives good counsel to the townspeople, telling them how they may escape from punishment, and teaches them the way in which they should go. Therefore "thou shalt not destroy its tree by wielding an axe against it", that is, by inflicting punishment upon him and brandishing the flaming sword over him, which slays other men. The verse then continues, "For from it thou eatest". Now we cannot possibly apply this to the destroyer, so we must translate, "for from it *she* eats", to wit, that mighty rock from which issue all great and holy spirits, for the holy spirit has no pleasure in this world save from the Torah of that pious one, who, if one may say so, sustains her and gives her food in this world more than all sacrifices. Since the Temple has been destroyed and the sacrifices have ceased, the Holy One, blessed be He, has only those words of the Torah which this man expounds. Therefore "it thou shalt not cut down": be careful not to touch him, "for man is the [202b] tree of the field"; this one is called "man", being known as such above and below; he is the mighty tree of that field which the Lord hath blessed. "To be besieged of thee": these words are connected with the earlier part of the verse, "thou shalt not destroy its tree", namely, him who gave advice to the townspeople and prepared them to withstand a siege before thee, counselling them to amend and to blow the trumpet for repentance, to avoid thee and come before God. "In siege": this is the place to which higher and lower angels cannot enter, but where repentant sinners may enter. If they accept this advice then I pardon them their sins and they are received into favour before Me. Happy, therefore, are those who study the Torah, for they are great in this world. See what God has done, how He has planted these trees, not one only, but three spreading their branches on all sides. May it be the will of heaven that these trees shall never depart from this place, nor this fountain. And in truth those trees and that fountain are still there, and men call it "the plantation of R. Phineas b. Jair".'

U

R. Simeon then discoursed on the verse: "And he lifted
up his eyes and saw the women and the children, and said:
Who are these with thee ? And he said, The children which
God hath graciously given thy servant" (Gen. XXXIII, 5). 'The
wicked Esau', he said, 'had his eye on women, and therefore
Jacob took precautions against him, putting in front the
handmaids and then their children, for whom he had more
regard, then Leah and her children behind her, and then
Rachel, and behind her Joseph. But when they drew near
and bowed down, it says that "Joseph came near and Rachel",
putting Joseph first. This indicates that Joseph, being a
good and loving son, was afraid for his mother, and so kept
her behind him and covered her with his arms and his body,
so that Esau should not look at her. Now it says of Balaam
that "he lifted up his eyes and saw Israel dwelling according
to their tribes" (Num. XXIV, 2). The tribe of Joseph and the
tribe of Benjamin were there: the tribe of Joseph, over whom
the evil eye has no power, and the tribe of Benjamin, who
also has no fear of the evil eye. Now Balaam had said: I will
cross this line which is of no account and look well at them.
Rachel was there, and when she saw that his eye was sharp-
ened to do them hurt, she went forth and spread her wings
over them and covered her sons. Hence it says, "The spirit
of the God came upon him" (Ibid.), to wit, upon Israel, whom
He was protecting, and straightway Balaam retired. So at
first the son protected the mother and later the mother
protected the sons; for so God had said at the time when
he saved his mother from the eye of the wicked Esau. To
return to our text: the words "And he lifted up his eyes and
saw the women" contain a mystery of wisdom. On the Day
of Atonement, when mankind is on trial and Israel repent
before the Almighty to obtain forgiveness of their sins, and
the Accuser comes forward to destroy them, they send him
a gift and he becomes their advocate. He lifts up his eyes
and sees the Israelites all fasting and barefoot, along with
their wives and children, and pure and stainless, [203a] and
he says, "Who are these with thee ?", referring to the children,
as much as to say: I understand you, the grown-ups, fasting
because you have sinned against the King; but what are

these children doing here ? Then the holy spirit answers
him: "They are the children which God hath graciously
given to thy servant", to wit, to that officer of thine to put
them to death though guilty of no sin. When He hears
the mention of those children, he at once goes up to the
Holy One, blessed be He, and says: Sovereign of the Universe, all Thy ways are justice and truth. Now if punishment
impends over Israel it is because of their sins. But their
children who have not sinned—why hast Thou delivered
them up to be slain without guilt ? God then takes note of
his words and has mercy on them, and at that time there is
no whooping-cough among the children. The Accuser is
then jealous of his subordinate, saying: To me God has
given those who are clad in sin and guilt, and to my subordinate He has delivered children without sin who know
not the taste of guilt. Straightway he goes to rescue them
from his hands that he should have no power over them.
Thus the holy spirit rescues them from the hand of the
servant. Then it "passes before them" when the prayers of
Israel ascend on this day before the Holy One, blessed be
He, and "bows down seven times", corresponding to the
seven grades above it, so as to include them with it, "until
he reaches his brother", the grade of Mercy, to whom it
makes known the distress of their sons below, and then both
enter the secret and hidden palace of the Day of Atonement,
their Mother, and beseech pardon for Israel. So now with
the wise children here to whom God has communicated
the secrets of the Torah to be crowned and perfected therewith, the evil eye has no power over them because of the
good eye, the holy spirit of R. Phineas which rests upon
them.' R. Phineas then approached and kissed him, saying:
'Had I taken this journey only to hear these words it would
have been worth my while. Blessed is this journey which
led me to thee, and God is here who has agreed with us.
This well is a symbol of the supernal Well which is hidden
and concealed. These three trees represent the three cedars
which are called the Cedars of Lebanon, the emblem of the
Patriarchs. Happy is our portion at this hour'. The trees then
inclined themselves, one over the head of R. Simeon, one

over the head of R. Phineas, and one over the head of R. Eleazar, while the branches spread on every side over the heads of the Companions. R. Phineas wept for joy, saying: 'Happy is my lot and blessed my eyes that see this. I rejoice not only for myself and for thee, but also for our son, R. Eleazar, who is esteemed before the Holy King as one of us.' He then arose and kissed him, and R. Simeon said: 'Eleazar, stand up and repeat before thy Master His words.'

R. Eleazar then rose [203b] and opened a discourse on the verse: "O my people, remember now what Balak king of Moab consulted", etc. (Mich. VI, 3). 'God', he said, 'is merciful to his sons like a father to his son. A father beats his son and yet he does not leave his evil ways. He rebukes him, and still he does not listen to him. Says the father to himself: I will no longer treat my son as I have done hitherto. When I beat him, his head is hurt and his pain is my pain. When I rebuke him, his face becomes distorted. What, then, shall I do? I will go and plead with him, and speak gently to him so that he will not be vexed. So God tries all ways with Israel. He begins to beat them, but they pay no attention; he rebukes them and they pay no attention. He then says: I see that my beating has hurt their head. Alas, because I also feel their pain, as it is written, "In all their trouble he had trouble" (Isa. LXIII, 9). If I rebuke them, their looks are distorted, as it is written, "Their visage is blacker than a coal, they are not known in the streets" (Lam. IV, 8). Now, therefore, I will plead with them gently, "My people, what have I done with thee and wherein have I wearied thee?" My son, my only one, beloved of my soul, see what I have done for thee. I have made thee ruler over all the inmates of my palace; I have made thee ruler over all the kings of the world; and if I have done aught different to thee, "testify against me. My people, remember, I pray thee, what Balak king of Moab counselled", etc.' [204a]

R. Eleazar discoursed on the verse: "O Lord, in the morning shalt thou hear my voice", etc. (Ps. V, 4). 'When daylight comes', he said, 'that "Morning" of Abraham awakes, and then is a time of grace for all, both virtuous and wicked, and therefore it is the hour to offer prayer to the Holy King, since all the prisoners of the King then have respite. And most of all is it the time for those who repent to offer their prayer before the Holy King, because at that hour a certain Chieftain named Raphael goes forth to the side of the South having all manner of healing medicines in his hand, and from the side of the South comes forth a certain spirit which meets that keeper of the medicines. When the prayer reaches the Holy One, blessed be He, He enjoins His court not to hear accusations, because life is in His hand and not in theirs. And since it is a time of grace, God desires to justify that man if he is engaged in prayer or repentance. At that time the twittering of birds is heard praising and lauding the Holy One, blessed be He, and the Hind of the morning awakes and says: "How great is thy goodness which thou hast laid up for them that fear thee" (Ps. xxxi, 19). Then that emissary goes forth and does all that he was enjoined. When we said that he had medicaments in his hand, this was not quite correct, as really they are only in the hand of the King. But when God ordains healing for that man, the emissary goes forth and all the accusers who bring sicknesses fear him, and then that spirit that journeyed from the South is handed to that man, and thus there is healing, though all is in the hands of the Holy One, blessed be He. Our text continues: "In the morning will I order my prayer unto thee and keep watch". Why is the word "morning" repeated ? One refers to the morning of Abraham and the other to the morning of Joseph. [204b] The words "I will order" mean, I will prepare thy lamp to give light, and refer to the morning of Joseph. Why does David say, "I will keep watch" ? Surely all men watch and hope for the kindness of God, and even the beasts of the field ? I inquired concerning this, and was given the following answer, and it is a right one, and very recondite. The first light that God created was so bright that the worlds could not endure it. God therefore made another light as a vestment to this one, and so with all the other lights, until all the worlds could endure the light without being dissolved. Hence grades were evolved and lights were wrapped in one another until they reached this "morning of Joseph", which was a substratum to all

the higher lights. And since all the higher lights converge
on it, its brightness goes forth from one end of the world
to the other, so that the worlds below cannot endure. David
therefore came and prepared this lamp as a covering to this
"morning of Joseph", so as to preserve the lower worlds, and
therefore he said, "I will prepare the morning for thee and"
(as we might translate the word *azapeh*) "overlay it".'
R. Abba came and kissed him, saying: 'Had I made the
journey only to hear this it would have repaid me.'

As they were going along a pigeon approached R. Eleazar
and commenced cooing in front of him. He said: 'Worthy
dove, thou wast ever a faithful messenger, go and tell him
that the Companions are coming and I am with them, and
a miracle will be performed for him in three days, and he
should not be afraid as we are approaching him in joy.' He
replied again, saying: 'I am not very glad; in fact, I am sore
distressed on account of a certain full pomegranate which has
been sacrificed for him, and Jose is his name'. The dove went
on in front and the Companions left them. Said R. Abba:
'I am greatly amazed at what I see.' He said to him: 'This
dove came to me on a message from R. Jose, my father-in-
law, who is lying ill, and I know from this pigeon that he
has been delivered, and a substitute has been found for him,
and he has been healed'. As they went along a raven came
and stood before them, croaking loudly. R. Eleazar said:
'For this thou art here, and for this thou art come; go thy
way, for I know already.' Said R. Eleazar: 'Companions,
let us proceed and do an office of kindness with a pomegranate
that was full of juice, R. Jose of Pekiin was his name, for he
has departed from this world and there is no one to attend
to him, and he is near us.' So they turned aside and went
there.

When the townsfolk saw them, they all came out to meet
them. The Companions then went into the house of R. Jose
of Pekiin. He had a young son who would let no one approach
the bed of his father as he lay dead, but he himself kept close
to him and wept over him, putting his mouth to his mouth.
He exclaimed: 'Sovereign of the Universe, it is written in
the Torah, "If a bird's nest chance to be before thee . . .

thou shalt surely let the dam go" (Deut. XXII, 6). Sovereign
of the Universe,' he said with sobs, 'fulfil this word. We
were two children to my father and mother, I and my
younger sister. Thou shouldst have taken us and fulfilled
the injunction of the Torah. And if Thou shouldst say, It
is written "mother" and not "father", he was both, father
and mother, for my mother has died and Thou didst take
her from her children. Now the father who was our protector
has been taken from the children; where is the justice ?'
R. Eleazar and the Companions wept to hear the tears and
sobs of the boy. R. Eleazar started to quote the verse, "The
heaven for height and the earth for depth" (Prov. xxv, 3),
but before he could complete it a pillar of fire parted them,
while the child still had his lips pressed to the mouth of his
father. Said R. Eleazar: 'Either God desires to work a
miracle, or He desires no other man to attend to him; but in
any case I cannot bear the words and the tears of this child.'
As they sat they heard a voice [205*a*] say: 'Happy art thou,
R. Jose, for the words of this young kid have ascended to
the throne of the Holy King and sentence has been passed
and God has assigned thirteen men to the Angel of Death
in thy place, and an addition has been made to thy years so
that thou mayest teach the Torah to this excellent kid,
beloved before the Holy One, blessed be He.' R. Eleazar and
the Companions rose and would not let anyone stay in the
house. Forthwith they saw that pillar of fire depart and
R. Jose opened his eyes, the boy's lips still being pressed
close to his. Said R. Eleazar: 'Happy is our lot that we have
seen the resurrection of the dead with our own eyes'. They
drew near to him and found the boy sleeping like one dead
to the world. They said: 'Happy is thy portion, R. Jose,
and blessed is God who has wrought a miracle for thee for the
weeping and sobbing of thy son. For the sake of his beautiful
words with which he has knocked at the gate of heaven and
of his tears they have added years to thy life.' They then
lifted up the boy and kissed him, weeping for joy, and they
took him out of the house to another house, and were careful
not to tell him at once. They remained there three days, and
expounded many points of the Torah with R. Jose. Said

R. Jose to the Companions: 'I am not permitted to reveal what I saw in the other world till twelve years have passed. But the three hundred and sixty-five tears which my son shed have all been counted before the Almighty, and I assure you, Companions, that when he quoted that verse three hundred thousand chairs in the Academy of the firmament were shaken, and all stood before the Holy King and besought mercy for me and offered themselves as surety for me. And God was filled with mercy towards me, being well pleased with those words and his offer to sacrifice himself for me. There was one Guardian who said: Sovereign of the Universe, it is written, "Out of the mouth of babes and sucklings hast thou established strength" (Ps. VIII, 3). May it please Thee for the merit of the Torah and for the merit of that child who offered his life for his father, that Thou mayest spare him so that he be delivered. So He assigned him thirteen men in my place and gave him a pledge to save me from this sentence. Then God called the Angel of Death and commanded him to return for me in twenty-two years. And so, Companions, because God saw that you are truly virtuous, He wrought a miracle before your eyes.'

R. Jose then discoursed on the verse: "The Lord killeth and maketh alive, he bringeth down to the grave and bringeth up" (1 Sam. II, 6). 'This verse', he said, 'raises a difficulty. Can it be said that the Lord killeth, seeing that this name is the elixir of life to all ? We have, however, to ask how He kills. You might think it is by merely departing from a man, because so long as He is with him all the Accusers of the world cannot harm him, but so soon as He leaves him they at once have power over him and he dies. This, however, is not the real meaning. Who is it really that the Lord kills ? It is that influence of the evil "other side". So soon as the influence of the evil side sees the splendour of the glory of the Holy One, blessed be He, it dies straightway and cannot survive an instant. And so soon as that influence of the "other side" dies, at once God "brings to life". Whom does He bring to life ? The influence of the spirit of holiness which comes from the side of holiness. All this the Holy One, blessed be He, does at one and the same time. As for the words "He bringeth down to the grave and bringeth up", this means that He takes that spirit of holiness down to Sheol and there baptizes it to purify it, after which it ascends to its rightful place in the Garden of Eden. Now, Companions, at the time when I departed from the world, my spirit left me and slept for a little while till God revived me, my body being dead. When my son uttered those words, his soul flew away and met my soul as it was coming up from its purification to a certain place where its sentence was pronounced, and they gave me twenty-two years of life for the sake of the tears [205b] and words of my son. From this time forward I must occupy myself only with what I have seen, and not with the affairs of this world, since God desires that naught of what I have seen should be forgotten by me.'

He then discoursed on the verse: "The Lord hath chastened me sore", etc. (Ps. CXVIII, 18). 'David said this in reference to all that had befallen him in this world, to his having been pursued and taken refuge in the land of Moab and the land of the Philistines, in order to strengthen his assurance of the other world. He said: If I have sinned in this world I have been smitten in this world and received my punishment and been purified, and nothing of my punishment is left for the next world after death. Hence assuredly "God has chastened me" in this world, "but he hath not given me over to death" in the next world. So I, too, have been purified once in this world, and from now onward I must be careful that I do not incur disgrace in the world to come.'

His son then discoursed on the verse: "Our father died in the wilderness, and he was not among the company", etc. (Num. XXVII, 3). 'Why did the daughters of Zelopehad so particularly state that their father had died in the wilderness, seeing that so many thousands of others had also died in the wilderness ? Men are at a loss to explain this, and some say he was the man who gathered sticks on the Sabbath, and others say other things, but what I have learnt is this—my father taught it me on the day when he fell ill. We must take the word *midbar* (wilderness) here in the sense of "saying". Zelopehad was one of the principal men of the sons of

Joseph, but because he did not know the ways of the Torah
sufficiently he did not become their prince. His fault was
that he was not careful of his speech and his tongue in front
of Moses. Hence, because he sinned in his speech against
Moses, his daughters thought that Moses bore a grudge
against him, and therefore they drew near "before Moses
and Eleazar and all the princes", and spoke with Moses only
in their presence, because they were afraid of his anger. From
this we learn that one who is afraid of a judge should bring
a large audience before him in order that they may hear
him judge and he may be afraid of them and conduct the
case properly. Otherwise, he should not be allowed to
conduct the case. They did not know that Moses "was
exceedingly meek, above all the men on the face of the earth"
(Num. XII, 3). When Moses observed that a whole gathering
of the leading men of Israel and all the heads of the fathers
and all the princes were assembled round him, he at once
resigned the case, and so it says, "And Moses brought their
cause before the Lord" (Num. XXVII, 5), as if to say: This
case is not for me. This shows the modesty of Moses, for
other judges would not act so.' R. Eleazar and the Companions were delighted, and the boy continued: 'The tonal
accent (*zarka*) on the word "our father" resembles in
shape a serpent drawing its tail into its mouth, being an
indication of the One who presides over him above; for "he
died in the wilderness" through the utterance of his mouth.'
At this point the boy became frightened and clung to his
father's neck, weeping and saying: 'Zelopehad died through
words, and thou, father, hast been restored to this world
through words.' His father in turn kissed [206a] and embraced him, and R. Eleazar and the Companions all wept,
and his father with them, and they lifted him up and kissed
him on his mouth and his head and his hands. R. Eleazar
said to him: 'My son, since you have said so much, tell us
what is meant by "but he died in his own sin".' He replied:
'It means, by the sin of that serpent. And what is that ? The
speech of the mouth.' R. Eleazar then clasped him tightly
to his breast, and all the Companions wept. He said to them:
'Rabbis, leave me here with my father because my spirit

is not yet properly restored.' R. Eleazar then asked R. Jose how many years and days old the boy was. He replied: 'I beg of you, Companions, not to ask this, because five years have not yet passed over him.' 'God forbid,' said R. Eleazar; 'I desire to turn only a good eye on him, and your five years are "the five years in which will be no ploughing or reaping" (Gen. XLV, 6), an omen that you shall never reap him.' Said R. Eleazar to R. Abba: 'Let us stay here seven days, till the house becomes settled, because for seven days after the soul has left the body it goes about naked, and now though it has returned it will not be settled in its place till after seven days.' R. Abba replied: 'It is written, "Thou shalt surely open thine hand unto thy brother, thy poor, thy needy, and to thy poor in thy land" (Deut. XV, 11), and we have learnt that this is a lesson that one should not abandon his own poor to give to another. Now R. Jose, your father-in-law, is sick; let us go and visit him, and when we return we will go in here, and all the time we are going and returning on this journey we shall see the resurrection of the dead.' Said R. Eleazar: 'That is assuredly so.' So they kissed the boy and blessed him and departed. Said R. Abba: 'I am amazed at the young children of this generation, what capacities they show, being already mighty and lofty rocks.' R. Eleazar replied: 'Blessed is my father, the master of this generation. In his days God has been pleased to establish His two Academies and to create for us a great and noble academy, for there shall not be another generation like this till the Messiah shall come.'

So they went their way. As they were going, R. Abba said: 'We have learnt that for eleven things the plague of leprosy comes upon a man, and these are they: for idolatry, for cursing the Name, for fornication, for stealing, for slander, for false witness, for perversion of justice, for false swearing, for encroaching on the property of a neighbour, for harbouring evil designs, and for fomenting quarrels between brothers. Some add also, for the evil eye. [206b] All these were found in the wicked Balaam. Fornication and idolatry, as it is written, "Behold these caused the children of Israel to commit trespass against the Lord

through the counsel of Balaam in the matter of Peor"
(Num. XXXI, 16). False witness, as it is written, "Balaam the
son of Peor sayeth . . . which knoweth the knowledge of the
Most High" (*Ibid*. XXIV, 16), while he did not know even
the knowledge of his ass. He perverted judgement, as it is
written, "Come and I will advertise thee" (*Ibid*. 14). He
encroached on a domain which did not belong to him, as it
is written, "And I offered oxen and rams on the altar", and
also, "The seven altars I have prepared" (*Ibid*. XXIII, 4).
He fomented discord between brothers, between Israel and
their Father in heaven. As for slander, there was no other
to equal him. And so with the rest.'

R. Jose quoted the verse: "Eat thou not the bread of him
that hath an evil eye" (Prov. XXIII, 6). 'This', he said, 'is
Balaam who blessed Israel. "Neither desire thou his dainties": this was Balak, whose burnt offerings were not
accepted by the Almighty. When Balak observed that Sihon
and Og had been killed and their land taken away, he foresaw
in his wisdom that he and five princes of Midian and his
people would fall by the hand of Israel, and not knowing
what to make of it he approached Balaam, whose power was
in his mouth, just as the power of Israel was in its mouth.
Balaam was even more anxious to attack them than Balak.
The knowledge which he acquired was at night time, because
the lower crowns and the asses are at large only in the first
watch of the night. Therefore he had an ass to attract [207a]
the asses to her in the early part of the night. It is true that
it says, "*Elohim* came to Balaam in the night", but we have
explained this to refer to the Chieftain appointed over
them. It was on this account that Balaam said to the princes
of Balak, "Tarry here this night". Balaam went to his she-
ass and performed his rites and uttered his spells, and the
ass then told him and he did the requisite act for that spirit
to rest upon him. Then someone came and told him things
through the agency of the ass. It may be asked, if he told him
in one night, "Thou shalt not go with them", why did he
try a second time ? The fact is that these powers are subject
to a higher control, and we have learnt, "In the way in
which a man desires to go he is led". At first he was told,

"Thou shalt not go with them". When God saw that he was bent on going, He said to him, "Arise, go with them, only the thing that I tell thee", etc.

'All that night, therefore, Balaam was pondering and saying in his mind: What honour is it for me if I am tied to someone else ? He cast about all that night and found no side in which he should be his own master save that of his ass. R. Isaac has told us in the name of R. Judah, that among those lower crowns there is a right and a left, on the left side being she-asses. R. Jose said that those of the right are all merged in one called "ass", and that is the ass of which it is written, "thou shalt not plough with an ox and an ass together" (Deut. XXII, 10), and that is also the ass which the King Messiah shall control, as we have explained. There are ten on the right and ten on the left which are included in *kesem* (divination), and ten others on the right and ten others on the left which are included in *nahash* (enchantment), and therefore it is written, "For there is no enchantment with Jacob and no divination with Israel" (Num. XXIII, 23); why ? Because "the Lord his God is with him". Balaam, therefore, finding no way out save through his ass, straightway ROSE UP IN THE MORNING AND SADDLED HIS ASS to attain his own ends and the ends of Balak through it. And therefore "the anger of God was kindled because he went", as much as to say, because he was following his own bent and breaking loose from the one who said to him, "only the thing which I shall tell thee", etc. Said the Holy One, blessed be He, to him: [207b] Sinner, thou makest ready thy weapon to escape from my control; I will show thee that thou and thy ass are in my power. Straightway THE ANGEL OF THE LORD PLACED HIMSELF IN THE WAY. Said R. Abba: 'He left his own function to take up the function of another, for this was an angel of mercy, and this bears out what R. Simeon said, that sinners turn mercy into judgement.' R. Eleazar, however, said: 'The angel did not change, nor did he leave his own function, but because he was from the side of mercy and stood in his way he nullified his wisdom and frustrated his intention. Thus he was "an adversary to him", but to others he was not an adversary.' 'We have learnt', R. Simeon

said, 'how clever was Balaam with his enchantments above
all others, because when he sought to escape from the control
of the Holy One, blessed be He, he found no means save
the ass, and therefore "he loaded his ass" with all the
enchantments and divinations that he knew of in order to
curse Israel. Straightway, "the anger of God was kindled
because he was going". What did God do ? He sent an
angel of mercy to meet him and to nullify his enchantments.
Note that here for the first time in this passage the name
"Lord" is mentioned, showing that this was an angel of
mercy sent to frustrate his wisdom and to turn his ass aside
from the way, namely, that way on which he was bent on
going. Said the Holy One, blessed be He: Sinner, thou hast
loaded thy ass with thy enchantments to bring down all
kinds of punishments on my sons; I will turn thy load into
something else; and straightway He sent the angel of mercy
to stand in his way.'

AND THE ASS SAW THE ANGEL OF THE LORD, ETC.
Said R. Isaac: 'Why did she see while Balaam, who was so
wise, did not see ?' R. Jose replied: 'It was not to be thought
of that that sinner should behold the vision of holiness.' Said
the other: 'What, then, are we to make of the words, "Falling
down and having his eyes open" (Num. xxiv, 4) ?' 'Regarding
that', he said, 'I have not heard anything, so I can give no
explanation.' Said R. Isaac: 'I have heard that when it was
proper for him to behold, he used to fall down and see, but
now it was not proper for him to behold.' 'If that is so,' said
the other, 'he was in a grade superior to that of all the true
prophets, since when falling with open eyes he beheld the
glory of the Holy One, blessed be He. R. Simeon, however,
has told us that through his enchantments Balaam knew
only the lower Crowns beneath, and was entitled only a
"diviner". And R. Simeon also said that through one vision
which he was granted exceptionally, as it says, "And the
Lord opened the eyes of Balaam", his eyes were stricken.
How, then, can you say that he saw with open eyes and gazed
on the glory of God ?' He said: 'I simply answered your
question. Both your statement and mine require to be cleared

up. Of a truth the mysteries of the Torah are deep, and not to be penetrated, and therefore one should not make any statement about the Torah until he has heard and understood it properly.' They therefore went to R. Simeon and laid the matter before him. In reply he cited to them the verse: "What is man that thou art mindful of him, and the son of man that thou visitest him ?" (Ps. VIII, 5). 'The exposition of this verse', he said, 'is that it was uttered by those in charge of the world at the time when God expressed His intention of creating man. He called together various companies of heavenly angels and stationed them before Him. He said to them: I desire to create man. They exclaimed, "Man abideth not in honour", etc. (Ps. XLIX, 13). God thereupon put forth His finger and burnt them. He then set other groups before Him, and said: I desire to create man. They exclaimed, [208a] "What is man that thou shouldst remember him ?" What is the character of this man, they asked. He replied: Man will be in our image, and his wisdom will be superior to yours. When He had created man and he sinned and obtained a pardon, Uzza and Azael approached Him and said: We can plead justification against Thee, since the man whom Thou hast made has sinned against Thee. He said to them: Had you been with them you would have sinned equally, and He cast them down from their high estate in heaven. Now to come to your question. How are we to explain Balaam's saying of himself, "Falling and with eyes open" ? For if this was merely an empty boast, how comes a false statement in the Torah ? And if it is true, how could that sinner attain to a degree higher than that of all the true prophets, especially as the holiness from above rests only on a spot qualified to receive it ? The fact is, however, that after God cast Uzza and Azael down from their holy place, they went astray after the womenfolk and seduced the world also. It may seem strange that being angels they were able to abide upon the earth. The truth is, however, that when they were cast down the celestial light which used to sustain them left them and they were changed to another grade through the influence of the air of this world. Similarly the manna which came down for the Israelites in the wilderness

originated in the celestial dew from the most recondite spot, and at first its light would radiate to all worlds and the "field of apples", and the heavenly angels drew sustenance from it, but when it approached the earth it became materialized through the influence of the air of this world and lost its brightness, becoming only like "coriander seed". Now when God saw that these fallen angels were seducing the world, He bound them in chains of iron to a mountain of darkness. Uzza He bound at the bottom of the mountain and covered his face with darkness because he struggled and resisted, but Azael, who did not resist, He set by the side of the mountain where a little light penetrated. Men who know where they are located seek them out, and they teach them enchantments and sorceries and divinations. These mountains of darkness are called the "mountains of the East", and therefore Balaam said: "From Aram hath Balak brought me, from the mountains of the East", because they both learnt their sorceries there. Now Uzza and Azael used to tell those men who came to them some of the notable things which they knew in former times when they were on high, and to speak about the holy world in which they used to be. Hence Balaam said of himself: "He saith, which heareth the words of God"—not the *voice* of God, but those things which he was told by those who had been in the assembly of the Holy King. He went on: "And knoweth the knowledge of the Most High", meaning that he knew the hour when punishment impended over the world and could determine it with his enchantments. "Which seeth the vision of the Almighty": this vision consisted of the "fallen and the open of eyes", that is Uzza, who is called "fallen" because he was placed in the darkest depth, since after falling from heaven he fell a second time, and Azael, who is called "open of eye" because he was not enveloped in complete darkness. [208b] Balaam called both of them "the vision of the Almighty". At that time he was the only man left in the world who associated with them, and every day he used to be shut up in those mountains with them.'
Said R. Simeon: 'How often have I repeated this, and yet the Companions do not pay attention, that the Holy One,

blessed be He, does not let His divine presence rest save in
a place which is meet that it should rest therein. Happy is
the portion of Israel in that God has sanctified them that
He may abide among them, as it is written, "For the Lord
thy God walketh in the midst of thy camp", etc. (Deut.
XXIII, 14). Happy, too, is the portion of the true prophets
who are holy and are permitted to make use of the celestial
holiness.

'And THE ASS SAW THE ANGEL OF THE LORD STAND-
ING IN THE WAY: in that way which Balaam had chosen.
WITH HIS SWORD DRAWN IN HIS HAND. If the angel went
to meet the ass, why did he require a sword, and if he went
to meet Balaam, why did his ass see and not he himself?
All, however, was arranged by Providence. The angel was
sent by Providence to lead the ass out of that way in which
it was being driven, and to thwart Balaam in order to punish
him for wanting to go his own way.' R. Jose said: 'The
question now arises, if his words came from the side of the
lower crowns and not from another side, why is it written,
"And God (*Elohim*) came to Balaam?"' R. Isaac replied:
'What we have learnt is that *Elohim* in this passage designates
an angel, being the place that comes from the side of stern
judgement, to which is attached the strength and power
of those lower crowns which were employed by Balaam.
Hence it says, "And *Elohim* came to Balaam", etc., because
sometimes the angel is called by the superior name.

'AND THE ASS TURNED ASIDE OUT OF THE WAY. That
is, from the way of stern judgement against Israel. How did
Balaam see that she had turned aside?' Said R. Simeon:
'Even on the way he sought to do harm to Israel through
the power of his ass, and when he saw that he was not
succeeding he smote it with his staff, which is a symbol of
stern judgement. AND WENT IN THE FIELD: in the straight
path on the side of "field". AND BALAAM SMOTE THE
ASS TO TURN HER INTO THE WAY: that is, to turn her
out of that way of the field. When he saw he was not
able, then "he smote the ass with a staff", as has been
explained.'

X

AND THE ANGEL OF THE LORD STOOD, ETC. Said R. Abba: 'These verses have [209*a*] a profound symbolical meaning, and it was not for nothing that the angel went forth to appear to an ass and to meet it now here and now there. All was designed by the Holy One, blessed be He, to protect Israel from the domination of the evil species. We have learnt that from the side of the Mother when she is crowned there issue in her crowns fifteen hundred sides graven in her ornaments. When She desires to unite with the King she is crowned with a diadem of four colours, which flash to all four sides of the world, each one three times, making twelve graven boundaries. On the top of the crown there are four walls with towers, on each of which are three doors fixed in precious stones on each side. Under the crown are bells of gold, a bell on this side and a bell on that, and a pomegranate in which are a thousand bells, each one flashing white and red. This pomegranate is divided into four quarters and is open so that the bells can be seen. There are three hundred and twenty-five bells on each side, and all four sides of the world are illumined with the radiance of each quarter. There are four wheels on the four corners to bear the crown. Their voice is heard through all the firmaments, and at the sweet sound of them all the hosts of heaven are excited and inquire of one another until they all say: Blessed is the glory of the Lord from His place. When the King joins the Matrona, this crown ascends and settles on the head of the Matrona. Then there comes down a supernal crown studded with all kinds of precious stones and with garlands of lilies around it. It comes with six wheels to the six sides of the world, borne by six wings of eagles. In its quarters are fifty grapes round about traced by the supreme Mother, set with precious stones, white and red and green and black and blue and purple, six hundred and thirteen corners to each side. There are a thousand and six hundred turrets on each side, moistened by the supernal Mother with her oil of anointing. Then the Mother silently sends down noble gifts and fixes them in that crown, which thereupon lets fall streams of oil of holy anointing on the head of the King, whence it flows down on to his precious

beard and from there on to the garments of the King. Then
the supernal Mother crowns Him with that crown and
spreads over Him and the Matrona precious garments. Then
there is joy among all the sons of the King, to wit, those
who come from the sides of Israel, since none associate with
them save Israel, who are of their household, so that the
blessings which issue from them are for Israel. Israel take
all and send a portion thereof to the other peoples, who
thence derive their sustenance. We have learnt that from
between the sides of the portions of the Chieftains of the
other peoples there goes forth [209b] a narrow path whence
is drawn a portion to those lower ones, and thence it spreads
to many sides, and this is called the "residue", which issues
from the side of the Holy Land, and thus the whole world
drinks from the residue of the Holy Land. And not only the
heathen peoples, but also those lower Crowns drink therefrom. This is indicated here by the expression, "a hollow
way between the vineyards", the path of the Princes of the
other peoples, from which they are blessed. Therefore
when the angel saw that Balaam had made his ass turn aside
into that path, straightway he STOOD IN THE HOLLOW
WAY BETWEEN THE VINEYARDS, in order that the other
heathen peoples and the lower Crowns should not furnish
him assistance. There was A FENCE ON THIS SIDE AND
A FENCE ON THAT SIDE.' Said R. Abba: 'The angel would
not have been able to block up the path had he not received
assistance from the Holy One, blessed be He, and the
Community of Israel.' R. Judah said it was the Torah that
assisted him. Then the ass THRUST HERSELF INTO THE
WALL, the "wall" here symbolizing the protector that
guarded them. Also, instead of assisting Balaam she "pressed
his foot against the wall", hinting the same thing to him.
Then HE SMOTE HER AGAIN, on this side, AND THE
ANGEL OF THE LORD WENT FURTHER AND STOOD IN A
NARROW PLACE, thus closing all paths to her, so that she
could not assist Balaam in any way at all. Then SHE LAY
DOWN UNDER BALAAM, and BALAAM'S ANGER WAS
KINDLED AND HE SMOTE HER WITH A STAFF, as we
have explained.'

AND THE LORD OPENED THE MOUTH OF THE ASS.
R. Isaac said: 'What did she say that was of any consequence
either to Balaam or to herself or to Israel?' R. Jose replied:
'She made him ridiculous in the eyes of the nobles who
were with him. When they came to Balak they said: Have
you sent to honour that fool? You will find nothing in him
or his words. Thus through the words of the ass he became
degraded.' R. Ḥiya said: 'Had not the ass spoken thus,
Balaam would not have given up his attempt, but through
the words of the ass he knew that his power was broken.'
R. Abba asked: 'Why does it say here that "God opened
the mouth of the ass", while in an analogous passage it
says that "the earth opened its mouth" (Num. XVI, 32).'
'The reason', he said, 'is that there Moses decreed the
opening and the earth carried out his injunction, for it
would not be fitting that God should do so, but here there
was no one who gave the order, but it was the will of God,
and therefore it is written that "God opened the mouth of
the ass".'

R. Judah said: 'We have carefully examined this section
and these words, and we find that they are not words of any
consequence. Yet after it says that "God opened the mouth
of the ass", those words ought to have been words of pro-
fundity and wisdom. Why, then, did God trouble to open its
mouth for merely such words?' R. Abba replied: 'Assuredly,
through those words we learn the mind of Balaam, that he
was not worthy for the holy spirit to rest on him, and we
learn that there was no power in his ass to do either good
[210a] or harm. We also learn from this ass that animals are
not capable of receiving a rational mind. SHE SAID UNTO
BALAAM, WHAT HAVE I DONE UNTO THEE. As much as
to say: Was it in my power to do good or evil? Not so, for
beasts can only do as they are directed. And that beast, too,
though it struck a deeper note, was still in the power of
Balaam. AND BALAAM SAID UNTO THE ASS, BECAUSE
THOU HAST MOCKED ME. He ought to have laughed at
her, but he answered her in her own tone, and it was then
that they mocked him and he became contemptible in their
eyes, and they knew that he was a fool. They said: He

pretends he can kill peoples with his mouth, and yet he cannot kill his ass without a sword. We learn from here that
beasts are not capable of receiving another spirit. For should
men say: If only beasts could speak, what they would have
to tell the world, learn from this ass of Balaam; for God
opened her mouth, and see what she said !'

AND IT CAME TO PASS IN THE MORNING THAT BALAK
TOOK BALAAM, ETC. R. Isaac said: 'Balak was cleverer at
enchantments than Balaam, only he did not know how to
fix on the right hour for cursing. AND HE BROUGHT HIM
UP TO THE HIGH PLACES OF BAAL. He examined by his
enchantments from what side he could best attack them,
and he found that they would one day make high places
and serve Baal. He saw the princes of the people and their
king serving him. Straightway he said: BUILD ME HERE
SEVEN ALTARS. R. Jose and R. Judah differed as to the
significance of this number. One said it corresponded to the
seven built by the patriarchs. The other said that it was
based on cosmological grounds, because the portion of Israel
is attached to seven grades. A man had a friend who was left
to him from his father, and on account of whom men were
afraid to attack him. One day a man wanted to pick a quarrel
with him, but he was afraid lest the friend would protect him.
He therefore sent a present to the friend. Said the latter:
What does this man want with me ? It must be because of
the son of my friend. I will therefore not accept this gift, but
give it to the dogs. So when Balaam desired to attack Israel,
seeing that he would not be able to prevail against them on
account of their friend, he began to prepare a gift for him.
Whereupon God said: Sinner, what have I to do with you ?
You want to attack my son; here is your gift for my dogs.
So it says, "God met Balaam", the word *vayikkar* (met)
having the connotation of "uncleanness" and also of "uprooting".' [210b] R. Simeon said: 'The loathsomeness of
Balaam may be seen from the fact that in all the section it
never says, "The Lord said" or "spoke" to Balaam. What
it says is, "The Lord placed a word in the mouth of Balaam",
like one who places a bit in the mouth of an ass. God said to

him: Sinner, think not that through you the blessing of my
sons will be confirmed or otherwise. They do not require
you; but return to Balak, and when you open your mouth, it
will not be to say your own words, but *Koh*[1] (thus) will
speak out of your mouth.'

COME CURSE ME JACOB. R. Jose said: 'This means: Cast
them down from the grade in which they stand, for then
they will be uprooted from the world. COME, PROVOKE
ISRAEL; that is, the supernal Israel, so that wrath may be
aroused. FOR FROM THE TOP OF THE ROCKS I SEE HIM.'
R. Isaac said: 'These are the patriarchs. AND FROM THE
HILLS I BEHOLD HIM: these are the matriarchs. From
neither side can they be cursed.' R. Jose said: 'It means:
Who can prevail against Israel, since he is attached to the
source whence all rocks, that is, all forceful deeds, issue. LO
IT IS A PEOPLE THAT DWELL ALONE: as it is written,
"The Lord did lead him alone" (Deut. XXXII, 12). WHO
CAN COUNT THE DUST OF JACOB: this "dust" is the
place whence the first man was created, and from that dust
issue many hosts and camps, many flames and arrows and
catapults and lances and swords. OR NUMBER THE FOURTH
PART OF ISRAEL: this refers to David, who was the fourth
foot of the Throne. [211a]

'BEHOLD THE PEOPLE RISETH UP AS A LIONESS. What
people is strong like Israel ? When the day dawns the Israelite
rises like a lion refreshed for the service of his Master with
songs and praises, and then occupies himself with the Torah
all day. And before he lies down at night he sanctifies the
supreme Name and declares its kingship above and below.
How many officers of judgement are bound hand and
foot before them when they open their mouths on their
beds with "Hear, O Israel," and seek compassion from the
Holy King with many appropriate Scriptural verses !'
R. Abba said: 'This people will one day rise against all the
heathen peoples like a mighty lion and throw themselves on
them. It is the way of the lion to lie down with his prey, but
this people will not lie down till he has eaten of the prey.

[1] The Shekinah.

Or, again, we may explain, "he riseth up as a lioness" to offer burnt-offerings and sacrifices before their king on the altar. "He shall not lie down": these are the sacrifices of the night, like the burnt-offerings. AND DRINK THE BLOOD OF THE SLAIN: because God makes war upon their enemies.' R. Eleazar said: 'What is the meaning of "he shall not lie down" ? It means that when a man walks in the precepts of his Master he never [211b] lies down upon his bed at night before he has killed a thousand and a hundred and twenty-five of those evil species that abide with him.' R. Hizkiah said: 'Corresponding to the three times that Balaam smote his ass and directed it by his sorceries, Israel were blessed three times.' R. Ḥiya said that Israel were blessed three times correspondingly by having to appear three times before the Holy King.

AND WHEN BALAAM SAW THAT IT PLEASED THE LORD TO BLESS ISRAEL, HE WENT NOT AS AT THE OTHER TIMES TO MEET WITH ENCHANTMENTS. R. Jose said: 'The first two times he went with all his enchantments. When he saw what was God's purpose, and that he was only the mouthpiece of *Koh*, he sought to look upon them with the evil eye. He scrutinized the two grades of Jacob and Israel to see through which he could harm them with his enchantments, and that is why all the blessings were bestowed both upon Jacob and Israel. Having, therefore, abandoned his enchantments, he began under another impulse to praise Israel, the impulse of a certain spirit from the side of the left under which were made fast those species and enchantments of his.' Said R. Eleazar: 'We have learnt that even at that time the spirit of holiness did not rest on him.' Said R. Jose to him: 'Why, then, is it written on this occasion that "the spirit of the Lord came upon him", which we do not find before ?' He replied: 'It is written, "He that hath a bountiful eye shall be blessed" (Prov. XXII, 9), or, as we read, "shall bless", and Balaam had an evil eye like no other. Now there is a saying that if a man is taking his child through the street and is afraid of the evil eye, he should cover his head with his scarf, and then he will be safe from the evil eye. So here, when Balaam saw that he was not able to harm Israel with his enchantments and sorceries, he sought to look upon them with the evil eye, and therefore "he set his face towards the wilderness", that is, as the Targum renders, to the calf which they made in the wilderness, in order to find some opening for doing them harm, and had not God provided in advance some remedy for them, he would have destroyed them with the glance of his eye. What was this remedy ? It is indicated in the words, "And there was upon him the spirit of God"—upon him, that is, upon Israel; as when a man spreads his scarf over the head of a child in order that the evil eye should not injure him. Then he began to say: "How goodly are thy tents, O Jacob". Observe that anyone who desires to look at anything with the evil eye has first to praise and laud the thing which he desires to curse with the evil eye, as by saying: "See how good this is, how beautiful this is". So here he said: How goodly are thy tents, how many [212*a*] goodly shoots spring from them, resembling those which God planted in the Garden of Eden. He was like a man who, seeing another with beautiful hands, takes hold of them and begins to praise them, saying: How fair and beautiful they are ! See these fingers of divine form ! Then he goes on: Would that these hands were encased in precious stones and in purple in my box that I might have the use of them ! So Balaam, after beginning to praise them went on: "Let water flow from his buckets", or as we may read, from his poor ones (*dalav*), as much as to say: Let this fair shoot, the shoot of the Torah, come only from the poor among them. God said to him: Wretch, thine eyes cannot harm them, since the veil of holiness is over them. Then he went on: "God bringeth him forth out of Egypt", etc.: the whole world cannot harm them because a mighty power from above takes hold of them.' R. Eleazar said: 'No man was so skilled in inflicting harm as Balaam. For at first he was in Egypt, and through him the Egyptians fastened upon the Israelites fetters from which they thought they would never escape. Balaam therefore now said: How can I harm them, seeing that it was I who devised that they should not escape from the bondage of Egypt for ever. But "God brought them out of Egypt", and no enchanters could prevail against them.

'BEHOLD I GO UNTO MY PEOPLE. When the Israelites left Egypt, and Balaam heard that all his enchantments and divinations and magical fetters had not availed anything, he began to tear his flesh and pluck out his hair, and he then betook himself to the "mountains of darkness". Now when a man first approaches those mountains, Azael, who is called "open of eye", sees him and tells Uzza. Then they give a shout and certain huge flaming beasts gather to them. They send to meet the visitor a little creature like a cat with a serpent's head and two tails and tiny legs. When the man sees it he covers his face and throws in its face some ashes from the burning of a white cock which he has brought with him, and it then accompanies him to the top of the chains. This top is stuck in the ground and the chain extends thence to the abyss, where it is made fast to a pole stuck in there. When the man reaches the chain he strikes it three times. The others thereupon call him and he falls on his knees and closes his eyes till he reaches them. Then he sits before them with all the beasts around him, and when he opens his eyes and sees them he trembles and falls on his face before them. They then teach him enchantments and divinations and he remains with them [212b] fifty days. When the time comes for him to depart the small creature and the beasts go before him till he emerges from the mountains and from the thick darkness. When Balaam came to them, he informed them of what had happened and he sought means of assailing Israel so as to bring them back to Egypt, but God confounded all his wisdom. Now, too, when he saw that he could not harm Israel, without waiting to be asked he gave Balak counsel, namely, regarding the women, as we learn from what Moses said later, "Behold these caused the children of Israel through the counsel of Balaam", etc. (Num. XXXI, 16). God therefore showed to that power which rules over enchantments the end of days, and that is how Balaam came to speak of far-off events, for the words were really spoken by the power which controlled him.

'I SEE HIM BUT NOT NOW: since some of these things were fulfilled at that time and some later, while some are left for the Messiah. We have learnt that God will one day build Jerusalem and display a certain fixed star flashing with seventy streamers and seventy flames in the midst of the firmament, and it will shine and flash for seventy days. It will appear on the sixth day of the week on the twenty-fifth of the sixth month, and will disappear on the seventh day after seventy days. On the first day it will be seen in the city of Rome, and on that day three lofty walls of that city shall fall and a mighty palace shall be overthrown, and the ruler of that city shall die. Then that star will become visible throughout the whole world. In that time mighty wars will arise in all quarters of the world, and no faith shall be found among men. When that star shines in the midst of the firmament, a certain powerful king shall arise who will seek domination over all kings and make war on two sides and prevail against them. On the day when the star disappears the Holy Land will be shaken over an area of forty-five miles all round the place where the Temple used to be, and a cave will be laid open beneath the ground from which shall issue a mighty fire to consume the world. From that cave shall spread a great and noble branch which will rule over all the world and to which shall be given the kingship, and the heavenly saints shall gather to it. Then will the King Messiah appear and the kingship shall be given to him. Mankind will then suffer one calamity after another, and the enemies of Israel will prevail, but the spirit of the Messiah shall rise against them and destroy the sinful Edom and burn in fire the land of Seir. Hence it is written, "And Edom shall be a possession, Seir also shall be a possession of his which were his enemies, while Israel doth valiantly". And in that time the Holy One, blessed be He, shall raise the dead of his people, and death shall be forgotten of them.' R. Abba said: 'Why is it written, "For in joy ye shall go out" (Isa. LV, 12) ? Because when Israel go out from captivity the Shekinah will go forth with them and they with Her.'

PINḤAS

Numbers xxv, 10–xxix, 40

Phineas the son of Eleazar the son of Aaron the priest. R. Simeon said: 'Israel deserved to be destroyed at that time, and were only saved by that deed of Phineas.' Said R. Simeon: 'If a man receives a soul in the course of its transmigration and it does not properly fit into him, he as it were belies his trust to the King, and I apply to him the verse: "If he find something lost and deny it and swear falsely" (Lev. vi, 3). We have learnt that a completely righteous man is not thrust aside, but one who is not completely righteous may be thrust aside. A completely righteous man is one who does not receive migratory souls out of their course, who builds on his own inheritance, and digs his wells and plants his trees there. The righteous one who is not completely so builds on another's inheritance: he labours but does not know if what he produces will remain his. In respect of himself he is called good and righteous, but not in respect of that inheritance. He is like a man who builds a fair building, but when he examines the foundation he finds that it is sloping and crooked. His building in itself is good, [213b] but in respect of its foundation it is bad, and therefore is not called a perfect building. Note that if one is zealous for the name of the Holy One, blessed be He, even though he is not qualified for greatness, he nevertheless obtains it. Phineas at that time was not qualified for greatness, but because he was zealous for the name of his Master he rose to the greatest heights, and all was made right in him,[1] and he was invested with the high priesthood. Hence the word "son" is mentioned in connection with him twice. [214a] Phineas merited reward in this world and in the next. He was granted to outlive all those who went forth from Egypt and won the high priesthood for himself and his descendants. Now it is a rule that a priest who kills a human being becomes disqualified for the priesthood, and therefore

---

[1] i.e. the souls of Nadab and Abihu entered into him, *v. infra.*

by rights Phineas should have been disqualified. But because he was jealous for the Holy One, blessed be He, the priesthood was assigned to him and to his descendants in perpetuity.'

As R. Eleazar and R. Jose were once walking in the wilderness, R. Jose said: 'When it says of Phineas, "Behold I give him my covenant of peace", it means peace from the Angel of Death, so that he should never have power over him and that he should not suffer his chastisements. As for the tradition that Phineas did not die, the truth is that he did not die like other men, and he outlived all his generation, because he kept hold of this supernal covenant, and when he departed from the world it was with celestial yearning and beauteous attachment.' R. Eleazar cited the verse: "And he showed me Joshua the high priest standing before the angel of the Lord", etc. (Zech. III, 1). 'The "filthy garments", as explained elsewhere, are those with which the spirit was clad in this world. It has been asked: When a man is doomed to Gehinnom, what are the garments with which they invest him ? And the answer is given in the words, "Now Joshua was clothed with filthy garments, and standing before the angel" (*Ibid.* 3). This was the angel appointed over Gehinnom, and from this we can learn that the evil deeds of a man make for him these filthy garments, and so God said afterwards to him: "Behold, I have caused thine iniquity to pass from thee and I have clothed thee with rich apparel"; he was clothed in other proper garments through which a man may see the glory of the Shekinah. So Phineas did not depart from this world until there were prepared for him other garments pleasing to the spirit for the next world.' [214b]

As R. Simeon was once studying this portion, his son, R. Eleazar, came and asked him: 'What is the connection of Nadab and Abihu with Phineas ? If Phineas had not been born when they died and had afterwards come into the world and taken their place, I could understand, but he was alive at the time, and his soul was already in its place ?' He replied: 'My son, there is a deep mystery here. When they departed from the world they were not sheltered under the wings of the holy Rock, because they had no children, and they were therefore not fitted for the high priesthood. Now when Phineas rose up against the adulterers, when he saw all the hosts of the tribe of Simeon gathering around him, his soul fled from him, and then two souls which were flying about naked joined it and they all became one and thus united entered into him, so that he took the place of Nadab and Abihu to become high priest, and therefore it is written, "Phineas *son* of Eleazar *son*".'

R. Ḥiya expounded the verse: "He causeth grass to grow for the cattle" (Ps. CIV, 14). 'The "grass",' he said, 'refers to the sixty thousand myriads of angels who were created on the second day of the Creation, being all of flaming fire; and they are called "grass" because they are constantly being cut down and restored. They are food for the "Cattle", over which rules the "Man".'

R. Abba and R. Jose once rose at midnight to study the Torah. As they were sitting they saw a shadow hovering over them and going to and fro in the house, and they marvelled greatly. Said R. Abba: 'Jose, my son, I will tell you what once happened to me with the Sacred Lamp. Once we were walking in the Valley of Ono, studying the Torah. [218*a*] To escape the heat of the sun we sat down in the hollow of a rock. I said to him: Why is it that whenever sinners multiply in the world and punishment impends over the world, the virtuous among them are smitten for them, as we have learnt, that for the guilt of the generation the holy and righteous are seized upon ? Why should this be ? If because they do not reprove mankind for their evil deeds, how many are there who do reprove but are not listened to (though the righteous do humble themselves before them) ? If it is in order that there may be no one to shield them, let them not die and let them not be seized for their sins, since it is a satisfaction to the righteous to see their destruction. He replied: It is true that for the guilt of the generation the righteous are seized upon, but we may explain this on the analogy of the limbs of the body. When all the limbs are in pain and suffering from sickness one limb has to be smitten in order that all may be healed. Which is the one ? The arm. The arm is smitten and blood is drawn from it, and this is healing for all the limbs of the body. So men are like limbs of one body. When God desires to give healing to the world He smites one righteous man among them with disease and suffering, and through him gives healing to all, as it is written, "But he was wounded for our transgressions, he was bruised for our iniquities . . . and with his stripes we are healed" (Isa. LIII, 5). A righteous man is never afflicted save to bring healing to his generation and to make atonement for it, for the "other side" prefers that punishment should light upon the virtuous man rather than on any other, for then it cares not for the whole world on account of the joy it finds in having power over him. Yet withal another virtuous man may attain to dominion in this world and the next; he is "righteous [218b] and it is well with him", because God does not care to make atonement with him for the world. I said to him: If all suffered alike, I could understand, but we see a righteous man in one place who is sick and suffering, and a righteous man in another who enjoys all the good things of the world. He replied: One or two of them are enough, since God does not desire to smite all of them, just as it is sufficient to let blood from one arm; only if the sickness becomes very severe is it necessary to let blood from two arms, and so here, if the world becomes very sinful all the virtuous are smitten to heal all the generation, but otherwise one is smitten and the rest are left in peace. When the people are healed the righteous are healed with them, but sometimes all their days are passed in suffering to protect the people, and when they die all are healed.

'We arose and went on our way, the sun becoming stronger and more oppressive. We saw some trees in the wilderness with water underneath, and we sat down in the shade of one of them. I asked him: How is it that of all peoples of the world, only the Jews sway to and fro when they study the Torah, a habit which seems to come natural to them, and they are unable to keep still ? He replied: You have reminded me of a very deep idea which very few people know. He pondered for a moment and wept. Then he continued:

Alas for mankind who go about like cattle without understanding. This thing alone is sufficient to distinguish the
holy souls of Israel from the souls of heathen peoples. The
souls of Israel have been hewn from the Holy Lamp, as it
is written, "The spirit of man is the lamp of the Lord"
(Prov. xx, 27). Now once this lamp has been kindled from
[219a] the supernal Torah, the light upon it never ceases
for an instant, like the flame of a wick which is never still
for an instant. So when an Israelite has said one word of the
Torah, a light is kindled and he cannot keep still but sways
to and fro like the flame of a wick. But the souls of heathens
are like the burning of stubble, which gives no flame, and
therefore they keep still like wood burning without a flame.'
Said R. Jose: 'That is a good explanation; happy am I to
have heard this.' [220a]

The shadow returned as before and went to and fro in
the house in the shape of a man. R. Abba fell on his face.
R. Jose said: 'I remember that I once saw R. Phineas b. Jair
in this place standing in this spot and discoursing on the
verse, "Phineas son of Eleazar son of Aaron the priest", etc.
God at that time, he said, was debating how to give this
covenant to Phineas, because it belonged of right to Moses,
and it would be an insult to him to give it to anyone else
unless he consented. God therefore commenced to speak
with Moses, saying: Phineas son of Eleazar son of Aaron
the priest. Said Moses: Sovereign of the Universe, what of
him ? He replied: Thou didst risk thy life many times to
save Israel from destruction, and now he has turned My
wrath away from the children of Israel. Moses thereupon
said: What wilt Thou of me? All is in Thy hand. He replied:
Nay, all is in thy hand. Tell him that it (the Shekinah) will
abide in him. Moses replied: I am willing with all my heart
that it should be with him. God then said: Declare aloud
that thou deliverest it to him with all thy heart. Hence we
read in the text, "Say, Behold I (viz. Moses) give unto him
my covenant", and not, "Say *to him*". Yet think not that
it was taken away from Moses: it was like a light from which
another is kindled without loss to itself.'

The shade then came and sat down and kissed him. They

heard a voice saying: Make way, make way for R. Phineas b. Jair, who is with you, as we have learnt: Any place in which a righteous man has given some new explanation of the Torah he visits when he is in the other world, especially when there are in it other righteous men discoursing on the Torah. So R. Phineas b. Jair came to revisit his place and found those righteous men repeating his own remark. R. Abba gave a further exposition in the name of R. Phineas b. Jair of the text: "Whatsoever thy hand findeth to do, do it with thy might" (Eccl. IX, 10). 'It is fitting for a man', he said, 'that while the lamp is burning over his head he should strive to do the will of his Master, because the light of that lamp is the might that rests upon him, as it is written, "And now I pray thee, let the power of the Lord be great" (Num. XIV, 17). The "power of the Lord" is the might that rests on the heads of the righteous, and of all who strive to carry out the will of their Master, and therefore we have learnt that when one makes the response, "Amen, may his great name be blessed", he should do so with all the might of his limbs, because through that effort he awakens that supernal holy might and breaks the power and might of the "other side". [220b] The verse continues: "Because there is no work nor device nor knowledge nor wisdom in the grave whither thou goest". In that "might", however, there is work, namely, effort in this world, which is called "the world of work"; "device" in the world that depends on speech, "knowledge" of the "six sides", which are called "the world of Thought", and wisdom on which all depends. Hence a man who does not labour with his "might" in this world to bring it into "work and device and knowledge and wisdom", will eventually enter into Gehinnom, where there is no work nor device nor knowledge nor wisdom. For all men go down to Sheol, but they come up again at once, save those sinners who never harboured thoughts of repentance, and who go down and do not come up. Even the completely righteous go down there, but they only go down in order to bring up certain sinners from there, to wit, those who thought of repenting in this world, but were not able to do so in time before they departed from it. The righteous go down and bring these up.' Said R. Abba to R. Jose: 'How fair is the jewel that you obtained from the company of the holy saint who is with us! I would add that assuredly it is not right to send a woman to stay in another place until her husband gives her permission. Her husband must therefore first be told and persuaded to give her permission. So God persuaded Moses to say, "Behold, I give him my covenant of peace", and until Moses gave it permission to go there it would not go. Similarly the Righteous One of the world gives Her permission to abide among the righteous ones of this world; in the evening She comes in to her spouse, and in the morning She returns to the righteous of this world, but She is ever in the charge of her Spouse. So Moses gave the gift to Phineas on condition that it should be subsequently restored; and it was through this covenant that Phineas obtained the high priesthood, and without it he would not have been linked to the grade of the priesthood.'

R. Abba said: 'I remember a certain thing which I heard from the Sacred Lamp, and which he said in the name of R. Eleazar. One day a certain clever non-Jew came to him and said: Old man, old man, I want to ask three questions [221a] of you. One is, how can you maintain that another Temple will be built for you, whereas only two were destined to be built, the first and the second. A third and a fourth you will not find mentioned in the Scripture, but it is written, "Greater shall be the glory of this latter house than of the first" (Haggai II, 9). Again, you maintain that you are nearer to the King than all other peoples. Now, one who is near to the King is ever in joy and free from sorrow and oppression, but you are ever in sorrow and oppression and anguish, more than all the rest of mankind, whereas we never suffer sorrow or oppression or anguish at all. This shows that we are near to the King and you are far away. Again, you do not eat *nebelah* and *terefah*,[1] in order to protect your health, but we eat whatever we like and we are healthy and strong, whereas you who do not eat are all weak and sickly beyond other peoples. You are a people who are wholly hated of your God. Old man, old man, don't

[1] Flesh of animals not killed according to Jewish rites.

Y

say anything to me, for I will not listen to you. R. Eleazar raised his eyes and looked at him, and he became a heap of bones. When his wrath subsided he turned his head and wept, saying: "O Lord, our Lord, how excellent is thy name in all the earth" (Ps. VIII, 2). How mighty is the power of the Holy Name, and how beloved are the words of the Torah, since there is nothing at all which cannot be found in the Torah, and there is not a single word of the Torah which does not issue from the mouth of the Holy One, blessed be He. These questions which that wretch put to me I also one day asked Elijah, and he told me that they had been raised in the celestial Academy before the Holy One, blessed be He. The answer given was as follows. When Israel left Egypt, God desired to make them on earth like ministering angels above, and to build for them a holy house which was to be brought down from the heaven of the firmaments, and to plant Israel as a holy shoot after the pattern of the celestial prototype. Thus it is written, "Thou shalt bring them in and plant them in the mountain of thine inheritance, the place, O Lord, which thou hast made for thee to dwell in"—this is the first Temple—"the sanctuary, O Lord, which thy hands have established" (Ex. XV, 17)—this is the second Temple; and both were to have been the work of the Almighty. But as they provoked God in the wilderness they died there and God brought their children into the land, and the house was built by human hands, and therefore it did not endure. In the days of Ezra also on account of their sins they were forced to build it themselves and therefore it did not endure. All this time the first building planned by God had not yet been set up. Now of the future time it is written, "The Lord buildeth Jerusalem" (Ps. CXLVII, 2)—He and no other. It is for this building that we are waiting, not a human structure which cannot endure. The Holy One, blessed be He, will send down to us the first House and the second House together, the first in concealment and the second openly. The second will be revealed to show all the world the handiwork of the Holy One, blessed be He, in perfect joy and gladness. The first, which will be concealed, will ascend high over that which is revealed, and all the world will see the clouds of glory surrounding the one which is revealed and enveloping the first one which ascends to the height of the glorious heavens. It is for that building that we are waiting. Even the future city of Jerusalem will not be the work of human hands, all the more so then the Temple, God's habitation. This work should have been completed when Israel first went forth from Egypt, but it has been deferred to the end of days in the last deliverance. [221b] As for the second question, assuredly we are nearer to the supernal King than all other peoples. God has made Israel as it were the heart of all mankind, and as the limbs cannot endure for a moment without the heart, so the other nations cannot endure without Israel. And what the heart is among the limbs, such is Israel among the nations. The heart is tender and weak, and it alone feels sorrow and distress, since in it alone is intelligence. The other limbs are distant from the king, which is the wisdom and intelligence situate in the brain, but the heart is near. So Israel is near to the Holy King, while the other nations are far away. Similarly in regard to the third question, Israel being the heart, which is tender and delicate and king of the members, takes for its food only the most purified part of all the blood, and leaves the remnant for the other members, which are not particular. They are therefore strong, as we see, but they also suffer from boils and from other ailments from which the heart is quite free. So God takes to himself Israel, who are clean and pure without any blemish.'

NOW THE NAME OF THE MAN OF ISRAEL THAT WAS SLAIN, WHO WAS SLAIN WITH THE MIDIANITISH WOMAN. R. Isaac said: 'We should have expected the text to run "whom Phineas slew". The reason why it is put in this way is because God, having raised Phineas to the high priesthood, did not wish to associate his name with the killing of a man, which does not beseem a high priest.'

R. Simeon was once going from Cappadocia to Lydda with R. Judah. R. Phineas b. Jair was coming the other way with two men behind him. Suddenly the ass of R.

Phineas came to a stop and would not budge. Said R. Phineas: 'Let him be, he must have scented some newcomers here, or a miracle is to be wrought for us.' While they were there R. Simeon emerged from behind a rock, and the ass immediately began to move forward. 'Did I not tell you', said R. Phineas, 'that he scented some newcomers?' He got down and embraced him, saying: 'I saw in a dream the Shekinah coming to me and giving me beautiful presents. Now I see it.' R. Simeon said: 'From the sound of your ass's hoofs I know that you are wholly joyful.' Said R. Phineas: 'Let us sit down in a suitable spot, since the words of the Torah require coolness.' They found a spring of water and a tree and sat down. R. Phineas said: 'I was reflecting that, in the resurrection of the dead, God will reverse the way of this world so that what is now first will then be last. We know this from the bones which God revived by the hand of Ezekiel, as it is written first, "And the bones drew near, each bone to his fellow", and then, [222a] "And I saw, and behold there were sinews on them and flesh came up and skin formed on them above, but there was no breath in them" (Ezek. XXXVII, 7, 8). Thus we see that what a man is divested of here first will there be last, for here the breath is lost first and then the skin and then the flesh and then the bones.' Said R. Simeon: 'The ancients also marvelled at this. But the truth is that these bones which God revived were treated in an exceptional manner. What will really happen is indicated in the verse: "Remember now that thou hast made me like clay and will restore me to dust", and then, "Wilt thou not pour me out like milk and congeal me like cheese?" (Job x, 9, 10). At the time of the resurrection of the dead, God will melt that bone which remains of a man [for all time] and pour it out like milk and then congeal it and shape it like a cheese, and then skin and flesh and bones and sinews will be drawn over it, and lastly the spirit of life will be put into them, as it says, "and thy charge preserved my spirit" (*Ibid.*), the words "thy charge" referring to the Matrona of the King, in whose charge are all spirits and by whom they are preserved.' R. Phineas wept, and said: 'Did I not tell you that the Shekinah gave me beautiful presents ? Happy is my lot to have seen and heard this.' He then said: 'So much for that bone, but what about the other bones that will then be in existence ?' He replied: 'They will all be put together with that bone and made into one dough and shaped with it.' [231a]

R. Judah said: 'Pray tell us some of your fine ideas on the New Year.' R. Simeon thereupon discoursed on the verse: "And it fell on a day, and the sons of God came", etc. (Job I, 6). 'The expression, "And it fell on a day",' he said, 'always refers to a day on which there is trouble, here, the New Year. The "sons of God" are the great Beth Din, the seventy Chieftains who always surround the King. "To stand before the Lord": this indicates that sentence is first passed on those who do not heed the honour of the Holy Name to save it from being profaned in the world. The ancient pillars of the world were divided in opinion in regard to Job, some holding that he was of the saints of the Gentiles, and some that he was of the saints of Israel, and that he was smitten to make atonement for the sins of the world. On that day of New Year seventy seats are set for hearing the judgement of the world, some inclining to the right to acquit and some to the left to condemn. [236b] Now Phineas stood before the stern judgement of Isaac to shield the world and to close the breach, and therefore Phineas here corresponds to Isaac,[1] and here the Left was united with the Right.

'HE TURNED BACK MY ANGER, ETC. We have here mentioned the three chiefs of Gehinnom, "Destruction", "Anger", and "Wrath". When he saw the wrath stretching forth from the side of Isaac, he invested himself with [the might of] Isaac and seized that wrath like a man who [237a] takes hold of another and turns him back. And this was FROM THE CHILDREN OF ISRAEL, for he saw that Wrath coming down upon the children of Israel. He saw the letter *mim* descending upon them, which is the sign of the Angel

[1] The reference is to the fact that there is here in the text an extra *yod* in the name *Pinhas*, which makes it numerically equivalent to *Yiẓhak* (viz. 198).

of Death, so he snatched it and drew it to him and at once
the Angel of Death drew back. It may be asked, How can
it be said that Phineas turned back the wrath of God from
Israel seeing that so many died of the plague ? The fact is,
however, that not one of the children of Israel died save
from the tribe of Simeon, for when the mixed multitude
came they associated with the women of the tribe of Simeon
after they had become proselytes and bore sons from them;
and of these some died on account of the golden calf, some
by plague, and some now. And because Israel and all the
holy seed kept themselves clear, they were now numbered
to show that not one of them was missing. In the same way
all those that died at the time of the calf were from the
mixed multitude, and to show this Moses was afterwards
commanded to assemble "all the congregation of the children
of Israel" (Ex. xxxv, 1), and to take from them only the
free-will offering.' R. Eleazar said: 'Father, this would be
a very good explanation if there were not something which
conflicts with it.' He said to him, 'My son, say it.' He
replied: 'It is written, "And *Israel* was joined (*vayizamed*)
to Baal Peor" (Num. xxv, 3), which we explain to mean,
"like the ornament (*zamid*) on a man's arm".' He replied:
'Eleazar, that is true; Israel were joined to Baal Peor. But
I did not say that Israel were clear of that sin, but that they
were not condemned to death.' He rejoined: 'But it is
written, "Take the heads of the people and hang them".'
'Yes,' he replied, 'the heads of the *people*, but not the heads
of the *children of Israel*. Hence it is written, "And Israel
were joined to Baal Peor", that is, only lightly, but it goes
on to say, "And the *people* ate and worshipped" (*Ibid*. 2),
but not "the children of Israel". [240a]

'COMMAND THE CHILDREN OF ISRAEL AND SAY UNTO
THEM, MY OBLATION, MY FOOD FOR MY OFFERINGS,
ETC. It is written: "Hath the Lord as great delight in burnt
offerings and sacrifices as in obeying the voice of the Lord ?"
(1 Sam. xv, 22). It is not God's desire that a man should
sin and bring an offering to atone for his sin; the offering
brought without sin is the perfect offering.' R. Abba cited

here the verse: "The sacrifices of God are a broken spirit",
etc. (Ps. LI, 18). 'This verse', he said, 'has been explained
as showing that God does not desire a sacrifice from man
for his sin, but a contrite spirit. I have heard from the
Sacred Lamp that when a man is inclined to defile himself
with sin, he draws down upon himself a spirit from the
side of uncleanness which has complete sway over him, but
if a man makes an effort to purify himself he is helped to
do so. When the Temple existed and he brought his offering,
his atonement was held in suspense until he had repented
and broken the pride of that spirit and humbled it, and then
his offering was favourably accepted, but if not, it was given
to the dogs.' R. Eleazar said: 'There is a mystery relating
to the offering in the verse, "I have come to my garden, my
sister, my bride . . . eat, O friends, drink, O beloved" (S.S. v,
1), which I have seen in the book of Enoch.' Said R. Simeon:
'Tell us what you have seen [240b] and heard.' He said:
'God says, "I have come into my garden" because all
offerings when they ascend go into the Garden of Eden at
the beginning of the sacrifice when a man confesses his sins
over it, and, as it were, his own blood is poured out on the
altar. Now, it may be asked, How do the holy spirits find
enjoyment in this, and what is the reason for the offering
of an animal ? Would it not be more reasonable that a man
should humble himself and repent ? The inner reason is
that there is an animal which sprawls over a thousand
mountains the produce of which it eats every day, and concerning it we have learnt: "There is a beast which consumes
beasts made of fire, all of which it licks up at one swoop,
and it swallows at one draught as much water as flows down
the Jordan in six years". Now all these are the basis and
foundation of these beasts of the earth, because the spirit
is spread from them below, and that spirit is formed below
in the beasts, and so when a man sins he brings a beast for
an offering and that bestial spirit rises and returns to its
place and all that belong to that species come together and
feast on the flesh and the blood which is the vestment of this
spirit, and so become advocates on behalf of that man.
Therefore it is that an offering is brought from the animal.'

R. Simeon said to him: 'That explains the offering of the animal, but what of the offering of birds?' He replied: 'I have not seen nor heard anything different from this of the beasts.' He said: 'Eleazar, my son, you have spoken well, but the mysteries of the offerings are many and should only be revealed to the truly virtuous. The sacrifices do in fact contain a hidden reference to the holy Beasts (*Hayoth*). Four forms are engraved on the Throne—of an ox, of an eagle, of a lion, and of a man. From those archetypal forms myriads without number are spread above and below. From the "face of an ox" a spirit is spread to four species closely connected, namely, bullocks, sheep, he-goats, and rams. These are appointed for offerings; and because those holy powers which spread from the "face of an ox" are akin to them, they draw near to their foundation and partake of that foundation and vestment of theirs in the same way as the holy Shekinah derives satisfaction from the spirits of the righteous. From the "face of an eagle" a spirit is spread to the birds in two directions, right and left, and therefore not all birds of the clean side are brought for offerings, but only pigeons and turtle doves, which are faithful to their mates [241a] more than all other birds, and are preyed upon but do not prey; and so those holy spirits come down and partake of their basis and foundation. You may ask how the little that comes from this pigeon or turtle dove can be shared among countless powers, and the same may be asked of a single animal. The answer is that it is in the same way as a little light fills the whole world or a thin stick will light a conflagration. So much for the offering from two of the sides engraved on the Throne. And in reality there is an offering from the other two also, although it does not seem so. When the sacrifice is completed, the Lion comes down and enters into the fire and feasts himself. Also the supernal Man derives benefit from the earthly man, who offers there his spirit and soul, and so each kind partakes of its own kind and basis. In the same way the priest who unifies the Holy Name is brought near to the supernal Priest, the Levites with their song rejoice that side to which they belong, and the lay Israelites, who offer prayers alongside of the sacrifice, awaken the supernal holy Israel. Thus the lower grades arouse the upper grades, but none of them is permitted to eat or to have any enjoyment of the sacrifice until the supreme King has eaten and given them permission. All this is hinted in the verses, "I have gathered my myrrh with my spice, I have eaten my honeycomb with my honey, I have drunk my wine with my milk; eat, O friends, drink, yea, drink abundantly, O beloved". [241b] This is the real secret and mystery of the sacrifices.'

NOTE. From the beginning of the section *Pinḥas* to the end of the Zohar, a large portion of the text in the original is taken up by the *Ray'a Mehemna;* hence the frequency of the omissions in the translation. On the section *Mattoth* there is only a short piece of Zohar of too allusive a nature to be made intelligible in a translation. There is no Zohar at all on the sections *Mas'e, Debarim, Ekeb, Re'eh, Shofetim, Ki Teze, Ki Tabo, Niẓabim,* and *Vezoth Haberakah.*

DEUTERONOMY

VAETHHANAN

Deuteronomy III, 23–VII, 11

AND I BESOUGHT THE LORD AT THAT TIME SAYING, O LORD GOD, THOU HAST BEGUN TO SHOW THY SERVANT, ETC. R. Jose adduced here the verse: "And Hezekiah turned his face to the wall and prayed to the Lord" (Isa. XXXVIII, 2). 'How great', he said, 'is the power of the Torah, and how it is exalted above all, since he who occupies himself with the Torah fears no adversaries either above or below, nor any evil haps of the world, because he is attached to the Tree of Life and eats therefrom every day. For the Torah teaches man how to walk in the right way, it gives him counsel how to return to his Master, so that even if sentence of death has been passed on him it is annulled and removed from him and impends not over him. Therefore he should occupy himself with the Torah day and night and never depart from it: for if he banishes the Torah from him or departs from it, it is as though he parted from life. Now it is a good counsel for a man that when he goes to his bed at night he should take upon himself the ycke of the heavenly kingdom with a perfect heart and hasten to entrust to God his soul. The reason, as we have explained, is that all the world then has a foretaste of death, as the tree of death is then present in the world, and all the spirits of men then leave them and ascend and are delivered to Him, but because they are given in trust they afterwards return to their places. Now when the north wind awakes at midnight and a herald goes forth, and the Holy One, blessed be He, enters the Garden of Eden to have joyous communion with the souls of the righteous, then all the sons of the Matrona, and all the denizens of the palace, prepare to sing praises to the Holy King, and then all the souls that were entrusted to her hand are returned to their owners; and most men awake at that time. Those who belong to the supernal Palace rise up in vigour and betake themselves to praisegiving in accordance with the Torah and join the Community of Israel until the

day is light. When the morning comes, She and all who
belong to the Palace go to visit the Holy King, they being
called the sons of the King and of the Matrona, as has been
explained. When the morning comes, a man should cleanse
himself and gird on his weapons[1] to pay suit to the Holy
King. For in the night he paid suit to the Matrona, and now
he should come with the Matrona to unite her with the King.
He goes to the synagogue, he purifies himself with [the
recital of the] offerings, he repeats the praises of King David;
he has the phylacteries on his hand and his head, and the
fringes at his side; he says "A psalm of David", and offers
his prayer before his Master. While he says this he must stand
like the heavenly angels,[2] who are also called "those who
stand", and concentrate all his thoughts on his Master as
he offers his petition. Note that when a man arises at midnight to study the Torah a herald proclaims concerning
him: "Behold, bless ye the Lord all ye servants of the Lord
which stand in the house of the Lord by night" (Ps. CXXXIV,
1), and now when he stands in prayer the herald proclaims
over him, "And I will give thee places to walk among them
that stand" (Zech. III, 7). When he has finished his prayer
with devotion before his Master, as already said, he should
deliver his soul with complete renunciation to the rightful
place. Thus there is good counsel for men for all occasions.
[260b] When prayer is being offered, all the words that
a man has emitted from his mouth during his prayer mount
aloft and cleave their way through ethers and firmaments
until they reach their destination, where they are formed
into a crown on the head of the King. The Companions
have agreed that the prayer directed by man to the Almighty
should be of the nature of supplication.[3] We know this
from Moses, of whom it is said, "And I besought the Lord"
(Deut. III, 23); this is the best kind of prayer. When a man
stands in prayer he should keep his feet together,[4] and
cover his head, and he should also shade his eyes so as not
to look at the Shekinah. In the Book of R. Hamnuna the
Elder it says that if a man opens his eyes at the time of

---

[1] i.e. fringes and phylacteries.   [2] v. T.B. Berachoth, 10b.   [3] Ibid., 28b,
Aboth II.   [4] T.B. Berachoth, 10b.

prayer or does not cast them on the ground he brings the Angel of Death on to himself before his time, and when his soul leaves him he will not behold the face of the Shekinah, nor will he die by a (divine) kiss. If one contemns the Shekinah, he himself is contemned in the hour of need, as it says, "Them that honour me I shall honour, and they that despise me shall be lightly esteemed" (1 Sam. 11, 30). This is he that looks at the Shekinah at the time of prayer. In fact, of course, one cannot look at the Shekinah; but what he should do is to know that the Shekinah is before him, and therefore there should be nothing interposing between him and the wall.

'Before a man stands in prayer he should first recite the praise of his Master and then offer his supplication. So Moses first said, THOU HAST BEGUN, ETC., and then LET ME GO OVER, I PRAY THEE.'

R. Judah said: 'Why did Moses say first "Lord" (*Adonay*) and then "God" (*YHVH*)? Because this is the proper order from the lower to the higher, so as to combine the measure of day with night, and of night with day, and to unite all fitly together.

'THOU HAST BEGUN TO SHOW THY SERVANT. Why is "beginning" mentioned here? Because Moses indeed made a new beginning in the world by being complete in all. It is true that Jacob was also complete and in him the tree was completed below after the pattern above. Yet there was that in Moses which was not in any other man, since his perfection radiated to many thousands and myriads of Israel in the Tabernacle, the priests, the Levites, the twelve tribes with their chieftains, the seventy members of the Sanhedrin— in fact, with the perfect body, Aaron being at the right, Nahshon at the left, he himself in the centre, as it says here "thy greatness", referring to Aaron, and "thy strong hand", referring to Nahshon. Thus Moses was a new beginning in the world. And if you ask, Who is the termination? the answer is, the King Messiah, for then there shall be such perfection in the world as had not been for all generations before. For then there shall be completeness above and

below, and all worlds shall be united in one bond, as it is
written, "On that day the Lord shall be one and his name
one" (Zech. XIV, 9).'

AND THE LORD SAID UNTO ME, LET IT SUFFICE THEE,
SPEAK NO MORE, ETC. R. Ḥiya said: 'God said to Moses,
It is enough for thee that thou hast been united with the
Shekinah; thou canst advance no further.' R. Isaac said:
'Long enough hast thou enjoyed the light of the sun that
was with thee; thou canst not do so any more, for the time
of the moon is come, and the moon cannot shine till the sun
is gathered in. Therefore "Charge Joshua and encourage
him and strengthen him"; thou who art the sun must give
light to the moon.'[1]

BUT YE THAT DID CLEAVE UNTO THE LORD YOUR
GOD, ETC. R. Jose said: 'Happy is the people whom God
chose from all the heathens and took for His portion and
blessed with His own blessing, the blessing of His Name.
All other peoples God has placed under the charge of
Chieftains who have control of them, but Israel the Holy
One, blessed be He, has taken for His own portion to be
united to Him, and He has given them His holy Law that
they may be joined to His Name.' [261a]

AND THE LORD SPAKE UNTO YOU OUT OF THE MIDST
OF THE FIRE: YE HEARD THE VOICE OF WORDS, ETC.
R. Eleazar said: 'What is meant by "the voice of words"? It
means, the Voice which is also called Utterance, because all
utterance proceeds from it. Hence also it says "ye heard" [and
not "saw"], because "hearing" corresponds to "utterance".

'BUT YE SAW NO FORM. They were not like Moses, of
whom it says, "And he beholdeth the *form* of the Lord".
Or we may say that "form" refers to the inner Voice which
was not seen at all. ONLY YE HEARD A VOICE: this is the
other voice, which we mentioned above. Hence there is a
higher *Hé* and a lower *Hé* ; the higher *Hé* is "the great voice

[1] *v.* T.B. Baba Bathra, 75a.

which did not cease", the flow of which never ceases, and all those "voices" were in it when the Torah was given to Israel. Now what is called "the repetition of the law" (Deuteronomy) was said by Moses in his own name. For the supreme Wisdom is called the summation of the Torah, and from it all issues through that inner Voice. Eventually it comes to rest in the place called "the Tree of Life", wherefrom depend the general and the particular, the Written Law and the Oral Law. And to show that both are one, the later (of the Ten) Commandments are in this version connected with one another by "and".'

R. Jose said: 'Why do we find here both "*thou shalt not covet*" and "*thou shalt not desire*"? Because they are two different grades. A man covets things which it is in his power to obtain (wrongfully), and through coveting he does try to obtain them. A man can desire things even if he sees no way of obtaining them.

'Go THOU NEAR AND HEAR, ETC. When the Law was given to Israel, all the Voices were present and the Holy One, blessed be He, was sitting on His throne, and one was seen within another, and the utterance of each came forth from the one above it, wherefore it is said, "The Lord spake to you face to face in the mount out of the midst of the fire" (Deut. v, 4), which means that the utterance came forth from the midst of fire and flame, which thrust it forth by the force of spirit and water; and fire, spirit and water all issued from the trumpet which contained them all. Israel were terrified and drew back, and therefore they said: Do thou speak to us; we do not desire to be spoken to by the mighty Power from on high, but only from the place of the Female, not higher. Said Moses to them: Of a truth ye have weakened my power, and also another power. For had not Israel drawn back and had they listened to [261b] the remaining words as to the first,[1] the world would never have been laid waste subsequently and they would have endured for generations upon generations. For at the first

---

[1] According to the Rabbis, the Israelites heard the first two commandments directly from God, the rest from Moses. T.B. Maccoth, 24*a*.

moment they did die, for so it had to be on account of the
tree of death, but after they revived and stood up God
desired to bring them up to the Tree of Life, which is above
the tree of death, that they might endure for ever, but they
drew back and were not willing; therefore was the power
of Moses weakened and another power with him. Said the
Holy One, blessed be He: I desired to stablish you in an
exalted place that ye might cleave to life, but ye desired the
place of the Female. Therefore Go, SAY TO THEM, RETURN
TO YOUR TENTS: let each one go to his female and join
her. And with all this, since Israel acted thus only through the
pious awe that was upon them, nothing worse was said of them
than "O that there were such an heart in them that they
would fear me", etc. From this we learn that if a man,
though doing an action which in itself is bad, does not turn
his mind and intent to the evil side, punishment does not
fall upon him as on another man, and God does not impute
it to him for evil.

'BUT AS FOR THEE, STAND THOU HERE BY ME. From this
point Moses parted from his wife completely and attached
himself to another higher place, of the male and not of the
female. Happy the lot of Moses the faithful prophet who
was favoured with the highest grades to which no other
man ever attained, wherefore he was called "good". But
was not David also called "good"? Of David it says that
he was "goodly to look upon": his goodness was in the
appearance, but Moses was absolutely good.'

R. Judah said: 'A man should place God before him in
all his acts. When a man walks abroad he should have three
objects in view, the highest of which is prayer, and higher
even than prayer is the converse of two or three companions
on matters of the Torah, for they shall come to no harm,
since the Shekinah accompanies them.' Thus R. Eleazar and
R. Ḥiya were once walking together, and R. Eleazar said:
'It is written, "And the Lord God made for Adam and his
wife coats of skins" (Gen. III, 22). Were they then divested
of that skin till then? Yes, for they were robes of glory.'
Said R. Ḥiya: 'Surely they did not deserve even coats of

skin. For you cannot say that this was before they sinned, since it is after they sinned that it is written, "And the Lord God made them coats of skins" '. He replied: 'At first they were like heavenly creatures, and divested of the earthly type, and heavenly light played around them. After they sinned they became of the type of this world, and the heavenly character was taken away from them, and then God made them coats of skin and clothed them with the character of this world. None the less the beauty of those garments was incomparable. It is further written, "And the eyes of both of them were opened" (Gen. III, 7), that is, to see the squalor of this world, which they did not notice before since their eyes were turned aloft. So of the future time it is written, "And I will bring the blind by a way that they know not", etc. (Isa. XLII, 16), which means that God will open eyes that are not wise to contemplate [262a] supernal wisdom and to attain to heights which they could not attain in this world, that they may know their Master. Happy are the righteous who are deemed worthy of this wisdom, since there is no wisdom like that wisdom, nor knowledge like that knowledge, nor attachment like that attachment.' As they were going along they saw some robbers following them with intent to harm them. R. Eleazar looked at them and two serpents came out and killed them, whereupon R. Eleazar said: Blessed be the Merciful One who has saved us.

'We have learnt as a profound mystery in the Book of Hidden Wisdom that three hollows of inscribed letters are disclosed in the Cranium of the Small of Countenance, and we have further learnt that there are three Brains enclosed in these hollows, but through the influence of the uppermost and hidden brain of the Ancient Holy One which spreads through that Small of Countenance they become four Brains. These spread throughout the whole of the Body, and these are the four compartments of the phylacteries which the Holy One, blessed be He, puts on. Therefore a man should put on the phylacteries every day, because they are the supernal Holy Name in its inscribed letters. The first compartment of the phylacteries contains the passage,

"Sanctify unto me every firstborn", which typifies the highest brain, to wit, Wisdom. The second compartment contains the passage commencing "And it shall come to pass when the Lord thy God bringeth thee".' R. Judah said: 'This typifies the brain which opens out through fifty gates, which in turn correspond to the numerous places where the going forth from Egypt is mentioned in the Pentateuch. We have learnt in the Book of R. Hamnuna the Ancient that God burst open many gates above and below which were closed with chains in order to bring forth Israel, for from the gates of that brain all other gates are unlocked and opened. Had not the gates of that brain been first opened, the others could never have been opened to execute judgement and to bring forth Israel from bondage. All is closed up in that which is called the Supernal Mother, whence power is derived to the Lower Mother. This one comes forth from the Supernal Mother, who is the second compartment, which is called the *Hé* of the Holy Name which opens out through fifty gates, and from this issues a spirit to one of the Nostrils. We have learnt, too, that the Jubilee in which slaves go forth to freedom is attached to this Brain, and the fifty days of the Jubilee further correspond to the fifty days of the Omer. Thus *Hé* stands for the appeasement of the spirit and its going forth to freedom, and thus the going forth from Egypt depends on this compartment and on the letter *Hé* of the Holy Name, as has been explained. Observe that from the side of the Father issues Lovingkindness and from the side of the Mother Force, and the Holy One, blessed be He, grasps both and crowns himself therewith as the letter *Vau*. [262b] The third compartment contains the passage commencing, "Hear, O Israel", the reference being to the patriarch Israel. R. Simeon, however, says that the reference is to the supernal Israel crowned from the side of his Father, to wit Abraham, and crowned from the side of his Mother, to wit, Isaac. We have learnt that he who loves the King does lovingkindness with all, and all the more so if he asks for no reward, which is a "kindness of truth", through which he increases lovingkindness in the world. Hence this passage goes on, "Thou shalt love". The fourth compartment contains the passage commencing, "And it shall come to pass if ye diligently hearken". This passage contains the words, "Take heed to yourselves . . . and the anger of the Lord be kindled against you", and this compartment typifies Might and stern judgement, and it comes from the side of the supernal Mother; for we have learnt that although She Herself is not judgement, yet from Her side issues judgement and force. These four does *Vau* take and crown himself therewith, and these are the phylacteries which the Holy One, blessed be He, puts on. We have learnt that this *Vau* ascends and assumes his crowns and grasps both sides and is crowned with all, and therefore *Vau* is the centre of all above and below to display complete Wisdom on all sides.'

R. Abba learnt: It is written, "Only the Lord had a delight in thy fathers" (Deut. x, 15). Commenting on this, R. Simeon said that the patriarchs are the holy chariot above. As there is a holy chariot below, so there is a holy chariot above. And what is this ? As we have said, the holy chariot is the name given to the Whole, all being linked together and made one. But the fathers are only three, and the chariot has four wheels. Who is the fourth ? It says: "And he chose their seed after them"; this includes David, who is the fourth to complete the holy chariot, as we have learnt: The patriarchs are the consummation of the whole, and the Body was completed through them and made one. Then King David came and perfected the whole and made firm the body and perfected it. R. Isaac said: 'As the patriarchs merited to be crowned with the holy chariot, so did David merit to be adorned with the fourth support of the chariot.' R. Judah said: 'It is written of David, "He was ruddy and withal fair of eyes". The "ruddiness" typifies his occupation (as a man of war), while "with fair of eyes" refers to the patriarchs. Note that while Jerusalem and Zion correspond respectively to Judgement and Mercy, yet it is written, "The city of David, that is Zion" (1 Kings VIII, 1).

'We have learnt: *Vau* takes those upper ones that we have mentioned, and those are the phylacteries which the Holy One, blessed be He, puts on, and therefore a man should

take a pride in them. Of such a one it is written, "And all
the people of the earth shall see that thou art called by the
name of the Lord" (Deut. XXVIII, 10)—literally. These are
the phylactery of the head. The phylactery of the arm is the
left, which is called "strong", and inherits from the "strong".
[263a] Therefore the second *Hé*, which is the left, takes
the four which are one body and entwined in one another,
to wit, *Tifereth*, *Nezah*, *Hod*, and *Yesod*.' Said R. Ḥiya:
'If that is so, this is what is meant by "Thou shalt see my
back" (Ex. XXXIII, 23), which, as we have learnt, means
the knot of the phylacteries.' He replied: 'So we have
explained, and this is the truth of the matter, and therefore
a strap hangs down below to show that all below are sustained by this, and therefore it is called a "sign", as it is
written, "And it shall be for a sign upon thy hand".'

HEAR, ISRAEL. R. Yesa said: 'This is the patriarch Israel.'
R. Isaac said: ' "Israel" here has the same meaning as
"heavens" in the verses "Hear, O heavens" (Isa. I, 2), and
"Give ear, O heavens" (Deut. XXXII, 1). "The Lord" here
indicates the starting-point of all, in the radiance of the Holy
Ancient One, and this is what is called "Father". "Our
God" is the deep source of the streams and founts that
flow forth to all. "The Lord" again is the body of the Tree,
the completion of the roots. "One" is the Community
of Israel. All form one whole linked together without
division.' R. Isaac learnt: 'The holy supernal chariot consists
of the four compartments of the phylacteries which are put
on by *Vau*, as already explained. There is another holy
chariot of four other compartments united into one which
are put on by the second *Hé*, as already stated.' [265a]
R. Simeon said: 'When a man rises at midnight and gets
up and studies the Torah till daylight, and when the daylight
comes he puts the phylacteries with the holy impress on
his head and his arm, and covers himself with his fringed
robe, and as he issues from the door of his house he passes
the *mezuzah* containing the imprint of the Holy Name on
the post of his door, then four holy angels join him and
issue with him from the door of his house and accompany

him to the synagogue and proclaim before him: Give honour
to the image of the Holy King, give honour to the son of the
King, to the precious countenance of the King. A holy spirit
rests on him and proclaims: "Israel in whom I will be glorified"
(Isa. XLIX, 3), and then ascends aloft and testifies concerning
him before the Holy King. Then the Most High King
orders the names of all the children of His palace, of all
those that acknowledge Him, to be written before Him, as
it says, "And it was written in the book of remembrance
before him, for them that feared the Lord and that thought
upon his name" (Mal. III, 16). The word *hoshebei* (that
thought upon) can also be taken in the sense of "making
designs"—designs of the phylacteries with their compartments, their straps and their writing; designs of the fringes
with their threads and the thread of blue; and designs of the
mezuzah, all for the sake of God's Name. God then glories
in them and proclaims through all worlds: See what my
son hàs done in my world. He, however, who leaves his house
to go to the synagogue without the phylacteries on his head
or fringes on his garment and who yet says, I will bow down
to Thy holy temple in Thy fear—of him God says: Where
is my fear ? he is bearing false witness.'

R. Jose said: 'Happy the portion of Moses who attached
himself to a higher grade than all the other faithful prophets.
For in connection with the verse, "Moses spoke and God
answered him with a voice" (Ex. XIX, 19), we have learnt
that this voice was the voice of Moses, the Voice to which
he was attached through his superiority over all the other
prophets. And because he was attached to this higher grade
he was able to say to Israel, "The Lord *thy* God", namely,
the grade called Shekinah which abode in their midst.'
R. Simeon further said: 'We have learnt that the curses in
Leviticus were uttered by Moses as coming from the mouth
of the divine Might, but those in Deuteronomy were uttered
by him as from the mouth of himself. What is meant by "as
from the mouth of himself" ? Can it be thought that Moses
said a single word of the Law of himself ? No: what it
refers to is the Voice to which he was attached, which is
called "himself", so that one set of curses were uttered from

the mouth of the divine Might and the other of that grade to which he attained in virtue of his superiority over the other prophets. Hence, while in all other places he says "*Thy* God", here (in the Shema) he says "*Our* God".

'Note how diligent men should be to devote themselves to the service of their Master so as to win eternal life. Under the throne of the Holy King there are supernal chambers; and in that place of the throne there is fastened a *mezuzah* to deliver men from executioners of justice [265b] who are ready to assail them in the other world. Similarly did God do to Israel, giving them precepts of the Law which they may observe to deliver themselves from many assailants and accusers that are on the watch for men every day.' R. Ḥiya said: 'If a man wishes to guard his steps, he should not step over water that has been poured out in front of a door, because a certain demon abides between the two posts of the door with his face to the door seeing all that goes on inside, and therefore a man should not pour water between the two doorposts.' (R. Isaac, however, said that if it is clean water it does not matter, provided it has not been poured out in contumely.) The reason is that he is authorized to do harm, and if he turns his head to the house everything on which he looks will be cursed. He has three hundred and sixty-five assistants, corresponding to the number of the days of the year, and all go forth with a man when he leaves his house.' R. Eleazar said: 'Against all this God desired to protect Israel, and therefore a man should inscribe on the door of his house the Holy Name in which all faith is summed up. For wherever the Holy Name is the evil species cannot come and are not able to accuse a man. The place of the door of the supernal House is called *mezuzah*, which is a necessary part of the house, and from it flee the emissaries of justice and punishment. Correspondingly when on earth a man affixes a *mezuzah* to his door with his Holy Name inscribed in it, such a one is crowned with the crowns of his Master and no "evil species" come near to the door of his house.'

As R. Abba was once coming away from a visit to R. Simeon he was met by R. Isaac, who exclaimed: 'Who is coming ? The master of light, the man who all day has been cleaving to a consuming fire. Behold, light abides with him.' R. Abba said to him: 'We have learnt that a man should go to pay his respects to the Shekinah every Sabbath and New Moon, and who is meant ? His teacher. All the more, then, is it incumbent on all people to pay their respects to the Sacred Lamp.' Said R. Isaac: 'I will turn back with you and pay my respects to the Shekinah and [meanwhile] taste of those excellent words of which you have tasted.' R. Abba then commenced a discourse on the verse: "A song of degrees, Unto thee do I lift up mine eyes, O thou that sittest in the heavens" (Ps. cxxiii, 1). 'The author of this psalm is not mentioned, and in all such cases we suppose the holy spirit to have uttered it concerning Israel in captivity. We have laid down that whoever desires to offer his supplication before the Holy King should pray from the lowest depth that blessing should be poured down below. This is indicated by the superfluous *yod* in the word *hayoshebi* (who sittest), the *yod* being the lowest of all; and therefore through it one should pray that blessings be poured down to the place called "heaven", that all may be fed from it. For when blessings are drawn from that spot most remote of all and collected in the place called heaven, then blessings abound among both higher and lower beings. "As the eyes of servants look unto the hand of their master": these are the Chieftains of the other peoples who are fed only from the remnants, the overhanging branches of the tree to which Israel cling, and when Israel receive blessings from that place they are all blessed from Israel. "As the eyes of a maiden unto the hand of her mistress": this, as already stated, is the handmaiden whose host God slew in Egypt, since she has no power of her own save when it is drawn to her from the Land of Israel, which itself [266a] is called "mistress". From the direction of this handmaiden issue many officials of judgement who bring accusations against Israel, but the Holy One, blessed be He, protects Israel from them as a father protects his son. God says to Israel: "Many are the accusers looking out for you, but be diligent in my service and I will protect you without, while within you will sleep safely in your beds. Now when the evil species come to the door of a man's house, and they raise their eyes and see the Holy Name written outside the *mezuzah*, namely Shaddai, which has power over all of them, they flee away in fear of it and do not come near the door.' Said R. Isaac to him: 'If that is so, a man should inscribe only this name on his door; why all the section?' He replied: 'This is quite right, because this name is crowned only with all those letters, and when the whole section is written this name is crowned with its crowns and the King goes forth with all his hosts stamped with the impress of the King, and they all flee from him in fear.' R. Abba said: 'Many holy hosts are present when a man fixes a *mezuzah* on his door, and they all proclaim, "This is the gate of the Lord", etc. (Ps. cxviii, 20). Happy is the portion of Israel, for then Israel know that they are the sons of the Holy King, for all bear His stamp. They are stamped on their bodies with the holy impress; their garments bear the stamp of a religious precept;[1] their heads are stamped with the compartments of the phylacteries with the name of their Master; their hands are stamped with the straps of holiness; their feet with the ceremonial shoes;[2] without they bear the stamp of the [precepts connected with] sowing and reaping, and in their houses that of the *mezuzah* at their doorway. Thus in all ways they are stamped as the sons of the Most High King.'

As they proceeded R. Abba said: 'What is the meaning of the verse: "They have forsaken me the fountain of living waters to hew out to them cisterns, broken cisterns that cannot hold the water" (Jer. II, 13)? This', he said, 'refers to one who is false to the sign of the holy impress. And how is he false to it? By letting it enter into an alien domain, which is called "broken cisterns". For so the idolatrous peoples are called, but Israel's God is called "a fountain of living waters". For the perennially flowing Stream waters all the Garden and replenishes every place, as we have already pointed out, until it comes to that place in the Garden which is called "the fountain of living waters",

[1] The fringes. [2] The shoe used in the ceremony of *ḥaliẓah*.

whence are sustained all creatures above and below. But all the sides of the Left Side are not watered from that Stream of running water because they are of the side of the other peoples, and they are called "broken cisterns". Hence he who is false to the holy impress cleaves to the "broken cisterns which do not hold the waters" because they do not enter into them, whereas he that is able to guard it is granted to drink of the waters of that stream in the world to come, and causes that supernal Well to be filled so as to pour forth blessings to higher and lower; happy is he in this world and the next: of him it is written, "And thou shalt be like a watered garden and like a spring of water whose waters fail not" (Isa. LVIII, 11). Woe to him who is false to the holy impress, for he is false [266b] to the most high Name, nay more, he causes blessing to be withheld from that Well, and we apply to him the words, "he hath brought up an evil name on a virgin of Israel" (Deut. XXII, 19); for so R. Simeon has expounded, that one who brings a false charge against his first wife and brings an evil name upon her is like one who casts aspersions on high. This, again, is in conformity with what R. Ḥiya said in the name of R. Jose, that a virgin inherits seven blessings, but not a woman who is married again; she, however, inherits the blessing of Boaz and Ruth.'

They came to a field where they saw a number of trees, and sat down beneath them. R. Abba said: 'Here is clear air for expositions of the Torah; let us stay here.' He then began a discourse on the verse: "And it shall come to pass in that day that a great trumpet shall be blown; and they shall come which were ready to perish in the land of Assyria, and they that were outcasts in the land of Egypt" (Isa. XXVII, 13). 'What is meant', he said, 'by "that day"? It is that day which shall be known to the Holy One, blessed be He, as it is written, "But it shall be one day which is known unto the Lord" (Zech. XIV, 7), or again, "In that day when Gog shall come against the land of Israel" (Ezek. XXXVIII, 19). "A great trumpet shall be blown"? What difference does it make whether it will be great or small? It refers, however, to that great trumpet through which slaves go forth to freedom; this is the trumpet of the supernal Jubilee, and it is very mighty, and when it is aroused all freedom is set in motion, and it is called "the great trumpet". "They that are perishing in the land of Assyria": because those who live in an alien land suck from an alien power, and, as it were, do not abide in the faith. They are lost from all sides, for when Israel dwell in the Holy Land they are ever virtuous in all, both above and below. According to another explanation, "those that are perishing" are the *Ẓaddik* and the Community of Israel. These are also called "lost", as it is written, "Wherefore perisheth the land" (Jer. IX, 12), to wit, the Community of Israel. The *Ẓaddik*, as it is written, "The righteous (*Ẓaddik*) perisheth" (Isa. LVII, 1). If it is asked, Whence are they to "come", the answer is, the Community of Israel from exile, and the *Ẓaddik*, as it is written, "When the Lord returneth *with* (*eth*) the captivity of Zion" (Ps. CXXVI, 1), which, as we have explained, means that He will return to His place and join the Community of Israel. "And they shall bow down to the Lord on the holy mountain, Jerusalem": this means, if we may say so, that Israel will not go out of captivity save with the Shekinah.'

R. Abba further discoursed on the verse: "The Lord shall keep thy going out and thy coming in from this time forth and for evermore" (Ps. CXXI, 8). He said: 'That God shall keep thy going forth we understand; but what need is there to say, "thy coming in"? For when a man goes into his house he is in no danger? What it means, however, is that he who affixes the holy sign to his house with the words of the Holy Name is protected against all danger. The one who dwells at the door of his house accompanies him when he issues forth, and when he returns it proclaims before him: Have a care for the honour of the image of the Holy King—all this on account of the Holy Name which is impressed on his door, so that not only is a man protected in his house, but God protects him both when he goes out and when he comes in, as it is written, "The Lord shall keep thy going out and thy coming in", etc. But as for the evil spirit that abides between the doorposts, [267a] woe to the man who does not know how to guard against it by impressing on the door of his house the Holy Name that it may be with him, for this spirit has three hundred and sixty-five assistants, one for every day of the year, which accuse him above and below, trying to mislead him by day and troubling his dreams by night. When he goes out they accuse him; when he comes in they place their hands on his shoulders and say: Woe to So-and-so who has thrown off the control of his Master, woe to him in this world and in the world to come! Therefore the sons of the true faith should be stamped throughout with the impress of their Master to scare away all the sides of the "evil species", that they may be protected in this world and the next.'

AND THOU SHALT LOVE THE LORD THY GOD. R. Jose adduced here the verse: "Now, therefore, what do I here, saith the Lord, seeing that my people is taken away for nought" (Isa. LII, 5). 'This', he said, 'shows the love of God for Israel, for although their sins caused Him to depart from them, and they were scattered among the nations, yet He avenges their wrong. When Israel were in their land, God used to delight Himself in His garden and draw near to Israel and hear their voice and glory in them. But since through their sins Israel have been banished from their land, the Holy One, blessed be He, does not enter His garden nor take delight in it, and He even exclaims, "What do I here, saith the Lord?" Since the day that Israel were banished from their land there has been no joy before the Holy One, blessed be He. Therefore because of the love which God shows to Israel it is written, "thou shalt love the Lord thy God", which means that man should bind himself to Him with very strong love, and that all service performed by man to God should be with love, since there is no service like the love of the Holy One, blessed be He.' R. Abba said: 'These words are the epitome of the whole Law, since the Ten Commandments are summed up here, as the Companions have explained. Nothing is so beloved of God as that a man should love Him in the fitting manner. How is this? As it is written, "with all thy heart", which includes two hearts, one good and one evil; "with all thy soul", one good and

one evil;[1] and "with all thy might". What lesson can be
learnt from the word "all" here ?' R. Eleazar said: 'The
word "might" refers to money, and "all" means both money
which comes to a man from inheritance and money which
a man earns himself.' R. Abba said: 'To return to the
words "and thou shalt love": one who loves God is crowned
with lovingkindness on all sides and does lovingkindness
throughout, sparing neither his person nor his money. We
know this from Abraham, who in his love for his Master
spared neither his heart nor his life nor his money. He paid
no heed to his own desires because of his love for his Master;
he spared not his wife, and was ready to sacrifice his son
because of his love for his Master; and he sacrificed his
money also by standing at the cross-roads and providing
food for all comers. Therefore he was crowned with the
crown of lovingkindness. Whoever is attached in love to
his Master is deemed worthy of the same, and what is more,
all worlds are blessed for his sake.'

Once when R. Jose was ill, R. Abba and R. Judah and
R. Isaac went to see him. They found him asleep lying on his
face. When he awoke they perceived that his face was
wreathed in smiles. Said R. Abba to him: 'Have you seen
some notable thing ?' [267b] 'Assuredly so,' he replied,
'for my soul went aloft and I saw the glory of those who
have sacrificed themselves for the sanctity of their Master,
how they were given thirteen streams of pure balsam, and
how the Holy One, blessed be He, held joyous converse
with them. I saw things which I am not permitted to tell.
I asked for whom was this honour, and they replied: For
those who loved their Master in the other world. My soul
and my heart were illumined with what I saw, and therefore
my face was wreathed in smiles.' R. Abba said: 'Happy is
thy portion. The Torah testifies of them saying, "Eye hath
not seen, O God, beside thee what he shall do for him that
waiteth for him" (Isa. LXIV, 4).' R. Judah said to him: 'The
Companions have already asked: Why is it written here,
"*he* shall do", and not "*thou* shalt do" ?' He replied: 'The
reason is to be found in the inner meaning of the words,

[1] T.B. Berachoth, 54a.

"To behold the beauty of the Lord and to inquire in his temple" (Ps. XXVII, 4). The "beauty of the Lord", as we have explained, is that which comes from the Ancient Holy One, and wherewith the Holy One, blessed be He, delights himself. So here, "*he* shall do" refers to the Ancient Hidden One on whom it depends.' He said: 'Assuredly it is so. Happy those to whom the love of their Master cleaves; there is no limit to their portion in the other world.' R. Isaac said: 'Many are the abodes of the righteous in the other world, one above another, and highest of all that of those to whom was attached the love of their Master, for their abode is linked with the palace that surpasses all, the Holy One, blessed be He, being crowned in this one. This Palace is called Love, and it is established for the sake of love. So it is too with the Holy Name, the forms of the letters of which are linked together, so that the whole is called "love"; wherefore he who loves his Master is linked to that Love. Hence it is written, "And thou shalt love the Lord thy God".'

AND THESE WORDS SHALL BE, ETC. R. Isaac adduced here the verse: "All my bones shall say, Lord, who is like unto thee, who delivereth the poor from him that is too strong for him, yea, the poor and the needy from him that spoileth him" (Ps. XXXV, 10). 'This verse', he said, 'refers to the time when the Holy One, blessed be He, will revive the dead, at which time He will prepare the bones and bring each one near to its fellow, as it says, "And the bones came together, bone to his bone" (Ezek. XXXVI, 7). They will then sing a psalm, namely, "O Lord, who is like thee", etc. And this song will be superior to that which the Israelites chanted by the Red Sea, for there they mentioned the Holy Name only after three words, as it is written, "Who-is like-unto-thee among-the-mighty, O Lord", but here they will put the Holy Name first. "He delivereth the poor from him that is too strong for him". This means that God delivers the good prompting from the evil prompting; for the evil prompting is hard like stone, whereas the good prompting is tender like flesh. What does the evil prompting resemble ?

When it first comes to associate itself with a man it is like
iron before it is placed in the fire, but afterwards like iron
when it is heated and becomes wholly like fire.' R. Ḥiya
said: 'The evil prompting is at first like a wayfarer who
comes to the door of a house and, finding that there is no one
to stop him, goes into the house and becomes a guest. Finding
that there is still no one to stop him he takes liberties and
acts as the master[1] [268a] until the whole house is subject
to him. From where do we learn this ? From the story of
David and Nathan. Nathan first said, "There came a
traveller to the rich man"—a mere traveller who passes the
door without any intention of staying there and meaning to
proceed on his way. So the evil prompting when it first
approaches a man prompts him to a petty sin, being still but
a chance visitor. Then the text goes on, "to prepare for
the guest that came to him". So the evil prompting incites
him to greater sins one day or two days like a guest who
stays in a house one or two days. Next it says, "And dressed
it for the man (*ish*) that was come to him" (the word *ish*
meaning "master", as in "the man, the master of the land"
(Gen. XLII, 30)). So the evil prompting becomes the "master
of the house" in respect of the man, who is now bound to
his service, and he does with him what he likes. Hence a
man should ever carry about with him words of Torah in
order that the evil prompting may be subdued by them,
since there is no opponent of the evil prompting like words
of Torah; wherefore it is written, "And these words shall
be upon thy heart" (*lebabeka*), that is, upon both thy
promptings, the good prompting that it may be crowned
with them and the evil prompting that it may be subdued
by them.' R. Judah asked: 'Why does the good prompting
need them ?' He replied: 'The good prompting is crowned
by them, and the evil prompting, if it sees that a man does
not repent nor seek to study the Torah, goes above and
points out his guilt.'

When R. Simeon came, he said: 'Assuredly in the section
of the Shema are hinted the Ten Commandments, as already
stated elsewhere, in the words "and these words shall be".

[1] *v.* Bereshith Rabba, 22b.

There are also ten commandments here corresponding to the other ten. They are as follows: (1) "Thou shalt teach them diligently to thy children", (2) "And thou shalt speak of them", (3) "When thou sittest in thy house", (4) "And when thou goest by the way", (5) "And when thou liest down", (6) "And when thou risest up", (7) "And thou shalt bind them for a sign on thy hand", (8) "And they shall be for frontlets between thine eyes", (9) "And thou shalt write them upon the doorposts of thy house", (10) "And upon thy gates". Hence this section is a fundamental portion of the Law; blessed is he who recites it completely twice every day, since then the Holy Name is fitly sanctified in his mouth.'

R. Aha once rose after midnight with R. Eleazar to study the Torah. R. Eleazar cited the verse: "For it is thy life and the length of thy days" (Deut. XXXII, 47). 'Observe', he said, 'that above all the stipulations which God made with Israel when they entered the Holy Land was the stipulation that they should study the Torah. Why so ? Because the Divine Presence finds a home in the land only through the Torah, and it finds a home above only through the Torah. For so my father has said: The Oral Law has been made known only for the sake of the Written Law, and the Shekinah finds a home above and below only through the Torah.' As they were sitting, R. Simeon bent his head and said: 'Assuredly it is so, and this secret I have found in the Book of R. Hamnuna the Ancient, who applied to the Community of Israel the verse: "Her food, her raiment, and her duty of marriage shall he not diminish" (Ex. XXI, 10); and if they are withheld from her, then it is written, "She shall go out for nothing without money". He that withholds the Torah from her is like one who withholds the raiment of his wife from her, so that she is left as a widow without being a widow.'

They sat and studied the Torah till daylight, when they resumed their journey. As they went along they saw a man going on the road with his head shrouded. When they came near him they found that he was muttering [268b] with his lips, and he made no answer to their greeting. Said R. Eleazar: 'Of a surety this man is consulting his Master.' R. Eleazar and R. Aha sat down and said their prayers, while the man stood upright in another place. They went on their way and the man went another way. Said R. Eleazar: 'Either that man is a fool or an evildoer.' He then said 'Let us occupy ourselves with the Torah, for it is time.' Before he could commence, the man came up to them. Said R. Eleazar: 'We must not interrupt our study, for he who studies the Torah becomes worthy of obtaining the heavenly inheritance in the glory of the supernal Holy King, and also of an inheritance in this world, which is called "the glory of the Lord". For when a man walks in the path of rectitude before the Holy One, and occupies himself with the Torah, he inherits that "glory of the Lord" for himself, and he has many protectors and advocates above who point out his merits before the Holy King, but if a man does not study the Torah nor walk in the way of his Master, then God appoints for him an accuser, who flies about in the air but does not at first go aloft, in case that man will repent of his sins. When he sees that he does not repent, and does not seek to study the Torah, he goes aloft and points out his guilt.'

He then discoursed on the verse: "And if the family of Egypt go not up and come not, neither upon them shall be the plague", etc. (Zech. xiv, 18). Why does it not say here, "not upon them shall be the rain", as in the case of all the other peoples? It is because, as the Companions have pointed out, the land of Egypt does not require rain, and therefore another punishment was decreed against them. But the Holy Land was ever watered from the heavens, and therefore when Israel studied the Torah it was watered properly, and he who withheld Torah from it was like one withholding good from heaven.'

They went into a cave which was by the road, and the man went in with them. They sat down, and the man opened a discourse on the verse, "And the Lord spake unto Moses face to face", etc. (Ex. xxxiii, 11). 'This verse', he said, 'does not seem to hang together properly; first it says, "God spake to Moses face to face", then, "Moses returned to the camp", then, "And his minister Joshua the son of Nun, a young man", etc. What does it mean?' Said R. Eleazar: 'Verily God desired to honour us, for now we are associated with the Shekinah, which has not departed from us. Let him who has opened the discourse continue it.' The man then proceeded: 'Moses was separated by many degrees from all the other prophets, who bore the same relation to him as an ape to a human being. Other prophets beheld visions in a glass that did not illumine, and even so they did not venture to lift up their eyes and gaze above, but were like Daniel, who said, "I was fallen into a deep sleep on my face, and my face was upon the ground" (Dan. x, 9); nor was their message given to them in clear terms. Not so was Moses, the faithful prophet: he saw his vision in a luminous glass[1] and still stood upright, and he dared to raise his head and gaze upwards, like one to whom his neighbour says: Lift up your head and look me in the face in order that you may know what I say. So Moses raised his head without fear and gazed [269a] at the brightness of the supernal glory without losing his senses like the other prophets, who when they prophesied were bereft of their faculties and became transformed and knew nothing at all of this world. Not so Moses, for even while he was in that exalted grade he did not lose his faculties, and straightway after gazing on the brightness of the heavenly glory he "returned to the camp" to speak to them concerning all their requirements, and his mind was as clear as before, and more so. "His minister Joshua the son of Nun, a young man", derived instruction from "the tent",[2] where he learnt to contemplate in the holy spirit. So long as he was with Moses he used to learn and derive instruction from "the tent" without fear, but after Moses departed from him and he was left alone, then we read of him that "he fell on his face on the ground and did worship" (Joshua v, 14), not being able to gaze even on the messenger of God; how much less so then on another place. There was a man with whom a king entrusted vessels of gold and precious stones. As long as they were with him the man's servant was able to handle them and examine them. When, however, the man died, the king would not leave anything with the servant and took back his deposit. Alas, exclaimed the

[1] T.B. Yebamoth, 49b.　[2] The Shekinah.

servant, for what I have lost! When my master was alive
I had the handling of all these. So while Moses was alive
Joshua used to suck every day from the "tent" without
fear, but when Moses died, then Joshua "fell on his face".
So I, being in your company, will examine the words of the
Torah and not be afraid. When, however, I leave you, I
shall not be able to examine them by myself. He then
continued:

'AND THOU SHALT TEACH THEM DILIGENTLY TO
THY CHILDREN AND SHALT TALK OF THEM, ETC. A
man should sharpen the intellect of his son on the words of
the Torah like a two-edged sword, so that he should not
be dull. THOU SHALT TALK OF THEM. Every word of
the Torah has each its separate way. A man should conduct and guide himself by them so as not to turn aside
right or left. WHEN THOU SITTEST IN THY HOUSE.
A man should conduct himself with due propriety in his
house, so as to set an example to his household, and he
should also be gentle with them and not overawe them.
AND WHEN THOU WALKEST BY THE WAY: to guide himself by the precepts of the Law and to direct himself by
them in the fitting manner, and to prepare himself like
Jacob for gift, for battle, and for prayer. AND WHEN THOU
LIEST DOWN: to conduct himself in the fear of his Master,
in holiness and humility, so as not to be bold of face towards
his Master. AND WHEN THOU RISEST UP: to give praises
to his Master for having restored his soul, in spite of his
many sins before his Master, who, however, shows him
lovingkindness and restores the soul to his body.

'AND THOU SHALT BIND THEM FOR A SIGN UPON
THY HAND. Our colleagues who dwell in the South have
explained the inner meaning of the four compartments of
the phylacteries in their own way, viz., that the passage
"sanctify to me every firstborn" is to correspond to the
Supernal Crown (*Kether*); "and it shall come to pass when
the Lord bringeth thee" to Wisdom; "hear, O Israel," to
Binah ; and "and it shall come to pass if thou hearkenest
diligently" to *Ḥesed*. Then they are all combined in one on
the left arm which is called Strength (*Geburah*). We, however,

do not accept this view, because the Supreme Crown comprises all and is not reckoned (among the grades). Further, the section "and it shall come to pass [269b] when the Lord bringeth thee" is connected with the going forth from Egypt, and so with that place in which is freedom for slaves.[1] Hence our colleagues are not right. We commence from Wisdom, and we hold that the Holy One, blessed be He, wears them, four above, four below, four in the place of the brain, and four in the place where the heart is, because one is linked with the other. Man should crown himself with them, because they form the supernal Holy Name, and whoever crowns himself with the supernal Holy Crown is called king on earth as the Holy One, blessed be He, is king in the firmament. AND THOU SHALT WRITE THEM ON THE DOORPOSTS OF THY HOUSE AND ON THY GATES in order that a man may be found complete in all, complete in the precepts of his Master, inscribed above and inscribed below. Happy is the portion of Israel.'

R. Eleazar then discoursed as follows. 'We find sometimes the expression "Thus saith the Lord of Hosts", and sometimes "Thus saith the Lord God". What is the difference ? A message opening with the words "Thus saith the Lord of Hosts" is one of mercy, whereas a message opening with "Thus saith the Lord God" is one of judgement. The reason is that in the first case the *Koh* (thus)[2] is blessed from the *Zaddik* and *Nezah* and *Hod*, which are called "the Lord of Hosts", and therefore the message is delivered in gentleness, since it comes from the place thereof. But in the other case it sucks from the side of judgement, from the side of the supernal *Geburah ;* and I have learnt from my father that it is then judgement with mercy. Thus the prophet was careful to give the source of his message, and the sons of the true faith knew whence it depended.'

R. Aḥa then discoursed on the verse: "Curse ye Meroz, saith the angel of the Lord", etc. (Judges v, 23). 'This verse', he said, 'contains a profound mystery. When the Holy King handed over his house to the Matrona, he placed in her hands all kinds of weapons and engines of war, and put Her

---

[1] *Binah.*   [2] A name of the Shekinah.

in command of all his warriors who are called "the mighty men of Israel, expert in war" (S.S. III, 7, 8); for when the Holy One, blessed be He, makes war, it is with these that He does so. We have learnt that when the Israelites vowed to uncover the holy impress on their flesh,[1] then that "sword that executeth the vengeance of the covenant" collected all its forces and armament to make war with Sisera, and the stars poured down fire from heaven, as it says, "The stars from their courses fought with Sisera" (Jud. v, 20). For God said to them: Be ready to execute the vengeance of my sons. I am going to exact a twofold vengeance from the enemy, once for the six hundred chariots which he lent the Egyptians to make war against Israel, and again for their oppression of my sons till now. Therefore they were judged with two punishments, one of fire and one of water. Among the stars was one which did not come to assist in the work of vengeance, and it was cursed for ever, so that when it commences to shine the other stars come and swallow it up with all its attendant stars, and they all vanish. Hence it says, "Curse ye Meroz, saith the angel of the Lord". It may be asked, Has an angel the right to say this ? This, however, is the one of whom it is written, "And the angel of the Lord that went before the camp of Israel removed", etc. (Ex. xiv, 19), for to him belong [270a] all wars, and this is also the one whom Jacob called "The angel that delivered me" (Gen. xlviii, 16). This one, too, will be supreme and glorious in the time to come, and through him the Holy Name will be magnified, and the Holy One, blessed be He, will take vengeance of the peoples.'

They went on until they came to R. Simeon, who on seeing them said: 'Behold, the Shekinah is here; of a truth we must show gratitude to the Shekinah.' He then discoursed on the verse: "Lo, it is yet high day", etc. (Gen. xxix, 7). 'This verse', he said, 'has been expounded to signify that when Israel shall turn in repentance before the Holy One, blessed be He, through the merit of the Torah they shall return to the Holy Land and be gathered from exile. For the captivity of Israel is only one day and no more. If, therefore,

[1] At the time of circumcision.

they do not repent, God says: Behold it is still high day, it is not time that the cattle should be gathered together—without merits or good deeds to their credit. You have, however, a remedy: "Water the sheep": study the Torah and drink of its waters, "and go and feed" in a restful spot, the desirable place of your inheritance. Or, again, we may take the "day" mentioned here to refer to the "day of discomfiture, of treading down, and of perplexity" (Isa. XXII, 5), when the Temple was destroyed and Israel went into captivity, and on account of their evil deeds that day is prolonged and drawn out. Therefore "water the sheep", as we have explained, with words of the Torah, for through the merit of the Torah Israel will escape from captivity. What do Israel reply ? "We cannot, until all the flocks be gathered together", that is, until the other supernal Days be gathered together, "so that they may roll the stone", roll away the stern judgement of that Day which commands the mouth of the "Well" that is in captivity with us. When that Well is released and the stone will no longer dominate it, then "we shall water the sheep". At the end of days God will restore Israel to the Holy Land and gather them from exile. This "end of days" is the "latter end of days" frequently mentioned in Scripture, which is also a name for the Community of Israel in exile. With this the Holy One, blessed be He, will execute vengeance, and He will also restore it to its place, as it is written, "And it shall come to pass in the latter end of days that the mountain of the Lord's house shall be established", etc. (Isa. II, 2). Just as when the Temple was destroyed the shadows commenced to fall, as it is written, "Woe unto us for the day declineth, for the shadows of evening are stretched out" (Jer. VI, 4), so at the end of the captivity the shadows will commence to pass. The extent of that shadow will be six fists and a half, measured by the hand of a man who is a man among men. The mnemonic for this mystery among the Companions is the verse, "For we are but of yesterday and know nothing, because our days upon earth are but a shadow" (Job VIII, 9): that is to say: We are but from yesterday in captivity, and we did not know that the shadow is for God to settle us upon the land. Happy he that sees it

and happy he that does not see it. Woe to him who will be
at hand when the mighty lion seeks to join his mate, still
more when they actually do join. Of that time it is written,
"The lion roareth, who will not fear", etc. (Amos. III, 8).
Of that time it is also written, "And the Lord God will turn
thy captivity", etc. (Deut. xxx, 3): the Community of Israel
will return from exile and the *Ẓaddik* will return to occupy
his place.'

VAYELECH

Deuteronomy XXXI, 1–30

AND MOSES WENT AND SPAKE THESE WORDS UNTO ALL ISRAEL. R. Hizkiah cited here the verse: "That caused his glorious arm to go at the right hand of Moses, that divided the water before them" (Isa. LXIII, 12). 'Happy', he said, 'are Israel in that God chose them, and because He chose them He called them sons, [283*b*] firstborn, holy, brothers, and came down to dwell among them and sought to establish them after the supernal pattern, and spread over them seven clouds of glory. Three holy brethren accompanied them, Moses, Aaron and Miriam, and for their sakes God gave them precious gifts. All the days of Aaron the clouds of glory did not depart from Israel, and Aaron, as we have stated, was the right hand of Israel, and therefore it is written, "that caused his glorious arm to go at the right hand of Moses": this refers to Aaron. Therefore Aaron being dead it says now that Moses "went", like a body without an arm, as it says, "and they *went* without strength before the enemy" (Lam. I, 5).

'All the days of Moses the children of Israel ate bread from heaven, but as soon as Joshua came "the manna ceased on the next day . . . and they ate of the produce of the land" (Joshua V, 12). What is the difference between them ? One is from the higher source and the other from the lower. As long as Moses was alive the orb of the sun was in the ascendant and illumined the world, but as soon as Moses departed the orb of the sun was gathered in and the moon came forth. We have learnt that when God said to Moses, "Behold my angel shall go before thee" (Ex. XXIII, 23), Moses said, "Shall the radiance of the sun be gathered in and the moon lead us ? I desire not the orb of the moon, but that of the sun". Then the orb of the sun shone forth and Moses became like the orb of the sun to Israel; and when Moses was gathered in the orb of the sun was gathered in and the moon shone and Joshua used the light of the moon. Alas for this degradation !

'AND HE SAID TO THEM, I AM AN HUNDRED AND TWENTY YEARS OLD THIS DAY. This bears out what R. Eleazar said, that the sun illumined Israel for forty years and was then gathered in, and the moon commenced to shine.' R. Simeon said: 'This accords with the verse: "There is that is destroyed without justice" (Prov. XIII, 23), which has caused some difficulty to the Companions. The explanation is this. It has already been stated that all spirits issue from heaven in pairs, male and female, and then separate. Sometimes the spirit of the female goes forth before the male which is her mate, and as long as the time of the male has not come to be united with her another can come and marry her, but when the time of the first one arrives to marry her, when *Zedek* (Righteousness) arises to visit the sins of the world, this other that married her is gathered in and the first comes and marries her. And even though his works were not particularly evil, he is gathered in before his time and not in accordance with judgement, and the doom of *Zedek* lights on him for his sins because the time of the other to whom she belongs has come.' R. Eleazar asked: 'Why should he die ? Cannot God separate them and let the other come and give her to him ?' He replied: 'This is the kindness that God does with a man, that he should not see his wife in the hand of another. Observe, too, that if the first [284*a*] is not deserving, even though the woman is his by rights, the other is not removed to make way for him. In the same way Saul obtained the kingdom, because the time of David, to whom it rightfully belonged, had not yet come. But when David's time arrived to come into his own, *Zedek* arose and gathered in Saul on account of his sins, and he had to make way for David. If it is asked, Could not Saul have lost the kingdom without also dying, the answer is that God did him a kindness in gathering him in while he was yet king so that he should not see his servant ruling over him and taking what was formerly his. So here too. Therefore a man should pray to God that he be not thrust out to make

way for another. So, too, God said to Moses: Do you want
to overturn the world ? Have you ever seen the sun serving
the moon ? Have you ever seen the moon shining when the
sun is still high ? BEHOLD THY DAYS APPROACH THAT
THOU MUST DIE, CALL JOSHUA; let the sun be gathered
in and the moon rule. Nay more, if thou enterest the land
the moon will be gathered in before thee and have no sway.
The time has come for the dominion of the moon, but it
cannot rule while thou art in the world.

'THAT I MAY GIVE HIM A CHARGE. We find, in fact, that
God gave no charge to Joshua, but only to Moses. Why, then,
does it say, "that I may give him a charge" ? What it means
is this. God said to Moses: Although thou liest with thy
fathers, thou wilt still be existing to give light to the moon,
just as the sun even after it has set continues to give light
to the moon. Therefore I will charge Joshua to be illumined,
and therefore it says also, "command Joshua and encourage
him" (Deut. III, 28): charge him, that is, to give light.

'FOR THOU SHALT BRING THE CHILDREN OF ISRAEL.
And previously (v. 7) it says, "thou shalt *come* with this
people". Why this variation ? One was to announce to him
that he would enter the land and remain on it, the other that
he would have sway over Israel.'

R. Simeon discoursed on the verse: "From the uttermost
part of the earth have we heard songs, glory to the righteous",
etc. (Isa. XXIV, 16). 'These songs are the praises uttered by
the Community of Israel before the Holy One, blessed be
He, at night, at the time when He holds joyous converse
with the righteous in the Garden of Eden. When is this ?
From midnight onwards. And for what purpose ? To be
united with the Holy One, blessed be He, [284b] and to be
sanctified with the same holiness. The verse continues: "I
pine away, I pine away, woe is me. The treacherous dealers
have dealt treacherously". Woe is me for the generation
and for the world ! For all are false to Him, and their children
inherit their treachery and add to it their own, and so become
defective both above and below. When Isaiah saw this, he

gathered all who feared sin and taught them the way of
holiness and the sanctity of the King that their sons might
be holy; and therefore the sons they bore were called after
his name, wherefore it says, "Behold I and the children
whom the Lord hath given *me* are for signs and wonders
in Israel" (Isa. VIII, 18). Another explanation of this verse
("From the uttermost part of the earth", etc.) is that when
the Israelites came into the land with the Ark of the holy
covenant before them, they heard from one side of the land
the sound of joyful praises and the voice of sweet singers
who were singing in the land. And this redounded to the
praise of Moses, that wherever the ark rested in the land
they heard a voice saying, "This is the law which Moses set
before the children of Israel". But woe is me that the traitors
have dealt treacherously, that Israel are destined to be false
to God and to be uprooted from the land, and because their
children persist in their falsehood they will be uprooted a
second time until their guilt will be expiated in a foreign
land.

'THAT IT MAY BE THERE FOR A WITNESS AGAINST
THEE. Three things [are recorded in Scripture as] having
been made witnesses, namely, the well of Isaac, the lot, and
the stone which Joshua set up. This song, however, is the
best witness of all.' Said R. Isaac: 'If so, there are four ?'
He replied: 'The term "witness" is not specifically applied
to the lot in Scripture, though it says "by the *mouth* of the
lot shall their inheritance be divided" (Num. XXVI, 55).'

AND MOSES SPAKE THE WORDS OF THIS SONG UNTIL
THEY WERE FINISHED. R. Eleazar asked: 'Why does it
say here, "*the words of* this song" and not simply "this
song" ? The reason is that all the words which Moses spoke
were traced with the name of the Holy One, blessed be He,
and then every word came to Moses to be traced by him
and remained before him. How is it, it may be asked, that
for the song of Solomon the masculine term *shir* (song) is
used, and for the song of Moses the feminine term *shirah ?*
Seeing that, as we have learnt, all the other prophets were

in comparison to Moses like an ape compared to a man, should not Moses have said *shir* and the other *shirah* ? [285*a*] The answer is that Moses was speaking not for himself but for Israel.' R. Simeon said: 'This is not so, but the truth is that this itself is a proof of the superiority of Moses. For Moses went up, from the lower to the higher, but they came down, from the higher to the lower. Moses said *shirah*, which is the song of the Matrona in honour of the King, and he was attached to the King. They said *shir*, which is the song of the King in honour of the Matrona, and they were attached to the Matrona; and thus the superiority of Moses was here displayed. We may also say that Moses used the term "*shirah*" to connect his words with the place from which judgement could be visited on them, since he had already said, "For I know their imagination", etc. (v. 21), and also, "For I know that after my death", etc. (v. 29). We find it also written, however, "And David spake unto the Lord the words of this song (*shirah*, 2 Sam. XXII, 1). It is to the honour of David that he attained to this grade of inditing a *shirah* from the lower to the higher. This was towards the end of his days, when he had reached a higher stage of perfection. And why was he worthy to indite such a hymn, from the lower to the higher, at the end of his days ? Because he had peace on all sides, as it is written, "On the day that the Lord delivered him from the hand of all his enemies" (*Ibid.*).'

R. Simeon said: 'What is the most perfect hymn ? One that is addressed both by the lower to the higher and by the higher to the lower, and which then combines the two. From whose example do we know this ? From this song of Moses. First the lower addresses the higher in the words, "For I will call on the name of the Lord", and again, "Ascribe greatness to our God", the reference being to the Most High King. Afterwards he traces the degrees from higher to lower, as it is written, "righteous and upright". Finally the knot of faith is tied in the words "he is". This should be the example for every man in arranging the praises of his Master. At first he should ascend from the lower to the higher till he carries the honour of his Master to the place whence issues the stream of the most recondite fountain. Then he draws it downwards from that moistening stream to each grade in turn down to the lowest grade, so that blessings are drawn to all from on high. Then he has to knit all firmly together with the knot of faith, and this is the man who honours the name of his Master by unifying the Holy Name. Of such a one it is written, "'Them that honour me I will honour" (i Sam. ii, 30), that is, them that honour Me in this world I will honour in the next. "But", the verse goes on, "they that despise me shall be lightly esteemed". This applies to one who does not know how to unify the Holy Name, to bind the knot of faith, and to bring blessings to the proper place; for whoever does not know how to honour the name of his Master were better not to have been born. R. Judah says that these words apply to one who does not answer "Amen" with devotion, since we have learnt: Greater is he that answers "Amen" than he that says the blessing.[1] For so we have explained in the presence of R. Simeon, that Amen draws blessings from the Source to the King and from the King to the Matrona; in the inscribed letters of R. Eleazar, from A to M and from M to N, and when the blessings come to N, from there [285b] they issue forth to higher and lower and spread through all, and a voice proclaims, "Drink from the stream of blessings that So-and-so the servant of the Holy King has sent forth". And when Israel below are careful to answer "Amen" with fitting devotion, many doors of blessing are opened for them above, many blessings are spread through all worlds, and great is the joy throughout. For this Israel receive a reward in this world and in the next. In this world because when Israel are oppressed and offer up prayer a voice proclaims in all worlds, "Open ye the gates that the righteous nation which keepeth truth may enter in" (Isa. xxvi, 2): as Israel open for you gates of blessing, so open the gates for them and let their prayer be received for deliverance from their oppressors. In the next world what is their reward ? That when a man who was careful to answer Amen departs from this world, his soul ascends and they proclaim before him: Open the gates before him[2] as he opened gates

every day by being careful to answer Amen. But if one hears
a blessing from the reader and is not careful to answer Amen,
what is his punishment ? As he did not open blessings below,
so they do not open for him above, and when he leaves this
world they proclaim before him: Close the gates in the face
of So-and-so that he enter not, and do not receive him—woe
to him and to his soul ! We have learnt that the sinners of
Gehinnom are in different storeys, and that Gehinnom has
a number of gates corresponding to those of the Garden of
Eden, each with its own name. There is one storey lower
than all the rest which consists of a storey on a storey, and
this is called the nether Sheol, "sheol" being one storey
and "nether" another below it. We have learnt that he who
descends to Abadon, [286a] which is called "nether", never
ascends again, and he is called "a man who has been wiped
out from all worlds". To this place they take down those
who scorn to answer Amen, and for all the amens which
they have neglected they are judged in Gehinnom and taken
down to that lowest storey which has no outlet, and from
which they never ascend. Of such it is written, "As the
cloud is consumed and withereth away, so he that goeth
down to Sheol shall come up no more" (Job VII, 9); this
refers to that nether storey.' R. Jose cited the verse: "For
my people have committed two evils: they have forsaken
me, the fountain of living waters, and have hewed them
out cisterns, broken cisterns, that can hold no water" (Jer.
II, 13). ' "They have forsaken me", by refusing to sanctify
the name of the Holy One, blessed be He, with Amen; and
their punishment is "to hew out broken cisterns", by being
taken down to Gehinnom storey after storey till they reach
Abadon, which is called "nether". But if one sanctifies the
name of the Holy One, blessed be He, by answering Amen
with all his heart, he ascends grade after grade till he is
regaled with that World-to-come which perennially issues
forth.'

R. Eleazar said: 'Israel will one day indite a chant from
the lower to the higher and from the higher to the lower and
tie the knot of faith, as it is written, "Then shall Israel sing
(*yashir*) this song" (Num. XXI, 17), from the lower to the

higher. "Spring up, O well, sing ye to it": that is, ascend to thy place to unite with thy Spouse. This is from the lower to the higher; then from the higher to the lower in the words, "The well which the princes digged"—for it was begotten of the Father and the Mother, "which the nobles of the people delved", as a place for the King to join her with blessings. And through what shall be their union ?" "With the sceptre": this is *Yesod ;* "And with their staves": these are *Neẓaḥ* and *Hod*. Thus we have from the higher to the lower. Then the song proceeds: "And from the wilderness to Mattanah and from Mattanah to Nahaliel and from Nahaliel to Bamoth": this is the complete bond of faith, the permanent bond wherein is all.'

R. Jose said: 'Israel will one day utter a complete song comprising all other songs, as it says: "And in that day shall ye say, Give thanks unto the Lord, call upon his name, declare his doings among the peoples" (Isa. XII, 4).'

HA'AZINU

Deuteronomy XXII, 1–52

GIVE EAR, YE HEAVENS, AND I WILL SPEAK, ETC.
R. Judah cited here the verse: "I opened to my beloved, but
my beloved had withdrawn himself and was gone", etc.
(S.S. v, 6). 'And just before this it is written, "I was asleep
but my heart waked" (*Ibid*. 2). Said the Community of
Israel: I was asleep to the precepts of the Law when I went
in the wilderness, but my heart was awake to enter the land
so as to perform them, since they all are meant for the land.
"It is the voice of my beloved that knocketh": this is Moses,
who administered many reproofs [286b] and rebukes, as it
says, "These are the words", etc. (Deut. I, 1), "Ye were
rebellious", etc. (*Ibid*. IX, 24). Yet withal he spoke only in
love for Israel, as it says, "Ye are a holy people", etc. (*Ibid*.
VII, 6). Said the Israelites: When we were about to enter into
the land and to receive precepts of the Law, then "my
beloved withdrew himself and was gone", for "Moses the
servant of the Lord died there". "I sought him but I could
not find him", as it is written, "There arose not a prophet
like Moses". "I called him but he gave me no answer", for
there was no generation like that of Moses, one to whose
voice God hearkened and for whom He did such wonders
and miracles. R. Isaac said: "I rose to open to my beloved":
this was in the days of Moses, during the whole of which
there was no need of angel or messenger to guide Israel.
"My beloved had withdrawn himself and was gone": this
was in the days of Joshua, as it is written, "Nay, but as
captain of the host of the Lord am I now come" (Joshua v,
14). Moses heard the voice of the holy supernal King without
trembling; "I came in the days of Moses thy master but he
would not accept me". Then did the children of Israel realize
the greatness of Moses; they sought the Holy One, blessed
be He, but He was no longer at hand for them as in the days
of Moses.'

GIVE EAR, YE HEAVENS, AND I WILL SPEAK. R. Ḥiya
said: 'Blessed is Moses in that he was superior to all other
prophets. For Isaiah being further removed from the King
said only, "Hear, heavens", but Moses being nearer to the
King[1] said, "Give ear". We have learnt that when Isaiah
said "Hear, heavens, and give ear, earth", many translucent
angels sought to break his head and a voice came forth saying:
Who is this that seeks to throw the world into confusion; and
he therefore made haste to say: I do this not of myself, but
"the Lord speaketh". In regard to Moses, however, it says,
"Hear, ye heavens, and I will speak"—I, and no other,
"and let the earth hear my voice"—mine and no other's.'
R. Jose said: 'There is a further difference between Moses
and Isaiah in that Moses said, "Give ear, *the* heavens", that
is, those highest heavens which are called the name of the
Holy One, blessed be He, and further, "and let *the* earth
hear", the upper earth, the land of the living. But Isaiah
said only "heaven" and "earth", meaning the lower heaven
and earth, and withal he was nearly punished.'

R. Isaac discoursed on the verse: "As the apple tree
among the trees of the wood, so is my beloved among the
sons" (S.S. II, 3). 'Just as the apple is superior in its colour-
ing to all other fruits, so the Holy One, blessed be He, is
distinguished from all forces, higher and lower. Observe
that the Holy One, blessed be He, is compared to the apple,
which has three colours, and the Community of Israel to the
lily, which has two, red and white.' [287a] R. Judah said:
'The Holy One, blessed be He, is called Heaven, and because
He is called heaven, therefore all the seven firmaments
which are included under this name when they are joined
together are also called heaven and are called the name of
the Holy One, blessed be He.'

R. Jose asked: 'Why is this discourse called "song"?'
R. Isaac answered: 'Just as [287b] a song is drawn from
heaven to earth by the holy spirit, so these words were
drawn from heaven to earth by the holy spirit. Observe that
Moses made a long exordium saying, "Give ear, ye heavens,
and hear, O earth, let my discourse drop as the dew", etc.

[1] *v.* Yalkut, Is. I.

Why all this ? "Because I will call on the name of the Lord".
We have learnt that when Moses said "Give ear, ye heavens,
and I will speak", all worlds were shaken. A voice came forth
and said: Moses, why dost thou shake the world, being but
a mortal ? He replied: Because I will call on the name of
the Lord. Forthwith they were silent and listened to his
words.'[1] [296b]

R. Jose said: 'God first called Israel "holy", as it is
written, "For thou art a holy people", etc. (Deut. XIV, 2).
Then He called them "holiness", as it is written, "Israel is
holiness (kodesh) to the Lord, the firstfruits [297a] of his
increase" (Jer. II, 3). What is the difference between the
two terms ?' R. Abba said: ' "Holiness" is higher than all,
for so we have learnt that when all sanctities are combined
they are called "holiness", and all assemble together to that
place which is called "holiness".' R. Eleazar said: 'The
beginning and end of all is comprised in "holiness", and
the supreme Wisdom is called "holiness", and when this
Wisdom shines forth the wisdom of Solomon is illumined,
the Moon being then at the full. When it is illumined from
Yesod we call it "holiness" when this illumines her fully,
but when it is not illumined completely we call it "the spirit
of holiness". And when it is blessed from Yesod and gives
suck to all below, we call it Mother, and we call them "holi-
nesses", and so it becomes "holy of holies".'

FOR I WILL PROCLAIM THE NAME OF THE LORD, ETC.
R. Abba said: ' "Ascribe ye greatness" refers to Gedulah ;
"The Rock, his work is perfect" to Geburah ; "For all his
ways are judgement" to Tifereth ; "a God of faithfulness"
to Nezah ; "and without iniquity" to Hod ; "just" to Yesod ;
"and right" to Zedek ; "is he" completes the holy name of the
Holy One, blessed be He.' R. Jose said: 'Then only did
Moses reveal this name to the children of Israel, as it is
written, "I am an hundred and twenty years old this day", etc.
(Deut. XXXI, 2). From this we learn that one in whom resides
divine wisdom, when his time arrives to depart from the
world, should reveal that wisdom to those among whom is

---

[1] Here in the original follows the Idra Zuta, v. Appendix.

the holy spirit. If he does not, we apply to him the words, "Withhold not good from them to whom it is due when it is in the power of thine hand to do it" (Prov. III, 27).' R. Ḥiya said: 'The end of this verse makes fast the knot of faith in the word "he", as if to say "He is all, He is one without division", and all the others mentioned are not diverse but are all united in One, who is, was, and will be. Happy is he who calls upon the King and knows how to call upon him fittingly. But if one calls without knowing to whom he calls, the Holy One, blessed be He, is far from him, as it is written, "God is near to all who call upon him, (to wit) to all who call upon him *in truth*" (Ps. CXLV, 18). Is there, then, one who calls upon Him in falsehood?' Said R. Abba: 'Yes; he that calls and knows not to whom he calls.

'THEY HAVE CORRUPTED THEMSELVES, THEY ARE NOT HIS CHILDREN, IT IS THEIR BLEMISH. We have learnt: Sinners, if one may say so, create a blemish above, [297b] in that through them all the divine adornments are not in their proper condition.' Said R. Jose: 'What is the blemish? That the Fathers do not obtain full blessing from the watering of the Stream, and even less of course the Children.' Similarly R. Simeon said: 'When sinners are numerous in the world, the Holy Name, if one may say so, is not blessed in the world, but when sinners are not numerous, the Holy Name is blessed in the world.' R. Abba said: 'This text also says so explicitly. Who is the cause of the corruption here mentioned? "A perverse and crooked generation." Hence, after Moses had expressed the Holy Name in fitting manner, closing with the words, "just and right is he", he went on, "but they corrupted themselves being not his sons", etc. Why? Because they were a perverse and crooked generation.

'DO YE THUS REQUITE THE LORD, to wit, for all those kindnesses that He has shown thee.' R. Eleazar said: 'Blessed are Israel above all heathen peoples, because although they have provoked their Master, the Holy One, blessed be He, was fain not to abandon them. For in every place to which they have been exiled the Holy One, blessed be He, is with them in their banishment, as it is written, "And yet for all that, when they be in the land of their enemies I will not reject them", etc. (Lev. XXVI, 44). Now how great is the love of the Holy One, blessed be He, for Israel, for although they brought exile upon themselves the Shekinah never leaves them, as it says, "and this (*zoth*) also (is with them) when they are in the land of their enemies". A king had a son who provoked him so that he condemned him to depart from him and to go to a distant land. The Queen on hearing this said: Seeing that my son is going to a distant land and the King casts him out of his palace, I will not leave him, but either we will both return together to the palace or both will dwell together in another land. In course of time the King sought the Queen and did not find her, because she had gone with her son. He said: Since the Queen is there, let them both return. But it is the Queen whom the King seeks out first, and for her sake he seeks out his son, as it is written, "I have heard the groaning of the children of Israel". Why ? Because "I remember my Covenant" (Ex. VI, 5).' [298*a*]

As R. Isaac was once journeying on the road, R. Ḥiya met him. He said to him: 'I see from the look of your face that your abode is with the Shekinah. Why is it written, "And I *am* come down to deliver them out of the hand of the Egyptians" ? Surely it should be, "And I *shall* come down" ? It means, however, "I went down at first", namely, when Jacob went down to Egypt; I then went down to deliver them from the hand of the Egyptians, since otherwise they could not have endured the captivity; and so it says, "I am with him in trouble, I will deliver him and honour him" (Ps. XCI, 15).' He replied: 'Of a truth wherever Israel dwell the Holy One, blessed be He, is among them, and wherever the wise of the generation walk the Holy One, blessed be He, walks with them. How do we know ? From Jacob, of whom it is written, "And Jacob went on his way" (Gen. XXII, 1), and then, "And Jacob said when he saw them, This is God's host". Now let us join one another and proceed, as I know we are going to the same place, to pay our respects to the Shekinah.' 'Assuredly so,' replied the other. As they went along, R. Ḥiya said: 'It is written, "These are the generations of the heavens and the earth" (Gen. II, 4). "*The* heavens" includes the Holy One, blessed be He, and "*the* earth" includes the Holy One, blessed be He, and all that is lower is called "the generations of the heavens". We have learnt that this world was created with *Hé* and the future world with *Vau*. From the Head of the King the streams issue forth to *Binah*, and thence they flow to all corners until finally they are collected in the place called the Great Sea, whence issue generations for all.' Said R. Isaac: 'When we studied with R. Simeon, all this was set forth explicitly and not by way of allusion.' He replied: 'R. Simeon is not like other men, for they are to him as the other prophets to Moses.'

As they went along, R. Ḥiya asked R. Isaac the meaning of the verse: "Can a woman forget her sucking child, that she should not have compassion on the son of her womb?" (Isa. LXIX, 15)'. Said the other: 'If in the company of the colleagues we could find no proper explanation for it, how can *I* say ?' He thereupon said: 'I once caught a hint of the meaning as I was going along the road, but I do not know who said it or exactly what he meant. For seven days I was troubled by this and did not eat anything, and now I am going to the Sacred Lamp in case he may be able to remind me.' Said R. Isaac: 'Perhaps it was the day when R. Eleazar was going to his father-in-law, and I was with him, and I can remember. For thus said R. Eleazar in the name of his father: Israel said before the Holy One, blessed be He: Since the day that we fell into captivity God has forsaken and forgotten us, as it is written, "But Zion said, The Lord hath forgotten me" (*Ibid*. 14). Whereupon the Shekinah replied: "Can a woman forget her sucking child, that she should not have compassion on the son [298b] of her womb ?" "Yea, *these* may forget"—to wit, those mentioned in the verse, "*These* are the generations of heaven and earth", "yet will not I forget thee". This shows that the Holy One, blessed be He, will not forsake Israel for ever. Further, there is a deep mystery here, since God said that "these" things are attached to His name, and just as the Holy One, blessed be He, cannot forget His name, which is all, so He does not forget Israel, who are attached to His very name.' R. Ḥiya thereupon became excited and said: 'In truth that is the thing. Blessed be God that I reminded you, so that now I know what it was and who said it. I ran four miles that day and could not find out who it was.' R. Isaac said: 'I heard it because I went into a cave where R. Eleazar was resting.'

REMEMBER THE DAYS OF OLD, CONSIDER THE YEARS OF MANY GENERATIONS. R. Abba said: 'The "days of old" are the six Days in which God made the world; and these Days know and are acquainted with all the years of the world, and all generations up to this generation to which we ourselves belong. ASK THY FATHER AND HE WILL SHOW THEE: this is the Holy One, blessed be He, who will reveal to thee the hidden depths of Wisdom, to wit, that when those six Days constructed the universe they did so only for thy sake that thou mightest come and perform the Law, as we have learnt, that God made a condition with creation that if when Israel came they would accept the Torah it should stand, and if not that it should revert to chaos. Therefore God assigned other peoples to Chieftains and Overseers, but of you it is written, FOR THE LORD'S PORTION IS HIS PEOPLE, JACOB IS THE LOT OF HIS INHERITANCE, since He assigned them to no Potentate or Angel or Chieftain, but took them for his own portion. Where did He find them ? IN A DESERT LAND AND IN A WASTE HOWLING WILDERNESS, as it is written, "Terah the father of Abraham . . . and I took your father Abraham", etc. (Joshua XXIV, 2, 3); and from there He guided Israel in every generation, never separating from them.'

AS AN EAGLE THAT STIRRETH UP HER NEST. R. Jose said: 'There is no creature so devoted to her young as the eagle, being as kind to them as it is cruel to others. THE LORD ALONE DID LEAD HIM AND THERE WAS NO STRANGE GOD WITH HIM: He alone, as it is written, "And the

Lord went before them", etc. (Ex. XIII, 21), and they were not led by an angel or any other Chieftain such as are called "strange god".'

O THAT THEY WERE WISE, THAT THEY UNDERSTOOD THIS. R. Jose said: 'All the verses of this section are reproofs addressed by Moses to Israel, with the exception of the Holy Name which he disclosed at the beginning of his discourse.' R. Abba said: 'Even his reproofs are included in the holy name, since there is no word in the Torah which is not comprised in the holy name. That the name [299a] of the Holy One, blessed be He, however, might be inscribed in this section, we have had to wait till here, where it is indeed written, "O that they were wise, that they understood this (zoth)", meaning that if Israel knew how zoth takes hold of judgement to punish sinners "they would consider their latter end", and take heed to be faithful to her. Or we may explain that She is united with Israel when they keep the precepts of the Torah and dwell with Her in peace, and then they know that this zoth is on their side to help them to punish their enemies. Israel who are the least of nations will then know "how one should chase a thousand and two put ten thousand to flight".

'EXCEPT THEIR ROCK HAD SOLD THEM AND THE LORD HAD DELIVERED THEM UP. Why so? Because "Of the Rock that begat thee thou art unmindful" (v. 18), and the divine adornments are not in their proper place.' R. Judah said: 'The "rock" here is Abraham, who said, "Let Israel be condemned to exile rather than to Gehinnom", and God consented, so that whenever Israel sin they are sent into captivity and their enemies rule over them.' R. Judah said: 'Why did Moses reprove Israel thus in this song? Because they were about to enter into the land where the Shekinah would dwell in their midst.' R. Isaac said: 'When the prophet said, "The Lord hath a controversy with Judah, and will punish Jacob according to his ways" (Hosea XII, 2), the nations of the world exulted, saying: "Now they will be utterly destroyed". But when God saw them rejoicing, He changed His mind, and it is written, "In the womb he took his brother by the heel", etc. (Hos. XII, 4). A woman had a quarrel with her son, and went to complain against him to the court. When she saw the judge condemning prisoners to stripes, to crucifying, to burning, she said: Alas, what shall I do with my son ? When the judge was ready he said to her: Tell me what I shall do with your son. She said: I was only shouting.

'HE FOUND HIM IN A DESERT LAND AND IN THE WASTE HOWLING WILDERNESS. Assuredly he afterwards made all those "shells"[1] subservient to him.

'Up to this point this section was transcribed in the Book of Kartana the physician. Then in a note to this verse were set down all the precautions that a wise physician should take for a person laid up in his sickness, among the prisoners of the King, for the service of his Master, the Lord of the Universe. When the wise physician goes in to him, he "finds him in a desert land and in the waste howling wilderness". Are we to say that because God has commanded him to be seized, no one should seek to help him ? Not so, for David said, "Blessed is he that considereth the poor" (Ps. XLI, 2), and the "poor" is one confined to a bed of sickness. What, then, is the wise physician to do ? He "compasses him about", finding means to protect him against the things that injure him, by letting blood and removing the bad blood from him. "He cares for him", examining the cause of the disease, and taking steps that it should not grow worse. Then "he keeps him as the apple of his eye", that he may be careful to prescribe for him the proper medicines, since if he makes a mistake in a single particular God imputes it to him as if he were to shed blood, for, although that man is among the prisoners of the King, yet God desires that his fellow man should tend him and help to release him from the prison. He used to say thus: God passes sentence on human beings above, whether for death or [299b] banishment or confiscation of goods or imprisonment. He who is liable to confiscation of goods falls ill and is not healed until he pays

[1] The *klifoth*.

all that is decreed against him. When he has paid his money
penalty he is healed and goes out from his prison, and therefore it is fitting that one should assist him to pay his fine
and be released. He who is liable to uprooting is seized and
thrown into the prison until he is completely uprooted,
though sometimes he is uprooted only from his limbs or from
one of them and is then released. But one who is liable to
death cannot save himself by any ransom whatever. Hence
a wise physician must do his best first to provide him a
healing for his body, and if he cannot do this he must try
to find a healing for his soul. This is the physician whom
God assists both in this world and in the next.' R. Eleazar
said: 'I never heard before of this physician and this book,
save once when a certain merchant told me that he had
heard his father say that in his days there was a physician
who on looking at a patient would say: This one will live, or
this one will die. He was said to be a virtuous God-fearing
man, and if a patient could not afford to get what he prescribed he would give him out of his own pocket. It was said,
too, that there was no physician so skilful as he, and that
he accomplished more with his prayer than with his hands.
I fancy this was that same physician. Said that merchant:
His book is indeed in my possession, as I inherited it from
my father's father, and all the words of that book are founded
upon hidden meanings of the Torah, and I have discovered
profound secrets in it and many remedies which he said
should not be administered save by one who was God-fearing,
they being of those which were employed by Balaam, who
used to utter an incantation over a sickness and heal it
forthwith. All this he explained in that book, saying: This
is forbidden and this is permitted to one who fears sin, since,
as he said, the cure of many illnesses depends on the incantation. These are from the side of enchantment, some of them
from the side of magic. All those which it is forbidden to
pronounce with the mouth or to do with the hands were set
down, and we found that certain diseases it was necessary
to excommunicate, which was a great wonder to us.' R.
Eleazar and the Companions were greatly interested to hear
this. Said R. Eleazar: 'If I had that book I would see what

it says, and I vow that I would show it to the Sacred Lamp'. We have learnt that R. Eleazar said: I had that book for twelve months and I found in it many illuminating things. When I came to the incantations of Balaam I was in some perplexity. One day I uttered one in a certain place, and letters went up and down and a voice said to me in a dream: Why dost thou enter into a domain which is not thine and not thy concern ? When I woke I was sore displeased with the hidden mysteries there. I sent to a certain Jew named R. Jose, son of R. Judah, and gave him the book. In the secrets of Balaam I had found some of the names of the angels which Balak sent to him, but not set down in the proper manner. I also, however, found a number of remedies which were based on arrangements of texts and secret mysteries of the Torah, and saw that they consisted of pious remarks and prayers and supplications to the Almighty. It must not be thought, however, that he performed healing with verses of the Scripture or with mysteries of the Torah; far from it. He used to pronounce mysteries of the Torah, and thereby he discovered secret healings the like of which I have never seen. I said: Blessed be God who has imparted to man of the supernal wisdom. I also took some of the words of Balaam, from which I could see that there never was a sorcerer like him. I said: Blessed be God for removing sorcery from the world, so that men should not be led astray from the fear of the Holy One, blessed be He.

APPENDIX

THE DIVINE NOMENCLATURE
OF THE ZOHAR

The reader of the *Zohar*, whether in the original or a translation, hardly needs to be told that with the mere understanding of the words he can in a great many passages by no means be sure of having penetrated to the sense. The *Zohar* has a way of using ordinary terms, including well-known proper names, in a sense peculiar to itself, often, too, when the reader, if not on his guard, might not suspect this; it deals largely in allegories of a very far-fetched and intricate character; and therefore a great part of it cannot be understood without some kind of a key. The appendices and glossaries in the first two volumes aimed only at giving such help as would make the main outlines of the *Zohar* intelligible. Now that the whole work of the translation has been completed, it seems proper to endeavour to provide a more effective clue to its mysteries.

Now, if there is one feature more than another which distinguishes the *Zohar*, it is the great variety of expressions which it uses to designate God and the divine essence in general. Not merely does it divide the Godhead into grades, but it has a number of names for each grade, besides other names which, strictly speaking, lie outside of the ideology of the grades. For the proper understanding of the *Zohar* nothing is more essential than the accurate distinguishing of these names; and an Appendix dealing with this matter in a systematic fashion will probably be found the most succinct means of providing a key, if not to the whole, at any rate to a great part of the *Zohar*, while it will incidentally afford occasion for a critique within limits of the theology of the *Zohar*, which is the aspect of it most likely to be of interest to the modern reader.

THE THREE APPROACHES TO GOD

An attentive study of the *Zohar* from this point of view reveals in it a complexity of a peculiar kind. It exhibits three distinct approaches to the God idea springing from distinct psychological needs and ministering to distinct religious requirements, yet all based upon the study of the Hebrew Scriptures and all consonant with Jewish faith and practice. The object of the *Zohar* in this field may in all cases be said to be the bringing of the individual Jew into communion with God. This, however, may be effected in three ways, according as the appeal is made to his sentiment of prayer and devotion, to his ethical impulse, or to his philosophical spirit. The *Zohar* recognizes—or postulates—that the individual may be materially assisted in this endeavour by being provided with suitable designations under which to represent to himself the Deity. It further recognizes the need of harmonizing these representations and showing how their diversity is consistent with the essential unity of God; and for this purpose further sets of designations are brought into play. Thus we find in the *Zohar* on the one hand three designations—or rather, sets of designations, for each has an alternative—which constitute what may be called the standard names of God, according as communion is sought by means of any one of the three approaches mentioned above; and on the other hand, a number of other designations grouped round these and serving to correlate them, and bring them, so to speak, into one frame. We may now proceed to specify these designations and the various aspects of the divine essence to which they are applied.

1. To designate God as the recipient of the Israelite's prayers and the object of his devotions, the *Zohar* commonly uses a term which the reader would not immediately suspect to have a divine significance, namely 'Community of Israel'. This term corresponds to what present-day writers call the 'national' or 'tribal' or 'particularist' God of Israel. Belief in such a God is based purely on historical grounds, especially on the election of the patriarchs. God as the 'Community of Israel' is the protector and guardian of the people of Israel in this world. In this capacity God is not only personal, but also localized. He is with the children of Israel wherever they are, whether in their own land or in exile. This union

was first effected at Mount Sinai; it was consummated by the building of the Temple, and was not broken even by the destruction of the Temple. But since that event God's protection of Israel is naturally much less efficacious. It will however, be restored to its former vigour in time to come, on the advent of the Messiah, which is frequently predicted in the *Zohar* with great circumstantiality.

If we ask, how does God manifest His presence in Israel, the answer is, through the Divine Light, the Shekinah. This light is the connecting link between the divine and the non-divine. For, according to the *Zohar*, God, the protector of Israel, is borne along by four *Ḥayyoth* or Holy Beasts, constituting His throne, and these are borne on other angelic beings, which again rest on higher firmaments, under which is the lowest heaven, to which belongs the earth and all its creatures.[1] Through this hierarchy an emanation of the Divine Presence is conveyed to earth, just as, on the other hand, the prayer of human beings is conveyed up to heaven. The Shekinah originally rested on the Tabernacle and Temple, but even now it accompanies the wise, especially when three study together.

The 'throne of God', consisting of the *Ḥayyoth*, is the instrument of God's providence on earth. For the *Ḥayyoth* are pictured as having each a human face, but with the aspect respectively of a man, a lion, an ox and an eagle. According, therefore, to the aspect through which he is looked upon from on high will be the providential care which a man receives here on earth. Here, too, intermediate beings come into play, and round this conception of the Godhead revolves most of the angelology of the *Zohar*. All this constitutes the more popular portion of the *Zohar*. Its Biblical basis is to be found in the first chapter of Ezekiel. It is essentially imaginative in character, and its main purpose is to afford consolation and encouragement to Israel in exile by assuring them that God's protection is

[1] It will be noticed that this hierarchy corresponds closely to the four 'worlds' of the Cabbalists—of Emanation, Creation, Formation and Completion. In the *Zohar* itself the worlds of *Aẓiluth* and *Beriah* are mentioned only occasionally, the others hardly at all.

still with them, as evidenced by the fact that the name
'Community of Israel' has both a human and a divine
application.

2. As the promoter of man's moral strivings, God is
usually termed in the *Zohar* 'The Holy One, blessed be He'.
In this capacity God is regarded as the source of animate
life, as the creator of species, as the vitalizing force in the
universe. Man knows of God in this aspect through his own
neshamah, the consciousness—based primarily on his
neshimah (breathing power)—of his own individuality, the
super-soul, the deeper self which transcends his *ruaḥ*
(spirit, intellectual faculties), and *nefesh* (physical vitality).
Through his *neshamah* man is capable of direct communion
with the Holy One, blessed be He, and also of ethical and
moral perfection or the reverse. The Israelites possess in the
precepts of their Torah the instrument for achieving this
perfection, and in proportion as they do so or fail to do so,
their *neshamah* is rewarded or punished after their death.
The place of reward is called the Garden of Eden, of punishment, Gehinnom. As the dispenser of reward and punishment after death, God is called the 'Holy King'. Another
name given to God from this point of view is the 'Tree of
Life', in the branches of which the souls of the righteous
are figured as resting. Hence, when an Israelite carries out
the Torah, he is said to be cleaving to the Tree of Life.
Round this conception of God as the Holy One, blessed be
He, revolves the whole Zoharic doctrine of the moral life,
of reward and punishment, of heaven and hell and their
respective denizens, and of the incarnation and transmigration of souls. This part of the *Zohar* is predominantly
emotional in tone, and the God-idea which it embodies
may be said to be based on an effort of introspection, or
on what in German philosophical language would be called a
Lebensanschauung. Its Scriptural basis is the second chapter
of Genesis.

3. The *Zohar* is not content to base the religious life
merely on the emotional side of man's nature. It seeks an
approach to God, not only introspectively, from the starting-
point of a *Lebensanschauung*, but also extraspectively, from

the starting-point of a *Weltanschauung*. The designation given to God for this purpose is 'Ancient Holy One'. This name designates God regarded as the First Cause of all existence and all movement. God in this aspect is purely impersonal, a fact somewhat veiled by the designation and of which the writers of the *Zohar* seem frequently to lose sight. It is, however, clearly brought out in another expression frequently used to describe God in this aspect, viz. 'That Hidden and Undisclosed' (or equivalent terms). It is a postulate of the *Zohar* that this First Cause is a kind of algebraical *x*, which for the sake of intellectual satisfaction must be sought for, but which can never be found. This attitude is summed up in the Zoharic interpretation of the Biblical text, 'See who created these' (Isa. XL, 26). The aspect of 'these'—the perceptible universe—points to the existence of a First Cause, but on inquiring into it we can get no further than the interrogation 'Who?' since the pursuit of an ultimate cause can be carried on to '*en sof*', without limit. In order, therefore, to find a beginning we posit an 'Ancient One' who differs from the 'Ancient Holy One' in being not absolutely absolute, so to speak, but containing the possibility of producing or becoming the non-absolute.

As the precepts of the Torah furnish man with the complete guide to the life of righteousness and moral improvement, so the first chapter of Genesis furnishes the complete guide to the quest of the Absolute. When pursued under such guidance, this quest is called *hokhmah*, wisdom, and constitutes the highest form of human activity, the mark of perfection in man. Naturally, in the eyes of the *Zohar* this quest is fundamentally a theological rather than a metaphysical activity, since the First Cause is *ex hypothesi* regarded as God, and has by some means or other to be identified not only with the personal God who enjoins the moral life, but also with the localized God who dwells among and protects the people of Israel. *Hokhmah* forms a link between man and the First Cause because *hokhmah* also governs the relation of cause and effect throughout the universe. And as the divine *hokhmah* determines the consequences to the soul of human conduct, so the human *ḥokhmah* embraces of necessity the moral life. Thus there can, in the system of the *Zohar*, be no conflict between philosophy and the moral law.

THE CORRELATION OF THE
THREE APPROACHES

From what has been said above, it will be seen that it is possible to distinguish three strata in the *Zohar* regarded as a theological work, which we may designate the devotional, the ethical, and the philosophical, and which address themselves primarily to the imagination, the emotions, and the intellect respectively. Each of these strata is, so to speak, dominated by its own designation for the Deity, representing God under a distinct aspect—in the one case as both personal and local, in the second as personal but not local, in the third as neither personal nor local. But the *Zohar* is not content to leave these aspects side by side, like the Scottish clergyman who commenced a prayer with the words, 'O Thou who art our eternal hope and ultimate hypothesis'. A great part of it—perhaps the most important—is taken up with an endeavour to correlate them by expressing each in the terms of the others. This involves a wide extension of the designations of God, which we have now to consider.

1. We have seen above that the providential care of Israel in this world is exercised, according to the *Zohar*, by God *qua* 'Community of Israel', while the recompensing of souls in the other world is carried out by God *qua* 'the Holy King'. Now, these two activities are pictured by the *Zohar* as being the same relation to each other as the management of the royal household to the management of the affairs of State. If the latter is assigned to the King, naturally the former is assigned to the Queen. Hence the Community of Israel is brought into relation with the Holy King by being designated the Matrona, or Queen, and they are pictured as consorting together in *ziwwug*, or wedlock. The pious are fancifully pictured as, by means of their prayers and studies,

preparing the Matrona for the union, and partaking in Her joy. Apparently this is possible even at the present time —a doctrine which it is not altogether easy to reconcile with the statement frequently made in the *Zohar*, that since the destruction of the Temple there has been 'separation' between the King and the Matrona.

Another way of bringing these two aspects into relationship is to picture the Community of Israel as the moon reflecting the light of the Holy One, blessed be He, who is the sun. Strictly speaking, we should compare them as sun *light* and moon *light*, and the moon, the opaque reflecting body, is formed by the souls of the righteous. God's activity in sending souls down to this world and resuscitating them in the next is like the light of the sun. But His providential care of Israel in this world, superadded to His care for their souls, is like the light of the moon, which is the light of the sun conveyed to a place to which it does not properly belong. And just as the moon is not always equally bright, so the Community of Israel is not always equally beneficent. It is the wicked who 'impair' the Moon, causing the Sun's light to be withdrawn from it, while the righteous restore it to fulness. In this way, then, King and Queen, and Sun and Moon are all designations in the *Zohar* of various aspects of the Godhead.

2. The question now arises, how does the *Zohar* unify the First Cause with the Holy One, blessed be He, and the Community of Israel ? The answer is, through the doctrine of the grades (*v.* Appendix to Vol. I). This is in essence the same as what is usually called by the Cabbalists the doctrine of the Sefiroth, but it is enunciated in the *Zohar* in a manner specially adapted for the purpose it has in view and with its own peculiar theological terminology.

When the *Zohar* speaks of 'grades', there is no question that ordinarily it means grades of the Godhead, and specifically of the Godhead regarded as First Cause. Seeing that it enumerates ten such grades, it in effect posits ten First Causes. This is apparently a contradiction in terms, and it must be admitted that the *Zohar*, while positing that the ten grades are in essence one, does habitually speak of them as if they were distinct entities capable of forming all sorts of relations with one another. The favourite method adopted by the *Zohar* for expressing their unity in diversity, or vice versa, is by picturing them as members of a human body or features of a human head; this method is elaborated in the 'Book of Concealed Wisdom' and in the two *Idras*. This, however, affords no satisfactory answer to our problem; for while it would be permissible, if we had some rational explanation, to illustrate it by the figure of the human frame, it is surely somewhat 'preposterous' (in the literal sense of the term) to seize on the figure of the human frame first and leave its precise application to be filled in afterwards.

Another explanation which is only adumbrated in the *Zohar*, but which is found more clearly expressed in other parts of the Cabbalistic literature, and has been adopted by Cordoveiro in his *Pardes Rimmonim*, is as follows. The First Cause is compared to a luminary shining on to a reflecting glass which in turn throws its light on to another from which it is cast on to a third, and so on through nine reflecting glasses (or it may be ten, for there is a difference of opinion as to whether the original light is reckoned among the ten or not). In this way there are ten lights of various grades of intensity which are yet all the same light. This figure explains the fact that there can be a gradation in the extent to which the human mind comprehends the First Cause. But it fails to explain the objective division of the First Cause into ten, which is certainly posited in the Cabbala, because it does not provide us with anything to which we can attach the figure of the reflecting glasses.

It would be possible to find such a basis of comparison in certain 'worlds' of which mention is made in the *Zohar*. We frequently come across such phrases as, 'there is re-joicing in all worlds', or 'all worlds are knit together'. Now, in later Cabbalistic works there is no doubt that by 'worlds' in such a connection would be meant the four 'worlds' of *Aẓiluth*, *Beriah*, *Yeẓirah* and *'Asiah* (*v*. Intro-duction). But, as we have seen, the *Zohar* does not seem to be really familiar with this idea, and certainly it hardly seems in place in the contexts where these expressions occur. It makes much better sense if we regard 'worlds' in these contexts as the 'opposite numbers' of the various grades, as the effects of the various manifestations of the First Cause. After all, if the First Cause is tenfold, it stands to reason that the universe must also be tenfold; and we may take this to be the doctrine of the *Zohar*, though it is nowhere expressly stated.[1]

This supposition, however, only carries the difficulty back a stage, and we have still to ask, how are we to understand the simultaneous existence of various worlds ? The key can perhaps be found in the Zoharic conception of the primordial 'Days'. Of the ten grades, six—from the fourth to the ninth—are regarded as functioning each within its own 'day'. Now it is obvious that these 'days' are not successive, since all the grades are evidently functioning concurrently. We must suppose, therefore, that when the *Zohar* says there are six 'days', what it means is that there are six *kinds of time*, what we might call six 'tempos' of existence, and in relation to each of these the First Cause assumes a different aspect, exhibits a different manifestation, becomes, in the Zoharic language, a different grade of itself. If we ask, how are we to imagine different kinds of time, it would be hard to find anything in the *Zohar* throwing light on this point, but it is not difficult to provide an answer, if we regard time as something not objectively perceived, but as subjectively felt. It might fairly be held that the animate world *feels* time in a manner different from the inanimate, and the higher branches of the animate world in a manner different from the lower. In this way the conception of various 'worlds' each with its own First Cause, yet all forming one, would become intelligible.

The 'day' as a definite kind of time, presupposes the existence of 'heaven and earth', that is, of an active cause and a material on which it works, originally one but differentiated by the action of the First Cause as a preliminary to the creation of 'worlds'. In this preliminary stage itself

[1] Of course, the three inferior 'worlds' of the Cabbalists would be contained in these worlds, though how exactly they are to be distributed is not easy to determine.

the *Zohar* distinguishes three grades, which it commonly refers to in a group as 'The Patriarchs'. It impresses upon us that these grades are totally beyond the realm of human comprehension, but this does not prevent it from speaking about them quite familiarly. The third of them is frequently called 'the Jubilee', a word which is meant to indicate the passage of timelessness into time, or, it may be, vice versa. The relation of the six Days of Heaven and Earth to the primordial First Cause is expressed by comparing them to six saplings trained in a nursery and subsequently planted out, the mnemonic being the verse of the Psalms, 'The trees of the Lord, the cedars of Lebanon which he hath planted' (Ps. CIV, 16).

The names given to the grades are the same as those given in Cabbalist literature to the Sefiroth—*Kether, Ḥokhmah, Binah,* then *Ḥesed,* etc. For Wisdom and Understanding one can perceive a certain reason; the rest seem more or less fanciful, and no reason for them is given in the *Zohar.* It should be observed that, strictly speaking, all these are names of God, regarded as first cause. That the *Zohar* always keeps this fact in mind it would not be safe to assert; it is hardly possible in many places to avoid the impression that we are dealing with a plurality of divinities, or again with mere attributes of the Deity. But either supposition reduces the Cabbalistic system to nonsense.

As there are grades prior to 'heaven and earth' and the six grades functioning in them, so there is a grade posterior to heaven and earth. Whence comes the energy which constitutes this 'day' ? This is a question to which it is difficult to find an answer in the *Zohar.* We might say, however, that it is constituted by a kind of reflex action, and consists in the activity of the First Cause in being conscious of itself and all that it has accomplished. This would explain why the specific function of the Seventh Day is to unite the human soul or consciousness (*neshamah*) with the body, and why, being outside of 'heaven and earth', it occupies a position apart from the previous six grades.

After what has been said it will not be difficult to understand how the conception of God as First Cause can be made to embrace the conceptions of God as Ruler of the world and Protector of Israel. The sixth grade, *Tifereth* or Beauty, is the one which functions in the third of the six days of creation, and therefore stands in the relation of First Cause to the earth as the basis of all animate existence and all activity of propagation. There is, therefore, obvious ground for identifying this grade with the Holy One, blessed be He, the dispenser of vital powers and the arbiter of life and death in both worlds. When the Ancient Holy One and the Holy One, blessed be He, are thus correlated, they are distinguished as *Arich Anpin* (Makroprosopus, lit. long of nostrils, i.e. long-suffering, forbearing), and *Ze'er Anpin* (Mikroprosopus, lit. small of nostrils, i.e. hasty), the reason being that suffering and pain issue directly from the latter, but not from the former.

If the Holy One, blessed be He, can be identified with the sixth grade, *Tifereth*, with equal right the Community of Israel can be identified with the tenth grade, *Malkuth*. The latter is the first cause of union of the human soul with the body; the former is God regarded as immanent in the human soul. A further resemblance lies in the fact that *Malkuth*, lying outside of the sphere of 'heaven and earth', acts only with a kind of borrowed energy, or, in the language of the *Zohar*, 'has no light of its own', while the Community of Israel also is regarded as but a moon shining with a borrowed light. Hence the transition from one to the other is easy and natural.

The connection between the various designations of God employed by the *Zohar* may be illustrated by the following figure. Imagine a long hall divided into three sections, of which one bears the title 'Community of Israel', the second 'Matrona', and the third '*Malkuth*'. The first section is open to the heavens; the second section has a somewhat lofty roof; the third a much lower roof. The roof of the second section forms the floor of another hall which extends over the third section also. That part of it which covers the second section of the lower hall, the Matrona, is entitled 'Holy King' and is open to the heavens; that part of it which extends over *Malkuth* is called *Tifereth*, and it has three storeys underneath it between itself and *Malkuth* and five storeys above it, of which the topmost—or it may be the three highest—is open to the heavens. If a man desires to have communion with God, he must enter the lowest hall, but he has his choice between its three sections. If he is content to base his belief in God on the teaching of tradition, he can immediately find communion with God through prayer and devotional exercises. If he seeks to base his belief on the consciousness of his *neshamah*, or higher self, then devotion is only a first stage and true communion is attained only by ethical practice. If, finally, he bases his belief on philosophical speculation, then even ethical practice is only the fifth of ten stages of intellectual cultivation which he has to pass through in order to attain his goal.

To complete this sketch of the divine nomenclature of the *Zohar* two things are still necessary. One is to fit into the above scheme the three pairs of categories to which attention was called in the Appendix to Vol. II, namely, Upper and Lower, Male and Female, and Right and Left. The second is to discuss the place occupied in the Zoharic system by the Holy Name or Tetragrammaton.

THE DESIGNATIONS AND THE CATEGORIES

1. *Upper and Lower*. According to the *Zohar*, the grades, as the name implies, constitute a hierarchy, each one being superior to the one which follows. The reason is that the activity of each is conditioned by the activity of the one above it, but not vice versa. This is expressed in Zoharic language by saying that each one *sucks* from the one above it. Hence the terms 'upper' and 'lower' applied to the grades are relative, save that the lowest grade is 'lower' and the highest grade 'upper' *par excellence*. It is no doubt in virtue of this conditioning that the *Zohar* lays down that whatever takes place 'above' also takes place 'below', since it is natural that the same First Cause working in different media should produce parallel results.

2. *Male and Female*. While each grade is responsible for its own world, in certain cases it is regarded as having received the seed thereof from the grade above, to which it accordingly stands in the relation of female to male. Thus the grades of Wisdom and Understanding are regarded as male and female in regard to the primordial 'heaven and earth' which are, properly speaking, the 'world' of the latter, and hence these two grades are commonly designated 'Father' and 'Mother'. Again, the world of the grade *Ḥesed* is commonly known as 'upper waters' and that of the grade *Geburah* as 'lower waters', the former being a fluid element and the latter fiery. These are regarded as being respectively 'male' and 'female', and out of their union issues the earthly element. The grades themselves, however, *Ḥesed* and *Geburah*, are not distinguished as male and female. Further, the lowest grade, *Malkuth*, is regarded as female in respect of the six grades of 'heaven and earth', and is often referred to simply as 'The Female'. More specifically, it forms a pair with the grade *Yesod* (Foundation) immediately above it. The two, when thus conjoined, are usually designated *Ẓaddik* (Righteous One), and *Ẓedek* (Righteousness), and out of their interaction issues the *neshamah* as the soul of man.

3. *Right and Left*. The distinction between 'right' and 'left' in the *Zohar* is of particular importance because it is the keystone of the Zoharic theory of good and evil. It is also more elusive and difficult to explain than the other categories. This is due to the fact that these terms are found on examination to embody three sets of ideas which in themselves are in reality quite distinct.

(*a*) In one sense, 'right and left' seem to be used in the *Zohar* simply as a variation of 'male and female'. *Ḥokhmah*, being 'male', is on the right, and *Binah*, being 'female', is on the left. Similarly, *Ḥesed*, being responsible for the 'male waters', is on the right, and *Geburah*, being responsible for the 'female waters', is on the left. The supreme grade, *Kether*, being beyond the division of male and female, is pictured as being in the centre. Similarly, *Tifereth*, which effects the union between male and female waters, is also placed in the centre. Thus it is possible to speak of a 'straight line' from *Kether* to *Tifereth*, and to designate *Tifereth* the 'central pillar'.

(*b*) A second use of the terms 'right and left' is based on the identification of the grade *Tifereth* with the Holy King, the Ruler and Judge of the world. The Holy King as judge can exercise either clemency or rigour, and it is a not unnatural figure to say that He exercises clemency with His right hand and rigour with His left. Now, as we have seen, the 'world' of the grade *Tifereth*, namely the earthly element capable of producing life, is formed by a union of the fluid and fiery elements which constitute the 'worlds' of *Ḥesed* and *Geburah*. It is assumed by the *Zohar* that the world of bliss which is reserved for the souls of the righteous after death in some way derives from the grade of *Ḥesed* and its element, while the world of punishment reserved for the souls of the wicked derives from *Geburah* and its element. Hence, by a natural transference, *Ḥesed* becomes the Right Arm and *Geburah* the Left Arm. A further elaboration of this idea is to regard *Ḥesed* and *Geburah* as two judges advocating respectively acquittal and condemnation, while *Tifereth* turns the scale. When thus grouped the three grades are designated Abraham, Isaac and Jacob.

(*c*) The distinction between 'right' and 'left' in the *Zohar* corresponds, not only to the distinction between reward and punishment in the next world, but also between good and evil, and specifically moral good and evil in this world. Samael, the power of evil, the tempter, the accuser, the evil Serpent, is placed on the left and is identified with the grade *Geburah*. Now Samael is represented as the opponent not of *Ḥesed* but of *Tifereth*. He is the Great Dragon, who on New Year swallows the Moon, that is, prevents the union of the Matrona with the Holy King, until Israel by their sacrifice on the Day of Atonement induce him to desist. He also, by means of his minions, Lilith and others, seduces men to defile their souls, contrary to the desire of the Holy King.[1] Thus one aspect of the

[1] It may be noted here that the *Zohar* distinguishes the *ẓelem* (form) and *demuth* (likeness) of man (*v.* Genesis 1, 26) as 'left' and 'right', and identifies the *demuth* with the *neshamah*.

distinction between right and left in the *Zohar* is a conflict between Samael and the Holy King. This conflict is obviously a very different thing from the conflict of view between *Ḥesed* and *Geburah*, though described in the same terms, and if we ask how it arises, the answer is by no means easy to find in the *Zohar*. A possible explanation is as follows. It has been mentioned above that each grade is regarded as 'sucking' from the one above it. Now it is not unnatural to suppose that the one which is 'sucked' should offer a certain resistance to the process, so that two opposite tendencies are always at work. This would seem to be implied in the somewhat obscure interpretation given by the *Zohar* to a text which it frequently quotes as containing a fundamental principle with reference to the grades, viz. 'To the place whence the rivers came, thither they are ever returning' (Eccl. 1, 7). On this principle there should be a conflict between all the adjacent grades; but we may suppose that the reason why the *Zohar* dwells on the conflict between Samael and the Holy King is because of its importance for the salvation of man's soul and the welfare of the people of Israel.

THE DIVINE NAME

It remains to say a few words on the place occupied by the Holy Name, the Tetragrammaton, in the scheme of the *Zohar*. In the Cabbalistic doctrine the name formed by the four Hebrew letters *yod*, *hé*, *vau*, *hé*, has a special and intimate connection with the grade of *Tifereth*, of which it is in the strict sense the proper name. We must understand this to mean that if one could grasp with sufficient clearness the nature of the grade *Tifereth*, especially as the originator of the *neshamah*, he would automatically perceive that this is the fitting appellation which should be given to it. To this grade of comprehension Moses and the other prophets actually rose, and this was the basis of their inspiration. There is, however, a difference between the inspiration of Moses and that of the other prophets. Moses was able to grasp the connection between the grade and the Name fully and clearly, but the others only through a haze, as it were, since their comprehension only reached fully to the two inferior grades of *Neẓah* and *Hod*, the two 'pillars' or 'willows of the brook', as they are fancifully called.

Apart from its importance as a vocable, the Tetragrammaton has a deep significance for the *Zohar* as a *written* word, through the symbolism of its individual letters and their shapes and qualities. Thus the point of the *Yod* symbolizes the grade *Kether;* the *Yod* itself stands for *Hokhmah* the Father, and the first *Hé* for *Binah*, the Mother. The *Vau*, having the numerical value of six, symbolizes the 'six ends', the grades of the six days, and more particularly *Tifereth*, the centre of this group. The second *Hé* naturally symbolizes *Malkuth*. Since the shape of the *Vau* combines features of the *Yod* and the *Hé*, it is fancifully referred to as the 'son' of these letters, and this designation of 'son' is sometimes transferred to the grade *Tifereth* which it represents, although we do not find that *Tifereth* as a grade is particularly associated with *Hokhmah* and *Binah*. Thus the Tetragrammaton in its letters sums up the whole doctrine of the grades, while as a name it is the pivot of the entire Holy Writ; and the *Zohar* therefore does not hesitate to declare that 'the whole of the Torah is the Holy Name'.

MAURICE SIMON